MW00627219

HITLER'S TROJAN HORSE

HITLER'S TROJAN HORSE

THE FALL OF THE ABWEHR, 1943-45

NIGEL WEST

FRONTLINE
BOOKS

First published in Great Britain in 2022 by
FRONTLINE BOOKS
an imprint of Pen & Sword Books Ltd,
47 Church Street, Barnsley, S. Yorkshire, S70 2AS

ISBN: 978-1-39907-603-6

CIP data records for this title are available from the British Library

For more information on our books, please visit
www.frontline-books.com, email info@frontline-books.com
or write to us at the above address.

Printed and bound by CPI Group (UK) Ltd, Croydon, CR0 4YY
Typeset by Concept, Huddersfield, West Yorkshire
Pen & Sword Books Ltd incorporates the imprints of Pen & Sword
Archaeology, Atlas, Aviation, Battleground, Discovery,
Family History, History, Maritime, Military, Naval, Politics,
Social History, Transport, True Crime, Claymore Press,
Frontline Books, Praetorian Press,
Seaforth Publishing and White Owl

For a complete list of Pen and Sword titles please contact
PEN & SWORD LTD
47 Church Street, Barnsley, South Yorkshire, S70 2AS, England
E-mail: enquiries@pen-and-sword.co.uk

Or

PEN AND SWORD BOOKS
1950 Lawrence Rd, Havertown, PA 19083, USA
E-mail: Uspen-and-sword@casematepublishers.com

CONTENTS

LIST OF PLATES

In Great Britain espionage is considered to be an occupation of gentlemen of high social standing, whereas in Germany the worst and most corrupt elements are recruited as agents.

Walter Schellenberg, Camp 020 Interrogation Report, 10 April 1945

It is not merely a matter of academic interest to obtain a complete picture of German counter-espionage work of this nature. There is reason to believe that the deception policy which they were then pursuing was not unsuccessful and we should profit by the present opportunity of ascertaining details of the German activities at that period in order to prevent errors made by this country in the past from being repeated.

Ian Wilson, Memorandum to Colonel Stimson, Camp 020,
8 August 1945

ACKNOWLEDGMENTS

The author acknowledges his debt of gratitude to those who have assisted his research, among them the late Bill Williams, Roger Hesketh, David Strangeways, Noel Wild, Juan Pujol (GARBO), Roman Garby-Czerniawski (BRUTUS), Harry Williamson (TATE), Frano de Bona (FREAK), Ib Riis (COBWEB), Dusan Popov (TRICYCLE), Ivo Popov (DREADNOUGHT), Eugn Sostaric (METEOR), John Moe (MUTT), Tor Glad (JEFF), Elvira de la Fuentes (BRONX), Lisel Gärtner, Hugh Astor, Len Burt, Christopher and Pam Harmer, Cyril Mills, John Maude, Gerald Glover, Peter Ramsbotham, Tommy and Joan Robertson, Susan Barton, Enriiquetta Harris, Sarah Bishop, Joanna Phipps, Peter Hope, Jim Skardon, Eric Goodacre, John Gwyer, Dick White, Victor and Tess Rothschild, Bill Magan, Russell Lee, Michael Ryde, Rupert Speir, Bill Luke, who shared their wartime MI5 experiences; and the late Sigismund Best, Philip Johns, Cecil Gledhill, Nicholas Elliott, Felix Cowgill, Peter Falk, Desmond Bristow, Rodney Dennys, Cecil Barclay, John Bygott, Eddie Boxshall, Euan Rabagliati, Charles Seymour, Andrew King, George Blake, Lionel Loewe, Walter Bell, Kenneth Benton, John Codrington, Lord Tennyson, George Young, Robin Cecil and John Cairncross, who all served in SIS. Also, from SOE, Ronnie Seth, Peter Kemp, Jack Beevor, Brian Stonehouse, Tony Brooks, Peter Wilkinson; and Al Ulmer, Bill Hood, Peter Sichel and Hugh Montgomery from OSS, Ken Crosby, formerly of the FBI Special Intelligence Service, Cleve Cram from the CIA and John Taylor from NARA. Finally, Halina Szymanska, Martin and Kim Dearden, Bill Kenyon-Jones, Gunter Peis, Rob Hesketh, Erich Vermehren, David Mure, Jock Colville and Bill Cavendish-Bentinck. David Kahn, Marco Popov, Roger Grosjean, Ladislas Farago, John Taylor, Jennifer Scherr, Sebastian Cody, Kim and Marton Dearden, Christian Linde, Frederick Solms-Baruth, Kathleen Ritter, Otto Weltzien, Charles Byford, Jim Lee, Nicholas Reed and Christopher Risso-Gill.

AUTHOR'S NOTE

Many of the documents reproduced in this volume originate from official files and have been redacted during the declassification process. Where possible the redactions have been restored, but where this has not been possible the redaction is indicated thus: [XXXXXXXXXXXXXXX]

The author has retained the convention of printing codenames in capitals but, for ease of reading, has restored capitalised surnames to ordinary lower case.

In the interests of consistency, some American-month/day style dates have been altered to the European day/month convention.

Many Allied and German military ranks have been deliberately omitted as they can be somewhat misleading for the uninitiated as they do not always accurately reflect seniority. In the German system the status of specialist (Sonderführer) was often granted to civilians who had no military background. The five designations (Sondeführer G, Z, K, B and R) were the equivalent, respectively, of an NCO, lieutenant, captain, major and colonel.

GLOSSARY
AND ABBREVIATIONS

@	Alias
104 SCI	Special Counter-Intelligence in Brussels
105 SCI	Special Counter-Intelligence in Paris
212 Committee	SHAEF double agent supervising group
Abt.	Abteilung
AFHQ	Allied Forces Headquarters
Amt	Office
B1(a)	MI5's section handling double agents
B1(b)	MI5's German espionage research section
B1(g)	MI5's Spanish section
B9	MI5's Irish section
BCRA	Bureau Central de Renseignements et d'Action
BdS	Befehlshaber der Sicherheitspolizei
BELINDE	Schloss Baruth
BISMARCK	B-Dienst HQ
BRAVERY	SOE circuit in Belgium
Camp 020	Latchmere House, Ham Common
CENTRO	KO Madrid's wireless station
CICI	Combined Intelligence Centre Iraq
CIS	US Counter-Intelligence Corps
CODAR	FBI counter-espionage investigation
CSDIC	Combined Services Detailed Interrogation Centre
CSS	Chief of the Secret Intelligence Service
DASD	German branch of the International Amateur Radio Organisation
D/F	Direction-Finding
DK	Etappen merchant shipping section
DLH	Deutsche Lufthansa
DNB	Deutsche Nachrichten Buro (German News Agency)

DORA	I/H West command at Rheda Castle
DSO	Defence Security Officer
EASTER EGGS	Abwehr II stay-behind sabotage plan
EDES	National Republican Greek League
ELAS	Greek People's Liberation Army
FA	Reichsluftfahrtministerium Forschungsamt (Air Ministry Research Office)
FAK	Nachrichten Fernaufklärungs Kompanie (long-range intercept company)
FAT	Frontaufklärungstrupp (tactical mobile reconnaissance unit)
Feste	Feste Nachrichten Aufklärungstelle (stationary intercept company)
FHW	Fremde Heere West
GC&CS	Government Code & Cipher School
GFP	German Field Police
GIS	German Intelligence Service
GOLFPLATZ	Abwehr codename for England
GV	German double agent
HAPAG	Hamburg-Amerika shipping line
Hastuf	Hauptsturmführer (captain)
HSSPF	Hoherer SS und Polizei Führer
Ic	OKW intelligence laision
I/H	Eins Heer
I/L	Eins Luft
I/LTW	Eins Luft Technik
I-M	Eins Marine
INTERALLIÉ	SIS network in occupied France
IRA	Russian official
ISBA	Intelligence Source British Agent ISOS subset
ISLD	Inter-Services Liaison Department (SIS cover organisation in the Middle East)
ISOS	Abwehr decrypts
IVORY	FBI counter-espionage investigation
JIC	Joint Intelligence Committee
KO	KriegsOrganisation
KOBU	KriegsOrganisation Bucharest
KONA	Kommandeur der Nachrichtenaufklärung
KONO	KriegsOrganisation Nehe Orient
KOP	KriegsOrganisation Portugal
KOS	KriegsOrganisation Spain

LRC	London Reception Centre
LVF	Legion of French Volunteers
MA	Military Attaché
MAMMUT	Abw II mission to Mosul in June 1943
MAS	Motoscafo Armato Silurante
MI5	British Security Service
MI6	British Secret Intelligence Service
MIT	Turkish Intelligence Service
MoI	Ministry of Information
MP	US Army Military Police
MSS	Most Secret Sources
ND	Nachrichtendienst
NID	Naval Intelligence Division
NKVD	Soviet intelligence service
NSCO	Naval Security Control Officer
OEDE	Organisation of Nationalist Forces in Greece
OKH/Chi	Oberkommando der Wehrmacht, Cipher Section
OKM/SKW	Oberkommando der Kriegsmarine, Seekriegsleitung
Ops B	SHAEF deception planning unit
OSS	Office of Strategic Services
OTU	Officer Training Unit
OVRA	Organisation for Vigilence and Repression of Anti-Fascism
PAIR	Mediterranean theatre codename for ISOS
PCO	Passport Control Officer
PF	Personal File
PILLOW	Allied plan to contact Abwehr personnel
PPF	Parti Populaire Français
PR	Photographic Reconnaissance
PVDE	Policia de Vigilancia e de Defesa do Estado
PWE	Political Warfare Executive
RDF	Raadio Direction-Finding
ROF	Royal Ordnance Factory
RSS	Radio Security Service
RVPS	Royal Victoria Patriotic School
SABENA	Belgian airline
SABOT	SOE circuit headed by Pierre Bourriez
SAFEHAVEN	Post-war OSS investigation of Abwehr funds
SCI	Special Counter-Intelligence Unit
SD	Sicherheitsdienst
SIM	Servicio de Información Militar
SIME	Security Intelligence Middle East

SIPO	Sicherheitspolizei
SIS	British Secret Intelligence Service
SIS	Italian Speciali Servizio Informazioni
SO 1	SOE's covert propaganda department
SOE	Special Operations Executive
THEODORA	Ast Munster mission
TICOM	Target Intelligence Committee
TRIANGLE	ISOS in the Middle East
V-Mann	Verbindungsmann
WIDO	Abwehr nest in Tripoli
X-2	Counter-intelligence branch, OSS
XX	Twenty Committee
Y	Wireless interception
ZbV	Zur besonderen Verwendung ('Special Purpose')
ZEPPELIN	Abwehr headquarters at Zossen

INTRODUCTION

Canaris is his own principal agent.

Major Richard Wurmann, January 1944[1]

As the military tide turned again the Axis the German military intelligence machine found itself beleaguered by a combination of factors that would ultimately prove catastrophic. The various components included a self-destructive rivalry with the SD, plummeting morale because of high-level defections, a lack of confidence in its own intelligence reporting, growing doubt about the integrity of individual agent networks and, perhaps most disastrous of all, clear proof that the Abwehr's senior staff had been at the very heart of the plot to assassinate the Führer.

The idea that at one of the most vital moments in the entire war, just as the Allies were fighting their way towards the Reich from Italy, Normandy and southern France, the Abwehr's management should be distracted by a scheme to mount a putsch in Berlin is itself remarkable. The fact that one of the principal Abwehr conspirators, codenamed WHISKY, should have spent the previous two years negotiating with his British counterparts is almost as astonishing as the secrecy that has prevented the link from being made public in the intervening 75 years. At the time, of course, there was an obvious political sensitivity and need to avoid antagonising Moscow and exacerbating existing fears, bordering on paranoia, that the Western Allies might be tempted to agree terms with a new German government to create an anti-Bolshevik front. The evidence suggests that knowledge of the relationship was tightly held within SIS and only became known to some Foreign Office officials, and MI5, *after* WHISKY's exfiltration from Lisbon. In the absence of any SIS documents, apart from those that slipped into his MI5 dossier, one can only speculate about the lack of a single reference to WHISKY or his accomplices in SIS's official centenary history, published in 2010. Indeed, the authorised history, *MI6: The History of the Secret Intelligence Service 1909-49*,[2] laid great emphasis on the organisation's connection with Colonel Richard Maasing, Estonia's pre-war director of military intelligence who had been recruited by Harry Carr of SIS's Helsinki station (based in Stockholm for most of the war) and codenamed OUTCAST, who was described in 1943 as 'the best source of information on the German interior produced so far in the war'.[3] Allegedly he 'belonged to a circle of Abwehr officers regarded as close to Admiral Canaris' and reported to Carr after each of his visits to Berlin. This is the official narrative relating to SIS's high-level contact with the Abwehr, which infers that the connection was limited to OUTCAST, who was not even an Abwehr officer but one of the organisation's agents, albeit one who appears to have been greatly trusted. As an intelligence professional, Maasing also supplied information to the Swedish military, the American OSS and even the Japanese through General Makoto Onodera. This last channel, betrayed by ISOS, proved too much for SIS and Maasing was flown to England where he died of tuberculosis in 1944.

SIS would only publicly acknowledge one other, indirect contact with Canaris, which was through his Polish mistress, Halina Szymanska, who was based in Berne. She was not only in personal touch with Canaris, who visited her in Switzerland and Italy, but she liaised with his representative, Hans Bemd Gisevius, who was under diplomatic cover at the Zurich consulate. However, Gisevius was *not* an SIS agent and his traffic was one-way, and not always entirely accurate. SIS averred that 'between August 1940 and December 1942 Geneva sent London twenty-five reports with information provided by him. Almost all of this was channelled through Szymanska'[4] but he never mentioned any assassination plot to her until he had managed to return to Switzerland, three months *after* the attempted putsch.

> One report, however, was based on a dinner Szymanska had with Canaris in Berne on 19 October 1941. This is the only recorded face-to-face meeting between Canaris and anyone reporting directly to SIS.[5]

Plainly this assertion is wrong, so why the subterfuge? In the post-war era SIS was anxious to dispel a widespread belief that the agency, or individual officers, had engaged in freelance, 'off-the-books' maverick operations which had been undertaken either with the Chief's tacit support or at least his Nelsonic eye. Most likely one can suppose that the reluctance to acknowledge its involvement in the 20 July plot was a manifestation of a policy intended to protect SIS's reputation and a need to conceal WHISKY's true identity, especially as in 1950 he would be nominated to head the Federal Republic of Germany's newly-created domestic security apparatus, the Office for the Protection of the Constitution. To have revealed that Otto John had been an SIS asset for the past eight years would have been utterly compromising for all concerned, and especially WHISKY himself.

In the first volume of this work, *Hitler's Nest of Vipers*, which covered the period from 1935 to 1943, the Abwehr expanded rapidly into a formidable organisation, especially in the counter-intelligence field where it mounted impressive operations to gain the upper hand in Holland, Belgium, France and the Iberian Peninsula. Almost as impressive as the Abwehr's development was its swift decline, documented in the pages that follow, and based on evidence drawn mainly from recently-declassified Allied documents which have been hitherto unavailable for public scrutiny.

Nigel West

DRAMATIS PERSONAE

Walter Aberle	Abt. II saboteur in Iraq
Donald Adams	Pre-war Abwehr spy in England
ADOLPHE	I/H stay-behind agent in Marseilles
Heinrich Ahlrichs	Pre-war Etappendienst agent in England
Sigurd Alseth	Abwehr spy landed at Lerwick in March 1941 to join SOE
Mori Aoki	Japanese Intelligence officer in Ankara
Pierre Arend	Belgian pilot codenamed FATHER
ARMOUR	Luigi Alassi, SIM officer and Abwehr stay-behind agent in Rome
ARTHUR	Abwehr codename for DOLEFUL
ARTIST	MI5 codename for Johannes Jebsen
ATOM	Stay-behind agent
Marc Aubert	French naval officer executed January 1939
Ludwig Kramer von Auenrode	Alias Fritz Cramer, Chief KOP
Prince Karl Adolph Auersperg	Resigned from the Abwehr in Berne, 1944
AUGUSTA	Abwehr spy in Lisbon Renato Roque Laia
Robert Baheshy	Abwehr candidate for MAMMUT II
Louis Bakos	Iraqi candidate for MAMMUT II
BASKET	MI5 codename for Joseph Lenihan
Friedrich Baumeister	Leiter, Astl, Paris, alias Colonel Rudolf
Johannes Becker	SD Chief in South America
Kurt Beigl	Abwehr defector in Istanbul, August 1944
Herbert J. Berthold	Abt. II deserter in Paris codenamed JIGGER
Ahmed Bey	SIME double agent DOLEFUL, ARTHUR to the Abwehr
Johannes Bischoff	Abwehr officer at Nest Bremen
Ludwig Bischoff	Abwehr cut-out in Dallas

BLACKGUARD	SIME double agent Hamdi Khaqqay alias Mirz Khan
Wolfgang Blaum	Alias Friedrich Baumann, head of Abt. II in Madrid until February 1945
BLAZE	Stay-behind agent in Munchen-Gladbach
Gunther Blume	SD officer and member of ANTON captured in Tehran, August 1943
Anthony Blunt	MI5 officer
Corneille Boehme	Dutch spy for the Abwehr detained at Camp 020 in January 1942
Carl Boemelburg	SD Paris
Paul Borchardt	Ast Munich V-Mann arrested in New York, December 1941
Pierre Bourriez	SOE agent arrested in January 1943
Juan Brandes	I/H KOP
Gertrud Brandy	Pre-war Abwehr spy in Dublin
Arthur Breuer	Abwehr agent landed in the US by U-boat in 1941
BRIZO SENIOR	Abwehr codename for Georg Hansen
Harald Bruhn	Abwehr agent detained in August 1940 on meteorological reporting mission
BRUTUS	MI5 codename for Roman Garby-Czerniawski
Erich Buecking	I/M Lisbon
Roberto Buenaga	Spanish officer and Abwehr agent
Karl Burger	Pre-war Abwehr spy in England
CABANON	I/H stay-behind agent in Toulon
John Cairncross	SIS Section V desk officer
Joachim Calca	Abwehr agent, Lisbon
CAMOUFLAGE	Stay-behind agent
Francis P. Campbell	Pre-war Abwehr spy in England
Joachim Canaris	I-H KOS
Wilhelm Canaris	Abwehr Chief until February 1944, codenamed GUILLERMO
CARELESS	MI5 double agent Edward Ejsymont
Goesta Caroli	Abwehr spy parachuted into Cambridgeshire, September 1940.
Mathilde Carré	SIS wireless operator codenamed VICTOIRE
Jean Carrere	SD double agent in Paris codenamed KEEL
CELERY	MI5 double agent Walter Dicketts
CHARLIE	MI5 double agent Charles Eschborn

CHEESE	SIS/SIME double agent Renato Levi
Charles Cholmondeley	MI5 officer
COLACO	SIS agent, Lisbon
Axel Coll	Abwehr spy detained in August 1940 while on meteorological reporting mission
COSSACK	Stay-behind agent
COSTA	Abwehr codename for British double agent, a member of PESSIMISTS
Jose Costa	SIS agent, British Consulate, Lisbon.
Fritz Cramer	Alias of Ludwig Kramer von Auenrode, Chief, KOP
Mrs Crookes	Pre-war Abwehr spy in England
CROW	Norwegian SD agent arrested in 1942
CRUDE	Turkish businessman and SIS double agent in Iraq
DARIEN	British double agent agent in Lisbon
G.H. Darragh	Pre-war Abwehr spy in England
DAVIT	French double agent in Paris stay-behind group
Françoise Deeker	Abwehr spy landed in Scotland, September 1940
Jose Antonio Del Campo	German spy in Madrid
DEPUTY	SD stay-behind agent in Antwerp
DERRICK	Stay-behind agent in Bruges
de Renzy	Pre-war Abwehr spy in England
Charles de Salis	SIS Section V in Lisbon
DESIRE	Albert Gabas, double agent in France, 1944
DICTIONARY	Abwehr defector Carl Marcus
Friedrich Dohse	SD Bordeaux
DOLEFUL	Ahmed Bey, ARTHUR to the Abwehr
DOMINANT	SD stay-behind agent in Antwerp
DOMINO	Abwehr codename for DOLEFUL
DON PEDRO	Bertie Koepke, Nest Barcelona
DOOLITTLE	Polish airman and double agent, recruited by MI5 in October 1940
DRAGOMAN	X-2 codename for double agent Jean Frutos in Cherbourg
DRAGONFLY	MI5 double agent Hans George, codenamed KILLIAN by I/L

Christopher Draper	MI5 double agent terminated in January 1933
Frederick Duquesne	Abwehr spy arrested by the FBI in New York in June 1941
Bernard Durrant	Pre-war Abwehr spy in England
ECCLESIASTIC	Olga Zemanova, SIS agent in Lisbon
Gunnar Edwardsen	Abwehr saboteur arrested in Soctland in October 1941
John Eikens	Stay-behind agent in Cherbourg codenamed PANCHO
Carl Eitel	I/M Lisbon, codenamed ELLERMAN by OSS
Edward Ejsymont	Polish pilot codenamed CARELESS by MI5
Heinz Engelhorn	Abwehr officer implicated in 20 July plot
Charles Eschborn	MI5 double agent codenamed CHARLIE
ELLERMAN	OSS codename for Carl Eitel
Vera Erikson	Alias of Vera von Schallburg, Abwehr spy landed in Scotland in September 1940
My Eriksson	Abwehr spy detained in London in September 1939
Arnold Evinsen	Abwehr spy posing as Norwegian refugee landed at Lerwick, January 1943
FAN	French double agent and former Fascist
FANK	SD stay-behind double agent in Brussels
Massud Farzad	Persian interpreter on ANTON mission
Waldemar Fast	SD in Istanbul
FATHER	MI5 double agent Pierre Arend
FEDERICO	Abwehr codename for Friedrich Knappe-Ratey in Madrid.
Mario Ferreira	Abwehr agent, Lisbon
Paul Fidrmuc	Czech fabricator in Lisbon codenamed OSTRO
Ulrich von Finkenstein	Abwehr agent on meteorological reporting mission, detained August 1940
FISH	Stay-behind agent
FOREST	Lucien Herviou, French stay-behind agent
FORGE	SD stay-behind agent
FRANK	SD double agent in Brussels
Richard Frauedorf	Etappendienst agent expelled from London in 1938
FREELANCE	Three parachute agents in France
Jean Frutos	X-2 double agent codenamed DRAGOMAN

Gilbertus Fukken	Abwehr spy, alias Willem Ter Braak, parachuted into Buckinghamshire in November 1940
Dieter Gaertner	Abwehr agent arrested in Ireland in July 1940
Lisel Gaertner	MI5 double agent codenamed GELATINE
Alfred Gaessler	SIS radio operator, defector to the Abwehr
GANDER	MI5 codename for double agent Karl Gross
GAOL	Stay-behind agent in Paris
Roman Garby-Czerniawski	Polish SIS agent codenamed WALENTY and BRUTUS
Hans Otto Gast	Czech spy in the Abwehr
GAT	French-controlled stay-behind agent
Ludwig Gehre	Abwehr Abt. III
GELATINE	MI5 double agent Lisel Gaertner
Wilhelm Gessmann	Alias Alexander, German spy in Lisbon
GILBERT	BCRA codename for André Latham
Karel van Gils	Belgian seaman detained at Camp 020
GIRAFFE	MI5 double agent Georges Graf
GIRRANT	Stay-behind agent
Hermann Giskes	III/F in Paris, The Hague and Brussels
Tor Glad	MI5 double agent codenamed JEFF
GLASS	Stay-behind agent
Hermann Goertz	German spy arrested in England in 1935
Willy Goetz	Hungarian journlist in Istanbul and SIME detainee, November 1944
GOLD	I/H source in Istanbul
GOLDFLAKE	Stay-behind agent in Marseilles
Hans Graepe	Member of the FRANZ mission to Iraq, March 1943
Georges Graf	MI5 double agent codenamed GIRAFFE
Georg Grille	SD member of the FRANZ mission to Iraq, March 1943
Martin Grimaldi	MI5 B1(a) officer
Andur Gross	Abwehr agent and SIME detainee, 1943
Karl Gross	MI5 double agent codenamed GANDER
Carl Grundell	Swedish seaman and I/M agent arrested at Gibraltar in February 1945
GUILLERMO	Abwehr codename for Admiral Canaris
GULL	Abwehr spy Elie Haggar, sent to Egypt December 1942
Viktor Guryevich	GRU illegal codenamed KENT

John Gwyer	MI5 officer
Andre Gyorgy	Alias of Andur Gross
Werner von Haeften	Aide to Colonel Count von Stauffenberg
Luipold Haffner	Abwehr defector in Mardid, August 1945
Elie Haggar	Abwehr spy in Egypt codenamed GULL
Jawad Hamada	Abwehr spy captured on the U-572
Mahmoud Hamada	Abwehr spy codenamed ROMEO in Syria
Willi Hamburger	Abwehr defector in Istanbul
Georg Hansen	Chief, Abwehr Abt. II, codenamed BRIZO SENIOR
Kurt Hansen	Danish Abwehr agent detained August 1940 on meteorological reporting mission
Kurt Harbers	SD radio operator for the ANTON mission captured in Persia in March 1944
HARDY	Abt. II saboteur Wilhelm Hoffmann
Hans Harnisch	SD representative in Argentina
HATCHET	MI5 double agent Albert de Jaeger
Osmar Hellmuth	Argentine envoy arrested in Trinidad
HELMUTH	SIME double agent SCEPTIC
Lucien Hervious	Stay-behind agent codenamed FOREST
Stephen Hill-Dillon	Allied Counter-Intelligence Chief. Mediterranean
Otto Hinrischen	Abwehr, Bilbao
HITTITE	MI5 double agent recruited by the German consul in New Orleans
Wilhelm Hoffmann	Abt. II saboteur in Iraq codenamed HARDY captured July 1943
Dr Holm	Czech spy in the Abwehr, alias Paul Thummel, arrested in March 1942.
Hans Holzapel	Radio operator on the FRANZ mission to Iraq, March 1943
HOSIERY	SIME codename for Willi Hamburger
HOST	Stay-behind agent
HOSTESS	Stay-behind agent
Gerhard Huntemann	III/F in The Hague and Brussels
Jack Ivens	SIS Section V, Madrid
JACQUES	I/M stay-behind agent in Marseilles
JAEGER	Abwehr codename for Otto John
Adolf Jaeger	Pre-war Etappendienst agent in England, expelled in 1938
Albert de Jaeger	Belgian detainee at Camp 020 codenamed HATCHET

Dietrich Jakobs	Pre-war Etappendienst agent in England
Josef Jakobs	Abwehr spy parachuted into Huntingdonshire in March 1941
Kurt Janhke	German intelligence officer
Ralph Jarvis	SIS Section V, Lisbon
JEANNOT	I/H stay-behind agent
Johannes Jebsen	Abwehr officer codenamed ARTIST by SIS
JEFF	MI5 codename for double agent Tor Glad
Paulino de Jesus	SIS source on the Abwehr in Lisbon
JIGGER	Herbert J. Berthold, Abwehr NCO in Paris
Invald Johansen	Abwehr spy landed at Lerwick in March 1941 to join SOE
Otto John	Abwehr defector codenamed WHISKY by SIS and JAEGER by Berlin
Otto Joost	Abwehr spy arrested in Nairn, October 1940
Franz Jordan	Abwehr agent arrested in Brazil in 1942
Jessie Jordan	Abwehr postbox in Dundee arrested in March 1938
Leon Jude	Belgian Sabena pilot and Abwehr spy detained at Camp 020, June 1942
JUNIOR	SIS codename for Abwehr defector Hans Ruser
Joe K	Kurt Ludwig
Ernst Kaltenbrunner	SD Chief
Otto Kamler	Amt. I, KOP
Cornelia Kapp	SD defector in Ankara
Richard Kauder	Abwehr officer alias Fritz Klatt
KEEL	Jean Carrere, SD double agent in Paris
KELLER	Stay-behind agent
Joseph Kelly	Pre-war Abwehr spy in England
KENT	GRU illegal Viktor Guryevich
KEYNOTE	Stay-behind agent
Mizra Khan	I/M agent codenamed SHAROCK
Charles van der Kieboom	Abwehr spy landed in Kent, September 1940
Bernie Kiener	MI5 double agent codenamed RAINBOW
KILLIAN	I/L spy Hans George codenamed DRAGONFLY by MI5
KINGPIN	MI5 double agent
KISS	Double agent Mohamed Salmassi
Fritz Klatt	Alias of Richard Kauder

Karl von Kleczkowski	Abt. III defector in Istanbul
Stella von Kleczkowski	Abt. III defector in Istanbul
Ernst Kleyenstubber	Leiter KOS from September 1944
Emile Kliemann	I/L Paris
Friedrich Knappe-Ratey	Abt. I officer in Madrid, codenamed FEDERICO
Simon Koedel	Ast Hamburg agent arrested in New York in March 1945
Ernest Kondgen	Abt. II wireless operator on ANTON mission, arrested in Tehran, August 1943
Georg Konieczny	Abt. II saboteur capured in Iraq in June 1943
Karl Korel	Abt. II wireless operator on ANTON mission to Iraq, 1943
Georg Kronberger	SD defector in Greece, September 1944
Wilhelm Kuebart	I/H Berlin
KUPPER	I/H source in Istanbul
Martin Kurmes	Leader of ANTON, committed suicide in March 1944
Josef Kuvett	SIS double agent codenamed MIMI
Ernst Lahmann	Etappendienst agent expelled from London in 1938
Erwin Lahousen	Chief, Abt. II until 1944
Fred Lang	Abwehr spy convicted September 1945
Ilya Lang	Associate of General Turkul
Alfred Langbein	I/M agent delivered to the US by U-213 in May 1942
LARK	Norwegian SD agent Herluf Nygaard
Andre Latham	BCRA double agent codenamed GILBERT
Joseph Laurenssens	Belgian seaman detained at Camp 020
LAZY	Stay-behind agent in Munchen-Gladbach
LEAGUE	Stay-behind agent
Josef Ledebur	Abwehr defector in Madrid
LEGION	Abt. III stay-behind agent
Wilhelm Leisner	Leiter, KOS until September 1944, alias Lenz
LENA	Abwehr operation to support 1940 invasion
Joseph Lenihan	MI5 double agent codenamed BASKET
Renato Levi	Codenamed CHEESE by MI5 and ROBERTO by the Abwehr
Renato Roque Liai	Portuguese spy in London
LIBERATORS	Abt. II mission to Iraq

Gerard Libot	Abwehr spy arrested in Plymouth, September 1940
Cecil Liddell	Head MI5's Irish section, B9
Guy Liddell	Director, MI5's B Division
LITIGANT	Stay-behind agent
Robert Lochner	I/M KONA
Walter Lohrey	Abwehr agent arrested in New Jersey in November 1944
Peter Loxley	Foreign Office Under-Secretary
LUC	I/L stay-behind agent in Dragignan
Kurt Ludwig	Abwehr spy 'Joe K' arrested in the United States in December 1941
Legwald Lund	Abwehr saboteur arrested in Scotland in October 1941
Richard Maasing	SIS double agent codenamed OUTCAST
Graham Maingot	SIS in Lisbon
Richard L'Estrange Malone	Pre-war SIS double agent
MARCHAND	I/H stay-behind agent in Grenoble
Carl Marcus	Abwehr defector codenamed DICTIONARY
Maria Marek	MI5 double agent codenamed THE SNARK
Hans Marschner	Alias adopted in Eire by Gunter Schutz
Otto Mayer	Abwehr officer captured in Yugoslavia
Franz Mayr	SD officer captured in Iraq September 1943
MEADOW	SD line-crosser
Albert Meems	Animal dealer and I/H Hamburg agent
Carl Meier	Abwehr spy landed on Kent coast September 1940
Rogerio de Menezes	Portuguese diplomat arrested in London
Merckl	Abwehr officer in Lisbon
Friedrich W. Meyer	Pre-war Abwehr spy in England
Cyril Mills	MI5 officer
MIMI	Josef Kuvett, SIS double agent in Istanbul
MINT	SD stay-behind double agent
MODEL	Stay-behind agent
John Moe	MI5 double agent codenamed MUTT
MONARCH	Stay-behind agent
MONOPLANE	Paul Jeannin, stay-behind agent in Marseilles.
MONTAG	Abwehr agent in Spain. Employee of the German-French Mining Co.
MONUMENT	Stay-behind agent in Paris

Ludwig Moyzisch	SD representative in Ankara
MULETER	Stay-behind agent
Gottfried Muller	Abt. II saboteur in Iraq codenamed TIGER, captured June 1943
MURAT	Abwehr codename for Otto Mayer
MUTT	MI5 codename for double agent John Moe
Dietrich Niebuhr	Abwehr representative in Argentina
Willem Niemayer	SIS agent arrested in Holland in 1942
Fritz Noak	Abwehr agent arrested in Brazil in January 1942
Henry Obed	Abwehr agent arrested in Ireland July 1940
Daniel Ocana	Detainee at Camp 020
Martin Olsen	Abwehr spy arrested September 1941
Waldemar Othmer	Abwehr spy arrested in Trenton, New Jersey in July 1944
OUTCAST	SIS double agent Richard Maasing
Arthur Owens	MI5 double agent codenamed SNOW
PABLO	Leiter, Nest Barcelona
Vaclav Pan	Head of Czech intelligence in Lisbon
PANCHO	John Eikens, double agent in Cherbourg
Heinz Pannwitz	Alias of Heinz Paulsen
PASCHA	Spaniard in Cairo represented in Istanbul by Guelfo Zamboni
PASTURES	MI5 codename for a German spy who arrived from Lisbon in June 1941
Gottfried Paul-Taboschat	Leiter, Nest Barcelona
Heinz Paulsen	Sonderkommando ROTE KAPELLE, alias Heinz Pannwitz
PEDRO	Alberto Koepke, I/H Barcelona
Jean Pelletier	SIS radio operator alias Lacoste and Abwehr spy arrested in London in April 1942
PENKNIFE	Stay-behind agent
PENNANT	Stay-behind agent in Paris
PERCY	Stay-behind agent
PERRIER	Stay-behind agent
PESSIMISTS	British-controlled network of double agents
Waldemar von Petroff	Chief agent of the Buro Jankhe
Robert Petter	Abwehr spy landed in Scotland, September 1940

Erich Pfeiffer	I/M Bremen
Kim Philby	SIS office in Secton V, then Section IX
PIE	Ferdinand Rodriguez-Reddington
PIGEON	British double agent in Lisbon
Isabel Pilderit	Abwehr agent in Valparaiso
PIP	Finnish seaman double agent
Kurt Pirwanko	SD radio operator for the ANTON mission captured in Persia in March 1944
POGO	MI5 codename for Miguel del Pozo
Sjoerd Pons	Abwehr spy landed on Kent coast, September 1940
Dusko Popov	MI5 double agent codenamed TRICYCLE
Walter Praetorius	I/Wi Ast Hamburg
PRECIOUS	SIS cdename for Erich Vermehren
Willi Preetz	Abwehr agent interned in Ireland July 1940
John Price	British double agent in Lisbon codenamed WASHOUT
Juan Pujol	V-Mann 319, codenamed GARBO by MI5; IMMORTAL and BOVRIL by SIS, ALARIC by the Abwehr
PUMPKIN	SIS agent in Lisbon
QUALITY	Abwehr stay-behind officer in Kaiserslautern
QUEASY	Stay-behind agent
RAINBOW	MI5 codename for Bernie Kiener
Nafti Rashid Ramzi	Iraqi interpreter arrested July 1943
Percy Rapp	London taxi driver and Abwehr spy
Heinrich Reimers	Abwehr agent in Valparaiso
Karel Richter	Abwehr spy paracuted into Hertfordshire in May 1941
Gene Risso-Gill	SIS, Lisbon
Jose Rist	Abwehr spy in Union City, New Jersey
T.A. Robertson	Head of MI5's B1(a) section
Werner Rockstroh	SD member of the FRANZ mission to Iraq in 1943
Ferdinand Rodriguez-Reddington	SIS agent codenamed PIE
Kurt von Rohrscheidt	Leiter, Amt III, KOS
William Rolph	Ex-MI5 officer, committed suicide in May 1940
George Romanov	General Turkul's assistant
ROMEO	Mahmoud Hamada

Gustav Ronning	Abwehr spy arrested September 1941
ROSIE	Stay-behind agent
Renato Roque Laia	Abwehr spy in Lisbon codenamed AUGUSTA
Rudilf Roser	Etappendienst agent expelled from London in 1938
Mirko Rot	Yugoslav spy for the Abwehr, arrested in London in December 1943
Gunther Rumrich	Abwehr spy arrested by the FBI in February 1937
Hans Ruser	Abwehr defector codenamed JUNIOR by SIS
Gilbert Ryle	Radio Security Service cryptanalyst
Olaf Saetrang	Abwehr spy landed at Reykjavik, September 1941
Charles de Salis	SIS Section V officer in Lisbon
Mohamed Salmassi	Double agent KISS
SCEPTIC	Notional double agent known to the Abwehr as HELMUTH
Peter Schagen	Abt. II defector in Madrid
Vera von Schallburg	Abwehr spy alias Vera Erikson
Fritz Scharpf	Pre-war Etappendienst agent in England, expelled in 1938
Walter Schellenberg	Chief, Amt VI
Gottfried Schenker-Angerer	I/L Istanbul
Ernst Schmidt	Abwehr, Oporto
Wolf Schmidt	MI5 double agent TATE alias Harry Williamson.
Gunther Schallies	Etappendienst agent expelled from London in 1938
Aloys Schreiber	I/H, then Leiter KOP
Erich Schroeder	SD Chief, Lisbon
Wilhelm Schulze	German journalist and Abwehr agent in London until August 1939
Gunter Schutz	Abwehr agent arrested in Dublin, March 1941
Berthold Schulze-Holthus	I/L stay-behind agent in Persia, freed in prisoner exchange.
Heriberto Schwartau-Eskildsen	Abwehr agent arrested by the FBI in October 1941
Otto Schwerdt	Radio operator of the FRANZ mission to Iraq, March 1943

Stanley Scott	Pre-war Abwehr spy in Southampton
Duncan Scott-Ford	British seaman and Abwehr spy executed in England
SHAROCK	Mirza Khan
Mario Shumann	Abwehr officer, Lisbon
SILBER	I/H source in Istanbul
Juan da Silva Purvis	Abwehr spy arrested in New Jersey in 1943
Arnold Silver	US Army interrogator
Ernesto Simoes	Portuguese spy arrested in England
Walter Simon	Abwehr agent expelled from England in March 1938, interned in Ireland June 1940
SISYPHUS	SIS agent in Lisbon
SKULL	Double agent Jean Senouque in Cherbourg
THE SNARK	Maria Marek, a Yugoslav domestic servant and MI5 double agent
SNIPER	MI5 double agent Hans Berrand, a Belgian pilot
SNOW	MI5 double agent Arthur Owens
Robert Solborg	OSS Chief in Lisbon, alias Charlie Grey
Thorleif Solem	Abwehr spy landed at Lerwick in March 1941 to join SOE
SOMER	Abwehr codename for Leiter, KOS
Dante Souza	SIS agent, British Consulate, Lisbon
George Speich	I/M officer
STANDARD	Stay-behind agent in Rouen
Claus von Stauffenberg	Failed assassin and 20 July conspirator
Florent Steiner	Dutch seaman and Abwehr spy arrested in Liverpool, December 1942
Michel Stockmann	I/M Paris
Richmond Stopford	SIS station commander, Lisbon
Adolf Striepe	Abwehr spy arrested in Jackson Heights, New York, in September 1945
STRIPE	MI5 double agent
Theodor Struenck	Abwehr officer implicated in the 20 July plot
SUMMER	MI5 codename for Goesta Caroli
Halina Szymanska	SIS agent in Berne
TATE	MI5 codename for Wolf Schmidt
Willem Ter Braak	Alias of Gilbertus Fukken
THISBE	Alst Paris agent arrested in London in July 1941

Hans Thost	Pre-war *Volkischer Beobachter* correspondent in London.
Paul Thummel	Alias of Dr Holm
Theodore Tietz	Pre-war Abwehr spy in England
TIGER	Abwehr codename for Gottfried Muller
Alphonse Timmerman	Belgian hanged in London in July 1942
TRICYCLE	MI5 double agent Dusko Popov
Herbert Tributh	Abwehr agent arrested in Ireland in July 1940
Anton Turkul	White Russian at KOBU
Robert Ulshofer	I/L Istanbul
Werner Unland	I/Wi Ast Hamburg spy in Dublin from August 1939 until arrested in April 1941
Klop Ustinov	MI5 agent U.35 alias Mr Johnson
Jack Verlinden	Belgian spy detained at Camp 020 in January 1942
Erich Vermehren	I/H defector in Istanbul, codenamed PRECIOUS
VICTOIRE	Mathilde Carré
VIPER	SIS double agent at the Hotel Aviz in Lisbon
Eduard Waetjen	Abwehr defector in Switzerland, 1944
Otto Wagner	Leiter, Ast Sofia, alias Dr Delius
José Waldberg	Abwehr spy landed on Kent coast in September 1940
WALENTY	Roman Garby-Czerniawski
Helmik Wallem	Abwehr spy posing as Norwegian refugee arrested in Scotland, May 1941
Werner Wälti	Abwehr spy landed in Scotland, September 1940
Ludwig Warschauer	Abwehr agent in London interned in 1940
WASHOUT	British codename for John Price
Erwin Wassner	Pre-war German naval attaché in London
WEASEL	Dr Hilaire Westerlinck, Belgian ship's doctor and MI5 double agent
Waldemar Weber	Abt. II spy in Iraq
Kuno Weltzien	Abwehr, Lisbon
Hilaire Westerlinck	MI5 double agent codenamed WEASEL
WHISKY	SIS codename for Otto John
Gerth van Wijk	Abwehr spy landed at Whitchurch in April 1941
Tarleton Winchester	Pan Am representative in Lisbon

Rita Winsor	SIS in Lisbon
Herbert Winterstein	Abwehr spy arrested in Brazil in January 1942.
William Wishart	Pre-war Abwehr spy in England
WITCH	Stay-behind agent
Bruno Wolf	SD in Istanbul
Friedrich Wolf	SD in Buenos Aires
YODLER	SIS double agent in Switzerland
Edgar Yolland	Abwehr spy in OWI Istanbul
Kurt Zaehringer	I/M Istanbul
Guelfo Zamboni	Italian journalist in Istanbul
Olga Zemanova	ECCELSIASTIC in Lisbon

Chapter I

NAVAL INTELLIGENCE

Strictest secrecy and the greatest restraint in time of peace, greatest activity and the relentless prosecution of their duties in time of war.

Generaladmiral Erich Raeder, Kriegsmarine Directive, 6 June 1936

In May 1935 Admiral Canaris took control of the Kriegsmarine's intelligence branch, the Etappendienst, and began planning for war. The naval intelligence organisation then in existence had its roots in the Kaiser's Admiralstab der Marine which had established a global network to collect shipping information for the fleet and to organise supplies for German warships when they were away from their home bases. Even after the Nazi collapse Allied knowledge of the Etappendiest was scanty, and based on a collection of captured documents assembled by MI5, combined with CSDIC interrogation reports relating to two prisoners, Werner Dietel and Horst von Pflugk-Harttung.

Born in Basle in 1889, von Pflugk-Harttung and his brother Heinz had been acquitted on charges of involvement in the assassination in January 1919 of the revolutionary leader Rosa Luxemburg, and he had been sent under journalistic cover, as the *Berliner Börsen-Zeitung* correspondent, by Canaris to build an Abwehr network in Denmark. He was arrested in Copenhagen in November 1938 and, together with fourteen Germans and Danes, was convicted of espionage. His network had successfully penetrated the Danish Army and, in particular, the detective branch of the Copenhagen police. Von Pflugk-Hartung was released from prison during the German invasion in 1940. In 1942 he was posted to Ast Bordeaux, and was taken prisoner by American troops in 1944. He remained in custody in Arizona until 1947 when he was repatriated.

Under interrogation Pflugk-Harttung revealed that his pre-war Danish spy-ring had helped manage a fleet of Spanish trawlers based at the German port of Emden which had operated on behalf of Francisco Franco's nationalist forces, and had been responsible for the loss of the SS *Cantabria* in international waters off the Norfolk coast in November 1938. The freighter, bound for Leningrad, was attacked by the auxiliary cruiser *Nadir* and sunk, the crew being rescued by the Hunstanton Lifeboat. This was but one of many episodes, wartime and pre-war, that Pflugk-Harttung clarified for his interrogators.

The other key source for information relating to the Etappen was Kapitän Dietel, who had been posted to the Abwehr in April 1935 as an expert on shipping companies, and would rise to become head of the sections dealing with North and South America, India and Australia. At that time the main etappen were located at Reval, Riga, Stockholm, Oslo, Vigo, Lisbon, Funchal, Las Palmas, Santa Cruz de Tenerife, Victoria (in Cameroon), Durban, Mombassa, Batavia, Singapore, Bangkok, Buenaventura, Valparaiso, Montevideo and Pernumbuco. According to an SIS assessment of September 1945, more 'independent' etappen were opened in Colombo, Madras, Calcutta and Wellington, and a pair of motorboats, the *Quito* and *Bogota*, were fitted with 40-watt short-wave transmitters and sent to Central America. By 1938 the number of agents employed abroad exceeded 200, a remarkable achievement considering that government policy dictated that none could be consular staff, Nazi Party members or any individual likely to attract the attention of the local security apparatus in the event of war. That last stipulation embraced other German intelligence agencies such as the Abwehr or SD. Furthermore, all were supposedly 'economically independent' volunteers, albeit encouraged by a regular monthly retainer of RM500 in return for two or three-weekly reports. In January 1940 they were informed that they had become official members of the Kriegsmarine, and were therefore exempt from being called up for military service in the Reich or in another of the armed services. One of the documents captured post-war encapsulated the intelligence collection priorities:

> The following classifications of types of intelligence which are of value should only serve the reporter as a guide; the possibility is in no way to be rejected that in addition, knowledge of events, facts, and conditions which are not catalogued here is of importance. Generally speaking it is correct to take the view that it is better to report too much than too little,

because much of the intelligence which will collect in the hands of the Etappenleiter, though if, viewed as individual reports, it seems to be unimportant, if put all together, it can in certain circumstances gives a true picture of events and lead to the correct conclusions.

Such intelligence, in order of importance, comprises the following:

(aa) Mobilisation, equipping and collection of enemy warships; presence of aircraft carriers; calling up of reserves, stocking of war materials and provisions.

(bb) State of preparation of enemy ships, anchorage, movements, intentions and state of enemy fleets, and of individual warships.

(cc) Preparation of railway transport, embarkation of troops and vehicles, armaments, and distinction of transport ships; collection of troops and war material in harbours, and also withdrawal from harbours of troops; diverting of enemy mercantile marine transport; immobilisation in neutral harbours.

(dd) Installation of new telegraphic and signal stations, laying out of new sea cables and their track; the difficulties in the conveying of intelligence; security of postal, telegraphic and cable communications.

(ee) Armament of auxiliary cruisers in enemy and neutral harbours.

(ff) Other phenomena in any way remarkable, such as changes in the colours of warships and merchant vessels.

(gg) Mining and other obstacles in waters; establishment of sentry and guard services outside the harbours; withdrawal and removal of markings of sea routes, or their replacement by different markings; changes or removal of landmarks and changes in the light frequencies of lighthouses.

(hh) Withdrawal and removal of sea markings or their substitution by different markings; alteration or removal of landmarks and changes in the frequency of light signals.

(ii) Events abroad; large political demonstrations; changes of opinion of enemy populations; cases of sabotage; notable rises in prices of essential foodstuffs; large scale purchases; freezings of export and of big business undertakings and important events on the stock exchange.

(kk) Installation of new aerodromes and seaplane bases and the state of preparedness of aeroplanes, armaments, raw materials and munitions.

(ll) Visits by high ranking statesmen or officers which are not known to the general public; the object of these visits.

(mm) Important export of war equipment and weapons of all kinds (machine guns, aircraft parts, motors, munitions etc.); export and route of the vessels allocated for this, change of flags, collections of escort vessels, their armament, and times of arrival and departure of transports and convoys.

(nn) All information about the personalities or nature of the enemy Intelligence Service; noteworthy activities of enemy agents.

(iii) Ways and means of sending reports.

Generally speaking the reporters, in obtaining intelligence concerning the topics previously set out, will only have to make use of the possibilities which are at the disposal of every reporter in a larger newspaper or telegraph office. First and foremost they must make use of the help which sea-going traffic offers them.

In towns on the coast reporters must try to collect information from the crews of arriving ships. In this respect harbour masters and customs and harbour officials employed on confidential work, can render good service, and they should be made as much use of as much as possible by reporters to this end. Aircraft, fishing boats, coastal steamers, and yachts under neutral flags are also possible helps who are able to obtain a good insight into the movements of enemy war vessels.

The reporter must decide for himself whether on occasion he can employ other persons, not Germans, who either from inclination or for other reasons want to undertake intelligence work, and also those whose only motive is the possibility of financial gain.

The services of persons sending reports directly from enemy territory are above all valuable in times of danger. It is their work to live unobtrusively in enemy countries and to observe all works which are undertaken towards war. If they are to communicate by telephone with reporters it must be by the use of previously agreed code words for certain terms.

Every reporter who is faced with this question of such agents does well to compile such a code with particular attention to the use of names of wares which are dealt in locally in peace, or at the latest in times of alarm. Often it will be desirable to allow two agents to work together, one of them doing the observing and the other bringing reports to the reporter.

The chief difficulty of their work will always be the task of communicating the intelligence which they have obtained on the subject assigned to them quickly and securely to the home country or to our own war vessels.

Even the preparations made in times of peace for a means of communicating intelligence are of the greatest possible importance. In this connection one must always be prepared for ways and means of communication to fail, whether that should be as a consequence of political events or legislation such as the establishment of censorship, or because of surveillance by the enemy Intelligence Service.

It is the duty of every reporter to search constantly for alternative possibilities for the transmission of intelligence, particularly via neutral countries which are sympathetic, and to report such limitations of means of communication, as for example, because of police or postal obstructions, as are to be expected.

The establishment and preparation of cover addresses for letters and telegrams as well as centres for sending all telephonic messages in the country in which a reporter is living, as well as in neighbouring countries which presumably will remain neutral, will require vigilant co-operation from reporters. In particular they should determine what is the traffic in letters, telegrams, telephonic messages and goods between firms of the country in which they are living and firms in the countries bordering on Germany, which presumably will remain neutral, and as the opportunity presents itself this traffic should be made use of for the communication of disguised reports.

Similarly they should examine with great care the possibilities of making use of couriers, such as those who travel regularly or frequently on steamers or aeroplanes between the countries in which they are resident and Germany, or neighbouring states which presumably will remain neutral.

The reporter must make exhaustive enquiries into the favourable opportunities which exist of sending information directly to Germany by means of commercial radio. He thus will have to inform himself on this matter while peace still exists, and learn with which countries the radio stations of his country exchanges messages, and how it is possible to send such messages via neutral foreign states to Germany.[1]

Supervising their communications was a naval officer, Friedrich Frisius, a former Kaisermarine motor torpedo boat commander in the Baltic who had used extended cruises on the light cruiser *Leipzig* to recruit his personnel across the globe. Having established a basic network, Frisius extended it with representatives in New York, Galveston, Mexico City, Puebla, Lima, Porto Alegre, Buenos Aires, Puerto Rico and Kobe. A further ten offices would be added at San Sebastian, Seville, Rio de

Janeiro, Bahia, Santos, Panama, Oahu, Sydney, Shanghai and Dairen. Originally the plan, based on the Kaisermarine's experience in the First World War, was to create a truly worldwide organisation to supply and fund naval operations conducted far from home bases in Germany.

> In addition to supplying cruisers with fuel, provisions and equipment, transmission of information on movements of enemy warships will be expected and the gathering of data on enemy merchant shipping, in some cases with cargo.[2]

In 1936 the Etappendienst was enhanced by a secret subsidiary, headed by Leutnant Otto Kreuger, designated DK, which consisted of the captains of German merchant vessels who, carefully selected, were employed to gather information and perform associated tasks, such as blockade-running.

As each individual component ettappe was headed by the relevant naval attaché who supervised networks consisting of German businessmen and shipping agents, the organisation underwent a dramatic restructuring in 1939 when, for example, the London Etappe was closed down in March and the Eastern Mediterranean section was dissolved four months later, just as there was pressure, on naval replenishment grounds, to re-open the Madrid Etappe which had been suspended during the Civil War when responsibility for reporting on shipping to 'Red Spain' or French ports was moved temporarily to Istanbul to monitor vessels transiting from the Black Sea. The system adopted during the conflict, which also monitored all shipping from Russia, the Baltic and the North Sea, was considered highly efficient and a model for future operations. During this period the Etappendienst also collected information from an office in Port Said on shipping destined for the Sino-Japanese war, and in September 1938, in the midst of the Munich crisis, a global survey was conducted to determine the exact location of all Royal Navy warships.

Similarly, the station covering the Dutch East Indies was closed when the Netherlands were occupied, and a Bordeaux office was established in the spring of 1941. Another significant change in July 1939 in anticipation of hostilities was the absorption of naval intelligence into the Abwehr's I/M. In reality those assets amounted to a large number of experienced agents across the world who were temporarily out of contact and a well-established relationship with the commercial shipping companies in Hamburg and Bremen, but only seven operational radios, linked to the Norddeich transmitter and to receiving stations at Mitte and Neuminster, located at Panama, Herta,

Sta Cruz de Tenerife, Las Palmas, Lisbon, Copenhagen and Istanbul, with plans to install more in Mexico, Cristobal, Valparaiso, New York, Buenos Aires, Rio, London, Madrid, Rotterdam, Antwerp, Oslo, Stockholm, Helsinki, Rome, Port Said, Walvis Bay, Monrovia, Durban, Mombasa, Batavia, Shanghai and Tokyo. In addition, I/M arranged for Siemens to design and build the 'Bayreuth', an ostensibly innocent radiogram which contained a concealed transmitter for distribution to selected agents. Later, stations at Swinemuende, Pillau and Ruegen were added by Werner Stouphasius to handle the growing volume of traffic. As well as employing its own special codes, the Etappen exploited amateur channels supposedly reserved for the DASD, the German branch of the International Amateur Radio Organisation.

The various schemes to develop the Etappendienst all terminated in a completion date in 1938 which coincided in mid-September with the Munich crisis, when the 'pocket battleship' *Deutschland* was deployed to southern Spain, supposedly on a goodwill cruise. In reality this was a dress-rehearsal for a wartime Etappen operation to charter neutral tankers through opaque Swedish intermediaries to refuel the warships, and position a Kriegsmarine replenishment vessel, the *Samland*, in the Atlantic as part of a strategy to extend long-distance raiders. Similarly, the *Schwabenland*, docked in Horta, was ordered to take on oil and leave her moorings in anticipation of a rendezvous with the *Admiral Graf Spee*.

According to the covert naval mobilisation plan, German merchant shipping would be instructed to avoid British, French and Russian ports (where they were susceptible to confiscation), and place themselves on a wartime footing. In addition, a small fleet of merchantmen and whalers fitted with extra-large tanks was acquired with secret funds and sent on missions in support of the Kriegsmarine's auxiliary cruisers. One such Etappe surrogate was the Waried Tankschiff Renderei, an ostensibly American-owned firm which ran twenty-seven Panamanian-flagged ships, crewed entirely by Germans. The fuel oil, already purchased from Standard Oil and the Spanish refinery CEPSA, had been bunkered by a Danish nominee in Malmo and Danzig. These precautions were intended to avoid the dangers of seized assets or frozen financial transactions, and the 1938 war alert demonstrated that the plans worked, apparently without detection or adverse consequences.

As war approached, the Etappendienst responded to a tour of inspection conducted in Madrid in April 1939 by undertaking a major reorganisation of the Spanish networks, appointing two officers to the embassy itself and establishing permanent posts at San Sebastian, Bilbao, Vigo, Seville, Barcelona, Palma de Majorca and Tetuan.

When, in August, the Molotov-Ribbentrop pact was signed, the Etappe ordered Erich Auerback, formerly of Istanbul, to Murmansk where he was allocated four supply vessels, known as V-ships. Two months later there was a further expansion with staff sent to Shanghai, Tokyo, San Salvador and Istanbul, with three V-ships, the *Elbe*, *Munsterland* and *Kulmerland*, equipped with special shortwave transmitters.

The post-war Admiralty Naval Intelligence Division (NID) assessment of the German naval intelligence networks, based on captured Kriegsmarine records, detailed their strengths and weaknesses: and gave an account of the clandestine supply organisation which

> in September 1938, by means of a very complicated use of intermediaries, the German Navy had at its disposal oil carried by Norwegian tankers chartered by a Swedish firm. And in September 1938 too the German captains of the tankers of the Waried Tanker shipping company (a company working under German management but with American capital, whose ships were run by the company but received cargoes and sailing orders from Standard Oil), sailing under the Panama flag, were enlisted and provided with a special code so that they might be given sailing orders from Germany to bring in their cargoes or make them available for supplies to German cruisers.
>
> The secrecy of the supply work from neutral countries had not only to be very strictly maintained for military reasons but it was, of course, necessitated by legal considerations connected with, for instance, the American neutrality law of 1935 and the Hague Convention in regard to the sale of supplies to belligerent powers and the use by belligerents of neutral bases. The Etappen eventually concerned in the supply work were Japan and China; Central and South America; Spain, Portugal and the Canary Islands; Bordeaux, from May 1941 after OKM/SKL had ordered that Bordeaux should be the home port for the equipment of the supply ships; Dutch East India, at the beginning of the war only, Murmansk, which was built up from October 1939 and operated with Russian consent until September 1940 when it was dissolved owing to the German acquisition of bases in the North of Norway; Italy. The files contain some evidence of assistance received from the governments of Japan, Spain, Russia and Italy.[3]

Although the Etappendienst records recovered included monthly operational reports until 1941, there was little left to indicate the scale of its activities during much of the war, although the Admiralty's NID assessed that after its agents had been taken over by I/M the organisation had concentrated on its covert supply role, rather than the collection of intelligence:

The organisation was clearly not designed to operate in enemy territory in wartime but for the purpose of collecting in neutral and friendly counties information which might be of use to the German war effort.

Whatever its achievements may or may not have been, it is interesting that this espionage network was able to be built up in peacetime and to operate in wartime under cover of a naval supply organisation, and it provides yet another example of the Germans' propensity for building up an espionage network under an elaborate cover.[4]

With the widespread deliberate destruction of Etappendienst files in Germany, the corresponding documentation in the overseas stations proved unrecoverable, so little information survived regarding specific supply operations beyond occasional hints. Evidently there was a considerable effort, at least until 1943, to replenish U-boats at night in some Spanish ports, as was noted by the NID analysis:

These operations were in some instances of considerable operational importance to the German Navy and the overall war effort; in 1940 Etappe Russia assured important fuel supplies from a German task force entering Narvik harbor; from 1940 Etappe Spain supplied German submarines with fuel and provisions; Etappe South America provided valuable shipping intelligence; by supplying and directing blockade-runners Etappe Japan was able to send into Germany scarce materials essential for war production.[5]

The extent and frequency of the Spanish replenishment project, considered illegal under international law, was the subject of conjecture for many years, in an almost complete vacuum of accurate information. Certainly the expedient of avoiding the necessity to undertake high-risk rendezvous at sea, or run the RAF Coastal Command gauntlet across the Bay of Biscay, made nighttime visits to the Spanish ports of El Ferrol, Vigo and Cadiz extremely attractive. By accident or design, five German merchantmen, the MV *Thalia* in Cadiz (but requisitioned in Seville); the MV *Bessel* in Vigo; the MV *Max Albrecht* in El Ferrol; and the MV *Corrientes* and the MV *Charlotte Schliemann*, both in Las Palmas, all of which appeared to have been trapped in neutral anchorages upon the outbreak of hostilities, potential victims of the Allied blockade, were available to participate in these covert operations conducted under cover of darkness.

Post-war research by NID 1 established evidence of twenty-three examples of U-boat replenishment in Spanish ports between January 1940 (the *U-29* at Cadiz) and December 1941 (*U-434* at Vigo), twelve of which were recorded in the relevant submarine's log. Four days after sailing from Vigo during her first war patrol, Wolfgang Heyda's Type VIIC *U-434*, based with the 7th U-boat Flotilla at Kristiansand in Norway, was attacked north of Madeira by the destroyers HMS *Blankeney* and *Stanley* while shadowing Convoy HG 76 from Gibraltar. Forced to the surface by depth charges, all but two of the crew of forty-four survived to be taken prisoner and, under interrogation, some revealed that days earlier, running low on stores after a voyage lasting six weeks, they had been refuelled and revittled in port by the *Bessel*, together with the *U-574*. A precise list of the provisions supplied to the submarine was recovered by the NID 1/P/W interrogators who learned that the supplies had been purchased recently in Madrid and included 36kg of marmalade and 11,000 cigarettes.

NID 1 concluded that although the Etappendienst's intelligence role would diminish as the war progressed, and the Kriegsmarine was 'driven from the seas', the 'vital activity of blockade-running' became all the more important, and in this field the Etappendienst proved highly effective.

When in 1946 the NID circulated its report on the Etappendienst, it took both MI5 and SIS completely by surprise, as neither knew very much about the organisation. Specifically, there was concern in March 1946 about references in the captured files to the man alleged to have been part of the Etappe London, Dietrich Jakobs, a naturalised British subject who had lived in Wimbledon with his wife Emma and daughter before the war.

In the absence of Jakobs, who reportedly had emigrated to South Africa in 1935 where he acquired a British passport, MI5's main source of information about the Etappendienst was a former German merchant navy captain, Heinrich Alhrichs, who was interrogated at Bad Nenndorf. Born in Bremen in April 1895, Alhrichs had commanded a Dutch liner in peacetime, and in the First World War had served on four U-boats, and for a period had been attached to the Turkish navy. Described as 'a great liar and extremely vociferous and boastful' by one of his interrogators, Alhrichs recalled that Kapitän Jakobs, who had also served on a U-boat during the First World War, had returned to England alone in December 1939 through Holland and had stayed at the Overseas Club in London, equipped with a code and cover-addresses in the Netherlands.[6]

MI5's belated post-war investigation of Jakobs, conducted mainly by Desmond Vesey, discovered that he had been in England in April 1936 on a mission to recruit representatives in Grimsby, Hull, Sunderland, Edinburgh, Aberdeen and the Shetland Islands, having already established Fritz Scharpf in Southampton and Adolf Jaeger in London. Scharpf was very familiar to MI5, which had initiated a file on him in April 1936 when he had been identified by Klop Ustinov as a spy undertaking clandestine missions for the German embassy.[7] Subsequently, he had connected him to Mathilde Krafft. Scharpf's large dossier shows that he arrived in England in June 1930 as a student and had found a job as a clerk assisting the German consul in Southampton, Colonel J.E. Dawe, who was a British shipbroker. He was then appointed deputy consul and, following a brief investigation conducted by MI5's Con Boddington, was expelled in May 1939 on suspicion of espionage, together with Jaeger, then employed as superintendent of the Hamburg Wharf in the London Docks, and four others: Rudolf Rosel, Ernst Lahrmann, Gunther Schallies and Richard Fraunedorf.

Both Scharpf and Jaeger had been compromised by another MI5 source inside the embassy, Wolfgang zu Putlitz, but not even he was aware of the Etappendienst, although he suspected a connection with the naval attaché, Erwin Wassner. The NID's post-war documents included Jaeger's instructions, issued in June 1935:

> He was to watch peacetime transports and exports to France; to collect data and photographs of French merchant ships and post installations, especially in the Channel zone; to examine the question of a systematic surveillance of the English Channel exit into the North Sea; to draw attention to persons for consideration as agents; to examine the possibility of obtaining letter and telegram cover-addresses in England; and, to examine the question of forming a 'Schiffsbefragungsdienst'.[8]

At that time the German plan was to find suitable recruits in Plymouth, Hull, Liverpool, Dublin and Belfast, but little progress was mentioned in the Etappendienst annual report dated July 1936. However, in the previous April Jakobs, codenamed W-536, had arrived in England to work for NordDeutscherLloyd, equipped to communicate with a cover-address in Copenhagen. He had visited Great Britain on several occasions, his first trip, lasting five weeks in the autumn of 1934, being to look for opportunities in Scotland. The files also disclosed that Jakobs had rented a large house at 76 Marryat Road in Wimbledon, and had received his salary through the Durban branch of the Netherlandsche Bank in South Africa,

Evidently the Etappendiest was quite successful in its pre-war operations in England, for in July 1939 it prepared a roster of its assets which were to be transferred to I/M control in Hamburg, Bremen, Wilhelmshaven and Cologne:

Ast Hamburg

London	Schmidt-Rex. Stephan, Helfert, Beuerburg, Kurt Dehn, Lang, Dr Markau, Heller, Prof. Bide, Zwanzig, Schmidt-Falkner
Southampton	Berndes, Henry Schubert
Leith	Däcker, Whitelaw
Glasgow	Konsul Werner Gregor
Gravesend	Löbbecke
Liverpool	Lahmann
Dublin	Müller-Duberow, Mohr, Wheeler-Hill

Ast Bremen

London	Baron Constant von Pilar, Dressler

Ast Wilhelmshaven

Hull	Hünecke
Aberdeen	Rhode

Ast Cologne

London	Seydel, Dr Salzmann, Dufour, Passbender, Neven-du Mont, hairdresser in the Carlton, Baron Schröder.[9]

This agent list, compiled by SIS's Miss Wells, was only read by MI5's management in June 1946, by which time it was judged by the authorities to be only of academic interest, but it nevertheless demonstrates that MI5's pre-war investigations may have penetrated the Abwehr networks, but came nowhere close to uncovering the Etappendiest's many assets. Among the many notable figures mentioned were several prominent Germans, all known to MI5, but not as spies. Among them were Constant von Pilar, the NordDeutscherLloyd chairman in London; Dr Werner Gregor, the consul in Glasgow since August 1937, denounced by Klop Ustinov as engaged in espionage; the City banker Kurt Dehn, described by MI5's Ronnie Haylor as 'a moral pervert'; Baron Schröder of Schöder's Bank; and Dr Karl Markau, president of the German Chamber of Commerce. The precise role played by these individuals remains unclear from the surviving files, but it would seem that each had been approached to authorise the employment of men such as Scharpf who required cover to enter, or remain, in the country. In the case of Henry Schubert, a dual national born in London but brought up in Germany, who was only investigated by MI5 after the war, there were suspicions about his perceived divided loyalties and his wartime service with the Luftwaffe, which he claimed had been under duress.[10]

* * *

Many of the post-hostilities naval intelligence interviews and much of the recovered documentation were derived from TICOM, a group of Anglo-American cryptographers and other personnel with related skills, known as the innocuous-sounding Target Intelligence Committee, deployed to seize sites of interest before they could be destroyed. An early TICOM discovery was that the Combined Naval Cypher No. 3, used by the US Navy and the Royal Navy for North Atlantic convoy operations, had been read 'almost 100 percent by the Germans from the end of 1941 through the middle of 1942. The solution of this system was perhaps for the Allies the most disastrous signal Intelligence success achieved by the Germans. Allied convoy shipping losses suffered during this period were six times as great as during any other comparable period.'[11]

The Kriegsmarine's signals intelligence branch was the Funkbeobachtungsdienst (B-Dienst), a combined interception and cryptanalytical organisation created in 1934 to undertake the traffic analysis, cryptanalysis and evaluation of British, American, Russian, French and Swedish naval traffic. Initially based in Berlin's Tirpitzufer, and commanded from November 1941 to January 1944 by Heinz Bonatz, the headquarters was bombed out in December 1943, when it moved to a bunker outside the city, codenamed BISMARCK. Later, following heavy Allied air raids, it was evacuated to Eberswalde, 50 miles northeast of Berlin in Brandenburg.

The B-Dienst produced instant results, partly because the British Admiralty's reluctance to adopt the TypeX machine. Instead, the navy had relied upon a five-figure Administrative Code for routine communications, and a four-figure Naval Cipher for the use of officers. Both consisted of frequently-used terms, which were altered by means of super-encipherment subtraction tables that were themselves subject to frequent change. The B-Dienst would eventually grow to employ some 5,000 staff and more than 40 intercept and direction-finding stations spread from the Crimea to Brest and the northernmost point of Norway.

13

a) Four detachments in Flanders, Brittany, Wilhelmshaven and Pomerania engaged in cryptanalysis on low-level systems, interception and direction-finding. Each detachment had a total complement of 200 men, including 100 intercept operators and 10 cryptanalysts.

b) Eighteen 'primary direction-finding stations', whose main duties were interception rather than direction-finding. Each station had a strength of 100, including 60 intercept operators, and 5 cryptanalysts.

c) Twenty-five 'secondary direction-finding stations', whose duties were direction finding and traffic analysis. Each station had a strength of 26 persons.

d) Small detachments were occasionally set up for special missions.[12]

The methodology adopted to reconstruct the Administrative Code had been a comparison of the known movements of particular, named, merchantmen with the routes of the ships as published in the *Lloyd's Weekly Shipping Report*. This procedure was a time-honoured routine requirement to signal the details of every merchant vessel sighted at sea and it enabled the B-Dienst to guess the likely content of many messages, which in turn led to the discovery of up to half of the relevant subtraction systems currently in use. The B-Dienst's knowledge was also greatly enhanced by wreck recoveries, such as the depth-charging in January 1940 of three British submarines, the *Undine, Seahorse* and *Starfish,* in the Heligoland Bight by German patrol craft. All three sank in shallow waters and were promptly visited by divers who retrieved the invaluable subtraction tables for the Admiralty's codes. Soon afterwards, in April, during the Norwegian campaign, another set of tables was recovered from HMS *Hardy.* The destroyer's commander, Captain Warburton-Lee, was killed by overwhelming enemy gunfire during his third attack on the harbour and his ship ran aground on the beach of the Ofot Fjord, enabling German troops to climb aboard and find the ciphers. Then, during the chaotic evacuation of Bergen, the Merchant Navy Codebook fell into the enemy's hands, together with a copy of the Foreign Office's Inter-Departmental Cipher.

The Admiralty became aware of some of the compromise and responded by introducing new encryption procedures, but one, which required the super-encipherment of the Naval Cipher, actually assisted the B-Dienst cryptanalysts. Because of the logistical problems of sending new subtraction tables all over the world and manufacturing the necessary quantities of one-time pads, the Admiralty simply ordered the Naval Cipher, which had hitherto resisted decryption by the enemy, to be subjected to the same subtraction method as the Administrative Code. As soon as the B-Dienst discovered the new procedure, it was able to read the greater part of the navy's two separate signal systems. Eventually, on 20 August 1940, the Admiralty managed to replace the compromised Administrative Code with a four-figure Naval Code No. 1, and the Naval Cipher with Naval Code No. 2. Because the five-figure version had been scrapped, the two had identical characteristics, causing the B-Dienst to experience great difficulty in telling one, codenamed BLUE, from the other, BROWN. The TICOM assessment completed in May 1946 described the B-Dienst's principal achievements, acknowledging that the solution of Naval Code No. 2 had revealed the entire 'wartime organisation and disposition of the British Fleet' in 1939, and conceding that 'in the spring of 1940 it obtained complete information concerning the proposed British and French Norway expedition (Operation STRATFORD)'.

> This was done by solution of British Naval Cypher No. 4. The German invasion of Norway followed immediately. During the subsequent Norwegian campaign, solution of traffic sent in British Naval Cypher No. 4 gave detailed information on Allied countermeasures, such as proposed British landing-fields, transport arrival schedules, and the disposition of British and French surface forces.
>
> Throughout 1942 and part of 1943 it provided important intelligence on Atlantic convoys by a current (and nearly 100%) solution of Combined Cypher No. 3 used by British and US North Atlantic Convoys. The average monthly Allied shipping losses in the Atlantic during this period were approximately six times the average monthly losses in later periods.[13]

The TICOM analysis listed other, relatively minor successes accomplished by the B-Dienst, including 'the solution of the British Inter-Departmental Cypher; solution in 1943 of a Royal Air Force torpedo-bomber transposition cipher used for practice exercises in the English Channel; and solution of various minor Navy and Merchant Navy codes and ciphers'.[14]

As well as enjoying considerable cryptographic success, the B-Dienst developed traffic analysis skills and

> carried out direction-finding activities against Allied naval and merchant ships, plotted their positions and movements, and passed the information to local commanders. Detachment Flanders, at Bruges, assisted in the 1942 'escape' of two pocket battleships [sic] Scharnhorst and Gneisenau when they made their dash from Brest through the English Channel to Kiel. This same detachment read British naval traffic to advantage during the Dieppe raid.[15]

The B-Dienst acquired further cryptographic material from HMS *Sikh*, a destroyer sunk in Tobruk harbour during Operation AGREEMENT, a Commando raid on the port in September 1942, but the access only continued until November 1943 when the TypeX was fully introduced across the fleet. That expedient, enhanced by special ciphers dedicated to particular operations, such as the landings at Anzio, served to limit further naval cryptographic exploitation, as was established by Allied interrogators who questioned the headquarters staff, then headed by Max Kupfer. Among the materiel his men surrendered to the British Army at Flensburg in May 1945 were twenty-six volumes of a file containing agent rosters, annual reports, lists of cover-addresses and a war diary, detailing the activities of the Etappendienst before and during the war. Until that point, the Admiralty had almost no notion of the relative success of German naval intelligence.

Chapter II

WARTIME OPERATIONS

Between the work of Abw. Abt. III and RSHA Amt. IV, (i.e. the Gestapo), the Allied intelligence services in the Low Countries were deeply penetrated at the beginning of the war, and throughout the history of resistance movements in occupied territory there were many instances of effective German penetration, some of them on a large scale.

SHAEF Report, December 1945

Colonel Friedrich Baumeister was already on his way to Madrid to take command of the KOS when he was recalled to Cologne in June 1940 by his old friend Colonel Oster. Born in Goslar, Lower Saxony, in September 1892, Baumeister was a monocle-wearing cavalry officer of the old school, having been commissioned into the 9th Dragoons in February 1912, who had joined Abwehr II in September 1924.[1] Posted to Munster, from September 1923 until recently had he been in charge of Ast Cologne where, according to HARLEQUIN,[2] he had supervised the great coup of the theft of the French mobilisation plans. At the time responsibility for collection against France was divided between the Abstellen at Wiesbaden and Cologne. In early July 1944 he had been transferred to Berchtesgaden to join the OKW staff, but was arrested on 26 July and accused of complicity in the attempted putsch. He was released for lack of evidence in September, but re-arrested in November, tried by a court-martial and sentenced to three years' imprisonment. He was finally released in April 1945 and was taken prisoner at Flensburg five months later, and interrogated at CSDIC in November.

As an intelligence professional, Baumeister had been known to SIS, the Belgian Sureté and MI5's Edward Hinchley-Cooke since September 1930 when he was discovered to be using the alias Rudolph and running agents in France and Belgium through a cover-address in Münster, Westphalia. This development prompted an investigation of the London-based Nazi journalist Karl-Heinz Abshagen who purported to represent the *Hamburger Nachrichten*, among several other German titles, concentrating on economic affairs. Shortly before war was declared he moved to The Hague and spent much of the conflict in Tokyo and China as a newspaper correspondent. After the war he collaborated with Ian Colvin to write a biography of Admiral Canaris, for whom his brother Wolfgang had worked in Lisbon.[3]

Simultaneously, MI5 ran a double agent, Richard L'Estrange Malone, against Rudolph, and the interception of mail compromised their means of communication, revealing in April 1933 one of several highly incriminating questionnaires produced by Baumeister which revealed his collection priorities. As SIS reported to MI5, referring to Malone as 'X':

RUDOLPH informed 'X' that he had agents in Belgium and that his work was to obtain information with regard to France, Belgium and Poland; that he proceeded to Cologne once a month and that his Chief lived in Berlin. He verbally gave 'X' a special questionnaire, as follows:

1, To obtain all possible information with regard to the results of the French autumn manoeuvres, especially with regard to mechanical transport and tanks, together with the latest tests etc.
2. Texts and possible amendments to Franco-Belgian Treaty, together with the possibility of any changes.
3. Latest gas analysis and possible antidotes used in French and Belgian gasmasks.
4. Anything in connection with orders that have been given to aviation pilots with regard to mobilisation in the case of outbreak of war.
5. Anything which may be secret or confidential with regard to the result of the Marseilles air manoeuvres.

If 'X' were able to obtain any documents bearing on the above points RUDOLPH expressed himself as ready to pay a deposit upon them as received; they would then be examined by experts who would decide their value.[4]

Although the investigation of Baumeister and Abshagen did not lead to any arrests, with the details securely filed away in various classified registries, it was a milestone event on several levels. There was the cooperation between the British and Belgian authorities, the evidence of German espionage and, for the first time, some identified suspects to keep under surveillance. Hitherto, as MI5 had complained, SIS's information about such matters invariably had been too vague to act on. Although both MI5 and SIS were keen to exploit their advantage and pursue a double-cross strategy employing Malone, the very detailed nature of Baumeister's questionnaires (see Appendix I) made answering them imprudent.

Although Baumeister was unaware of it, and never travelled further than Belgium to meet his agents, his lengthy questionnaires had utterly compromised him. On the other hand, of course, it was not until Baumeister was interrogated in 1945 that MI5 realised who 'Colonel Rudolph' really was.

In 1935 Baumeister was chosen by Canaris to reorganise Ast Frankfurt, where he worked with two subordinates, Waag and Schmidt, who would accompany him on his subsequent postings. According to Baumeister, he was informed by Hans Oster during a meeting in Cologne that Canaris had cancelled his transfer to Spain and decided to place him in administrative charge of operations in France, and Baumeister had suggested that the new organisation should be

> designated 'Abwehrleitstelle' (Alst) as he envisaged it was the superior Abw organisation under which the various nests in France would function. Canaris, however, considered that one Leitstelle should not run four Asts and a compromise was reached. The four Asts remained under the direct command of Amt Ausland Abwehr, but the Alst was to be kept informed of all important matters and to receive information on request.[5]

While in Paris Baumeister divorced his wife to marry his 34-year-old secretary, Fraulein Juhl, who was also his mistress. In July 1944 she was posted to KOS and would meet Baumeister twice a month in San Sebastian. His reputation would be damaged by his association with Otto Brandl who ran a large black-market business in Paris known simply as OTTO. This corruption of the Alst's role came about because theoretically the military occupation was not legally entitled to requisition anything except weapons and petroleum products, thus requiring the occupation troops to pay for everything else. This created an opportunity for OTTO to act as an intermediary between French vendors, who sought the security offered by Brandl's unquestioned status, and their German clientele. With intelligence collection devolved to the individual Abstellen, and actual operations left in the hands of the individual Abteilung, being mainly I and III, the Paris headquarters in the Hotel Luletia at 43 Boulevard Raspail became the hub of a business empire.

Although Alst Paris's involvement in the black market might have appeared to undermine the Abwehr's professionalism, self-enrichment was not necessarily the only motive, as the SD's Friedrich Dohse explained to his post-war interrogators. Dohse, who had been posted to Paris for six months from June 1941, recalled that OTTO

> bought everything that was obtainable on the French market. As the Germans printed the necessary French money themselves, the price did not matter, but the result was that the Black Market in France had so high prices that it was a catastrophe to the French state, nearly. A clear head in Abt. V got the idea to form an organisation of purchasers, which should range under the German criminal police. These purchasers should go out in the country and buy all the goods they could obtain on the Black Market. The price did not matter. The custom was to pay for the goods, when the lorry, brought along by the purchaser, was loaded. When this had happened 2 or 5 German policemen appeared suddenly. They required an explanation from the seller and from the buyer, and the latter, who worked for the Germans, confessed immediately that it was a Black Market business. Then the German criminal police confiscated the goods, in favour of the Germans.
>
> Here too was a keen co-operation with the French police. There was a special police corps: Police Economique, which was to fight against Black Market trades. A special arrangement was made with this section. The policemen, who seized Black Market dealers and occupied goods, received a provision of the Germans. They got 10% of the value of the goods, calculated at Black Market prices.[6]

France would be divided, administratively, into north and south zones, and be covered by nineteen Asts and Nests at Andernos, Angers (with outstations at St. Avertin, Angouleme and Tors), Arras, Bayonne, Biarritz (with an outstation at Hendaye), Bordeaux (with outstations at Cap Ferrat, Lucanau, Minizan, Royan and Souac), Boulogne/ Wimereux, Brest, Cherbourg, Dienay, Dijon (with outstations at Dienay and Pontarlier), La Roche, La Rochelle, Le Havre, Libourne, Lille, Lyon, Maison-Lafitte, Marseille, Mauleon, Nice, Perpignan, Poitiers, Rocquencourt, Strasbourg, Toulon, Toulouse and Vichy.

A Section V assessment of the Abwehr in France assembled and circulated in July 1944 by John Day set out the organisation's complex structure:

2. The form adopted by the Abwehr in a given country depends upon whether that country is occupied or unoccupied. If it is occupied, it depends upon (a) the status and location of the Wehrmacht commands and of the military administration, if any, (b) the decree to which the country continues to be controlled by Asts in Germany, which are generally those interested in it before its occupation. Hence, between the Armistice and the present time, its organisation in France has been determined by the following main factors:

(a) The establishment in Paris shortly after the Armistice of a supreme military commander, later to become Oberbefehlshaber West or a Tilitaerbefehlshaber for the Zone Nord, and of an Admiral i/c Submarines. This rendered necessary the establishment there of an Abwehrleitstelle exercising administrative and often intelligence control over other stations, including Asts, in the occupied territory, and passing the reports of its network direct to these commands. Similarly, the location and importance of other Abwehr stations has been determined by the establishment at various times of important operational commands elsewhere, notably at Bordeaux and Toulon.

(b) The existence of a conquered, but not occupied, zone which did not become occupied territory until 11 November 1942. Here, up to the time of the total occupation, the Abwehr was obliged to adopt an ad hoc organisation, and after the total occupation, to introduce the type of organisation prescribed for occupied territory.

(c) At the time of the Armistice three German Asts, Hamburg, Stuttgart and Wiesbaden, had interests in France which were probably of long standing. As, however, Alst France consolidated its position, it took over progressively the functions formerly exercised by Hamburg and Stuttgart, while Ast Wiesbaden was replaced by an Abwehr division of the German Armistice Commission HQ. Hamburg still exercises intelligence control over certain subsidiaries of Paris; but Stuttgart had been completely superseded by the end of 1941. Muenster/Cologne, however, whose interest in France also dates back to before the war has maintained outposts in Paris. Further, Ast Brussels controls two subsidiary stations in France, but this is simply because the departments Pas de Calais and Nord, in which they are located, have been included in the administrative area of the German Military Command in Belgium.

3. At the time of the German entry into France, Hamburg was the Ast most active in naval espionage and all operations against the Western Maritime Powers. Thus, during the invasion there was attached to IV Army HQ an Einsatzkommando under an officer of Hamburg's Nest

Bremen, which established a chain of some ten intelligence posts along the northern and western coastline of France. From the Channel ports in particular, operations against the UK were actively directed by Hamburg during the invasion period in close collaboration with Brussels, Hamburg's principal forward base for these purposes. When the invasion project fell into abeyance, the majority of them, however, were dissolved and only Boulogne/Wimereux, Le Havre, Brest and Bordeaux achieved permanent status. Of these Boulogne/Wimereux passed under the Brussels system while Le Havre, Brest and Bordeaux, later carrying out I/M and II work against the UK until mid 1941, were effectively taken over by Alst France, though Hamburg still retains a measure of intelligence control over them. The later activities of Hamburg in France have not been very significant. They include the establishment in mid 1942 of an outstation in Paris and of a communications centre at Andemos and, in about April 1943 an outstation in the Toulon area.

4. The Alst France network began to take shape very shortly after the Armistice. The Alst was certainly in existence by August 1940, had established the majority of its stations by mid-1941, and towards the end of that year took over Dijon from Stuttgart. From the end of 1942 it assumed control of some five stations of the German Armistice Commission system which had been superseded as a result of the total occupation.

Finally, at the end of 1943, Arras and Cherbourg were set up under it. Hence Alst France now controls, under Berlin HQ, every station in France with the exception of Strasbourg, and of the two subsidiaries of Brussels; even in those stations in which Hamburg has an interest the control clearly lies with the Alst. A final organisational feature deserving comment is the specialisation of function among the subsidiaries of Alst France. Thus, La Roche and Bayonne are virtually outstations of Alst France Gruppe II and Brest and Le Havre of Alst France I/M.

5. Stuttgart appears to have been principally interested in the area of the Franco-German and Franco-Swiss frontiers. Only three of its stations – Dijon, Strasbourg, Nancy – were of any importance, the rest, consisting of some half-dozen outposts, were responsible for the security of the Franco-Swiss frontier. The system lapsed about the end of 1941, when Dijon passed under Alst France, and Strasbourg under the Reich system as a result of the virtual incorporation with Germany of Alsace-Lorraine.

Brussels, for the reasons given above, controls two stations in France: Boulogne/Wimereux, which it took over from Hamburg in the early part of 1942 and Lille which first came to notice in August of that year.

6. The Zone Sud and French North Africa constituted a separate problem as territory which, albeit conquered, was unoccupied and to which

neither the Ast nor the KO system could be applied. Hence the Abwehr made use of a third type of organisation under which its officers were attached to the Armistice Commissions and sub-Commissions set up after the cessation of hostilities. The controlling authority for the Zone Sud and French North Africa therefore became the Abwehr division of German Armistice Commission HQ located at Wiesbaden under Oberstleutnant Hebeler, which was in the closest relations with Ast Wiesbaden. Within the Zone Sud, and to some extent in the Zone Nord also, the German Armistice Commission set up a number of military, air and economic inspectorates, commissions and sub-commissions to which Abwehr officers were on occasion attached, and some ten Abwehr stations are known to have been established under this cover. Further, Abwehr officers were attached, under cover of liaison, to the Italian Naval Delegations forming part of the Italian Armistice Commission, which had been allotted the supervision of the Mediterranean coast. In April 1942 the Zone Sud organisation was completed by the establishment of a control centre at Bourges which exercised a general authority over stations within the area. An analogous organisation existed in French North Africa, where Casablanca played the part of Bourges, and Oran, Algiers and Tunis corresponded to the Zone Sud stations which Bourges controlled. Indeed the analogy may be extended to the efforts made in both cases by the Abwehr officers to oust the Italian intelligence officers to whom they were attached, or at least to relegate the functions of the latter to a role of quite secondary importance.

7. On 11 November 1942 the German armed forces occupied the Zone Sud with the assistance of three Gruppe II Abwehr kommandos – mobile intelligence units originally formed in anticipation of an Allied landing in the Zone Nord – which were used as being the only mobile units available to strike against intelligence targets in the newly occupied territory. The effect of the total occupation was to place the Zone Sud in the same category as other occupied territory and to remove all further occasion for an ad hoc Abwehr organisation within it. Hence, following upon a conference held at Marseille on 30 November 1942 presided over by Canaris and attended by Rudolph and Hebeler, the Wiesbaden system passed into liquidation. At the end of December all stations in the Zone Sud were reporting to Alst France, and not as hitherto to Bourges; and by April 1943 the Bourges station had itself ceased to exist. The Wiesbaden outstation in Paris, however, has remained and now constitutes the only survival of the earlier system. The more important Zone Sud stations – Lyon, Toulon, Marseille, Toulouse and Perpignan – have passed under Alst France, and there is evidence that Lyon now holds the controlling functions formerly exercised by Bourges on behalf of Wiesbaden. A number of the less important stations were closed down, whilst the Italian Naval Delegations have disappeared

and the Abwehr liaison officers with them. Above all, the security duties which were the primary responsibility of the Wiesbaden stations have now been largely assumed by the Sipo and SD. None the less, the German Armistice Commissions themselves do not appear to have been withdrawn, and as they may still be carrying on local espionage their records will deserve attention.

OBJECTIVES

8. Although the Abwehr in France has been concerned with all forms of secret service work, the most active sections have been I, II and III.

9. Military Espionage. The most active sections have been those of Dijon and Alst France, while Angers and Bordeaux have also contributed. Here the principal objective has been French North Africa and the method adopted has usually been the infiltration of agents, who are often Arabs, through Spain and Spanish Morocco. Up to the total occupation, a good deal of espionage of a general operational character was also directed against the Zone Sud, principally by Paris, Angers, Tours, Dijon, Bordeaux, Nantes, Biarritz and Chalons-sur-Saone. The objectives were the French Army and Fleet, concealed munition dumps and airfields, and resistance organisations. In general, agents of a low type were employed, those of the Koenig organisation being typical. In addition, all the German Armistice Commission stations of the Zone Sud employed similar agents both locally and, on occasion, in North Africa.

10. Naval Espionage. Until the need arose for an Abwehr organisation adequate to meet the requirements of the supreme military commander in the event of an Allied invasion, by far the most important operational assignment was the supply of naval intelligence for the important submarine and long-range aircraft bases on the Western and Mediterranean seaboards. Hence the naval sections of Bordeaux, Toulon and, above all, Paris have acquired considerable importance. As, however, those stations would have been unable, either singly or in combination, to supply all the information required, they have also made use of that provided by more distant stations, particularly KOs Spain and Portugal, which cover a much larger area than the French stations themselves can reach – e.g. the Straits of Gibraltar and the Cape route to Egypt; while Toulon has similarly made use of the KO Bulgaria network in the Eastern Mediterranean. Paris has, however, established its own outstations in the Rio del Oro and the Canaries; its satellite stations, Le Havre and Brest, have covered the Channel and the Bay of Biscay; while Bordeaux and Toulon have run their own espionage undertakings. Le Havre, while specialising on a local reporting system conducted by W/T equipped agents from fishing trawlers, has also attempted transatlantic espionage and enterprises in the area of the Straits of Gibraltar, while

the Hamburg outstation in Toulon has recently organised a network which extends to South Italy and Lisbon and which makes use of agents on Red Cross ships. On the other hand, the activities of Brest and Bordeaux have, in general, been local only. Finally I/M Paris has been active in the dispatch of agents to Allied Countries, including French North Africa, with a view to obtaining intelligence of other than immediate value.

11. Air and Air Technical Espionage. The active sections have been above all Paris I. Luft and I/TLw and Bordeaux I/T.Lw; while the objectives have been Great Britain, French North Africa and the USA.

12. Economic Espionage. The most important section has been the outstation of Cologne I.Wi. in Paris, but Bordeaux possesses an economic section of some importance, and so, to a lesser extent, do Lyon, Dijon and Marseille. The most common objectives have been French North Africa, the USA and the Iberian Peninsula. Prior to the total occupation, economic espionage was also a secondary interest of the German Armistice Commission stations in the Zone Sud, the object being to discover evasions of the Armistice terms on behalf of the Economic Delegation of the German Armistice Commission and of the Sonderstab HKW, Berlin.

13. Sabotage and Subversion. If we except the early II operations of Brest, Boulogne and Bordeaux against the UK, all of which had come to an end by mid-1941, sabotage and subversion has been handled exclusively by Gruppe II Paris with the aid of its outstations at La Roche and Bayonne and its depot at Rocquencourt. The section is a strong one and has interested itself above all in French North Africa, the UK and possibly the USA. Paris exercises general control and recruits agents, particularly Arabs, while La Roche, Bayonne and Rocquencourt are mainly occupied with training, La Roche being the most important establishment of this kind which the Abwehr possesses.

14. Security and Counter-Espionage. Gruppe III has always been a most important section in view of the need which the Germans have had to protect themselves in an occupied but powerful country, the great majority of whose inhabitants are hostile to them. Since 1942, however, it has declined somewhat in importance. Its duties are being increasingly taken over by the Sipo and SD, both in the Zone Nord, and, since the total occupation, in the Zone Sud, where security had hitherto been the chief responsibility of the German Armistice Commission stations. None the less, the III/F sub-section is very active in Boulogne and Lille, which cover respectively the vital Channel sector and the Belgian frontier; in the Angers network which watches the Cherbourg peninsula; in Biarritz, Toulouse and Perpignan which guard the refugee routes into Spain; and

in Marseille and Toulon, Lyon and Dijon, which are responsible for the control of the Mediterranean coast and the Italian and Swiss frontiers. In general, the security work of the stations, of which – apart from Paris – Angers, Lyon and Biarritz deserve especial notice, takes the form of an unending struggle against underground movements and Allied, Patriot and Communist agents. They have received material assistance from the large and efficient D/F'ing units of WT/FU based on Paris and Lyon.

15. Technical Sections. The Leiter of Alst France is also Funkleiter France and is responsible for all W/T matters in the country. There is a W/T centre at Libourne which is of vital importance in this connection.[7]

The Section V document concentrated on Paris, seeking to explain the Alst's anomalous position within the Abwehr:

1. By far the most important station in Paris is Alst France, which came into existence shortly after the Armistice, and which is, according to a well-informed source, inferior in size only to the Abwehr HQ Berlin. Some idea of the degree to which its work overshadows that of other stations in France is given by the fact that, of all the espionage operations known to have been mounted by French stations, Alst France has initiated over 70. But it is to be expected in a station of such importance, all sections are substantially represented, and it is well equipped with training schools, places of interview and other such facilities.

2. The history of the relations of the Alst to Berlin HQ and to the other French stations is the recent history of the Abwehr in France.
    Paris contains, in addition to the Alst, a number of dependencies of other stations. An outstation of the German Armistice Commission HQ, Wiesbaden first came to notice in December 1940, and continues to operate, probably under cover of the Economic Delegation of the German Armistice Commission. There was evidence of the existence of a dependency of Stuttgart at the same period, but it was probably closed in the course of 1941. Since early 1942, Cologne has maintained an important office in Paris; an outstation of Hamburg was first reported in August 1942; and Angers opened a Meldekopf there early in 1943. There is also evidence that Ast Munster is interested in the work of Alst France Gruppe II. Finally, paragraph 7 below refers to a number of miscellaneous organisations which, though they cannot be classed as parts of the Alst, undoubtedly work on behalf of its officers.

3. The objectives of Paris have been:-

    (a) To secure a regular flow of operational intelligence to the submarines and aircraft based on the Atlantic and Mediterranean coasts.

(b) To maintain the security of German interests against the activities of allied and indigenous agents.

(c) To obtain information about the military intentions of the allies in the UK and French North Africa, latterly with a special view to defence against invasion.

(d) To effect sabotage and subversion in the Arab world generally, with particular attention to French North Africa; and to a much lesser extent sabotage against the UK.

(e) To obtain economic and technical aerial intelligence from the UK, the USA and French North Africa.

(f) Prior to the total occupation, espionage in the Zone Sud.

4. Gruppe I. Leiter: Oberstleutnant Waag.

I.H. The interests of Alst France I/H. are known to be wide. In the Spring of 1942 Waag was jointly concerned with the Leiter II/M in the establishment of a station at Villa Cisneros in the Rio de Oro, in the anticipation that this would provide a valuable base for infiltrating agents into French West Africa and French Morocco. Interest in French North Africa is also illustrated by the case of a Frenchman, an agent of Paris I/H, who began to work in Algiers at the beginning of 1943 through the intermediary of the Abwehr organisation in Spanish Morocco, his mission being to report on Allied military activities in the area. Again, it is known that in 1943 I/H was proposing to send an agent to Brazil. Typical of the methods of the section is the case of an agent sent to Egypt in July 1942. This was an Egyptian who had for some years prior to the war carried on a flourishing legal practice in France. Early in 1942, feeling his position in the Zone Sud insecure, he applied to return to Egypt, and was a result of this application brought into touch with agents of the Abwehr. Having accepted the mission proposed to him on advantageous financial conditions, he was trained in W/T and secret writing at a well-known espionage school in Paris. He left that city in March 1942 with orders to proceed to Cairo via Lisbon and Lourenco Marques in the guise of a returning national, and equipped with a W/T transmitter/receiver, secret ink and a code. His instructions were to undertake subversive political activity against the British military forces in Egypt, and to report by W/T and secret writing. He was given useful contacts in Palace circles. It was also probably intended that he should report operational intelligence. The case provides a good illustration of the use to which the Abwehr puts Arab residents in Metropolitan France.

The Hamburg outstation in Paris has been running a military espionage organisation since shortly before the Allied landings in North Africa. Its agents appear to have been selected for the most part from among Frenchmen in the Zone Sud, who have business contacts with the Allies in the Peninsula and North Africa, and intelligence has thus been obtained from Allied commercial circles, Consulates, etc. To a lesser extent the Hamburg organisation has attempted to penetrate the British Intelligence Service through members of the Deuxieme Bureau operating in the Zone Sud. Its objective has been intelligence regarding Allied invasion intentions, and military dispositions in North Africa and the Middle East. Whilst it is known to have sent agents to these areas, it has relied for the bulk of its reports on agents in the Zone Sud in relations with the Peninsula and French North Africa. There is also some evidence of contacts in the Balkans. The standard of intelligence thus collected has been uniformly low.

A minor interest of I/H, which has probably ceased since the total occupation, has been to supplement the activities of the German Armistice Commission sub-stations by running agents to the Zone Sud. I/H is known to have been engaged in this work since the early part of 1941, and it is probable that the activities of the Koenig Organisation in the Zone Sud and French North Africa were undertaken at the instigation of Paris I/H.

I/H. Leiter: Fregattenkapitan Huebener.
Section I, paragraph 10 refers to the importance of this section and the operational reasons therefor. There is evidence that Paris I/H enjoys an outstanding position among the naval espionage centres of the West, and thus when it has been necessary to hold conferences Paris has generally been selected for the purpose. The chief aim of Paris I/H having been to provide a regular flow of intelligence, it has been obliged to turn its attention to areas remote from France. Within Metropolitan France, it secured its objectives soon after the Armistice as a result of the activities of Brest, Le Havre with its ancillary at Vigo, and Bordeaux with its subordinate stations on the Atlantic coast. Similarly, the stations at Toulon and Marseille kept watch on the Mediterranean and the French fleet. It soon became apparent, however, that its services would be greatly improved if it obtained the reports of the intelligence networks based on Madrid and Lisbon, and set up stations under its own control in the area controlled by the latter. As a result, Paris succeeded in obtaining a regular supply of intelligence especially on the Gibraltar Straits area, from the I/H sections in Spain and Portugal. It also established stations of its own in the Canaries and the Rio de Oro. In addition to this, its most important if passive role, Paris 1/H has been active in the dispatch overseas of a number of agents who were to obtain intelligence of longer-term interest. Thus, in January 1942 it sent an agent to the USA via Argentina. Of Jewish origin and a German agent in the 1914-18 war, this individual was recruited in Holland shortly after the invasion of that country by the then Leiter I/H Paris who happened to be an old acquaintance. He was trained partly in The Hague and partly in Paris; it appears that the chance to escape to the USA was considered sufficient inducement for him to undertake the mission. Details of his instructions

28

are not known, since we are to believe that they would only have been made available after he had established contact with his masters from the USA. It is at least certain that he was supplied with secret ink, reagent, and microphotographic W/T instructions, and was told to proceed to the USA in the guise of a Jewish refugee via Iberia and Argentina.

On 5 October 1943 Paris I/H dispatched an agent from Toulon by submarine to Algeria; he was landed at Cape Khamis at 0400 hrs. on 9 October 1943 where he was shortly afterwards detected and arrested. A former professional naval W/T operator, this individual fell into the power of the Abwehr as a result of his shady and unsuccessful financial dealings. Having agreed to work on very advantageous financial terms, he was given three weeks' training in Paris at the end of August 1943 in W/T, codes and naval intelligence. He was dispatched as described on 5 October 1943, equipped with a W/T set, forged identity card, and money, with instructions to obtain information in the Oran area on naval, military and supply matters, with particular reference to Allied invasion intentions. His cover story was that he had arrived as a refugee from Spain in a Spanish fishing vessel. It is worth commenting that the conduct of the agent on landing, and the inadequacy of his forged documents, made his capture virtually inevitable.

The same officer, Stokheim, responsible for the above venture, was also the author of a similar undertaking in the same area and time. The strategic bearing of the two missions is obvious. On 20 September 1943 he dispatched an agent from Paris to Corsica by air from Pisa, who landed at Bastia on 24 September 1943 where he was captured by Fighting French Forces on 5 October 1943. The background of this agent is interesting. Prior to the war he had relations with Arab nationalists, and later became an active member of the Breton Nationalist Party. After the occupation of France he came into touch with the Gruppe II organisation in Brittany, and was instructed to form a party Intelligence Service. From that date he remained in constant touch with the Abwehr, and in September 1942 Paris I/H projected for him a mission to French North Africa, which, however, was called off as a result of the Allied landings. As preparation for this mission he underwent in Paris in that month training in W/T and codes. A year later he was hurriedly dispatched on the Corsican mission, equipped with W/T, codes etc., with instructions to remain in Corsica after the German forces had evacuated the island, and to report all military developments by W/T. The case is of peculiar interest as illustrating the type of post-occupational agent likely to be encountered in Metropolitan France.

The latest undertaking of Paris I/H known to us is reminiscent of the first case quoted above, it involved the recruiting in mid-October 1943 of two Dutchmen resident in Paris who hold prominent positions in the film industry. Their mission was to proceed to Spain and, making use of their connections with the Metro-Goldwyn Meyer Corporation, contrive to visit the USA and report on their return. No details of the mission are available.

(c) I/L. Leiter: Major Kliemann.
The energies of this section have been devoted to securing, firstly, regular reports for the use of the German Atlantic Coastal Command and of the Oberbefehlshaber Sud and, secondly, intelligence of a longer term interest from the UK and the US. As regards the first objective, it has made use of the Peninsular reports, whilst it has also attempted to establish a reporting service of its own, based on France and French North Africa. Thus, in the latter half of 1942, it succeeded in establishing a fairly extensive organisation in those territories, probably consisting of French officials with collaborationist sympathies. There is, however, no evidence of its continuation beyond the end of 1942. Similarly it is known to have been interested since the end of 1941 in sending agents to Liberia and French West Africa.

As regards the second objective, I/Luft is known to have attempted to send an agent to the USA in March 1942, and Kliemann has also sent three agents to the British Isles: one to England in December 1940, with instructions to report by W/T on air matters generally; a second was parachuted in July 1941 into Eire, with the primary mission of weather-reporting by W/T; a third to England in November 1943. It is also possible that Kliemann was responsible for sending here two agents, former French pilots, in September and December 1942 respectively, with instructions to enlist in the Allied Air Forces, take advantage of their position to steal an aircraft of latest type and fly it back to German-occupied territory bringing back with them also general operational intelligence. All these ventures revealed a low standard of conception and execution, and the third case adequately illustrates Kliemann's methods. This agent, a White Russian resident in Paris, had some contact with the Nazi movement before the war, and in 1937 was invited by an Abwehr officer to spy for Germany in the Spanish Civil War, an offer which she refused. After the fall of France she re-contacted the Abwehr and volunteered her services as an agent, intending to acquire intelligence of value to the allies. On the strength of her contacts in the UK and other qualifications, she was readily accepted and paid a substantial salary. Although trained in W/T in Berlin and Paris in 1941, it was not until two years later that she was finally dispatched. Her mission was to proceed to the UK via Spain in the guise of a volunteer for the Fighting French Forces who wished to rejoin her relatives in this country, and to report by W/T on matters of air and military interest. A transmitter would be sent to her later, disguised as a gramophone; it is typical that the same device had been employed in the case of the agent sent by this section to this country in December 1940. In an emergency she was to communicate in secret writing to cover addresses in Spain and Sweden. A well-informed source has stated that Kliemann enjoys a considerable reputation for incompetence in the Abwehr, and certainly the evidence of the undertakings he has sent against the British Isles supports this verdict.

(d) I/T Lw. Leiter: Dr. Sonnet.
There is abundant evidence of the activities of this section, which was responsible for the dispatch to the USA as early in 1943 of an agent with very high technical qualifications who was to report in secret writing on American aircraft construction, to the particulars of which his prominent position might have ensured him ready access, after which he was to proceed to the UK and steal an aeroplane. This agent was handled by the Leiter I/T Lw Berlin as well as by Sonnet, Leiter I/T Lw. Paris, and considerable attention was paid both to his training and to the method by which he was to send back reports. The reward, which was proportionate to the services which he was to render, was to have been four million francs.

The most active organisation in this field, however, is one which, though clearly working for I/T Lw, Paris, is equally to be regarded as a dependency of the Barcelona station. Its chief, Alberto Koepke, is second in command at Barcelona, and other prominent members are Loewschin and Katzen. It has been extremely active in sending agents to the UK and to French North Africa, and its methods show the uniformity so often to be observed in Abwehr practice. Koepke specialises in the employment of French ex-pilots who, from disillusionment or any other cause, have volunteered to join the LVF for action on the Eastern Front. The procedure is then as follows. The selected volunteer is introduced by Constantini or one of his lieutenants to Westrich, Counsellor of the German Embassy, Paris. Westrich suggests, as alternative to service on the Eastern Front, a mission on advantageous financial terms to the UK or French North Africa. If the offer is accepted, training in secret writing follows, after which the agent is instructed to proceed to Spain as a refugee and there to volunteer his services as a pilot in the Allied Air Forces in the UK or French North Africa. On arrival he is to report in secret writing to cover addresses in Barcelona the answers to a general questionnaire. He may also be instructed to steal an aircraft and fly it back to German-occupied territory. Six agents are known to have been sent by this channel to the UK since September 1942, and four to French North Africa. According to a German estimate, probably tendentious, twelve such agents were sent out in the six months between April and October 1943. It should also be noted that this method of penetrating the Allied Air Forces in the UK and French North Africa is not peculiar to Barcelona/Paris. Sonderfuehrer Dr. Rachwitz, Leiter I/T Lw Ast Brussels, for example, similarly makes use of former Belgian pilots. The technique employed being in all cases so similar, one will suffice to illustrate the point.

This agent, a Frenchman of intelligence and education, was a regular officer of the French Fleet Air Arm. On 24 November 1942 he joined the LVF from idealistic motives. At the end of February 1943 he was brought into contact with Westrich, who suggested a mission, and on his acceptance passed him over to Loewschein, who in turn introduced him to Koepke. In May 1943 Koepke took him down to Barcelona by car. He was there instructed in secret writing, given a secret ink, and instructed in the cover story he was to tell to the Allied authorities in that city. His instructions were to volunteer his services as a trained pilot, proceed in that capacity to the UK or French North Africa, and report thence by secret writing to a cover address in Barcelona the answers to a general military questionnaire. If occasion offered, he might later escape back to German-occupied territory by stealing an aircraft. It is to be noted that this agent, who agreed to the mission through idealistic motives, accepted no remuneration, and it is a point of some importance that this concentration on former service men constitutes a considerable danger, inasmuch as it enables Koepke to obtain material of considerable higher quality than the common run of Abwehr agents. In compensation, the Abwehr are frequently in error over the sincerity of their converts' motives.

(e) I/Wi. Leiter: Major Geck.
This section works in the closest co-operation with the related outstation in Paris of I/WI, Nest Cologne, under Dr. Becker. Not only is the I/Wi section at Cologne the most important section at that station, but it also controls I/Wi sections in other stations. Thus, there is evidence of the existence of I/Wi Cologne representatives in Madrid and Lisbon independent of the respective KOs, and it was the Leiter I/Wi Cologne who, about April 1943, was selected to succeed as Leiter I/Wi Berlin. It has sent numbers of agents to many countries. Cologne's most important outstation is that in Paris, the personnel of which travel frequently to Cologne, and which has been used for two principal purposes: (i) to obtain for them the station intelligence in areas such as the Zone Sud and French North Africa to which Paris has ready access, and (ii) to supply agents for the projects of I/Wi Cologne further afield. The Arab population of Paris is of especial use for this second purpose, and in September 1942 Paris was required to supply agents with a knowledge of Persian and Arabic for operations in Iran and Iraq,

There is also evidence that Paris I/Wi is represented in Spain, and like Paris I/H, it has been found a convenient centre for conferences of all I/Wi sections in the West. Such a conference was held in November 1943 in the Hotel Lutetia, which was attended by the economic officer of the Barcelona station. We possess detailed knowledge of two operations mounted by Paris I/Wi. In September 1941 the section sent to the USA via Spain and Argentina a former SD agent in the guise of a Jewish refugee, with instructions to report in secret writing to cover addresses in Europe on all matters of economic interest; further instructions were to be sent to the agent in micro-photographic form after his safe arrival. The second case, that of an agent sent to French Morocco in February 1942, is altogether representative. This man, an unsuccessful Belgian broker, was recruited in Paris in August 1940 at the customary financial rate. From March to September 1941 he was trained in W/T, codes and secret writing at Cologne, and in February 1942 was dispatched from the Zone Sud to French Morocco together with another agent, ostensibly as representative of a radio firm. His mission was to report by secret writing to cover addresses in Italy and the Zone Sud, and later by W/T, the answers to a comprehensive economic questionnaire.

(f) <u>Technical</u>. As is to be expected in a station of such size, Paris has its own technical sections. I/g is headed by Hauptmann Ackermann, and I/i by Oberstleutnant Rauh, who is also Funkleiter France. Paris is also reliably reported to have at its disposal an extensive D/F'ing organisation with a number of fixed posts and some eighty mobile units based on the suburb of Vanve.

5. <u>Gruppe II</u>. Leiter: Oberstleutnant E Schwege.
This section, which is very large and active, is stated to have a separate HQ at 6, Rue Kichel Ange, and its own sabotage training schools at Rocquencourt, North of Versailles (see Rocquencourt). Moreover, Nest La Roche and Nest Bayonne should also be regarded as extensions of Paris Gruppe II, a doubtful source has also alleged that it possesses a further sabotage training school at Orleans and a training School at Chatillon-sur-Seine. Very recently there has come into existence another outstation in the Marseille area, sending to Paris Gruppe II in the same relation as La Roche and Bayonne.

The work of Paris Gruppe II is primarily directed to supervising the work of its outstations, but it is, and always has been also occupied with the dispatch of numerous agents overseas, particularly to French territory in North Africa, and to a less extent to the UK, for purposes of sabotage and subversion. The specialist in this field is Dr. Schuster (see also Angers). We also know of the operation since August 1942 of an extensive Gruppe II organisation, also for the training and dispatch of Arab agents to North Africa. Gruppe II has maintained a number of recruiters in Paris to obtain agents, principally from among the ranks of the PPF for sabotage training in Berlin and later employment in Algeria.

In April 1941 Schuster made an unsuccessful attempt to send two trained saboteurs to Great Britain or French North Africa via Spain under cover of volunteers for the Fighting French Forces. Those agents, together with a third, who was intended to see them safely into Spain, were, however, arrested in the Zone Sud by the French Securité Militaire, and found to be in possession of detonators concealed in their property. Gruppe II was probably also the author of a venture which involved the landing of an agent by submarine in the Rio de Oro in January 1943. This agent, a patriotic but Anglophobe Frenchman, was recruited in Paris. He was trained in W/T in November 1942 in the neighbourhood of Munster, and in December 1942 at Berlin in secret writing, codes and sabotage, but refused any reward for his services. He was hurriedly embarked on a submarine at Bordeaux at the beginning of January unequipped and in circumstances of some confusion, and was duly landed by rubber boat in the Rio de Oro. Although the exact nature of his mission remains obscure, it is probable that the intention was that he should organise subversion and sabotage by the Arab population of French Morocco, using the Rio de Oro as a base, and possibly with the assistance of the Paris-controlled station located at Villa Cisneros. In the event, he gave himself up at Port Etienne on landing. A large-scale and ambitious project that is almost certainly to be ascribed to Gruppe II Paris materialised in mid-October 1943, when a party of four agents landed by parachute from a German aircraft in the area of Oudjda, French Morocco, and was immediately arrested. Three were high-grade agents, the fourth a W/T operator. Whilst full details are not available, it appears that the operation was run by Paris. The three principal agents, all French nationals, were recruited by the Abwehr through the agency of Gostini, described as Intendant-Directeur of the LVF. Previously they had been, respectively, a regular officer with specialist knowledge of Morocco, a fighter pilot, and an official of collaborationist sympathies who had served in French North Africa. Training appears to have been done in part in Berlin, possibly with the assistance of Munster, It will be recalled that the latter feature appeared in the case of the Rio do Oro agent cited above, and may indicate some connection between Gruppe II Munster and Gruppe II Paris. The party was equipped with a powerful W/T apparatus, revolvers, lists of contacts, rubber stamps for all Moroccan administrative offices for which they might require passes, and 200,000 francs in Moroccan notes. It is worth noting that the documentation revealed a number of errors. The departure was made from Bordeaux, the party flying over Spanish Morocco. Their mission appears to have been to establish for themselves a permanent base in the farm of a PPF member, himself a German agent, south of Meknes, and make contact by W/T, presumably with Paris. They were to apply themselves to military, political and economic espionage, attempt to start an Arab rising by propaganda, and at a later stage perform acts of sabotage and violence with the aid of arms and explosives which would be dropped by parachute. Communication with Paris was also to be maintained in emergency by secret writing to cover addresses in Spanish Morocco. The case is of some interest as shewing the methods by which Gruppe II attempts to counter the threat of invasion by action against the enemy's bases. The use as agents of malcontent French officers, and the role of the LVF and PPF groups will not be overlooked. Even in the inadequacy of the documentation, the hand of Gruppe II Paris stands revealed, for it is notable that in all its operations of which we have knowledge, quality has been in inverse ratio to quantity.

It is known that Gruppe II originally intended to employ as agents the two French pilots who arrived in the UK on 15 September 1942 and 7 December 1942 respectively; at a later stage, however, it appears to have handed them over to another section. In addition, it was responsible for sending an agent who arrived on 2 May 1943. This individual was a courageous Gaullist who was captured by the Germans on 19 June 1943 whilst on a mission for Combined Operations in Crete. After a period of imprisonment at Dulag Luft, Oberursul, he was escorted to Paris at the instance of the Abwehr, and on 13 January 1943 signed a contract with an officer of Gruppe II. Although the truth about subsequent developments has never been obtained, he admits to having received sabotage instructions at Rocquencourt, and there can be little doubt that he was intended to proceed to the UK as an escaped prisoner, and there perform unspecified acts of sabotage.

6. <u>Gruppe III</u>. Leiter: Oberstleutnant Reile.
The general significance of Gruppe III in France and of the Paris section in particular are discussed in Section I, paragraph 14 above. Its greatest successes were obtained in the Zone Nord in the first half of 1942. Acting in close co-operation with Gruppe III Angers, and making full use of the extensive D/F facilities at its disposal, it obtained very substantial successes in breaking up a number of allied organisations. Thus, early in 1942, Paris was able to claim the capture in the past months of 40 enemy W/T sets, leaving two only operating in the Zone Nord. Gruppe III was also a force in the Zone Sud; and it is known, for example, that two months prior to the total occupation, Paris III/F was operating a large D/F station in Lyon for the purpose of locating Allied agents in the area, with the aid of the Sipo and SD.

Gruppe III has also attempted to expand outside Metropolitan France. Thus, in October 1943 Madrid complained to Berlin of the existence in Spain of a Paris Gruppe III organisation working against Great Britain and the USA. The Gruppe III cases of which we have detailed knowledge reveal two important characteristics. First, the activities of sub-section III D in exploiting captured sets and agents for purposes of deception and penetration. Second, the fact that Gruppe III does not confine its attention to the security of France in the narrow sense, but dispatches agents overseas. The first tendency is illustrated by the following cases. From the end of 1940 to the end of 1941, the Allies were operating a large and valuable organisation in France, based on Paris. The two agents in question were the chief of the organisation and another member, at one time the chief's mistress. Towards the end of 1941 it became known that the organisation was being systematically broken up; treachery was suspected as the cause. On 28 February 1942 the woman arrived in the UK, her journey having been facilitated by the service in this country responsible for the activities of her organisation. Since the suspicions regarding responsibility for the break-up of the organisation rested on her, she was carefully examined, as a result of which it emerged not only that she had in fact betrayed her colleagues, but also that her present journey to the UK was German-inspired, the objective being to obtain intelligence about military intentions and the organisation of the British Intelligence Service which was to be reported over the W/T set in London controlling her organisation in France. In August 1942 there arrived in the UK the chief of the organisation himself. He declared that he had been imprisoned at the time of the break-up, but had managed to escape from Fresnes prison at the end of July 1942. It was not until a month after his arrival that he confessed that his 'escape' had been contrived by the Germans, and that he had in reality been released with instructions to build a W/T set in the UK for which he was given a crystal, to report thereby on matters of military interest, and also to try to persuade members of his own Government in London to collaborate in the German New Order in Europe.

The second tendency is illustrated by the following cases. On 13 April 1943 Reile parachuted into Tunis from Sicily a party of six agents. The leader was a former French regular officer of good family and sometime Colonel of the Legion Tricolore. The remainder of the party consisted of his second in command, two W/T operators, and two PPF members, the one being intended to arrange the party's contacts with the local PPF organisation in Tunisia, the other to liquidate the leader in case his allegiance to the Germans wavered. The party was equipped with three W/T sets, false papers and a large sum of money. The primary aim of this considerable undertaking was to set up, with the aid of the local PPF, a post-occupational network against the impending German collapse in Tunisia; operational reports were to be made by W/T to Sicily, with particular reference to Allied landing intentions; and reinforcements of men, money and instructions were liberally promised. There is evidence that the post-occupational network was intended to be completed by a similar organisation based on Tangier and designed to cover French Morocco. There were also subsidiary missions of sabotage and economic espionage. a similar type of case is that of an agent who was dispatched by Reile to Algeria, landing by parachute at Bouira (50 miles south-east of Algiers), having started from Sardinia. This agent, a Frenchman and professional W/T operator with the familiar PPF background, was enlisted into the Abwehr in November 1942 in Paris, whither he had gone from Algiers to attend the PPF conference of that month, undergoing training in W/T, codes and secret writing at Freiburg in July 1943. Equipped with a W/T set and code and traffic instructions in micro-photographic form, he was duly parachuted into Algeria as described above. His instructions were to proceed to Algiers, of which town he was normally a resident, and report operational and meteorological information by W/T; longer term economic and supply intelligence was to be reported by secret writing to cover addresses in the Peninsula. The main purpose of the mission was, of course, to obtain information on the next allied move in the Mediterranean.

Both these last two cases are of peculiar interest as indicating the kind of methods employed by Paris Gruppe III against an area about to be used as a base for enemy operations.

7. Other Organisations.

(a) The Keller/Eyden Organisation. According to a reliable report, Dr. Hermann Keller is an agent of what is described as the German Military Police in Occupied Territory. He appears to have extended these functions to include espionage, his HQ for this purpose being at 5 Avenue MacMahon, which is also occupied by his associate, Count Eyden. In August 1941 he sent a minor agent to the UK via Lisbon under business cover, with instructions to obtain naval, military and political intelligence, to be reported on his return to the Continent. The evidence is that Keller deals only in low-grade and disreputable characters, and that his activities are of no great significance. His relations with the Abwehr or the Sipo and SD have not yet been elucidated.

(b) The Koenig/Wilhelm/Kirscheder Organisation.
HQ, 28 Rue de la Faisanderie, XVIeme.
18, Rue du Colonel Bonnet, address of Wilhelm and Kirsheder

This organisation, which is undoubtedly affiliated with the Abwehr both in Paris and in Dijon, first came into prominence in October 1941. Its function appears to have been to supplement the work of the German Armistice Commission sub-stations in the Zone Sud and French North Africa by spying on the military and economic activities of the Vichy Government and the activities of Allied and patriot agents. It is known to have operated on a large scale. In October 1941 the BST arrested 100 of its agents in the Zone Sud alone, and in April 1942 another 25. Its agents, however, have all proved to be of low quality. Since the Allied occupation of North Africa and the German occupation of the Zone Sud the organisation has lost its raison d'etre, and there is little or no evidence of its activities since November 1942. We possess detailed knowledge of four North African and one Zone Sud cases: the latter will serve to illustrate the organisation's methods. The agent, an ineffective wastrel, found himself in trouble in Paris in April 1942 owing to lack of money and his fear of reprisals by Keller (see above) from whom he had accepted money, but whose commission he had failed to execute. In this predicament he was easily recruited by Kirsheder. His instructions were to make journeys of two weeks duration to the Zone Sud under business cover. He was to collect air and military intelligence in the Toulon region, reporting to Kirscheider on return, and was promised 5,000 francs per trip for his services.

(c) <u>The Lafont Organisation</u>.
HQ, 29, Rue Lauriston, 16ᵉ.
Chief: Henri Lafont.

This is a large organisation which works both for Reile, Leiter Abwehr III, and for Boemelberg, head of Sipo and SD Abt. IV, and is known to have been in existence since December 1942. It is also stated to have a branch at Bordeaux. Its activities consist of tracking down Allied and patriot agents in the Zone Sud and in French North Africa. Its agents are gangsters drawn from the Paris underworld, who indulge in the lowest forms of denunciation and Gestapo work. Lafont, condemned by the French for espionage before the war, is stated, inter alia, to have amassed an immense fortune at the expense of the Jews.[8]

According to the Section V analysis, which was the most comprehensive document on the subject, Ast Angers, located in the Hotel d'Anjou in the Boulevard du Marechal Foch, had a particularly significant role:

1. Ast Angers, which has always been an important station, is known to have existed since early 1941, but was probably established shortly after the Armistice. Its active Gruppen appear to be I and III. There is no evidence of a Gruppe II.

2. For administrative purposes Angers is subordinate to Alst France with which it has always been in close relations, particularly in the field of counter-espionage. It was also closely connected with Ast St. Germain until June 1942, when this station was dissolved. Since January 1943 it has maintained its own Meldekopf in Paris, and the activities of this sub-station will be treated as forming part of its work. It also runs out stations at Angouleme, Tours and St. Avertin, and has shown interest in the work of La Roche and Brest. Outside France it maintains two important outposts at Seville and Barcelona in connection with its interests in the Iberian Peninsula and North Africa.

3. The objectives of Angers have been, in order of importance:-
(a) Counter-espionage in the Zone Nord, especially against Allied and patriot agents in North-West France.
(b) The dispatch of agents abroad and particularly to French North Africa.

4. Gruppe I. Leiter: Oberst Weber.
Angers Gruppe I has revealed a wide range of interests in despatching agents to the UK, the Union of South Africa, South America and the Canaries; we have detailed knowledge of the first three of these cases, which will suffice to illustrate the methods of this section of the station. On 4 May 1942 there arrived in the UK by air from Lisbon a Polish Countess, who had ostensibly escaped from the Zone Nord to Portugal and come to the UK to rejoin her husband and her many friends in Polish Government circles, and in order to deliver a document on behalf of a Polish resistance organisation. On arrival she confessed to the following: after the Polish defeat, she escaped with her children to the Zone Nord whore she enjoyed good relations with the German authorities, inter alia the SD in Paris, and later herself served in the German Military Administration. Notwithstanding this, she also continued to work throughout for the Polish organisation mentioned above. In December 1941 she permitted herself to be recruited for a mission to the UK by an officer of Ast Angers, whom she had met by chance some three months earlier, the inducement being the chance to rejoin her husband with her children, and to preserve the family estate in Poland. She was trained in January 1942 at St. Avertin in codes, and in March 1942 at Tours in secret writing. The following month she 'escaped' to Lisbon, her confessed mission being to reach the UK as a refugee and report on the British security control system and on troop movements from the UK, especially to Syria; it is probable that she was also told to try and spread collaborationism in Polish Government circles, to which she had ready access. Communication was to be two-way, in secret ink and code through the Polish Diplomatic Bag; she was told to procure her ink and reagent on arrival.

In November 1942 the Meldekopf of Angers in Paris sent an agent to the Union of South Africa, This individual, a British subject of Afrikaaner origins and sympathies, found himself at the beginning of 1942 interned at St. Denis, Paris. Largely through disgust at the conduct of his fellow British internees, he fell victim to German propaganda, and volunteered his services. He was accepted and trained in W/T, radio construction, codes and secret writing at Paris, Karlsruhe and Hamburg. His mission was to proceed to Spain in the guise of an escaped internee, get himself repatriated to the Union, and there construct a W/T set with which to transmit military, economic and general information. He was equipped with a micro-photograph containing his traffic instructions, and in the event of W/T communication breaking down, he was to write in secret writing to cover addresses in the Peninsula. This agent is one of the few who have accepted a German mission from motives of idealism, refusing any reward for his services.

The South American agent was a young Frenchman of good family resident near Tours. Largely owing to the influence of his father, he permitted himself to be recruited by Ast Angers in August 1942, and was subsequently trained in secret writing. His mission, on which he at last started from Bilbao on 5 August 1943, was to proceed to Spain and thence to Uruguay as an arboricultural expert. He was instructed to report on military and economic matters in Brazil and/or Uruguay in secret writing either direct to cover addresses in Spain, or to a head agent in Buenos Aires, who would relay his information by W/T to Angers. He was equipped with secret ink and dollars, but was not to be paid more than his expenses until results were achieved. It is almost certain that the head agent in Buenos Aires was a Spaniard who had been in the employment of Angers since March 1942, having worked previously for Madrid. It is known that Angers proposed to send him on a mission to the Argentine at the same time as the agriculturalist was to go to Uruguay. From March 1942 to March 1943 this agent had operated a W/T set on behalf of Angers in Las Palmas; this fact, taken in conjunction with Angers' interest in shipping reports from Seville, may indicate the existence of an 1/M section at Angers.

The outstations of Angers at Seville and Barcelona are valuable not only as bases for operations further afield, but for obtaining intelligence on the spot. Thus, the Seville agent is expected to report on shipping movements in the port, and on information gleaned from Spanish travellers. Similarly, one of Angers' chief agents in Barcelona succeeded in November 1943 in obtaining a report from a well-disposed officer of the Spanish General Staff, and on a subsequent occasion reports from Spanish sub-agents in the Balearics.

An important use to which these Peninsular bases have been put is the penetration of French Morocco via Spanish Morocco. Prominent in this work is Dr. Schuser, who is known to have sent out a number of such agents, including Arabs, between mid-1941 and mid-1942. Another Arab agent was dispatched by Angers on 12 May 1942 to Spanish Morocco to penetrate French Morocco and report to a Spanish cover address in secret ink. Another agent, a former Spanish artillery officer, residing in Madrid and in low financial water, was recruited in that city at the end of 1941 by an officer of Angers. Thereafter his case was managed by the Seville outstation, the agent receiving his training in secret writing in Spain. He was given his first mission, to carry out espionage from Spanish Morocco against French and Allied military dispositions in French Morocco, in March 1942, and was to report in secret ink to a cover address in Spain. Since that date he has received a number of similar missions in the same area.

After the Allied landings in North Africa, Angers began to shew an interest in Algeria and Tunisia. In November 1942 an Angers agent was to have been sent to Tunis to form a part of a post-occupational network, though in the end this fell through. A further attempt was made towards the end of January 1943 but this second agent does not appear to have got beyond Rome. A little later a third agent, a Corsican resident in Paris, was likewise dispatched from Paris to Rome for post-occupational work in Tunisia, and in April 1943 Angers was shewing anxiety to get a good French W/T agent into Algeria before it was too late. In all these cases the intention was probably to parachute the agents from Sicily, whither they would report back military information by W/T both during and after the campaign. Similar enterprises wore organised by Alst France at the same period and for the same purpose.

Angers has also been interested in running post-occupational agents since the opening of the Italian campaign and both in September and November 1943 reports were received that its agents were operating in Sicily.

5. Gruppe III, Leiter III F: Oberstleutnant Dernbach.
Counter-espionage, especially against Allied and patriot organisations in North-West France, has always been the chief occupation of Angers. Its busiest period was the first half of 1942, when, in conjunction with III/F Paris, an effective drive was made against all enemy agents in the Zone Nord; it was probably as a result of these successes that Dernbach was promoted Colonel in March 1942. As is the case in Paris and elsewhere in France, it is sub-section III/F, of which Dernbach is Leiter, which conducts the great part of the Gruppe III business of the station. There is also evidence that Angers exercises some security responsibilities for the Abwehr in France as a whole; thus, in conjunction with Central Registry, Berlin, it vets proposed employees, and may have responsibilities in the granting of exit permits from France.

It is a fair inference that Angers III has now lost some ground to the Sipo and SD; whether from this or other causes, it is less active now than in 1942.

Like Paris, Angers has exploited its numerous captured sets and agents for purposes of deception and penetration. An instance of the latter activities is afforded by the following case. This agent reached the UK on 5 November 1941 from the Zone Sud via Lisbon, and told the following story. On 13 January 1940, she had left England for France to join her husband who was stationed at Nantes; she was unable to give a satisfactory account of the activities of herself and her husband during the next five months. She refused to leave France during the German advance, despite facilities being offered her to do so. She was not molested, however, and began to take advantage of her continued liberty to collect intelligence likely to be of use to the Allies. In due course she was caught

41

and rigorously cross-examined by Dernbach. She was rescued from this predicament by Dernbach's personal assistant, a mysterious figure and opponent of the Nazi regime, who obtained her release, ostensibly in order to work for him in the Zone Sud, in reality to make contact with the British Intelligence Service, to whom he would then supply information through her. On 5 April 1941 she left for Marseille, and was successful in getting herself recruited as an agent by the British, her instructions being to maintain her relations with her German case-officer in order to obtain the promised information; she did in fact make a number of journeys between the British Intelligence Service in the Zone Sud and Ast Angers' agent in the Zone Nord, In October 1941, however, she found that it had come to the notice of the Vichy security authorities that she was an agent, as a result of which both her own position and that of her contact in the British Intelligence Service was compromised. She accordingly left the Zone Sud for the UK via Lisbon. Although the whole truth of the affair has never been obtained, it was soon apparent that her story as told above was unacceptable. It is considered almost certain that the real explanation of the case is that it represents an attempt by Dernbach to penetrate the British Intelligence Service in the Zone Sud and induce the Vichy authorities to close it down, and probably also at a later stage to penetrate the British Intelligence Service in London.[9]

Following the extension of the German occupation to the entirety of metropolitan France in November 1942, the military priorities were largely unchanged, in terms of the suppression of the Resistance, a task which fell largely to III/F, and preparation for the inevitable Allied landings, a challenge for I/H. The key participants interrogated on these subjects after the war were Oscar Reile,[10] Hans-Joachim Rudloff,[11] Herman Giskes[12] and Giskes' assistant, Gerhard Huntemann.[13]

In 1943 the SD acquired documents which compromised large parts of the Resistance, and 'discovered the existence of Plan Rouge, Plan Vert and Plan Noir', together with details of the personal messages broadcast by the BBC, and carefully monitored the growing strength of the various target organisations in Belgium, Holland and France, being principally the Armée Secrete, the Franc-Tireurs and Partisans and the Armée Blanche in the months before D-Day. Reportedly, from 1 June 1944 III received and understood at least twenty-five BBC messages warning of D-Day within 36 hours and passed on the news, but only the Fifteenth Army acted upon the information, with the Seventh Army ignoring it. It was also alleged that several play-back W/T sets were operated successfully by a FunkAbwehr unit headed by Kieffer, and that Colonel Bottingen's contacts inside the Resistance also provided valuable information about Allied intentions.[14]

In pursuit of operations aimed against the Resistance, III established two training schools in Germany, at the spa town of Bad Ems and at Rodt an der Weil, for deployment in France. Hans Rudloff described the students as PPF volunteers who were trained in parachuting and wireless in anticipation of being dropped behind the Allied lines after the invasion.

Naturally, the British interrogators were keen to unravel the complexities of the extent to which the enemy had penetrated its field organisations, and in particular the truth behind the many SOE disasters in France. This was a subject upon which Friedrich Dohse, who served with the SD in Bordeaux from January 1942 until his evacuation in August 1944, was cross-examined after his capture in Denmark in August 1945:

The detainee tells that he succeeded in getting into touch with British agents in France and make them work for the Germans. He could do so, partly because he threatened them with a pistol and said that now they had to work for the Germans or they would be taken to a concentration camp, and in order to tempt then further, he offered them more money. The British agents in France were not very well paid, so it was rather easy for him, to make them turn round and work for the Germans. One of the first persons he contacted with was a man called Palloc at Pau, who at that time, November 1942, was stationed in the occupied part of France. The detainee had succeeded in getting one of his own V-Männer into Palloc's organisation, which was rather big. So the detainee knew something about this man already before Germany occupied the last part of France. On the night between the 11th and 12th of November 1942, when the Germans entered the non-occupied part of France, the detainee arrested this British agent, and took him to Bordeaux, where he was handed over to Hauptmann Gartner from Ast Bordeaux, He did so, because counter-espionage ranged under Abwehr. Hauptmann Gärtner succeeded in enlisting Palloc for the Germans, and the detainee knows that Palloc immediately received 100,000 francs. By examining him they found many pounds on him (more than 100,000 francs), this amount was given back to him. A sub-agent, a doctor called Grandier, was arrested together with Palloc. 3 – 4 other sub-agents were arrested too, but they were released immediately, as they agreed to work for the Germans together with their leader. All the material Palloc received from the British, he handed over to Ast Bordeaux or the detainee, while Ast Bordeaux supplied Palloc with forged information, which the latter re-forwarded to the British. Palloc worked for the Germans to the very end.

In the beginning of 1943 Hauptmann Gartner got into connection with a captain from the French Intelligence Service at Toulouse. This event was credit to one of Gartner's V-Männer. The captain, who was

43

possibly called Bordenhave, was also working for the British. The V-Mann succeeded in persuading the captain to work for the Germans. The captain was in charge of a line of the intelligence service, through which the courier-mail to England via Spain passed. Having agreed to Hauptmann Gartner's proposal, the captain now photo-copied the mail, and Hauptmann Gartner received a copy. In cases where the mail contained letters which were detrimental to the Germans, thus of a special military importance, these letters were simply removed and forged letters were placed instead of. Behind the captain was a very large intelligence organisation, which worked for France and England, but as it was the French captain only, who had joined the Germans, the organisation continued to act as hitherto. As far as the detainee knows, the captain was bribed with an amount of 100,000 francs.[15]

One of the largest SOE disasters, the wholesale arrest of the SCIENTIST circuit in Bordeaux, had been attributed to a traitor, André Grandclément, and Dohse gave his version of events, which must have made for uncomfortable reading. The network was betrayed in September 1943 by Grandclément, and Charles Hayes, codenamed YVES and on his second mission to France for F Section, was arrested in October. The organisation's other leaders, Roger Landes, codenamed ARISTIDE, and Claude de Baissac (DAVID) narrowly escaped capture and returned to England.

The German Intelligence Service, especially in the districts near the Spanish border, had during a longer time been aware of the fact that an organisation, called [ ] was in existence The only task of this organisation was to take British, American and Canadian pilots, who had been shot down, across the border to Spain· As far as the Intelligence Service knew, this organisation was under charge of a British major, who used the cover name *Aristide*. This British major was the head of the whole Resistance Movement, and he had his HQ at Aroachen. One day the detainee received a letter of the following contents:

'I suppose you are interested in the American, British and Canadian pilots, who had been shot down. I may be able to effect that all the Allied pilots, shot down, are handed over to you. At present attempts are made to take then across the Spanish border. To prove that I am telling the truth, you can tomorrow at 7a.m. send a French car with a civil-dressed driver to the corner of this and that street. Four pilots will enter the car, and you can do with them, whatever you like. For this trouble I claim 500,000 francs, and a driving license for the whole of France. I use the watch-word PHILIPPE HENRIOT REVANCHE.'

The detainee showed this letter to the German commander, but the latter thought it was without importance. However, the detainee was of another opinion, and he decided to act upon his own risk. Before sending the car away the next morning, he had ordered all roads out of town to be barred and armed guards were placed at various places. At the fixed hour the car appeared, and a civil-dressed man accompanied 4 men up to the car. The four men entered the car, and the civil-dressed person disappeared. The car drew out of the town along a predestinate route, where it was stopped by the detainee's guards. It proved to be 4 British pilots, and one of them was a wing commander. In the afternoon the detainee was phoned by a man, who asked how the plan had collapsed. The detainee told him, and the man claimed his money. The detainee answered that he could not give him so much, but he promised to send some money. They arranged that a car should appear in front of Credit Lyonnais Court d'Intendant at a certain time, then the money was handed over, the Germans would get two more British pilots. The detainee sent a car along at the fixed time, and an envelope containing 50,000 francs was given to the driver. The detainee appeared near the place of meeting, as he wanted to see the man, who was behind this game. Then the car stopped, a man, wearing the leader-uniform of the French Labour Service, went up to the car. The envelope with the money was given to the man in uniform, and two civil-dressed persons entered the car. It was two British pilots. This method was repeated. The unknown man, who still used the watchword 'Philippe Henriot Revanche', phoned up, arranged where to meet, the money was brought along, and British pilots were handed over to the Germans. A few days before the invasion the man phoned the detainee and said that he was going to have a conversation with *Aristide*, and asked the detainee if he was interested in getting some information about this organisation and this man. The detainee answered that he was, but such things could not be arranged over the phone, as the conversation might be tapped. He would prefer for a personal conversation with the unknown man. The man answered that it was impossible at present, but he would go down to *Aristide*, and when he returned from this meeting, he would arrange a personal meeting with the detainee, A few days later the man phoned again and said that he was ready to meet the detainee. They arranged to meet in a certain cafe at Bordeaux, but in the evening the detainee received a marching order. He should appear at the invasion front, so it was impossible for him to meet the unknown man. He has never spoken with him, he has only seen him from the distance, and he thinks that the man occupied a leading position within the French Labour Service. He says that at least 40-50, maybe 60 Allied pilots have been handed over to the Germans in this way. The detainee says that those pilots have been correctly treated. They got food and cigarettes when they were staying in the office at Bordeaux, before they were handed over to the Wehrmacht, whereafter they were taken to prisoners' camps in Germany.

The intelligence section in Southern France had during a longer time noticed that many British planes were flying over the country every night. These planes were most likely dropping arms to the French Resistance Movement. It was decided to try to stop this organisation. It was known that British officers, who stayed in France, were in charge of this organisation. It was furthermore known that the district around Bordeaux, was called *David*. They knew that the head was a major called Claude de Baissac, 1st Regiment Intelligence Corps. He was a French born nobleman, but had emigrated to England. Second in command was Charles Hayes, captain, 1st Regiment Intelligence Corps. Finally, it was known that the head of the French Resistance Movement in this district was an agent of an insurance company. His name was André Grandclement, a son of the famous admiral. The head himself was a lieutenant in the reserve. By assistance of Vertrauensmänner they succeeded in penetrating the organisation, and in the autumn 1943 they succeeded in arresting about 500 members of the organisation, but the French leader escaped. The British leader escaped too, whereas Charles Hayes was still there.

The detainee knew that the only effective way to bring the Resistance Movement to a stop, was to get hold of the French leader, so he ordered his best agents to find him. They had an idea about the fact that the leader was in Paris which is why they started a search of this town. Restaurants and bodegas were searched by German agents. One night in October one of the V-Männer phoned the detainee and said that he was together with Grandclement, and they arranged to meet the next day at 4 pm in a restaurant. The detainee tried to get hold of a plane, but failed so he ordered that Grandclement should be arrested if he appeared at the meeting. Grandclement arrived and was arrested and he was immediately taken to Bordeaux, where the detainee interrogated him. The man proved to be very anti-Communistic-minded, and on this base the detainee got on speaking terms with him. Grandclement was worried about the 300 arrested members of his organisation. Because of this the detainee succeeded in making the arrangement that all the arrested members would be released at once, if Grandclement could effect that the rest of his organisation in the district around Bordeaux, would hand over their weapons voluntarily. Through V-Männer the detainee sent a message to the Resistance Movement. A meeting was arranged, and the detainee and Grandclement should negotiate with the present members of the Resistance Movement. They met in a wood far from inhabited places.

The detainee and Grandclement gave the proposal to the head of the Resistance Movement, and after having thought it over for a day, they agreed. The detainee had arranged with his superiors, who had sanctioned the plan, that 189 arrested members should be released, as soon as the arrangement was a fact. The detainee says that the plan had been sanctioned by BdS in Paris. The release took place, and when the Resistance Movement saw that the Germans kept their promisses, they kept their part of the agreement too.

During the next 14 days 182 weapon depots, containing 8,600 machine-guns, and about 40,000 kilos of ammunition, explosives, hand grenades etc., were handed over to the Germans, who fetched the material in big lorries. The detainee and Grandclement had negotiated with a French Captain Andre Malhayran and a Lieutenant Roland Chazeau. These two officers were heads of the group of the dropping of arms in this district, and they saw that the arms were handed over to the Germans.

When this action was brought to an end, the detainee would try to get hold of the British leader Captain Charles Hayes. By assistance of V-Männer he succeeded in finding out where Charles Hayes was staying. Together with 7 – 8 men he appeared in a little village near Langón, south of Bordeaux, A V-Mann showed him the house, and the detainee went over and knocked at the door. From a window on 1st floor a whole magazine from a machine-pistol was fired at the same moment. However, the detainee was not hurt. A fight was commenced between the escort and the people in the house. The fight started at 4 am, and at 7 am, a white flag appeared in the window. Charles Hayes came out and said that a woman had been wounded in her stomach, and she was about bleeding to death. He asked if the woman could be taken to a hospital. The detainee complied with this, but said that the fight had to stop immediately. Charles Hayes himself was wounded in one of his arms and in one of his legs, which was bleeding rather strongly. The detainee said that he would take the woman and Charles Hayes to a hospital, if they would stop fighting.

After some negotiations Hays agreed to this proposal, and the two wounded persons were immediately taken to a hospital. Hayes was later on transferred to a German prisoner's camp.

The detainee wants to point out that Hayes denied to give any kind of information during the interrogation. The detainee did not force him, but told him what they knew about his organisation, so that Hayes could understand that they had been well informed. In this way the detainee succeeded in making an armistice between the anti-Communistic Resistance Movement and the Germans in south-west France,

The detainee did try to make an agreement with the Communistic Resistance groups. The before-mentioned Lieutenant Roland Chazeau tried to get into connection with the Communistic Resistance groups, which he succeeded in doing, but when the detainee and Chazeau met, somebody fired at them, and Chazeau was killed. The detainee escaped by running into a wood, and his persecutors were put on a false scent, and he reached a smaller German force, who guarded a prisoner camp.

When this action was brought to an end the detainee decided to try to come to an agreement with the complete French Resistance Movement. He wanted to stop the 'Kleinkrieg' (little war) which was in force between the Resistance Movement and the Germans. The Resistance Movement did ail sort of things. e.g, blew up lazaret-trains, pushed female Germans out on the rails in the Metro, so that they were killed, killed single Germans, when they were walking in the streets, etc.

The Germans would not accept the members of the Resistance Movement as soldiers, and they therefore treated then as partisans. Shot them immediately or sent then to concentration camps. As the Resistance Movement again and again during interrogations and per letters, complained to the detainee about the treatment of the members of the Resistance Movement, who were treated as partisans and not as soldiers, which they thought they could demand, the detainee tried to have the warfare humaniated by assistance of Grandclement.

From Grandclement and from V-Männer, he had learnt who were the leaders within the French Resistance Movement, and by assistance of Grandclement he succeeded in getting a conversation with a professor from the university at Bordeaux. The professor was called Joubert. The professor was the political head of the Resistance Movement in south-west France. The detainee told the professor about his plan, which met with approbation from the latter. However, he declared that he could not take a final decision in so important a question. He thought it had to be placed before General de Gaulle, but the latter was staying in Africa, and the professor did not know how to get into touch with him. The detainee declared that he was able to arrange that.

The detainee returned to Paris, where he had a conversation with his highest superiors, amongst others, der Höhere SS und Polizeiführer, General Oberg whom he told about his plan, and how far he had got, Oberg assented the plan, and Professor Joubert arranged a meeting between the detainee and one of the most important leaders within the French Resistance Movement. The detainee and Professor Joubert were blindfolded and taken to a place in Paris, where the detainee during the whole night discussed the questions with an abbot, who was called Pere Le Fevre (Cover name).

Gradually they came to an agreement, but it was still an assumption that General de Gaulle should take the final decision. A short time before Christmas 1943 Professor Joubert and Colonel Thinnieres were taken to St. Sebastian by the detainee. They were hidden in a big trunk, which was placed on the back of the detainee's car. The two men were taken to the British Consulate at San Sebastian, and the detainee knows that they went to Algiers via Madrid and Gibraltar, where they were taken to General de Gaulle.

During the course of the negotiations treason took place. Over the wireless an agent told the detainee that de Gaulle had arrested the two men as traitors. Furthermore it proved that his superiors in Paris, in the meantime had considered that the thing too dangerous. Der Führer had ordered no negotiations with partisans must take place. They should be treated as partisans and nothing else. The result was that the detainee was left alone, and his plan came to nothing.

The detainee explains that his department, Abt. IV N at Bordeaux, had a rather big developed intelligence within the French Labour Service. Members of the disorganised French army had formed a corps of volunteers, who worked for the Germans on the Atlantic coast. In that part of France where the 1st German Army was stationed, 10,000 Frenchmen were working for the Germans. These men were divided up in military formations, and they were wearing uniforms. The partisan movement was very widespread in the vicinity of Bordeaux, and again and again the Wehrmacht claimed that Gestapo should provide proofs against the partisans and against the members of the volunteer Labour Service. It was feared that the Labour Service at a certain time, would be supported with arms from the air, and then start to fight the German army from the rear. Raids took place very often, executed by the German Wehrmacht, and that the partisan movement was rather big, could be seen, as it was not unusual that they got about, 2,000 – 5,000 prisoners during the raids.

The people, used as informers, were French.[16]

Clearly Dohse was seeking to minimise his own role in the suppression of the French Resistance, and in particular his own part in the SCIENTIST debacle. For instance, he mentions the wounds sustained by the SOE agent Charles Hayes, and asserts that Hayes was transferred to a prison camp. He neglects to say that Hayes was actually executed at Gross-Rosen concentration camp in August 1944. Dohse was also asked about penetration:

In the district around Bordeaux where the detainee was serving, many parachute agents were dropped. Because of a very wide intelligence net and because the French police co-operated with the Germans, they succeeded in arresting nearly all the agents. However, it proved that those who got into the hands of the French or the German police, committed suicide by poisoning themselves. In one case the detainee got hold of a parachute agent called Bordin. But in the beginning of the interrogation, the agent poisoned himself and [ ] in front of the writing table. The French police had manacled the agent, and he had been examined thoroughly, so the detainee supposes that he had a tablet in his mouth.

4 or 5 million francs were found on him. The detainee used this money for his own intelligence service.

The agent used the cover name HYPOTENUSE, and the detainee knows that he should report to the head of the French Section in War Office in London, Colonel PASSY. The agent's telegraphist had been taken prisoner at the same time, and he was in possession of a code and 1.8 million Francs. The code was later on handed over to Abwehr, and the detainee thinks that a false co-operation was started by means of this code.

The two parachute agents were arrested because a Frenchman in an inn saw that the telegraphist was in possession of a lot of money which he had in a portfolio. The man thought it was a Black Market dealer and called for a French policeman, who arrested the agent and took him to the French criminal police. The portfolio was examined and the code was found. The telegraphist told the French police that he was a French patriot and British parachute agent, but even in spite of that, the criminal police phoned the detainee and informed about the man. Then the detainee arrived at the police station, he had poisoned himself. Bordin was denounced by a French informer.

A few days later BBC warned the patriots in the district around Bordeaux against the detainee.

In the district around Bordeaux GFP worked co-ordinate to Gestapo and Abwehr, A special group had been established for this object. It was called GFP Trup Nr. 644, and the head was Feltpolizei Kommissar Schultze. Then confronted with the fact that it was rather unusual that GFP was occupied in such cases, the detainee explains that the work with the French Resistance Movement and the English agents demanded so many men that the detainee could not manage this job alone. The main task of Trup 644 was to counteract the French Resistance Movement and their British connections. The Trup had its own intelligence section of Frenchmen, who undertook arrests and interrogations. However, the cases passed through the hands of the detainee, when GFP had finished their part of them.

The detainee has no further knowledge of the staff of this Trup, but he states it here, because he thinks, it must be of interest to the Allies, to know how far reaching the German intelligence service was in the district of Bordeaux. He adds that 65 Germans were employed in the GFP Trup; how many Frenchmen there were, he cannot say.[17]

Dohse's recollection, unaided by documentation, served to remind the Allied counter-intelligence analysts of the extraordinary success III/F had achieved with its policy of hostile penetration. Certainly the Germans had exploited counter-espionage leads provided by the local police in areas under occupation, and the Milice in Vichy had proved itself to be an enthusiastic collaborator, but even before the end of the war, and as early as 1942, there had been growing evidence that the Abwehr had energetically embraced a policy, not just of inserting informers into escape lines and Resistance groups, but had made quite sophisticated attempts to insinuate agents into SOE and SIS in Britain.

In terms of counter-intelligence doctrine, the Abwehr set itself the objective of destroying its adversary from within, whereas the Allies, dependent on ISOS, actively avoided the recruitment of enemy personnel as agents in place. MI5 became aware of IIIF's strategy in February 1943 as B1(a)'s Christopher Harmer noticed some common denominators in four recent cases, being BRUTUS, LARK, ANCHOR and CROW, which he set out in a paper entitled *Escape Cases*:

1.GENERAL

There are an increasing number of cases of British or Allied agents returning to this country after having been captured by the Germans and imprisoned, and subsequently having escaped. In two such cases which have been dealt with by B1(a), the agent, on returning, has confessed that his escape was arranged by the German authorities on condition that he accepted a mission for them to be performed in this country. Two further cases are under review by B1(a), but no such admission has yet been obtained, although a strong probability exists in one case that the escape was similarly arranged. As it appears that a great number of enemy agents who come to this country start their intelligence life as agents working against the Germans, the following memorandum is put forward setting out various principles which can be derived from our investigation of the two cases and the difficulties of dealing with them, and suggested methods of approach to similar cases in the future.

2. The BRUTUS and ANCHOR Cases

The two cases to which reference has been made above are shortly as follows:

(a) BRUTUS. This man was an Allied officer who ran a very large espionage organisation in Paris from the end of 1940 to the end of 1941. He was then arrested and imprisoned. He received no harsh treatment from the Germans, nor was he interrogated in any detail, but this fact is not very surprising in view of other developments within his organisation. About a week after his arrest he was allowed to see in prison his mistress, who urged on him, on behalf of the Germans, the advisability of collaborating with them in working against the Allies. She was accompanied by a German officer who then left them alone for half an hour. The reply of BRUTUS was that no collaboration would be possible, as it would react solely to the detriment of his compatriots. After three months of imprisonment, during the latter part of which the Germans arranged considerable improvements in his living conditions, the matter was brought up again, probably on BRUTUS' initiative. Discussions then took place for about three months and ultimately BRUTUS accepted a mission on behalf of the Germans on condition that his escape from prison was arranged. The basic factors of his mission were the following:

(i) The Germans admitted that his main loyalty should be to his own country, but persuaded him that in working for them he was helping his country.

(ii) The Germans made him sign a declaration agreeing to work for them and acknowledging their right to hold relatives and his fiancee as hostages.

(iii) The Germans prepared his escape story, but it was not put into effect, i.e. he did not go through the motions of escaping as in the case of ANCHOR.

(iv) He was given W/T crystals to bring to this country to enable him to construct a W/T set. His mission was to give military information and also to try and persuade leading circles in his own government in London to collaborate with the Germans in the new order in Europe.

(v) From and after his release from prison his movements were practically unsupervised and he was allowed to make his own arrangements for escaping from occupied territory.

BRUTUS 'escaped' from the Fresnes prison on 29 July 1942. His story was that he was being taken to an interrogation at the Gestapo Headquarters. He was travelling in a civilian motor car with a driver and an escort. The escort arrived late and the driver was in a hurry so that he should not be late for his appointment. He therefore drove recklessly and finally had an accident, when he became involved in a column of marching soldiers, it being the day of a great military parade in Paris. Finally, in order to prevent a collision the driver was forced to swerve violently and jam on all his brakes, which threw both the occupants in the back of the car on to the floor and enabled BRUTUS to 'escape'. BRUTUS dived through the ranks of the soldiers, thereby placing the marching column between himself and the escort. He then escaped and ultimately found his way to unoccupied France, Spain and Gibraltar. BRUTUS continually emphasized his extreme weakness at the moment of his escape and therefore told the story of having proceeded initially in short stages, first of all resting in a waiting motor car, then in a public convenience and then on a seat in the park.

On arrival in England, BRUTUS, who as an agent had worked under the direct orders of his own Intelligence Service, was examined by them for over a month. On arrival, he told his chief that he would have important information to impart in a month's time. He was treated, naturally, as an honoured guest and no search was carried out, and his crystals were therefore not found. His story was taken down in very great detail by his own government service, who formed the conclusion that the escape had been arranged by the Germans, but that he, in view of his previous record of faithful service, did not know about it. They suspected some subtle and indirect gesture on the part of the Germans, About a month after his arrival, however, he wrote out the correct story of his escape and offered to work for the British. It can be said that although his story left a vague feeling of uneasiness in the minds of everybody, he would probably have got away with it if he had not confessed.

(b) ANCHOR. ANCHOR is a young Norwegian who escaped from Norway and came to this country, and was recruited to go back as a secret agent to organise an underground movement there. He returned to Norway by sea, operating in the spring of 1942. He set up his headquarters in his home town and carried out valuable service in training local teams in guerrilla tactics. At the beginning of May 1942, he was arrested in his home by the Gestapo, tried to escape and was badly shot up. For many weeks he lay in a perilous condition, but ultimately recovered sufficiently to be interrogated. He was seen by [Siegfried] Fehmer, the chief of the Gestapo in Oslo, who impressed on him the advantages of collaboration with the Germans and finally allowed him to see in prison and alone an elderly Swede who had also been caught in Norway and whose life had been spared as a result of his collaborating fully with the Germans. ANCHOR stated that after this he pretended to break down and told the story which was accepted by the Germans, with the result that his treatment improved and their confidence in him was built up. Finally, at the end of September, he told them that he would show them an arms dump in the woods near Oslo and was taken out there by two Gestapo men. All this time he had pretended to be very weak in the legs and was supported by one man on each side. At an appropriate moment he knocked down the two guards and disappeared in the woods, finally finding his way back to Oslo where he hid and then escaped. In actual fact Fehmer's tactics broke him down completely and he told everything. He was then allowed to escape on condition that he accepted a mission in England. The basic factors about his mission are the following:

(i) It was emphasized that he was accepting the mission not for Germany but in order to help the cause of Norway, which was only being damaged by agents sent from England.

(ii) He was told that if he confessed his mission on arrival in England we would shoot him as a traitor and also the Germans would shoot his relatives and fiancee.

(iii) The Germans not only prepared this escape story, but he also carried it out in every detail, including knocking down the two Gestapo agents who were escorting him.

(iv) He was given the mission to come to this country where he was to report on the organisation of the underground movement in Norway and the names of agents going back, and also the names of agents provocateurs known to the British as working for the Germans. He was to give this information in code in letters which he could give to agents going back and ask them to post. If possible he was to receive training in W/T and communicate with Oslo in code.

(v) Having escaped he was left entirely to his own devices, in organising his journey to Sweden, and no real supervision appears to have been exercised by the Germans over his movements from that time.

On arrival in this country, ANCHOR was treated as BRUTUS, and told the false story of his escape. Once again the interrogators were left with a strong feeling of uneasiness, but the character of ANCHOR was such that it appeared impossible that he should he a German agent. After many weeks of investigation therefore, the case was about to be closed down when reliable information was received from Norway which enabled ANCHOR to be broken when he confessed his true story.

It is unnecessary to draw attention to the similarity between this case and the case of BRUTUS, but it should be observed that it was, if anything, better prepared in that the actual events of the 'escape' took place.

2. The Advantages to the Germans of this Method of Recruiting Agents

The evidence of these two cases and the extreme similarity of approach, starting off with the visit to the prison of an independent person urging him to collaborate, justifies one in drawing a conclusion that the Germans are working on a pre-arranged plan. Psychologically this appears to be absolutely right. They get hold of an agent who is in a very queer emotional state, having had instilled into him an enormous amount of propaganda about Gestapo frightfulness. They then set about showing a mixture of harshness and friendliness and set about persuading him that he is not a traitor to his own country by collaborating with them. In this, way they satisfy his conscience at the prospect of making terms with them. They then force him to accept a mission on condition that he is released, at the same time ensuring that they hold hostages against whom they will act if he betrays his mission. They then, as in the ANCHOR case, give him a story which he can tell and which so far as the escape is concerned, is the literal truth. They reason, quite rightly, that on arrival in England he will not be searched and therefore can bring in with him all the impediments of a spy, that he will be treated in an informal and friendly manner and that any sort of hostile interrogation of an agent who has risked, and almost lost, his life in our service, is extremely distasteful and improbable, that in telling his story there will be no point on which he will have to lie and therefore no possibility of ever catching him out and that the agent will be debarred from telling the truth to the British, not only by his feeling of shame at having betrayed them but also for fear of reprisals against himself and against the hostages who remain in German hands. It may be that they also think that the effects of their propaganda will remain after he arrives in this country and he will genuinely feel that he is serving his own country's good. In the BRUTUS case the Germans have communicated with him on a few occasions and go out of their way whenever possible to stress that he is serving his own country by carrying out his mission. It cannot be overstated that the above sort of escape story is an extremely difficult one to break. One may be left with all sorts of vague suspicions, but they are practically impossible to prove and over and above everything will remain the feeling that it is inequitable to imprison a man who has rendered faithful service in the past as an agent. It is considered therefore that the Germans are acting very cleverly in their approach to these cases though whether any of these sorts of agents would actually work for them is another matter. The problem, however, is to us as a security service a very graver one in that it relates to returned agents who are not strictly within our province. This note will therefore set out various suggestions for dealing with these cases.

1. Suggested Methods for Dealing With These Cases

In the BRUTUS case after he had confessed his true mission, his own government set up a military court of enquiry in pursuance of a rule of military law that any man taken prisoner by the enemy has got to have his conduct examined by a court of enquiry. This court of enquiry then set out to answer the question whether an agent was justified in accepting a mission in order to escape, and answered the question in the affirmative subject to three conditions which were the following:

(i) That no other means of escape was open to the agent.
(ii) That he did not save his life at the expense of betraying other people, particularly subordinates.
(iii) That he told the whole truth immediately he was out of enemy hands.

Both the setting up of a court of enquiry and the above statement of principle appear to be sound although it is difficult for a person who recruited an agent to be tough with him, it is always possible for a military court under the guise of extreme formality to do so. The first principle therefore, which I feel should be accepted by both the two intelligence services concerned is that any man who has ever been in the hands of the enemy should have an investigation of this nature.

The second point is that I feel fairly confident that the main reason for withholding the true story in other cases will not be so much the fear of reprisals against the subject's family in occupied territory, but the feeling of shame, and the fear of the consequences over here. This can, I am certain, be overcome if the matter is presented properly to the escaped agent on arrival. It is obviously rather a tricky business, because one cannot make promises to him, but if it could be put somewhat along the lines of an enunciation of the principles set out by the court in the BRUTUS case, coupled with a suggestion that in order to save the relatives over there the mission might still be carried out under the orders of the British, it might well be possible to induce the right state of mind for a full confession.

2. Proposals

I was not asked to make any specific proposals but for what they are worth I suggest the following:

(i) That both SIS and SOE should be asked for particulars with regard to all returned agents who have escaped from the enemy.
(ii) That the possibilities of a complete search of all returning agents should be investigated.
(iii) That all agents who have escaped from the enemy should be made in the first instance, before being allowed complete liberty, to write out a full account of their escape.
(iv) That if this discloses any possibility of having been an arranged escape by the Germans, they should then be dealt with in an extremely formal way in interrogation. In this connection I feel that the approach that they are only being interrogated in order to obtain useful information which will be of vital use to agents going

into the field, etc is the wrong one. It must be impressed on them that their conduct is upon enquiry and they must in all cases at some stage be bluffed.

Appendix

Short Particulars of the CROW and LARK Cases

A. CROW

This man is a Norwegian who came to this country from America after the capitulation of Norway. He was recruited and trained as a wireless operator to go back as part of an organisation working in Norway. He was given away by ANCHOR and caught by D/Fing from the air on 23 July 1942. In prison he was broken by the Gestapo (the case being under the control of Fehmer) and agreed to operate his set under the orders of the Germans which he did for several months. Meanwhile he had independent knowledge that he was working under control and played him along with stories of assumed contacts who were coming. This enabled him to persuade the Germans to release him, so that he could appear to be at liberty if the contacts checked up before approaching him. He was allowed his liberty on condition that he worked for the Germans in Norway. He was told that his relatives would be victimized if he double-crossed the Germans. He worked and lived in close relations with the Gestapo. At Christmas time 1942 hearing that a very large number of the Gestapo were going back to Germany for Christmas leave he escaped into Sweden with his mother, wife and family. He has been very closely examined, but so far it has not become apparent that his escape to Sweden was arranged. It would certainly be out of keeping with the other cases for the Germans to allow him to bring with him the only people they could hold as hostages. This is more important in the particular case of CROW who is obviously an unreliable character and not the same type as ANCHOR.

B. LARK

This man is a Norwegian who was recruited in the field in the spring of 1942, brought over to England and after a short training of a month or so, sent back to his own town in Norway under his proper name. He was captured by the Gestapo in Trondheim on 16 December 1942 at the home of a W/T operator. He states that he was held in prison for three days, during which time he was beaten up severely and finally confessed to having had some dealings with an underground organisation. He states that he told a false story and that the Germans had no idea that he had been sent from England. They accepted his story subject to checking and decided to move him from the cells in the Gestapo headquarters to the local prison. He was marched through the streets on the evening of Saturday, 19 December, loosely chained to another prisoner with an armed German guard following him. On arrival at the steps of the prison he allowed the guard to draw level and then slipped his chain and disappeared, ultimately finding his way to Sweden.[18]

Harmer's abbreviated version of the BRUTUS case highlighted the problem of dealing with SIS agents, but diplomatically avoided a discussion of SIS's role in managing enemy double agents, especially those that were known to have fallen under the enemy's control. In those circumstances SIS had a policy of maintaining radio contact with assets known to have been compromised, and the organisation had even insisted on taking responsibility for SOE personnel in similar positions. In the BRUTUS example, the picture had been further complicated because he had also been acting for the Polish Deuxieme Bureau, so there were other considerations to be taken into account. While Harmer was interested in the German technique, rather obviously deployed too often, of the 'fake escape', there was an underlying issue concerning the Abwehr's apparent determination not just to send spies to the UK, but more specifically to place their agents inside SIS and SOE. Hitherto the Abwehr had dispatched spies into England on an ad hoc basis, on short-term missions in answer to an OKW intelligence requirement, such as SEELOWE during the invasion summer of 1940, or the rather over-optimistic objective of the theft of an Allied aircraft by French or Belgian pilots. However, in March 1943 MI5 B1(b)'s Patrick Day discerned an altogether more sinister theme, in a paper entitled *Attempted Penetration of SOE and SIS*:

> The following five cases which have been handled by this section illustrate how the Abwehr has attempted to penetrate SOE and SIS by means of double agents for purposes of counterespionage and/or deception. These cases have been selected as offering the more striking and representative illustrations of this technique. They fall naturally into two categories: first, attempts to penetrate SOE operations against Norway; second, attempts to penetrate SIS operations against France.

2 Norwegian cases: SOE

a. The Case of the M/V *Olaf* (Johansen, Solem, Alseth)

On 16 January 1941 the M/V *Olaf* arrived at Lerwick, Shetlands, having left Trondheim on 4 March 1941. There were persons aboard: Ingvald Johansen, a Norwegian seaman; Thorleif Solem, a Norwegian seaman; and Sigurd Alseth, a Norwegian. The party were found satisfactory from the security standpoint and duly allowed their liberty. Two of the party then took service with SOE, namely Johansen and Solem. Johansen was recruited shortly after his arrival, and continued in this employment until November 1941, when he was captured together with a number of other agents whilst in Norway on a mission for SOE. His function over this period was to skipper the vessels plying between the Shetlands and Norway in the interests of SOE. Solem served only in a minor capacity from 16 April 1941 to 2 June 1941 when he was discharged as wholly unsuitable.

On 29 November 1941 Special Source information was received which made it plain not only that the Abwehr had imprisoned Johansen and his companions and were proposing to court-martial them, but also that on his original journey to this country Johansen had been charged with a mission for the Abwehr. On the strength of this intelligence, the cases of Johansen's companions on that journey, Solem and Alseth, were reexamined and found profoundly unsatisfactory. They were arrested, closely interrogated, and duly broken.

In the absence of Johansen, it has not been possible to elucidate with any distinctness the objectives of the German mission, since Solem and Alseth maintain that this was known to Johansen alone. The following facts were, however, established by the examination. Solem admitted that he was a German agent, having been engaged in counterespionage work for the Trondheim station against patriots in Norway from July 1940 down to his journey to this country. As for the purpose of that journey, Solem alleges that he and Johansen were told by the Abwehr officer in charge to observe on the way over the route through the mine-barrier at Lerwick, the position of any naval units seen en route, and the recognition signals used by aircraft. They were to allege that the purpose of the journey was to purchase whiskey, and having done this with the money with which the Germans had provided them, they were to return in the *Olaf* to Norway. It was clearly hoped by the Abwehr that having broken the ice in this manner the *Olaf* would be in a position to ply regularly between Shetland and Norway.

Manifestly, this story is unsatisfactory, and it is felt that the real purpose of the journey was to enter the service of SOE in order to ply, ostensibly on their behalf, between the two countries, whilst really putting the position to the advantage of the Germans. It should be emphasised, however, that in the absence of Johansen, this conclusion has of necessity remained a speculation. SOE have maintained that Johansen, whilst in their service, was in fact loyal, witness the facts that none of his expeditions gave any grounds for belief that he had double-crossed SOE, and that he is known to have been genuinely imprisoned by the Germans, not merely arrested for cover purposes.

But whilst these considerations may fairly be taken to have established that Johansen did not in fact act as a double agent in the German interest, they of course in no way invalidate the speculation above as to the nature of the original Abwehr intention. The case, therefore, is primarily of interest as shewing with what ease two accredited German agents were enlisted in SOE, in all probability on German instructions. For this the responsibility was found to lie with MI5 inasmuch as it was discovered, when the case was reopened on the basis of the Special Source information, that the security examination of the party on arrival had been quite inadequate.

b. The case of the M/V *Hernie* (Wallem)

On 8 July 1941 the M/V *Hernie* arrived at Lerwick, Shetland, having left Bergen on 5 July 1941. There were aboard three persons: Helmik Wallem, Norwegian, professional W/T operator; Ingard Nilsen, Norwegian; and Georg Lunde, Norwegian. The arrival of the vessel was preceded by information from Special Source shewing that she was carrying an unidentified German agent with a mission for this country. The party were closely examined, as a result of which Wallem confessed to being the agent in question. His story is briefly this.

He was recruited in March 1941 by the Bergen station of the Abwehr and had been employed down to June 1941 on contre-espionage work against patriots and Allied agents inside Norway. In the middle of June 1941 he was instructed to proceed to England in the guise of a refugee together with two selected dupes, Nilsen and Lunde. On arrival he was to get himself recruited by the British Intelligence and in this capacity return to Norway with a transmitter and code which he was to hand over to the Abwehr, who would play back the set to the British control.

The case is therefore a straightforward attempt to penetrate SOE. It is worth remarking that the Abwehr apparently held that, in view of his W/T qualifications, Wallek would experience no difficulty in getting himself constituted a British agent.

c. The case of the M/V *Reidar* (Evensen)

On 8 January 1943 the M/V *Reidar* arrived at Lerwick, Shetland, having left Aalesund on 6 January 1943. There were aboard three persons: Arnold Evensen, Norwegian, baker; Louis Westhum, Norwegian, seaman; and Gunnar Pedersen, Norwegian, student.

The arrival of the vessel was preceded and followed by copious evidence from Special Source, shewing that the arrival of *Reidar* was the realisation of a project the Abwehr had been entertaining since March 1942, and that she had aboard an unidentified German agent.

The party have therefore been closely examined, and although the investigation is far from complete, the main outlines of the story are sufficiently clear for present purposes. In the course of a statement freely made at the beginning of the examination, Evensen admitted that he was the German agent in question. His story, as given on this and subsequent occasions to date, is briefly as follows.

In July 1942, Evensen became an accredited agent of the Abwehr in Trondheim, and in this capacity was entrusted, at the end of the year, with a mission to proceed to England in the guise of a refugee, together with the dupes Westrum and Pedersen. Westrum was known to have contact in Norway with a certain resistance organisation which stood in need of a transmitter in order to establish contact with this country. This intention of Westrum's, and the activities of the organisation were known to the Germans, who had, for this reason, arranged for him to be included in the *Reidar* party. Evensen's instructions therefore were to ingratiate himself with Westrum in the course of the voyage and thus contrive to get himself sent back to Norway by the British Intelligence together with Westrum in order to supply the necessary transmitter to the organisation with which Westrum was in contact. He was also given a subsidiary straight espionage mission to cover the period of his stay in this country. It was supposed that, having hitched his wagon in this manner to Westrum's star, he would find no difficulty in returning with a set, which would then of course be handed over to the Abwehr in order to be played back. It is necessary to add that the foregoing is a considerable simplification of this involved case, which is complicated by the difficulty of establishing Eversen's good or bad faith. In brief, whilst he maintains that his whole long connection with the Abwehr is to be explained by his intention to double-cross them on his eventual arrival in England, there are strong grounds for believing that this claim is not wholly true. Doubts thus being shed on his good faith, it is felt to be possible that, in telling the story outlined above, he has been acting on German instructions; and in thus readily revealing his double-cross mission he is only concealing some still undisclosed assignment.

Whilst no conclusion can yet be pronounced on the general question of Eversen's claim to have acted consistently in the Allied interests, it can safely be said that any hypothesis as to a triple-cross mission can be emphatically rejected as over subtle. That is to say, it is felt that Eversen's account of his mission as summarised above is substantially true, and this being so, the case is clearly an attempted penetration by means of a double agent, exactly similar in type to that of Wallem.

3 French cases: SIS

a. The case of Stella Lonsdale

Mrs. Stella Lonsdale, British, arrived at Whitchurch on 5 November 1941 by air from Lisbon, having escaped by stages to Lisbon from Occupied France via the Unoccupied Zone. She had not been in England since 12 December 1940. She was treated on arrival as a suspect agent of MI9 for reasons which will appear in the sequel. MI9, MI5 and SIS quickly formed an impression that their suspicions were well-founded, and a careful joint examination of Lonsdale was undertaken, as a result of which the following story was obtained.

On 13 January 1940 she landed in France for the purpose of proceeding to Nantes to join her husband, John Lonsdale, who was stationed there. There is independent evidence of her presence there till immediately prior to the German occupation of Nantes. This, and her own story, convey a highly confused picture of what she was actually doing in these four months, in as much as it seems highly probable that Lonsdale and her husband were engaged in secret intelligence work of some kind, though on whose behalf is not clear. Lonsdale refused to leave France as the Germans advanced, with the result that the story of her doings from the occupation of Nantes down to her arrival in Vichy territory rests exclusively on her own words. That story is as follows. The Germans, on their arrival in Nantes, did not molest Lonsdale, and she soon began to take advantage of her continued liberty to engage on her own account in collecting Intelligence for the benefit of the Allies. On 15 November 1941 she was caught by the Germans *flagrante delicto*, arrested, rigorously examined by the head of the Abwehr contre-espionage department for North West France located at Angers, and thrown into prison. From this predicament she was rescued by the efforts of one 'Rene', described as personal assistant to the head of the Angers station and a pre-war acquaintance of Lonsdale's. Rene obtained her release on condition that she worked for the Abwehr; this condition she duly accepted to save her life. Curiously, Rene at the this point revealed himself as an opponent of Germany, and implied that his real reason in engaging Lonsdale as an Abwehr agent was that she should collaborate with him in passing on to the British Intelligence the valuable information Rene possessed. Accordingly, on 5 April 1941 she left for Marseilles, ostensibly on an Abwehr mission, actually to contact, on Rene's instructions, the British Intelligence, and to give certain information of which Rene had already apprised her. In Marseilles she attempted to obtain a quick passage to England, but failed. She aroused the suspicions of certain British authorities in that city by her conduct, but this did not prevent her putting her story across [Ian] Garrow of MI9, who, as a result, recruited her as an agent to act as go-between to Rene. On Garrow's instructions she returned in June 1941 to the Occupied Zone in order to recontact Rene and bring back any further information he might have accumulated, and in the course of the next month she plied regularly between the two zones as Garrow's liaison agent with Rene. In July 1941 a further complication was introduced in that the Vichy authorities tumbled to the activities of Garrow, Lonsdale and other MI9 representatives. This was regulated by a compromise, the IIieme Bureau chief agreeing to leave Lonsdale at liberty on condition that she supplied him with any intelligence from Rene bearing on German secret intelligence activities in Vichy territory.

About 10 September 1941 Lonsdale learned through a secret ink letter from Rene that she was blown, since the Abwehr had learnt that she was working for the French. This was closely followed by information from the IIieme Bureau chief that the Germans had applied for her arrest and extradition, and by the arrest of Garrow on 2 October 1941. Lonsdale therefore found her position untenable, and left France on Garrow's instructions, in order to convey an account of the whole affair to London and to distract attention from such of Garrrow's subordinates as had escaped the round-up. She accordingly flew to Lisbon and arrived in this country on 5 November 1941. In view of the fact that her own part in the arrest of Garrow was not clear, she was treated as suspect.

Lonsdale followed up this story with repeated requests to be enlisted as an agent of the British Intelligence to be sent back in this capacity to France in order to transmit direct the valuable intelligence she would obtain from Rene. A close observation of Lonsdale's character and activities after her arrival, combined with the utter improbability of there existing a traitor in the Abwehr in the form of Rene, led to an unhesitating rejection of both Lonsdale's story and her offer of services. Although the true story has never been obtained, there is little doubt that Lonsdale arrived here for the purpose of penetrating SIS in the German interest and establishing a deception mechanism in the guise of reports purporting to emanate from the traitor Rene. In qualification of this view of the case, however, it is necessary to add that the information Lonsdale alleged Rene had supplied to her for passing to the British Intelligence was found, on reference to SIS, to be quite accurate and indeed important. Although of course it is possible to interpret this as signifying that the Rene's story is true, it seems more probable that this represented the Abwehr's attempt to build up Lonsdale as a double agent, and the comparative importance and accuracy of the information sacrificed in building her up is a valuable indication of the importance the Abwehr attached to Lonsdale's own potentialities as a double cross agent.

b. Pelletier

On 15 April 1942 Pelletier, French and accredited agent of the Fighting French Forces, arrived at Liverpool from Vichy territory via Gibraltar. He was treated on arrival as suspect, for reasons which will appear in the sequel, and duly arrested, examined and broken by the French in the same day. At this point the case was handed over to MI5.

His story of his doings in France subsequent to his arrival as revealed by his confession is as follows. For the first three months he occupied himself in contacting a number of agents in the Free Zone as instructed. On 28 June 1942 instructions were received from London that he was to proceed to Paris for the purpose of making a contact there. For some reason with which he is unacquainted, the contact never materialised, and in consequence he decided to return to the Unoccupied Zone. On 29 July 1942 he was caught whilst crossing the demarcation line in the neighbourhood of Bourges. Although on Pelletier's story there is no reason for believing that the Germans at this stage possessed any information about him other than that he was a mere transgressor of the demarcation line. He was at once removed to Fresnes Prison at Paris. Here he was submitted to a rigorous examination, as a result of which he broke and confessed. He states that the principal reason for the German success in thus breaking down his resistance was that they possessed so much information about the activities of de Gaullist agents in the Occupied and Unoccupied Zones that to continue in his denials appeared to him pointless. Having confessed, the Germans put to him the proposition that he should work as an agent in their interest, for the purpose of double-crossing the British Intelligence. He accepted this proposition, largely because of the pressure the Germans put on him in informing him that his parents, who were still living in Paris, were in their power and would suffer if Pelletier did not meet their wishes.

On 23 October 1942 an escape was arranged for Pelletier by the Germans, the outline of which was that he was taken away from the prison by ambulance to hospital, pretending to suffer from appendicitis, later 'escaping' from the hospital. His instructions, as given to him by the Germans were as follows. In the first place he was to return to the Unoccupied Zone and rejoin his network, and transmit to the Germans in Paris full information, especially W/T and cryptographic, about the operations and identities of these other agents. He was also equipped with secret writing materials and postboxes for this purpose. In the second place he was told that if he performed this first function satisfactorily he would be contacted in the Free Zone by a German agent who would give him detailed instructions for a mission to England. Although this contact was never made Pelletier knows that the general nature of his assignment in this country was to have been to get himself introduced into the wireless section of the British Intelligence organisation running agents in the Free Zone, and, from this position of advantage, transmit to the Germans by one of the British sets information respecting the traffic, arrangements, identities of new agents in training, and identities of the controlling organisation in London.

After his release he proceeded as instructed to the Unoccupied Zone, and it is significant that two Free French agents, his former colleagues, whom he happened to contact shortly after his release, were immediately arrested by the Germans. On 17 November 1941 he decided to make his way back to England for a reason which is not, on his own statement, entirely clear. It is at least known that during his residence in the Free Zone he aroused the suspicion of his Fighting French colleagues, and was in periodic communication by secret writing with the Abwehr, Paris. He successfully reached Gibraltar, after a stay of 3 months in Miranda

Concentration Camp, and returned to this country in the manner already stated. Meantime, the information of the suspicions entertained against Pelletier by his former colleagues had reached London, and it was for this reason that Pelletier was treated on arrival as suspect.

4 The following general conclusions may be drawn from this survey.

It is clear that in their attempts to penetrate SOE and SIS the Germans use two different types of agent. First is the accredited agent of either of these two organisations, who has been caught by the Germans and turned round. Mr. Harmer's note, which is concerned exclusively with this type of penetration agent, emphasises that there is a common element in all of them in the 'escape' story they are told to tell, which is supposed by the Germans to account for the agents having been in touch with the Germans. It will be seen that the case of Pelletier and, to some extent, that of Lonsdale too, fully support Mr. Harmer's conclusion on this point.

A second type is the agent who is not already an accredited member of either of the two organisations in question, and of these Wallem and Evensen afford examples. Since agents of this type do not fall within the category of accredited agents of SOE or SIS it of course follows that the responsibility for their examination on arrival in this country lies with the LRC in just the same way as does the case of any other normal arrival. It is therefore clear that in this matter MI5 has a responsibility to SOE and SIS in order that agents of this class shall not be allowed to succeed in their penetration intentions, the case of the *Olaf* being a striking illustration of how matters can go wrong in this respect. From the foregoing survey it seems that the following inferences can fairly be made, which may be of assistance to the LRC in detecting this type of penetration agent. In the case of Wallem the Germans appear to have relied simply and solely on his excellent W/T qualifications, and his professed willingness to return to Norway in the British service. In the case of Evensen a rather subtler technique is apparent, inasmuch as he was told to ingratiate himself with Westrum, who was, in turn, associated with a resistance organisation in Norway. It was clearly the German view that his connection with Westrum would constitute in the eyes of the British Intelligence an additional reason why Evensen should return to Norway. It therefore appears that the LRC should treat with strong suspicion any arrivals who profess willingness to return to occupied territory as British agents, especially when they attempt to emphasise their qualifications for this work by pointing to a period of service or some other connection with a resistance organisation in Norway prior to their arrival here.

Whether it is within the capacity of the LRC to examine these cases with the care they require in the absence of full and up to date information from SOE and SIS as to the fate of such parts of their organisations as may at times come to the attention of the Abwehr is an open question. On the face of it, however, it would certainly seem that if SOE and SIS wish to ensure that MI5 does not clear agents of this type as sound from a security point of view, it is necessary that they should contribute to the common security machine, by making this information available to MI5 as and when they procure it.

There is, of course, one category which lies in between the accredited agent who has been turned round and the intended penetrator who does not enjoy accredited status, and that is the agent recruited by SOE or SIS in the field. It will be seen, however, that the cases which have so far come to our attention do not include any example of an agent recruited in the field being used as a penetration. It is none the less true that this category is a continual potential menace, and here again it seems very questionable whether the LRC can be in a position to deal with these individuals in the absence of regular and up to date information as to the security of the organisation ahead by which the agent professes himself to have been recruited.[19]

Day's report would turn out to be highly prescient, and alarmed the head of B1(a), T.A. Robertson, who, with a view to the invasion, recalled a highly relevant item from Stella Lonsdale's interrogation in a minute addressed to his colleague Jack Curry:

> It is of paramount importance to be certain the SOE agents and the SIS agents in the area which is going to be affected by the operations are not controlled by the enemy. [Friedrich] Dernbach, who is in charge of counter-espionage work at Angers, told Stella Lonsdale that it was his practice whenever an agent operating a wireless transmitter was captured by him, to try and turn it round in order to make use of it in misleading us by giving false operational information.[20]

Robertson's concern about Dernbach had been fuelled by ISOS texts which appeared to confirm that the Abwehr had penetrated the SABOT organisation, and prompted a warning in May 1943 to SIS's Valentine Vivian about the apparent link between Abt. III/F, concerned with counter-espionage, and IIID, which peddled false information.

> I attach a copy of a summary of the case of Pierre Bourriez with various aliases, but best known as SABOT. This summary is based mainly on information obtained at the LRC, but it only brings out the salient features and is far from representing the very voluminous information in our possession regarding the SABOT organisation at Montpellier, the LUC organisation in Belgium and various other associated organisations.

At the same time our information about both the Montpellier and the LUC organisations is in certain important respects incomplete; and it is insufficient for the purposes for which it has been prepared, i.e. to render as efficient as possible our machinery at the LRC for detecting enemy agents entering this country. It is clear that fuller information could be obtained if certain lines of enquiry were followed up, and no doubt, you have followed up the indications referred to below.

ISBA 115 dated 8 May 1942 refers to ZARATHUSTRA as a matter of interest to Abt. III.D which, as you know, is the organisation concerned with deception, and to IIIE in Dijon and Paris. From the text it appears that ZARATHUSTRA is a German agent or a German organisation in touch with 'the English Intelligence Service in Grenoble', and is using the latter as a vehicle to pass over misleading information on military matters, alternatively it may be a British or Belgian agent who has been turned round. Presumably this message, which received the approval of Heeresgruppe D, was received in this country by the Belgians or by your P Section; and you are therefore in a position to say by whom the attempt was made to put over this misleading information, i.e. you must know the identity of the agent or organisation concealed under the name of ZARATHUSTRA. In any case you will know whether the organisation at Grenoble is purely Belgian or whether your P Section is directly interested. Whoever is, or was, running whatever existed at Grenoble will presumably know how the deception material was 'put across', and therefore know something about ZARATHUSTRA. If there are any gaps in this part of the story it is possible that we may be able to assist through our indexed information. We should be interested, for instance, to learn whether Georges van der Valde whom we know as doing important work for the Belgians at Grenoble was in any was concerned, or SABOT's W/T man François de Weir.

There have been previous references to ZARATHUSTRA on 2 March 1943 which showed that Oberstleutnant Reile and Oberstleutnant Derkbach were concerned in putting over misleading information on a naval matter, as desired by the German Admiral commanding in France. On 12 November 1942 the material indicates that Alfred Genserowski asked Abteilung III to arrest ZARATHUSTRA, and the presumption from this is that it is an individual double agent rather than an organisation or any large group. Again, on 27 November 1942 Genserowski wanted Ruhrscheidt in Madrid to get from Berlin a short summary of their information about the LUC organisation for the purposes of ZARATHUSTRA. The details regarding the arrest of SABOT and his assistant, and the obtaining of information about the LUC organisation on 30 January 1943 and 7 February 1943 are referred to in the attached note on SABOT's case, and the evidence for 18 February 1943 would seem to show that they have succeeded in intercepting couriers' material; and that this interception is in some way connected with the British Consulate at Barcelona. Since then there has been a number of other seizures of couriers' material with serious results to the organisations in Belgium and France.

All this has no doubt formed the subject of suitable enquiry in the appropriate quarters, and the events of which we obtain an indistinct picture from the above material must have been to a great extent uncovered.

I should be grateful for a full account of the result of these enquiries, so that, in agreement with you, we may put an appropriately Bowdlerized form of it on record for the guidance of those parts of our organisation, on whom falls the responsibility for understanding what is happening in the way of penetration of British and Allied organisations in occupied territory, as material assistance to them in detecting penetrative agents of the enemy when they come to this country.[21]

In July 1943 Geoffrey Wethered reviewed the security situation at SOE and submitted a damning report.

General Report on SOE. Cases up to the end of June 1943

1 General

A great deal of damage has been done in recent months to SOE interests on the Continent and particularly in France. A very much greater number of SOE agents are operating in France than in any other European country. The degree of penetration of SOE organisations there seems to be partly accounted for by the number of agents used exceeding the powers of the London officers available. It is not possible on the information available to tell how far penetration has gone; in view of recent arrests as well as the batch of arrests which declined last April it would appear that penetration has gone fairly deep.

In other countries the situation is not so serious. A great deal of illegal activity continues apparently undetected in Norway, and in that country various SOE organisations have functioned without disaster for some time, while the chain of arrests which took place in the LARK Organisation and later in connection with Pastor Moe has not been repeated in recent weeks. In Denmark, in spite of the serious leakages which on two occasions in the last half of 1942 suggested that information was passing from this country to the Germans in Denmark, SOE organisations have apparently functioned recently without farther unfortunate results. This is to some extent capable of a double check as SOE do not have to rely only upon their agents in the field for reports but receive fairly regular information from an indigenous Danish organisation which has a courier service through Stockholm. In Holland there have been recently several arrests and a report on SOE activities in that country is now being prepared. The scene in Belgium has already become a tragedy in the spring of this year and activity in that country is still slight, though SOE contend that one or two recent operations have been successful. I have little detailed information about Poland where, of course, hardly any activity is possible from this country during the summer months. SOE, however, apparently co-operate with some success with native organisations and a recent report from a returned Polish agent suggests that underground activity in Poland is still on a large scale. In Germany itself nothing has been accomplished except propaganda work in collaboration with PWE. France has been mentioned above and a typical SOE French organisation will be referred to below. It is worth noting, however, that from information available from time to time at SOE the disasters which have applied to SOE organisations in the field have not greatly involved indigenous French organisations. It appears that operators of the Organisation LIBERATION continue to function, and a recent organiser of a separate organisation, CEUX DE LIBERATION, who has been interviewed in the last few days, has made a report which is encouraging in its statement of the effective potentialities of the Organisation he represented. This will also be referred to below.

It is easy to criticise SOE for concentrating on quantity rather than quality in respect of the agents they send to the field. There is considerable truth in this, particularly in the case of France. It should, however, perhaps be remembered that MI6 is apt to hear only of cases where penetration has been effected or is suspected. A great many successful operations are being performed of which we receive no notice. Whether or not the Germans are content to watch a certain number of such organisations and to take no action until the eve of invasion must remain to be seen. Apart from the operational side, SOE has been successful in obtaining a good deal of information from occupied territory which is useful to the Services, and other Ministries in this country; and of course they do a great deal of work in collaboration with PWE.

2 CEUX DE LIBERATION

The Organisation CEUX DE LIBERATION is referred to in some detail in the LRC *Monthly Summary* for June 1943. The story there set out can be taken a little further from SOE sources. Mederic, an organiser of CEUX DE LIBERATION and one Guerin @ GAUTIER, an SOE agent in touch with Mederic and the French Rex Organisation, have both been interviewed. Mederic gave a good deal of rather striking information about the scope of CEUX DE LIBERATION. He reported that this Organisation comprises approximately 50,000 men, of whom about 27,000 lived in the Paris region. The organisation has a good deal of arms but needs more, and in the opinion of Mederic, if these were

69

provided operations against the enemy on a very considerable scale would be possible. The Organisation has also got possession of several Gestapo cars and considerable number of lorries and transport of its effectives to a target, at some distance from Paris, would be possible. It would seem that the penetration which has affected so many SOE organisations in this part of France does not apply to any great extent to CEUX DE LIBERATION. Mederic also mentioned that a very strong resistance group in North France was constituted by the Communist Party. This group keeps its activities so secret that not even indigenous Gaullist organisations have much information about it. In many ways they appear to be the most efficient organisation operating in that part of France. The chief dangers to organisations of this sort seem to be the demands of the Relève [compulsory labour]. In the month of June the number of men demanded for the Relève was 250,000. The number will not be forthcoming but the demand has meant that a large number of men has had to go into hiding in the maquis in the south of France and in farms in the north

Guerin @ GAUTIER, referred to on page 3 of the LRC Summary, gave an account of his interrogation by the Special Section of SOE and to me of his arrest in company with Vivier and subsequent escape. Guerin was not himself strongly suspected of being an accomplice of Vivier and was therefore able to swallow all the incriminating papers in his possession. Both these men were taken to the Hotel de Cayre, Boulevard Raspail, a known Abwehr address, where they found three members of CEUX DE LIBERATION also waiting search and interrogation. Guerin was able to effect his escape by choosing an appropriate moment and felling the German guard to the ground. This enabled Vivier and the other three men to get away from the hotel also. The story has been confirmed from other sources and is thought to be accurate. Guerin was able to give some useful information about the activities of his Organisation which was an SOE one and has also ceased to function.

3 A Danish Organisation which supplies SOE with information from Stockholm recently sent to this country a copy of a German cypher and certain facts, many of which could be checked, which suggested that the German cypher might have been used for wireless transmission to the UK. The name of the German operator was supplied and it was found that this name was noted as a wireless operator in Jutland before the war. Although it seemed rather unlikely that the Germans would operate an espionage service of this sort independently of the Abwehr the above facts seem to link up with the serious Danish leakage referred to above. Suspicions had already turned upon a former SOE agent trained as a W/T operator who had been reported as making unauthorised use of his W/T set during 1942, and who would have been in possession of a set at the time of both leakages. It still seems conceivable that this man,

who was a first-class operator in Denmark before the war, may have been known to the German operator and might have established contact with him by pre-arrangement or by chance. The fullest enquiries are being made about the former SOE student.

4 A Polish woman who has been working for an indigenous Polish organisation since early 1941 was recently sent by this organisation through Germany, France and Spain to the US. She travelled under the name of Elizabeth Watson from the time she reached Spain and was entrusted with the mission of contacting the Poles in London and exchanging information with them. This lady has given information about conditions in Poland and in Paris which was previously known. She had an extremely eventful journey through France under the auspices of the Polish Organisation, which appears to have been extremely efficient. She was issued with several sets of identity papers, first as a Volksdeutsch living in Poland, and then as an Alsacienne since she spoke fluent German but no French. She had two brushes with the German Police in France and two with the Spanish Police after crossing the frontier. She appears, however, to have had both luck and a great deal of self-possession, and apart from the rigours of the journey and a brief period spent in hiding she made the whole enormous journey without being arrested or detained. Her account naturally needed a certain amount of checking but it was impossible to find any grounds for suspicion, although the whole affair lasted only from 9 February when she left Warsaw until 29 March when she reported to the British Consulate at Barcelona. This lady is to return shortly to Poland with the information which she has gained from the Poles in London, and it has been strongly recommended that she should travel by some different route in view of the fact that her description, or notes about her different brushes with the Police, may be compared and circulated. The case was chiefly of interest in showing how it is still possible for an individual with a good knowledge of German (and in this case a rather German appearance), to make such a long and complicated journey in safety.

5 BISHOP Organisation

A very full investigation has recently been made into SOE records in connection with an SOE Organisation in France which goes under the name of BISHOP. The ramifications of this Organisation are so large and varied that it is impossible to set out in a brief note the relevant facts; these have in any event been circulated within B1 as providing a useful example of SOE activities in the Field. The chief points to note as a result of this investigation seem to be as follows:

1. Security Investigations into SOE Organisations in the Field are made almost impossible by two main factors. The first is the

inadequacy of the Country Sections' records, most of which appear to be carried in the heads of individual officers, and secondly, the fact that the known agents who have been trained in this country invariably make contact with a number of other individuals who if they are referred to at all in traffic or courier reports, are called by some convenient sobriquet which cannot be checked. Agents in the Field are of course bound to enlist certain local inhabitants in the course of their job. They are not supposed, however, to make contact with other organisations. Unhappily it appears that in almost every case different parts of the same organisation and even different organisations are aware of each other's activities. Consequently, when as in the BISHOP case, penetration is effected in any one sector other sectors and other organisations may also be affected. The evils of this in the Field are obvious and in investigating the matter complications are considerable because of the various points at which penetration seems possible.

2. Although each agent going to the Field is instructed in the use of an identity check and a bluff check, so rare is it for these to be applied correctly that SOE Country Sections have almost ceased to set any store by the presence or absence of the necessary checks. Various suggestions as to the simplest and most foolproof type of check have been made and it is hoped that something more satisfactory may be introduced.

6 D/F-ing. There is no doubt from information now available that the Germans have had considerable success in occupied territory, particularly in Norway and France, in D/F-ing W/T sets. They appear to have brought this method of investigation to a high point of efficiency. Various returned agents have spoken of the number and effectiveness of German mobile units and detection vans. They also make use of a static installation complete with an aerial which is usually placed on high ground. Reference has also been made on more than one occasion to the presence of aeroplanes apparently engaged in detector work. It would appear possible that the Germans may have developed a system of D/F-ing from the air, though it is also possible that this method is a pretence in order to try the nerves of W/T operators in the area, particularly when some W/T set has been located but not found.

7 Cases continue to occur in which SOE material dropped by parachute from this country has turned up in German hands. It has now been suggested that SOE should make arrangements for each consignment to be marked with a different manufacturer's stamp so that if we should trace such equipment it would be possible to tell which SOE operation, or perhaps organisation, must have come under German control or attention.

8 More than one Frenchman recently interviewed by the SOE Special Section have referred to the problem of notifying the French of the eventual invasion, or, alternatively, telling the population to stay put when only a raid or similar operation is to take place. This problem, which is a very complicated one, applies of course to other occupied countries as well. It seems to be most probable that a large number of Frenchman whether or not they belong to resistance organisations would take strenuous action on any Allied landing, unless they were specifically ordered not to do so. If this should be done when in fact no invasion was intended it would obviously lead to reprisals and arrests. It might even cause the Germans to become aware of considerable underground activity which is so far unknown to them. The only method by which such directions could be assured would be by wireless broadcast, or, alternatively, by W/T messages to SOE and Allied organisations in the Field, The first is obviously impracticable as it would give the same information to the Germans. It would seem that the second would be attended by a similar danger, particularly in France where one cannot at present be certain of the continued effectiveness of SOE organisations.[22]

Patrick Day's conclusions, that the Abwehr had targeted SOE and SIS for penetration, and Harmer's opinion that under present conditions the two British organisations were very vulnerable to this strategy, caused MI5's senior management, in the form of Sir David Petrie, Guy Liddell and Dick White, to order further investigation by B1(b) in April 1943. The two-page brief set out the background, highlighting the challenge of addressing the problem without compromising ISOS, referred to as 'Most Secret Sources' which had to be protected from SOE.

The main report on this subject is based on information in the files of this office dealing with the interrogation of suspects, of agents who have been turned round and of well disposed persons passing through the LRC who have willingly helped us with information. This supplementary report is based on material of an extremely secret and delicate kind and cannot be sent outside this office without the consent of CSS.

2. Further enquiries made since the main report was prepared show that while there is an immense amount of material in this office to examine, it is not likely even if set out to lead us any further. The general nature of the material is similar to that already dealt with and, as has been mentioned, our information is, generally speaking, incomplete both in regard to the evidence dealing with individuals and in regard to the over-riding questions of the system, technique and policies of SOE and SIS. In the information at our disposal there are a number of gaps which can be filled in by them but not by us. In order to provide for a complete

enquiry it would, therefore, be necessary for this to be authorised by the heads of these two services.

3. Two points may, however, be emphasised. The first is that, as mentioned in the main report in para. 62, two of the most important factors contributing to the success of Abteilung III/F and the SD have been wireless interception and the use of agents for penetration purposes.

4. We know from Most Secret Sources that the Germans have a highly developed system of short range D/Fing which enables them to detect illicit transmitters; and we know that this work is done by a special section of Abteilung III/F which deals with wireless, acting in co-operation with a section of the Wehrmacht's Nachrichten Verbindungen. This branch of the Oberkommando der Wehrmacht, commonly known as WNV, deals with all wireless and other communications of the armed forces and also monitors illicit wireless, is in communication with the Abwehr on the subject and provides personnel to collaborate in the detection and location of such transmitters. There is good ground for believing that it is very unlikely that any transmitter can hope to exist for any length of time in Germany or German occupied territory without being detected, identified and located. If this is so it is, presumably, extremely dangerous for SOE or SIS to send an agent out equipped with a transmitter, but we do not know certain relevant facts. On the one hand we do not know how far they have been successful in maintaining transmitters for any length of time, or the proportion which come to grief and on the other we do not know exactly how the co-operation between the WNV, the Abwehr and the Gestapo in these matters is effected. It is, however, a reasonable inference that somewhere in their organisations they must discharge the same functions as our voluntary interceptors, 'general search' and, presumably, 'discrimination'; that they must be in a position to locate the stations in the UK from which messages are sent to agents abroad; and that the results of this work must be communicated to the Abwehr through the WNV and the above-mentioned wireless section of Abteilung III F. We also know that the OKW employs specialists in cryptographical work (just as they know that our services do the same).

5. It is understood that SOE are aware of the danger attached to the use of wireless transmitters, but that under present circumstances they feel compelled to continue to use them in spite of the losses they have incurred and that they are attempting to devise means of minimising these losses; it is not known, however, how far the real nature of the danger has been appreciated and it is not possible to arrive at a reliable estimate of the position on the basis of the material available in this office.

6. It will be obvious that we are here dealing with the point mentioned in para. 3, (ii) and (iii) of the main report and that this is a governing factor in the question of protecting the operations of SIS, SOS and their agents.

7. The success in the use of agents is illustrated in the main report and in the case of Pierre Bourriez. The attached summary of this case suggests that if they have not already done so Abteilung III/F and the Sicherheitsdienst – especially with the increasing control by Himmler and the SD – will be in a position by the time we invade the continent to cut off the heads of all the tall poppies, leaving the rank and file more or less disorganised and helpless. Whether or not Hitler will adopt a policy of waiting and pouncing, as they are known to have done in the past, may be in the nature of a hypothetical question, but it must be expected that they will act according to past form. It should be worthwhile to arrange for the action they now take to be carefully observed. If they have not, since the arrest of Pierre Bourriez in January 1943, and do not make a number of arrests of important people in Belgium, the inference that they intend to adopt this policy will be strengthened. The action which the Abwehr and the SD have recently taken to disrupt the ANDREE and Montpellier escape routes may have a sinister significance. If all the escape routes became closed it would become difficult to evacuate the leading personalities of the resistance movements, should that policy at any time appear desirable.

8. The second point to be emphasised and a serious aspect of the matter is that it cannot but be obvious to the Intelligence services of the Allied governments established in London that they have to deal with five different parts of the British Intelligence machine, i.e. SIS, Section V, SOE, the LRC and E Division of this office, and that the working of these parts is not only not co-ordinated, but in more directions than one is far from harmonious. The consequences of this are likely to extend to a high political level as well as to have a serious effect in matters of 'Intelligence'. In the first place, the Allied Intelligence services and their governments must inevitably attribute the loss of agents, that is to say very often the loss of the lives of their nationals, to this lack of harmony among the British organisations. If losses become more serious still, on the lines indicated above in the event of invasion, this cannot but have a serious effect on the political relations between this country and the Allies in the future and it must have a harmful effect on British prestige.

9. This is the apparent position as seen from this office, but it is possible, that this view may be to some extent modified when seen from a different angle in SIS and SOE and we must obviously be careful about jumping to conclusions when our knowledge of the whole subject is admittedly incomplete.

10. All the relevant information cannot be examined without the assistance of SIS and SOE officers. It is evident that if the matter is to be carried any further it will be necessary to arrange for a joint enquiry. It is suggested that the terms of reference should be (a) to set out in a convenient form, and if possible, on the basis of this report the relevant facts regarding the success of Abteilung III and the SD in effecting penetration, and (b) to make recommendations for a solution of the problems involved. The question of a solution vitally affects the interests of all three services but the functions of protecting our own organisations on an operational basis fall primarily within the scope of Section V of SIS.

Brief summary of the case of Pierre Bourriez @ MURET @ PIERRE @ LACANE © SABOT

Lieutenant Pierre Bourriez of the Belgian Army reported in September 1941 at the depot at Montpellier of an organisation under Major Branders. Bourriez had been dropped in France by parachute with a man named Francois de Weer, equipped with a radio transmitter and Branders was in charge of what was known as the 'E', ('Evades') Division with the function of evacuating Belgians of military age. The 'E' Division had been constituted by members of the Belgian Government residing in France in a formation of the staff of the Belgian Army in Montpellier dealing with Belgian war material abandoned or left in France after the departure of the Belgian troops. Officers on the active or reserve list and pilots, mechanics and petty officers of the regular Army were accepted in the 'E' Division, subject to their signing an undertaking to engage themselves on their honour to join the Belgian forces wherever they might be. The 'E' Division concerned itself with arrangements for the despatch of appropriate personnel, especially Belgian airmen, through France to the UK and in this connection Pierre Bourriez, who was directly responsible to M. Lepage in London through whom he received his orders from Minister Gut, proved himself highly efficient. Early in 1942 the influx of airmen reached embarrassing proportions and the Division encountered a number of difficulties, some of its men being arrested by the French and others becoming brulé. In particular, difficulties arose in connection with what was described as lack of flexibility and lack of liaison at Barcelona, where their representative was a certain M. Schul, who had an important part to play as he was the terminal of the escape route under Branders' control. Branders, who came over to this country in August 1942, mentioned that the organisation commanded considerable funds, that nearly 400 men had signed the 'E' Division undertaking and that in July about 100 airmen had been accepted. He said that Pierre Bourriez was indispensable and that his best colleague was a certain Lieutenant Lacombez, who was excellent at gathering information and undertook practically all the risky part of the work. Branders also mentioned that the Rexist Party in Brussels had been employed by the Germans to send several of their agents to France, with the obvious intention of penetrating this organisation. One of them had admitted that he belonged to a group of six and had been sent to unoccupied France with instructions to find out the number of Belgians, the means by which they travelled and the places where they were collected. The organisation also suffered from the activities of some disloyal Belgians who organised escape parties which were doomed to failure. Their victims were told that in case they were caught they should mention the names of Major Branders and his personal assistants in order to compromise the Montpellier organisation. As has been pointed out in the main report on penetration of SIS, SOE and Allied organisations, the principal movements in Belgium have been associated more or less closely in their activities, especially in connection with arranging escape routes. In this way the Montpellier organisation, based as it is on Belgian Army cadres, naturally came into touch with the Legion Belge and with organisations like LUC and ZERO. It was also in touch with individuals like Pierre Nottet, who was concerned in the evacuation of a number of Belgian airmen through Montpellier with the assistance of the Branders group. The LUC Organisation has already been briefly described in the report and, according to Jean Guricks, alias André CAUTIN, one of its founders, he was in contact with Gurickx, known as 'WALTER', the head of the ZERO Organisation, and these two organisations exchanged information. Gurickx, alias WALTER, has told us that the ZERO Organisation was started in July 1940 under the name of Service Jef, having been founded and led by Kerkhofs, a director of the Banque de Bruxelles. Kerkhofs is a man of standing not only on account of his position as a director of a bank but also because of his relations with the British Intelligence Service and even more so with unofficial military and political circles in Belgium. Kerkhofs left Belgium in October 1941 and at that time the organisation included sections dealing with the King and his entourage, political information, economic information, financial information, military information, air information, propaganda (e.g. *La Libre Belgique*), propaganda (tracts and posters), escape organisations (Belgian and British), supply of false documents, liaison with paramilitary organisations, communications (couriers), communications (Radio), security, assistance to parachutists, operations and codes and cyphers. We have details of the personalities in the different sections, who included a number of former ministers of the Belgian Government, prominent editors, lawyers, industrialists and others,Walter Gurickx was nominated by Kerkhofs as his successor.

Kerkhofs himself had maintained liaison with the Legion Belge, which he described as the only paramilitary organisation likely to have any real influence at the time of an attack on Belgium by the Allies. He stated that it had originally consisted of two groups and that he had helped to bring about a fusion between them in the late summer of 1941 with the assistance of Commandant de Hoover, one of his personal friends. According to Glazer, one of the chief leaders of the Legion Belge, it, like LUC, suffered considerable damage as a result of the alleged treachery of Jamart in 1941. The fact that LUC and the Legion Belge were both thought to have been so seriously affected by Jamart's disclosures is some indication of the close relation between them.

In 1941 a Belgian named Pierre P.T. Toppet was working in unoccupied France in connection with the evacuation of Belgians willing to serve as parachutists and saboteurs on behalf of the Allies. A friend of his, a Frenchman Kermarec who was secretary to the Office Belge in Montauban, had installed a transmitter in his loft. About the middle of December 1941 Toppet went to Montpellier to explain to Branders the difficult situation of Belgians interned in various camps and to try to find some way of evacuating them, and again in January 1942 he met Branders, Labwwyn, who went under the name of Firmin, and Pierre Bourriez. From that time until the middle of April Toppet worked in Montauban on behalf of Bourriez, but on 17 April he was arrested by the French Police and in the course of his interrogation was covertly informed by one of the French Police officers that he had been denounced by a man named Detal who had been associated with his work. In September 1942 Bourriez gave instructions to Toppet that he was to leave the country and he left by the escape route of the Montpellier organisation via Barcelona, where he was taken to the British Consulate and put in touch with Pierre Schul. He was hidden for a fortnight and then left Barcelona with a group of Belgians and reached this country, where he was well known at the RVPS as having worked for a long time helping Belgians to leave unoccupied France for Spain and Portugal.

On 3 January 1943 an individual named ADOLPHE was arrested by the French Police in Toulouse, together with his assistant, Sous-Lt. d'Ae, and five Belgians who were being sent to the UK by one of the escape routes. These five men told the Police that they had been sent by Kermanrec of Montauban. Consequently Kermarec was interrogated and had to leave France immediately afterwards and Bourriez had reason to fear that the organisation in Montauban had been given away. After ADOLPHE was arrested his wife telephoned to the German authorities at the Kommandatur in Toulouse and, in consequence of this, Reichnech, described as 'Chef de la Gestapo' in Toulouse, demanded his release in accordance with the terms of the Armistice Agreement. Pierre Bourriez regarded the circumstances as evidence of treachery on the part of ADOLPHE, who he learnt had made a statement to the French police to the effect that he was working for the Belgian SR, the French 2me Bureau and the Schutzpolizei and that he had passed escapees through in order to earn money. The details of his statement, of which

Bourriez obtained knowledge from associates in the French police, were in important respects incorrect. In addition to serving the needs of the various Belgian organisations, Bourriez established organisations in Paris, Toulouse, Montpellier, Montauban and elsewhere. The DELPA organisation in Paris was one of his. It supplied information of military interest which was sent on by courier.

It is known that Abwehr Abteilung III developed a project to penetrate the LUC Organisation, as a result of which Pierre Bourriez and Jules Lacomblez were arrested on 28 January 1943 and the circumstances under which Reichnech secured the release of ADOLPHE suggest the possibility that he may have been connected with this German attempt at penetration. Under the general supervision of Oberstlt Rohleder, head of Abteilung III/F in Berlin, and Oberstlt Rohrscheidt of Abteilung III in Madrid, an officer of Abteilung III named Alfred Genserowski, acting in co-operation with the SD in Toulouse and the Abwehr officers in Pau and Toulouse and with the SD and Abteilung III in Barcelona, was concerned in the arrangements which led to these two arrests. At the same time a quantity of incriminating evidence was seized and it appears that the enquiry was taken over by the SD in Paris, where Oberstlt Reile of Abteilung III also co-operated. As a result important information was obtained about the LUC Organisation. The Germans were able to arrange for a number of further arrests and they are also known to have planted another agent on the organisation, with the object of getting in touch with the British Consulate in Barcelona. At the same time there is reason to fear that the evidence obtained at the time of these arrests will have furnished them with information regarding other organisations in France and Belgium with which Bourriez was concerned. The Abteilung III organisation in Brussels was also concerned in the enquiry. We thus have a picture of a whole network of Abteilung III in Belgium, France and Spain collaborating actively with the SD to combat LUC and its associated organisations, and indications more or less definite of penetration by agents – including Belgian Rexists – in Montauban, Montpellier, Paris, Toulouse and Barcelona. The whole affair leaves a very strong impression that the Germans have now penetrated deeply into the most important groups in Belgium and that the opinion formed by Gurickx when he left that country in July 1942 cannot now hold good. He considered that the Germans had nowhere penetrated beyond the fringes.[23]

The eventual report drafted by MI5 produced further evidence that Abt. III had engaged in a widespread penetration scheme, against which the only defence was ISOS. The implications were especially grave as the Allied contemplated an invasion, and in August 1943 SIS obtained what it claimed was positive proof of what was termed 'large-scale Gestapo penetration of the resistance movements', disclosing to the Prime Minster and his intelligence adviser Desmond Morton that 'we have very recently obtained access by sure means to a Gestapo document which shows that the de Gaullist resistance movements, which had greatly centralised under the de Gaulle special delegate known as Rex, have been completely penetrated by the Gestapo, who know the names and identities of many leaders including the identities of some of those who are actually in England'.

'Rex', of course, was Jean Moulin, the charismatic chairman of the French Resistance Council who was betrayed at the end of June 1943 and arrested while conferring with other Resistance leaders in a village south of Lyons. This catastrophe occurred a few days after the arrest of General Vidal, the head of the Armée Secrete in Paris. Also detained in recent weeks had been Francis Suttill, head of SOE's PROSPER circuit, a disaster that resulted in more than 1,500 arrests. Apprehended within three days of his arrival in France in June 1943, Suttill made a deal with his captors that they would treat his organisation's membership as prisoners of war, and not as terrorists. Having received this assurance, Suttill revealed all he knew. In parallel, F Section's Air Movements Officer, Henri Dericourt, was benefiting from a pre-war relationship with Boemelburg, and under his sponsorship forty-three people had been delivered to France, and sixty-seven exfiltrated on twenty-one separate air missions. None had experienced the slightest difficulty with the Luftwaffe or hostile reception committees.

A damage assessment drawn up by SOE's Cyril Harvey acknowledged the scale of the debacle, 'It is unfortunately true that the Germans seized a great deal of material at the time of these arrests.' The verdict given by MI5's Geoffrey Wethered in September 1943 conceded 'It is undoubtedly an unfortunate fact that during the last three months untold damage has been done in France, both to SOE and indigenous organisations.'

Wethered had been studying German penetration of SOE since February 1943 when two Belgian circuits, SABOT headed by Pierre Bourriez and BRAVERY, were closed down by the enemy and mentioned in ISOS. In April he noted that BRAVERY had 'operated in Belgium and joined up with the SABOT organisation in the South of France. The channel for escapes and information then crossed the Spanish frontier and reached the British Consulate in Barcelona. It seems most likely that this route is now almost if not entirely blown.'

Very belatedly, SOE began to realise that its circuits in Belgium, France and the Netherlands had been thoroughly compromised by action taken jointly by the SD and Abwehr which meant that over several months the Germans had effectively sponsored SOE's clandestine flights, copied the contents of its courier pouches addressed to London, and was in control of numerous radio links.

* * *

During the month that MI5 was preoccupied with what were perceived to be security lapses in Belgium, France and Norway, the Abwehr pulled off an astonishing coup in the Netherlands by controlling up to fifteen SOE and SIS wireless sets simultaneously. Abt. III/F in Holland was led by Herman Giskes who was transferred from Alst Paris in November 1941. Born in Krefeld in the Rhineland in 1896 Giskes had volunteered for the 31st Field Artillery Regiment in 1914, and had been severely wounded at Verdun in July 1916. After the armistice in 1918 he was a PoW in Chateauroux, and upon his release joined his father's tobacco business. In September 1938 he rejoined the army and was posted to Ast Hamburg before running III/F at Alst Paris and then, from November 1941, the Netherlands.[24]

Giskes established his reputation as the Abwehr's principal spycatcher while he was in Paris, with his successful investigation of an espionage network and escape line run from the US consulate-general in Paris by a clerk-receptionist, Mrs Elizabeth R. Deegan, who was subsequently expelled and transferred to Rio de Janeiro. Also withdrawn were the consul, Leigh W. Hunt, and the first secretary, Cecil M.P. Cross, both implicated in accommodating RAF aircrew who had evaded capture and then passing them down an escape-line to the unoccupied zone and eventual freedom through Marseilles or across the Pyrenees.

Giskes was first alerted to the spy-ring by an Austrian socialite Freddie Kraus who, as a Siemens executive, had reported his suspicion that his fiancée, Princess Jacqueline de Broglie, was being cultivated by enemy agents, Michel Courtois and the Marquis Pierre d'Harcourt, described as then aged 'about 22, hot-headed and very indiscreet', whom she entertained at her home in Neuilly. The situation was delicate because Princess Jacqueline's mother was the Hon. Daisy Fellowes, whose husband Reginald was Winston Churchill's cousin.[25]

When interrogated in 1945, Kraus recalled that 'through Jacqueline de Broglie [he] came to meet most of Paris society' and in March 1941 was introduced to her friend Pierre d'Harcourt. The meeting, a chance one, took place in a café in Paris, and Kraus recounted that within five minutes of the introduction, D'Harcourt was asking him whether he would be prepared to work for the British Intelligence service.

In May 1941 Kraus became acquainted with Courtois who eventually declared himself to be an RAF officer with the rank of major. To make himself attractive as a potential recruit, Kraus espoused anti-Nazi views and claimed to have access to travel permits over the Demarcation Line into the unoccupied zone. Accordingly, having taken the bait, Courtois invited him to supply information on various topics:

(i) Constructional work being carried out at Brest, Lorient and the French coast in general;
(ii) Troops, their locations and movements;
(iii) The quantity of petrol coming into France monthly, and above all,
(iv) Details about troop concentrations on the Russian border.[26]

This questionnaire served to compromise Courtois but also provided III/F with valuable indicators about current Allied intelligence priorities. Additionally, Courtois gave Kraus a briefing on the recognition of military insignia, and as a security precaution introduced him to a cut-out, the Countess Colette ('Coco') Dampierre, to whom he was to deliver his reports. Having consulted Giskes, Kraus passed on his information which covered four topics:

(i) Details of bomb damage which Kraus was supposed to have seen or heard about during his visit to Berlin. Kraus had to learn these reports by heart and was required to pay particular attention to the definite order which they had been drawn out.
(ii) There was one report giving details of the performance of the performance of an aeroplane engine, possibly the 'Condor'.
(iii) At least one report concerning the number of U-boats at Lorient or the number which could be harboured there.
(iv) Finally, a blueprint of a tank chassis, possibly the 'Tiger' which was being turned out by the SOMUA (?) works in France.[27]

Clearly the 'chicken-feed' material planted on Kraus bore little relation to the SIS requirements set out in the Courtois questionnaire, and this rather unprofessional approach highlighted a systemic flaw in the Abwehr's somewhat hesitant attempts to develop and exploit double agents. Indeed, on one occasion Giskes recalled that, in the absence of an established protocol for passing secrets to the enemy, a disclosure relating to the location of an aerodrome had resulted in an air-raid and heavy Luftwaffe losses. Curiously, after the war the head of SIS's French Section, Wilfred Dunderdale, denied any knowledge of this operation, or of having received secret plans for the Tiger tank from his CARTWRIGHT network.

When Kraus handed over the allegedly classified tank blueprints, which he claimed he had acquired at Siemens, III/F kept the rendezvous under surveillance and watched as Courtois received the documents in the Ritz Hotel and drove them to a technician named Eglise to be photographed. Over the following weeks, as the quantity of material increased, Courtois put Kraus on a salary of 3,000 francs and employed Princess Jacqueline to type up his reports. At the end of June 1941 Courtois took up an offer from Kraus, who said he was to visit Marseilles on business, to deliver a package of reports to his local contact, an accountant named Spoldini at the Gibbs Soap factory. Another link, Michelene Carin, who was CARTWRIGHT's Polish courier, was exposed in Paris by Kraus, but the Abwehr failed to intervene as he passed her documents in a café.

Courtois was arrested in July 1941 and imprisoned at Fresnes where he was found to be carrying papers in his true identity, Lieutenant Michel Coulomb, an SIS agent codenamed EVE who had been parachuted in January 1941 near Chateauroux to join up with the BCRA's Hubert Moreau of the CARTWRIGHT circuit which he had established in August 1940. Ultimately, in August 1941, d'Harcourt was arrested in a Metro station immediately after he had dined in a restaurant in the Bois de Boulogne with Kraus. He too would be taken to Fresnes, but would survive incarceration at Buchenwald, as he described in his 1967 memoirs *The Real Enemy*.[28]

Finally, Giskes orchestrated a meeting between the Countess Dampierre and Mathilde Carré, the Abwehr agent who had penetrated SIS's INTERALLIÉ network. This episode ended with the arrest and temporary detention by III/F's Hugo Bleicher of both Kraus and Dampierre. Although the incident appears to have ended Kraus's espionage career, and exposed a lack of coordination within III/F, he was blamed by SIS for having compromised INTERALLIÉ. MI5 did not agree, and after Kraus had been interrogated at Camp 020, B1(a)'s Ian Wilson sent his verdict to G.H. Townsend of Section V in a letter dated 21 November 1944, referring to the penetration of INTERALLIÉ:

There is no evidence that Kraus was responsible for the break-up of this organisation. What he was responsible for was certainly the 'planting' of information on the organisation run by EVE, and probably he was at least in part responsible for the arrest of EVE and Richard [*sic*] d'Harcount. The INTERALLIÉ organisation appears to have broken down when the III/F officer Bleicher got onto the agent DESIRE in Cherbourg, through him got on to CHRISTIAN and through CHRISTIAN got on to WALENTY, VIOLETTE and VICTOIRE. With the help of VICTOIRE and papers captured at WALENTY's flat his almost complete round-up of the organisation followed. Kraus was not responsible for this.[29]

While SIS had been inclined to blame Kraus for betraying its INTERALLIÉ network, it was rather more likely that a sequence of arrests, beginning in Cherbourg, had led inexorably to the leadership in Paris, and specifically to Roman Garby-Czerniawki and his lover Mathilde Carré.

Although Giskes was posted to The Hague in November 1941 and replaced by Major Feil, Kraus remained in contact with him, and continued to exercise sufficient influence to obtain the release of his brother-in-law, Alexandre, Comte de Casteja, from the SD's custody. He also appeared occasionally in the ISOS traffic with the codename KURT, and for a period seemed to be attached to I/L Technik. As MI5's Helenus Milmo observed as Kraus was transferred to Camp 020 in November 1944, he had brought off 'what must clearly have been regarded as a coup of considerable magnitude'.[30]

Giskes was arrested by US troops in May 1945 while hiding in civilian clothes at the Abwehr's training school at Wiehl. Interrogated at Camp 020 from May 1945 to October 1946, Giskes and his subordinate Gerhardt Huntermann were completely cooperative, the former having been reminded that the circumstances of his capture had compromised any claim to PoW status, with the obvious consequences. Their version of events would form the basis of MI5's NORDPOL investigation (reproduced at Appendix II).

Together, Giskes and Huntermann gave detailed accounts of how they 'turned the SOE wireless operator' Hubertus Lawers after he had been arrested in The Hague when on March 1942 his transmitter was located by D/F apparatus. In return for a promise that his colleagues would not be executed, Lawers collaborated with his captors and laid the foundation for what the Abwehr codenamed NORDPOL, which would ensnare some fifty Dutch agents. The Germans also recovered his wireless and a quantity of his previous signals. Three days later, Thys Taconis was also taken into custody, and NORDPOL was underway.

Under cross-examination at Camp 020 Giskes disclosed details of the Abwehr's deception policy which, compared to its British counterpart, must have seemed primitive to his interrogators who drafted a paper on Abwehr doctrine in relation to the management of double agents entitled *Deception and Policy of XX Agents*:

German Policy and Procedure

The passing of 'Spielmaterial' to enemy intelligence services was a regular part of the functions of the Abwehr. All Diensttstelien carrying out this work kept on hand a regular stock of such material in order to be able to comply, within a reasonable time, with any requests for information that might be made by W/T by the Allies.

For definite deception purposes, prepared material was distributed by higher authority (C-in-C West, Ic Army Groups, OKW, Seekriegsleitung) to the III/F referats concerned for passing on to the Allies, where possible through several independent channels. Each time contact was made with the Allies, no matter in what manner, Abw. Abt. III had to be informed and authority obtained for maintaining this contact. All enemy requests for information had to be reported immediately to Abt. III, together with suggested replies. Material for drafting replies was collated by III/F with the help of other branches of the Ast, and had then to be submitted for approval to the relevant military authority, e.g. Luftgaukdo Holland. When this approval had been obtained, the suggested answer was telephoned to Abt. III D in Berlin for approval. If, however, time pressed, the information was often supplied and III D's authority obtained afterwards. All material regarding economic or political conditions in Germany, or the sphere of activity of another Ast, was supplied by III D.

When information on any specific target was required, a member of III F had to assume the role of the agent in order that only such information should be sent as could normally be procured by a real agent.

Deception

The intelligence branches of the highest military authorities in the occupied countries could give information to the relevant Ast for passing to the Allies, but in such cases the onus of informing III D lay with the originator, e.g., the intelligence branch of the service concerned.

Referat III D

This was a small section in the OKW at Berlin (Tirpitzufer) consisting of the Leiter Oberst Schaeffer on technical assistant and a female secretary. With the gradual eclipse of the Abwehr this section lost its importance and its role in the RSHA as III D was only a small one.

From 1943/44 onwards 'Spielmaterial' was distributed entirely by the 1c branch of the higher Wehrmacht headquarters, e.g. C-in-C West. Army Group B, etc.

There was apparently however no very fixed policy after the eclipse of III D with regard to 'Spielmaterial' and some very curious incidents occurred; for example in January/February 1944 Giskes heard that films seized in Brussels were forwarded through German Intelligence Service channels by mistake immediately after they had been developed.

One Source of Spielmaterial
In this connection Giskes claimed that genuine seized espionage material was always a good source of 'Spielmaterial'. The Dutch and Belgian Intelligence Services were in the habit of forwarding material in triplicate by three different means and if it was established that copies of the seized material had already been sent through other channels it was then forwarded in order to inspire confidence in the German-controlled channel.

NORDPOL Spielmaterial
During the NORDPOL affair, Giskes states, at various times which he cannot remember, information was used about the position of German warships, coastal batteries on the island of Beveland, the positions of HQ of divisions alleged to be in Holland; in addition reports on the Dutch armaments industries were also sent.

These reports were, of course, additional to the normal current traffic which was being sent over the various SOE links. For such routine traffic Giskes gave Huntemann a free hand and, unless it was necessary to forward answers to questions on specific military targets or troop movements, no other authority was required; but as has been stated above, this latter type of message had to be referred to the relevant authority in III D for their approval.

Copies of all signals sent or received had to be sent monthly to Abw. Abt. III.[31]

Lauwers was persuaded to use his radio to transmit, under German control, back to London on 12 March, and he was apparently confident that SOE would spot the tell-tale omission of his security check, the procedure of inserting a deliberate mistake at a predetermined position in every message to indicate that the operator was working under duress. Unfortunately, SOE not only acknowledged the signal, but announced the imminent arrival of another agent, Arnold Baatsen. A pre-war professional photographer, Baatsen landed on 27/28 March, and he was followed the very next night by a drop of two teams. The first, which landed safely, consisted of Hans Jordaan, a student who had been studying in England, and Gosse Ras, a trader in textiles, but the second pair failed. Their radio was smashed on impact and Jan Molenaar was fatally injured, leaving his companion Leonard Andringa, a 28-year-old divinity student, to administer a capsule of cyanide. Thereafter Andringa had made his way to Amsterdam where, devoid of contacts, he lived rough for a while. A third team, of Hendrik Sebes who was a veteran of Dunkirk, and Barend Klooss, recently returned from southeast Asia, followed on 5/6 April and had established themselves in Hengelo without incident. The next arrival, on 8/9 April, was Jan De Haas, who was landed by a British motor torpedo boat with the objective of linking up with Lauwers and Taconis, not realising both were already in German custody. His search failed but on 27 April Lauwers was instructed by London to go to Haarlem to meet De Haas. Instead the Abwehr cornered both De Haas and Leo Andringa, the trainee priest who had become increasingly desperate following the death of his partner and had been forced to seek help from his friends. Andringa was then coerced into attending a rendezvous on 1 May in a cafe with Ras, Jordaan and Klooss. Thus the Abwehr was presented with an ideal opportunity to run and exploit a second captured radio. This in turn resulted in another parachute operation, on 29 May, which delivered two saboteurs, Antonius van Steen and Herman Parlevliet, both former Dutch gendarmes, straight into the hands of the enemy and provided the Germans with a third and fourth active wireless link with SOE. More were to follow. Jan van Rietschoten, a technical college student who had rowed to England the previous year, and his radio operator, Johannes Buizer, arrived near Assen on 23/24 June and were forced to send a 'safe arrival' signal. Then, a month later, Gerard van Hamert dropped straight into an enemy reception committee and was obliged to hand over his radio. When they searched him, the Germans found some orders addressed to Taconis, whom they had imprisoned in March, which amounted to confirmation that London had not an inkling of the extraordinary deception game now underway involving six separate wireless channels. A seventh SOE transmitter followed when a South African, George Dessing, was dropped accidentally into the middle of an SS training camp on 27/28 February 1942. He casually walked out, giving Nazi salutes to the guards who assumed he was authorised to be there. Later he had another lucky escape when the Germans tried to use Leo Andringa to entrap him in a cafe. Sensing that something was wrong, Dessing had casually walked out, straight past Andringa's German escort, thereby narrowly avoiding capture for the second time. Realising that his friend Andringa was under enemy control, Dessing had decided to get out of Holland as soon as possible, but he was unable to warn SOE of what had happened because he had no independent means of communication with London. The agent who had been killed on landing, Jan Molenaar, had been intended to become his radio operator, and without him Dessing was powerless.

He did eventually make his way to Switzerland, but he would not reach London until the autumn of 1943.

In the meantime, the duplicity continued. On 26 June 1942 Professor George Jambroes, a senior and influential figure in the Dutch government-in-exile, and his wireless operator Sjef Bukkens were dropped straight into a German reception committee, and Bukkens's radio was used to report on the supposed low morale and security of the Orde Dienst resistance movement. On 4/5 September 1942 four more agents followed Jambroes: a young student, Knees Drooglever and an engineer, Karel Beukema, were taken, and the former's transmitter became the eighth to join the game; Arie Mooy and Commander Jongelie were next but the latter, a tough naval officer who had worked undercover in the Dutch East Indies, refused to co-operate so his captors sent a message to London indicating that he had been fatally injured in the landing.

On 11 March 1942 a Royal Navy motor gunboat delivered two SIS agents, a Dutch sailor named Maessen, and Angus Letty, to the Dutch coast but as they rowed ashore their craft capsized. A German patrol caught both men, and Maessen was subsequently shot.

During this period SIS's principal asset in Holland was Aart Alblas, a 21-year-old merchant seaman who had been operating independently there since his arrival on 5/6 July 1941. After the arrest of Hans Zomer, the naval cadet who had been caught by direction-finders in Bilthoven, SIS had decided that Alblas's codes might have been compromised and therefore had used a former naval signalman, Wim Van Den Reyden, to deliver a new set. This courier parachuted into north Holland in September 1941 and duly handed over the crypto-material, but in February 1942 was arrested in the company of another SIS agent, Wim van Der Reyden, whose radio had needed repairing. Van der Reyden had been delivered to Scheveningen by boat on 21 November 1941 but his wireless had fallen into the water. The arrest of Van der Reyden and the courier was a chance encounter for the SD and although they tried to raise London on the radio SIS spotted the absence of the all-important security checks and declined to acknowledge the signal. However, under interrogation Van der Reyden confirmed the existence of the third agent, Alblas, and his signals were monitored. Eventually, in early July 1942, he too was trapped, but when the Germans tried to exploit his transmitter, SIS spotted the ruse and signed off instantly.

In the coming months more SIS agents were swept up. Ernst De Jonge, who had been landed by boat in February 1942, was caught with ten other members of the Ijmuiden resistance on 18 May 1942. Once again, SIS refused to respond to De Jonge's transmitter when it was operated under enemy control. Soon afterwards three more SIS agents, Jan Emmer, Evert Radema and Felix Ortt, were arrested.

SIS responded to these losses by dropping Willem Niemeyer in the spring of 1942, but by October the former journalist had run short of funds and SIS had asked SOE to deliver a roll of banknotes to his agent. The courier was a Dutch naval officer, Aat Van der Giessen, who was also handed a set of emergency identity papers for Niemayer that contained his photograph. Accordingly, when Van der Giessen was received by the SD it did not take them long to trace Niemeyer. He was promptly arrested, but SIS would not respond to his radio signals, realising from his faulty security check that he had come under enemy control.

Still oblivious to NORDPOL, SOE dropped a further nine agents in October, with another four in November. By December 1942 the Germans had captured forty-three British agents, and were controlling fourteen different radio channels.

In 1943 SOE continued to despatch agents and by April another thirteen had arrived, as well as a woman from MI9, Beatrix Terwindt, whose mission had been to build an escape line like those that had developed in Belgium and France. She too was accommodated at the seminary in Haaren which the Abwehr and SD had acquired to isolate their prisoners. In May 1943 SOE delivered Anton Mink, Laurens Punt and Oscar de Brey into captivity, and thus gave an eighteenth radio link to the Abwehr.

However, the policy of securing all the NORDPOL victims together was jeopardised when Pieter Dourlein and Johan Ubbink escaped from Haaren on 30 August 1943. Realising that the entire deception was threatened by this resourceful pair, the Germans reported to SOE that they had actually been captured by the Gestapo and allowed to escape, having been turned. Dourlein and Ubbink eventually reached Berne on 22 November 1943, and gave a harrowing account of their experiences. For the first time SOE received word that eight British parachutists, including Dourlein who had arrived in March, had all been captured. Thus ended NORDPOL, although neither SIS nor SOE fully understood the scale of the debacle until its architect, Giskes, was interviewed by MI5 at 020.

In March 1944, with the reorganisation of the Abwehr, Giskes was transferred to Brussels to command a training unit, FAK 307, but, according to his MI5 interrogation report, 'Huntemann applied for permission to find out what had happened to the 42 agents locked up at Haaren. He discovered from Department IV E at Zeist that contrary to Giskes' promise, Lauwers and Jordaan had been transferred to

Oranienberg. He managed to visit Jordaan, but Huntemann was unable to find Lauwers.'[32]

Although Lauwers, Dessing and the two escapees survived the war, all the rest perished at Mauthausen early in September 1944. Of the SOE agents, only Lauwers, Dessing and the two escapees, Dourlein and Ubbink, endured the experience. According to a captured Abwehr report on NORDPOL dated 6 December 1943, of the forty-six agents listed as prisoners, only seventeen were described as not having collaborated in any way.

When questioned, Giskes asserted that he had accumulated a considerable amount of information about SOE, its personnel, communications and training schools, but when pressed he could only name two members of SOE's N Section, being Majors Blunt and Bingham, and two others, Lieutenant Knight and a Miss Bond. In reality, Blunt was the cover-name adopted by the Section head, Charles Blizard, while Seymour Bingham and Claude Knight had not worked under alias. More significantly, neither Giskes nor Huntemann could show any wartime penetration of any British Intelligence agency in London, despite the opinion of some vocal Dutch critics of SOE.

* * *

By the time Giskes had been posted to a training role for German stay-behind agents, counter-intelligence in occupied Belgium had scored a considerable success in exploiting enemy radio nets detected by AbwehrFunk D/F apparatus since June 1941. By September, more than 250 encrypted messages had been intercepted and stored, unread, and on 12 December the Abwehr raided a house at 101 rue des Atrebates where a GRU radio operator, Anton Danilov, and two women, Rita Arnould and Sophia Posnanska, were taken into custody. Posnanska committed suicide in St-Gilles prison but, while Danilov remained uncooperative and silent (and would perish two years later), Arnould betrayed a forger's workshop concealed in her house and, from a collection of passport photos, identified Leopold Trepper and Viktor Guryevitch as the key figures at the centre of a hitherto unknown Soviet organisation. On the day after the raid, while the Abwehr were still in occupation of the house, another unsuspecting visitor, Mikhail Makarov, was arrested. He also turned out to be a GRU radio operator and, because of his lack of cooperation, was transferred to Ploetensee prison where he is believed to have been executed in 1944. Soon after his capture, Moscow began signalling him, and a Kommando substitute maintained the link until mid-July 1944.

Having initially expected to arrest a group of black marketeers, it became evident that the Abwehr had stumbled across a major Soviet network, previously hinted at by V-Men CHARLES and ABBE, and when Harry Piepe delivered in person to Berlin some of the documents retrieved which referred to the CASE BLUE plans for an offensive to be launched on the Russian Front, agreement was reached by the Abwehr and the SD to launch a joint investigation, designated Sonderkommando ROTE KAPELLE, headed by Heinz Paulsen (alias Heinz Pannwitz) who was assisted by his deputy, Heinrich Reiser, and directed from Berlin first by Karl Giering, who would succumb to throat cancer, and then by Horst Kopkow. The Sonderkommando, based in the rue de Coucelles before moving to a suite of four rooms on the third floor of the old Interior Ministry at 11 rue des Saussaies, Paris, would conduct immensely complex, coordinated operations across Belgium, Holland and France, and would be the subject of immense interest from intelligence agencies for decades afterwards. Although Kopkow, who was arrested in May 1945 at Lubeck and interrogated for three months at Bad Nenndorf, provided the first detailed account of the ROTE KAPELLE, vital evidence was recovered from Brussels in 1947, known as the Henri Robinson papers, which formed the basis of the first major analysis of the Soviet espionage network which was conducted by MI5's Michael Serpell and Bob Hemblys-Scales.[33] This massive undertaking resulted in a lengthy report that formed the basis of all subsequent studies into what was then interpreted as the foundation of post-war GRU espionage across the West, as manifested by such examples as Rachel Dubendorfer, Allan Foote, Ursula Kuczynski, Ernest Weiss and Klaus Fuchs.

The West's understanding of the ROTE KAPELLE in terms of the organisation and the Sonderkommando's investigation would change in 1959 following Paulsen's release from ten and a half years' imprisonment in the Soviet Union and his debriefing by the Munich CIA base upon his return to Germany in January 1956. His extraordinary account (see Appendix III) would be incorporated into a final report for the CIA compiled by Donald Pratt.[34] A pre-war police professional, Paulsen advocated psychological techniques to win over potential double agents, and his unconventional views had landed him in trouble in Prague after he had opposed the savage reprisals taken against the Czechs following the Heydrich assassination, which he had investigated with Kopkow.[35] His vocal dissent had earned him a posting to the Eastern Front where he had scored a great success by recruiting Russian PoWs into special units for deployment behind the lines as anti-Soviet partisans around Leningrad. Paulsen's reward was a transfer to Alst Paris to work against Russian espionage with a staff of ten men, two cryptographers and one young Englishwoman, Antonia Lyon-Smith who 'made herself useful by making tea and sewing. She was allowed a fair amount of freedom but never went out unacccompanied and was obliged to sleep on the premses.' Aged 36, unmarried, and distinctive with his gold tooth, Paulsen easily won over his critics and his unit soon became known by his *nom-de-guerre*, 'the Soderkommando Pannwitz'.[36]

The first major spy to be caught by the joint Kommando was Johann Wenzel who had been noted as Communist activist in Germany since at least 1933. Known as 'the Professor', he was a skilled technician and trained numerous other radio operators. However, having spent so long in the field, he had not heard that the FunkAbwehr, which was known to run static goniometric D/F sites, had been experimenting with D/F equipment on aircraft which could pinpoint the source of clandestine transmisssions with unprecedented accuracy. When he was arrested at his home in Laeken at the end of June 1942 his current traffic, which was also seized, revealed that he was acting as a radio operator for a Soviet spy codenmed KENT who was in touch with a Luftwaffe officer, Harro Schulze-Boysen, in Berlin. Prompted by Wenzel's past messages, the material was decrypted by the FunkAbwehr's Wilhelm Vauck exploiting a carelessly discarded codebook. A broken man, Wenzel agreed to cooperate with his captors and resumed contact with Moscow, under the Kommando's control.

Although Wenzel escaped after just five months in custody and went into hiding until the liberation in October 1944, the past wireless traffic compromised addresses in Berlin for Schulze-Boysen's co-conspirators, his wife Libertas, Adam and Greta Kuckhoff, and Arvid and Mildred von Harnack. All would be executed, and eventually some eighty others were incriminated. Under considerable pressure, Wenzel agreed to contact Moscow and thus on 6 August began a funkspiel with the GRU which remained unaware that Wenzel was in custody. Meanwhile, the SD's occupation of Wenzel's home led to the arrest of Konstantin Effremov, a GRU radio operator who in turn compromised Leopold Trepper, a key figure in the organisation who would be caught in Paris on 5 December 1942 and agreed to operate under the Sonderkommando's control from a house in the rue de l'Aurore in central Brussels.

The extent to which this collaboration was either tolerated by Moscow, to keep Trepper alive, or was considered genuine, remains a matter of speculation, but for a period of more than two years the play-back appeared to be successful. Apart from KENT, the Kommando's principal asset was FRITZ who, supervised by Hans Kurfess and a former journalist, Dr Waldemar Lenz, lived under open arrest with his wife and child at Karl Boemelburg's sumptuous mansion in the Bois de Boulogne. According to Paulsen, when interrogated by the French in Austria in 1945, KENT had worked in the black market in Brussels with his GRU colleague Trepper who had fled to Marseilles in 1942. There he had been caught by Major von Wedel of the Alst Paris FunkAbwehr. Paulsen's French interrogators

> were unable to say whether it was thought that the Russians had discovered that [KENT] was being played back: it is clear that up to August 1943 when he was instructed to contact [Waldemar] Ozols, they accepted him as genuine. The question was discussed by Paulsen in summer 1944 and his opinion was that it was then a secondary matter, since the important thing was to keep a contact open for possible negotiations. When the withdrawal from France began to look up as a certainty, [KENT] was instructed by Moscow to remain behind in Paris and continue working. This he did not do![37]

On 17 August the Kommando, then based in the Rothschild villa in the rue Royale under the command of Adolf Goepfert, evacuated Paris and moved via Colmar to Bregenz on Lake Constance, where the unit was disbanded on 20 September, the staff being ordered to report to Berlin.

Apart from ISOS, which allowed the Radio Intelligence Section (formerly the Radio Security Service) to monitor Paulsen's movements, Allied knowledge of the Kommando was based on the interrogation of Henrik Mierseman, a radio technician captured in Brussels in September 1944, and Friedrich von Sartorius, an interpreter who deserted in the Tyrol in May 1945 and was arrested in Milan.[38] According to Rudolf Rathke, the Kommando in France concentrated on penetrating the Communist Party, and had little success in extending the funkspiel against the British, apart from a single example, 'operated by a Gestapo man, Eugen Grosz in Lille, which took place in May/June 1944 and yielded a parachuted delivery of ammo, radio equipment and food from Britain'.[39]

Although the Kommando had always been intended to target the Soviets, leads were followed up in Austria, Spain, Italy and especially in Switzerland where another of Trepper's networks was known to be active. In July 1943 MI5's Dick White acknowledged to Felix Cowgill that 'we know so very little about the Abwehr organisation in Switzerland', arguing that hitherto this lacuna had not mattered because of the country's geographic isolation, but in recent times the number of escape routes involving Swiss territory had increased, and MI5 was concerned about the volume of cover-addresses being used by the Abwehr. There was also a growing worry about penetration and manipulation of the International Red Cross. The situation was so bad that MI5's Kemball Johnston complained in May 1943 that SIS's 'only sources in Switzerland seem to be a few underpaid policemen who could give little or no help' to his enquiries. His section, B3(a), had become a pressing customer because of the recruitment of a Swiss embassy diplomat, Eric Kessler, codenamed ORANGE, whose invaluable information was generating dozens of useful counter-intelligence leads. However, with only a very limited, isolated staff at the SIS stations in Berne, Zurich and Geneva, all under ubiquitous surveillance, the opportunity for local enquiries was miniscule. Worse, because of the Swiss government ban on the use of transmitters by diplomats, the German legation depended on a landline teleprinter for its external communications, in preference to radio, so Section V's techniques were largely redundant.

SIS had assessed the head of the Abwehr as a well-connected aristocrat, Baron Max von Engelbrechten, who operated under diplomatic cover as press attaché at the consulate-general in Geneva, but by the end of the war a very different picture emerged as no less than five Abwehr officers underwent interrogation and one, Heinrich Eder, had served as a wireless operator throughout the war, from August 1939. In reality Alexander Waag had established a KriegsOrganisation Schweiz in the Berne legation as early as 1937, and this would become subordinate to Ast Dijon to create two Nests, at Geneva, running operations into France, and at Zurich. Later the KO would open more, in Lugano, targeting Italy, Basel and St Gallen, and have staff attached to the consulate in Lausanne. The KO itself, which would be headed from 1940 by Erik Knabbe, would employ some twenty staff, and was connected to Berlin by teleprinter to the Foreign Ministry, although in September 1944 Allied bombing forced communications back onto radio, on a circuit based at Loerrach in Baden, just over the border at Basle. According to Eder, the traffic amounted to between 80 and 100 messages a month, in either direction. The KO Schweitz commander, Karl Meissner, who had been appointed in March 1942, was questioned at Camp 020,[40] and Hans von Bohlen (I/H, Zurich), Major von Muehlen (I/H, Lugano), Alfred Geiler (KO), went to CSDIC at Bad Nenndorf.

Despite the geographic advantages for Germany, with a long land and lake frontier, a predominantly German-speaking population – 130,000 resident Germans nationals; 700 Swiss volunteers who had joined the Waffen SS in Stuttgart (later moving to a base in Bregenz); 350,000 Germans who had naturalised Swiss – an active local Nazi Party, titled the Nationale Front; and a ban on the Communist Party, which had no Soviet legation support it, Switzerland presented a challenge for the Abwehr which was responsible for collecting intelligence against their hosts in anticipation of a coordinated Axis invasion and occupation. This contingency soured relations with some Swiss intelligence personnel, who learned of the scheme from Count Ciano, and the Abwehr could not always rely on automatic, unquestioning cooperation from the federal authorities in Berne. Not surprisingly, the Bundespolizei was especially keen to find out who among their own citizens were slated to participate in a post-invasion puppet government.

In the spring of 1940 Abt. II's Major Kern and his assistant Dr Schaffert was instructed to launch a sabotage attack on Switzerland, apparently in retaliation for the loss of Luftwaffe bombers shot down by Swiss anti-aircraft batteries. A group of saboteurs assembled in Munich and crossed the frontier but they were apprehended before they could lay their charges on their targets, aeroplanes parked on airfields. All were arrested, including three Brandenburg Regiment soldiers, Bruenning, Freiberg and Helmuth von Thadden, who were sentenced to long terms of imprisonment. Their leader, Peter Schagen, evaded capture because of a plausible cover-story involving his claim to be a Portuguese refugee fleeing oppression in the Reich. According to Schagen, the prisoners were given life imprisonment, a sentence that was later commuted to detention for the remainder of the war, and Kern was dismissed from the Abwehr and returned to the Wehrmacht.[41]

Also targeting Switzerland were Ast Vienna and Ast Stuttgart, which the Bundespolizei were certainly aware of, as in mid-1942 a round-up was conducted in which around a hundred Abwehr agents were arrested. Three of the detainees (Hermann Grimm, Walter Laubscher and Ferdinand Infanger) were sentenced in October 1943 to be shot, and seven received long terms of imprisonment with hard labour, although six were exchanged for Swiss intelligence personnel detained in Germany.

In another incident the consul in Davos was expelled when it was discovered that a newly-opened tuberculosis sanatorium accommodated a transmitter for a local network.

According to Eder, the KO's I/H radio operator who was captured by the Americans as he crossed into Chiasso in June 1945, the KO's priorities were:

a) <u>Political</u>
Information derived from agents relating to the following matters:
i) Conversations between diplomats.
ii) Reports from London and Washington.
iii) Forecasts of international conferences, time and place. These were generally inaccurate, e.g. the Yalta meeting was professed to have been held at Cairo.
iv) Appreciations among Swiss diplomatic circles concerning relations between Russia and the Western Powers.
v) Forecasts of impending government changes in other countries (e.g. Italy).

b) <u>Military</u>
i) Effect of V1 and V2.
ii) Location and direction of pipelines.
iii) Troop and shipping concentrations.
iv) Aerodromes.
v) Division and troop movements forecasts, invasion forecasts were generally considered confusing and contradictory. Predictions including the Balkans, Denmark, Northern and Southern France. Source disagrees with the statement [....] that BOSSHART accurately forecast the date of Allied landings in Normandy, saying that neither locality nor date tallied exactly.

a) <u>Economic and financial</u>
Reports of war production.

b) <u>Internal matters and miscellaneous</u>
i) Queries to Zentral Kerlteiverwaltung about prospective agents.
ii) Indents for money, stationery and other requirements; transfer of foreign exchange.
iii) Monthly strength returns.
iv) Cover addresses for agents.
v) Enquiries about bomb damage and missing relatives in Germany.
vi) Notice of movements of personnel, requests for accommodation, etc.
vi) Reports of sentences passed by Swiss courts in espionage cases.

Source states that much was sent by wireless or teleprinter which could equally have waited for the mail service.

c) <u>Signal Control</u>
The above included frequent controls for checking the encipherment of signals. The standard of cipher work at Belzig was poor.

d) <u>Sources of Reports</u>

Among the sources of political and military reports the following figured prominently: BOSSHART, GEORGES, REISSER, ATAMANN. Of these, BOSSHART was by far the most important, particularly on the political side, to which he contributed at least 40% of all the information. Concerning this agent there was a considerable difference of opinion between the KO officials and Berlin, the latter having a much lower estimate of his usefulness. On the occasion Berlin sent a signal referring to a recent report of BOSSHART's and quoting an article in the *Neue Zürcher Zeitung*; it appeared that the former was a largely paraphrased rehash of the latter. After the receipt of a signal from Berlin during mid-1944 saying that [Walter] BOSSHART's military information was practically worthless, the quotations of his reports dwindles.

Generally source states that he cannot recall an outstanding political or military event taking place, the forecast of which he had previously enciphered for transmission to Berlin on the strenghth of an agent's report.[42]

Although of relatively junior rank, Eder proved to be an important source relating to the KO because of his role as a signaller, and his performance in Berne, where he had been based continuously, apart from occasional leave to his time in Munich. Details that he did not know, such as the identities of the KO's individual agents, were known to Meissner, who was more expansive and described twenty-two assets managed by his staff:

1 BENAVIDES	South American diplomat and contact of Muehlen @ BILIER
2 Boese, Max	Agent of I/H Berlin working in Switzerland
3 BOSSHARDT [*sic*] @ JACOB	Reserve office of the Swiss Intelligence Service
4 DRAGA	Agent sent to Switzerland by KO Italy
5 EDISON	Student and agent of Gerl @ BORIS
6 Franck, Karl Heinrich	Swiss businessman and a friend of Meissner
7 GOLIKORN 2	Swiss businessman and agent of Gerl @ BORIS
8 Haenseier @ RHENATUS	German working for League of Nations
9 KOPETSKI	Czech representative in Switzerland

10 LANGLOH	German agent previously working for Ast Hamburg
11 MESSERSCHILDT	German agent of Ast Stuttgart
12 von Moos	Agent of KO Portugal
13 von Moos or Moosdorf @ COLUMBUS	Agent of Muehlen @ ALBERT
14 Otttino, Prof Ricardo	Swiss scientist and agent of Muehlen @ ALBERT
15 REISSER	Ex-German diplomat with good political contacts
16 RUSCHEWEY or RUSCHEWEYI	German agent now living in Lucerne with Persian diplomat
17 Scharuk @ ATAMAN	Persian diplomat
18 Schmanska @ HANS	Polish woman contact of Gisevius for diplomatic reasons
19 Scheinberger @ AIGIR	Member of Swiss police and agent of [....]
20 'STEWARD' @ GOLDKORN	Seaman and agent of Meissner and ALBERT
21 Walther, Lt.	Swiss who offered fortification plans to AIGIR
22 Winkler @ LEOGON or COSMUS	Agent of Dernbach, III/F Lyons[43]

Meissner's list of KO assets is particularly interesting because it includes Canaris's Polish mistress, Halina Szymanska, as a contact of Hans Bernd Gisevius, an Abwehr officer posted to Zurich under consular cover in 1940. His efforts to develop a relationship with SIS in Berne would be rebuffed, later to be accepted by OSS, but Szymanska served to open a one-way channel between Canaris and SIS which he used to alert the Allies in May 1941 to Hitler's plans for BARBAROSSA.

According to Meissner, the KO's star agent was Walter Bosshard [*sic*], codenamed JAKOB, who had been run originally by Max von Engelbrechten until he was withdrawn at Swiss request in the early spring 1944. His replacement handler was III/F's Willy Piert who had been unimpressed with JAKOB's reporting which allegedly had been taken straight from Roger Masson's desk and included material such as V-weapon bomb damage supplied by PAUL in the Swiss embassy in London. Puzzled by Swiss interest in conditions in London, Bosshard had explained that he was merely checking on extravagant German claims of huge, widespread destruction.[44]

Despite some doubts about the quality of Bosshard's military reporting, the accuracy of which had been challenged by Berlin, he remained as a valued source for the status of his contacts, among then Allen Dulles, President Roosevelt's representative in Berne, and Freddie West, the British air attaché. Piert, who adopted the alias 'Hans von Pescatore', also disclosed that one of his subordinates, Loeff, had recruited an informant in the office of the US military attaché, General Rhett Legge. The source, Jacob Fuerst, had been embittered by a demotion following his exposure as a former member of the Nationale Front, and until March 1942 had removed sensitive documents and carbon copies of correspondence from the burn-bag. Among these secret papers intended for destruction had been a list of Legge's collection priorities, and another detailing his sources of information, and mentioning a German ex-officer named DONAU. Fuerst was eventually arrested, together with two of his associates, a barber named Knuettel and another legation employee, Napravnik, and were sentenced to long terms of imprisonment.

Liaison with the KO's Axis partners included regular contact with the Japanese, and the representative of the Italian Organisation for Vigilence and Repression of Anti-Fascism (OVRA) who was based in Geneva, and General Bianchi in Berne, where, until the armistice in September 1943, Major Dermidoff supervised a counter-espionage section later taken over by Colonel Denari. Thereafter SIM switched sides and the KO came to rely on Ast Milan for information.

Another of Meissner's contacts in Berne was the Japanese military attaché, General Kiyotomi Okamota, who relied on his well-informed consul-general in Zurich, Koda. Apparently Okamota, whom Meissner met twice a month, was on good terms with the head of Swiss military intelligence, Brigadier Roger Masson. Meissner disclosed that Okamota was probably the chief of Japanese Intelligence for the whole of Europe, and his principal tasks in Switzerland were 'to observe Germany and her European Allies' and 'watch the neutral countries'.

Like the KOs in Madrid and Lisbon, which did not exercise exclusive proprietorial rights over their respective territories, several other Abstellen, principally Dijon, Lyons, Stuttgart and Munich, operated across Switzerland independently of Berne. When the Sonderkommando ROTE KAPELLE came to pursue the Soviet organisation in Switzerland it did so with the benefit of information supplied by Trepper, enhanced with the more than 5,000 intercepts accumulated by the FunkAbwehr cryptographer Wilhelm Flicke, which demonstrated the existence of three separate clandestine transmitters based on Swiss territory, hence the term ROTE DREI.

Meanwhile, the SD, IV A 2, designated the investigation EDELWEISS, to reflect the Swiss element, and eventually MI5 would codename the organisation EQUAL. The network was headed by a Hungarian cartographer, Alexander Rado, who was compromised by having attended a rendezvous with Viktor Sukolov in 1939. In November 1942 Rado received a warning from Moscow that Sukolov, who knew him only as MANOLO, had been arrested. The second radio was in the hands of Alexander Foote, a British volunteer who had been recruited by the GRU upon his return to England from fighting with the International Brigade in the Spanish Civil War. Based in Lausanne, Foote had been lured to a rendezvous with a courier in April, and he learned that his contact had been substituted for an Abwehr agent. As Foote's MI5 file noted in narrative written by Michael Serpell in 1947, the Germans had showed signs of penetration at least seven months before he was arrested:

> In April 1943 Foote was instructed by Moscow to pay 15,000 Swiss francs at a specified rendezvous to a courier from France. The courier was found to have been replaced by a Gestapo agent and Foote was ordered to break contact with Rado and to take extra precautions, but to maintain w/t contact with Moscow. Contact with Rado was resumed in September 1943.[45]

Foote was asked to give his version of this encounter, which described uncharacteristically poor tradecraft which he later interpreted as the first evidence that the Abwehr was on his trail. Counter-intelligence analysts would also point out that Moscow's behaviour, in persuading Foote to continue his work even though he had fallen under suspicion and clearly was in danger from the Germans, suggested that 'the Direcktor' placed a high value on the material he was passing. Equally, this also meant that Berlin was motivated by an urgent need to plug a damaging leakage. As MI5's internal account remarked, 'as we know from German evidence, Moscow pressed the network to continue at all costs'.

> In the first part of 1943 the Centre gave me instructions to me to meet a courier. It was not stated where this courier was coming from, only later did I learn that it was from France. I was given two meeting places, one just inside the entrance of the funicular station at Ouchy, and the other inside the main entrance of the botanical gardens at Geneva. All meetings to take place at the same fixed hour of the day which I believe was 12 noon. I was to be wearing for all the meetings a dark blue felt

hat and a rolled umbrella on the crook of the right arm in the hand of which should be a pair of leather gloves. In my left hand I should have a copy of the English publication *Picture Post*. I was also advised what the courier would be wearing but cannot now recall the details.

Passwords and jargon were given, but I cannot recall these, however they were identical with those given me for an emergency meeting between CISSY and myself in the event of anything happening to ALBERT, and arranged by the former on the instructions of the Centre in 1941. The meeting place being also in this case the station of the funicular at Ouchy.

Nobody presented themselves at the Ouchy meeting place on the two occasions that I waited there, nor on the first date at the Geneva.

However at the last date a correctly attired individual gave the correct passwords etc.

I had been originally instructed to hand 15,000 dollars in Swiss francs to this person but as I had difficulty at this time risking transfers and had only 10,000 in course of transfer which I due to receive the day after the last arranged meeting with the […] I was forced to arrange a further meeting two days ahead, this inside the entrance of the railway station in Berne.

The courier readily acquiesced to this, stating in any case he would have required a further meeting with me in order to hand a parcel to me which at that moment he did not have in his possession. This surprised me because the Director had instructed me to hold no conversation with him and to limit my actions to the handing over the money. On travelling to Berne on the day agreed upon I was surprised to see the courier also travelling in the same train (from Geneva to Zurich) as he had desired the meeting between us to take place in Berne where he said he was staying. On handing the cash to him he stated that it was imperative I should see him again the next day as he would have very important, news to give me. He wanted to have the meeting near Geneva stating that he did not like to meet me in a crowded place, I declined this but made arrangements for a further meeting for one week ahead in the same place (entrance to the station at Berne). He also made arrangements (passwords, jargon, etc) in order that a third person could contact me in case he himself should be impeded. I was also alarmed by the fact that he had handed me a book enclosed in a bright orange envelope which, being too large to be concealed on my person would enable me to be easily followed.

I took evasive action before returning to my flat and reported suspicions to the Centre.

On examination the book which the courier had handed me was found to contain three cyphered messages between two pages which had been stuck together.[46]

This encounter was the first evidence noticed by Foote that he had come under hostile surveillance and was perhaps the target of a counter-espionage operation, likely conducted by the Germans, or the Swiss, or both. Later analysis showed that it took place a few weeks after the arrest by the Sonderkommando of Robinson's Swiss courier, Maurice Aenis-Haenslin, whose large apartment in Paris at 31 rue de l'Amsterdam was a centre of ROTE KAPELLE operations.

The Kommando's raid on the rue de l'Amsterdam in April 1943 followed a similar operation conducted on 21 December at a hotel close to 4 rue Gilbert, the home of the Soviet network's chief organiser, Henri Robinson. Under the floorboards of his hotel room the German searchers found a briefcase full of incriminating documentation, including four apparently authentic Swiss passports for Robinson under various aliases, and a large collection of his past messages to Moscow and to branches of his network in Switzerland, England and Bulgaria. Although Robinson, a French Jew probably of German extraction, had been born in France and had served in the French army in the First World War until he was a PoW and contracted tuberculosis, he had plausibly adopted Swiss nationality under numerous identities. His Sureté dossier suggested that he had been an active Communist Party organiser since 1922, and the mother of his 18-year-old son Victor was Klara Schabbel, also a Comintern agent, with a home address in the Berlin's Eichenstrasse.

According to the Kommando's records, Robinson had been betrayed by Trepper, who had been arrested on 5 December 1942 and pressured into setting up a rendezvous with his superior, where he was entrapped. A Kommando progress report to Berlin dated 24 March 1943 proved Trepper's role in their identification as Robinson, codenamed HARRY, as their next (albeit initially uncooperative) target:

> It is suspected – and partly confirmed by events so far – that there are at least three groups in Switzerland who had regular liaison as instructed with HARRY. The next step is to find out about this link. But there must also be liaison through Bulgaria, as in the most recent telegrams from Moscow they asked whether we were in a position to fetch money from Bulgaria and to make contacts there. Trepper cannot give details about this, but he thinks that HARRY certainly can, although the latter has up till now kept complete silence.[47]

Based on Trepper's information, the Kommando concluded that 'the organisation [Trepper's] was found to be built up centrally and composed of collateral, but entirely separate groups, in which only the head of the group ever had direct contact with Trepper. Liaison was made by similar rendezvous, and Trepper on his side was able to contact the group leaders through agreed cover-addresses; although they had no similar approach for him. Throughout the organisation particularly detailed and clever security measures were practiced.'

Trepper's willingness to ensnare Robinson was seen as proof of his genuineness. Furthermore, 'Trepper promises to explain to Hauptman Piepe III/F adviser, the set-up of his entire organisation in the West' including alleged relationships with the Polish and Vichy intelligence services. Thus, helped by Trepper, the Kommando's Harry Piepe learned of seven different groups, the first of which had been run by Robinson, which concentrated on military and political issues in France. Their output was transmitted to Moscow on three different wireless links, manned by Robinson, Henri Sokol and a Communist Party link at Le Peq.

Aenis-Haenslin had also acted as the principal link between Robinson and his Swiss branch, headed by Rachel Duebenorfer. Born in St Denis, Aenis-Haenslin was a pre-war member of the Central Committee of the Swiss Communist Party, and for years had distributed Moscow's funds to other European Parties. In 1937 he was monitored in Paris by the Sureté as he recruited volunteers to fight with the International Brigade in Spain. His knowledge was encyclopaedic, and his arrest in April 1943 effectively compromised the entire organisation, even if the GRU was reluctant to acknowledge the gravity of the situation. Also arrested was his mistress, Edwige Couchon, who would die in Ravensbruck concentration camp. Having been condemned to death in November 1943, Aenes-Haenslin would be released from Fresnes in a prisoner exchange arranged by the Swiss authorities. Certainly the Abwehr was well aware of his activities as records recovered from Ast Dijon after the liberation included a reference to him in a list of Soviet spies operating in Switzerland, dated February 1944:

> FOOTE, A.A. Cover name John. Lausanne, Longeraie, 2, Apt. 45
> Has a Comintern transmitter in his flat.[48]

Indeed, Foote, codenamed JIM, had appeared in sixteen messages exchanged with Moscow among the radio traffic examined by Wilhelm Flicke and dated from 31 October 1943 to 11 April 1944.

The third wireless was operated by Edmond and Olga Hamel in Geneva, and their apartment was raided on 14 October 1943 when their equipment was seized, together with 129 past messages. Simultaneously, the police arrested another suspect, Margaret Bolli at the home of her lover, an Abwehr III/F agent Hans Friedrich Peters, who was released. A hairdresser by trade, Peters supposedly was codenamed ROMEO and had deliberately cultivated Bolli, eventually learning that her codebook was *It Began in September* by the Austrian socialist and novelist Grete von Urbanitsky.

Another version, contained in Bolli's MI5 file, is that Peters was jealous of Bolli's relationship with Rado, who had recruited her as his courier in October 1941 when the 21-year-old had been employed in a Basle restaurant as a waitress, and had also become his mistress. Peters had reported his suspicions to his KO III/F handler, Hermann Haenseler, who in turn had alerted the Swiss police. When the raid took place, Bolli was actually in bed with Peters.

This version of events, that the Abwehr collaborated with the Bundespolizei to break up the ROTE DREI, would be disputed by the KO's III/F Leiter, Willy Piert, who was detained by the Americans on the Italian frontier as he was expelled from Switzerland in May 1945, and escorted to CSDIC in Milan.[49] In his account Piert claimed that one of his officers, named Hanseler, had been working to infiltrate agents into the Communist circles in Switzerland, but had not reached any accommodation with the Swiss. On the contrary, he asserted that the police suspected Hamel and Bolli had been acting for the Germans, even though, paradoxically, he had alerted the Swiss to the Soviet transmissions in the first place. This contradiction remains unexplained. Furthermore, Piert had offered the Swiss assistance, after the arrests, in decrypting the captured messages, but the suggestion had been rejected. However, the Abwehr's expert on Soviet espionage, Horst Kopkow, recalled that a Bundespolizei officer named Maurer had visited Berlin in 1944 to provide a briefing on the Swiss investigation. Naturally, Kopkow had been anxious to discover the ROTE DREI's sources in Germany and noted that Maurer had been 'asked to supply information regarding the sources of information in Germany; this however, he declined to give'. The intense interest shown in the ROTE DREI by the Germans would later be confirmed to Foote in Moscow when his GRU debriefer casually mentioned that documents recovered in Berlin when the city was captured by the Red Army had demonstrated the Gestapo's involvement.

On 29 November, soon after the raids in Geneva, Foote was arrested at his home in Lausanne by Inspector Pasche, just as he was transmitting a message to Moscow. Thereafter he was interrogated by a Swiss intelligence officer named Blazer who would himself come under suspicion of having an incriminating connection with the ROTE DREI. Blazer subsequently left the police and was employed by

Swiss Railways as its representative in Paris. The extent to which the Bundespolizei was assisted and encouraged by the Sonderkommando remains unknown, but for a while, probably not more than three months, there was an attempt to play-back all the three channels that had fallen into Swiss hands.

Ultimately, two issues would remain unresolved. Who were the network's German sources, and to what extent had the Swiss acted as Abwehr surrogates when they intervened and arrested Hamel, Bolli and Foote? Foote would later assert that information attributed to WERTHER originated from a Wehrmacht source, and that OLGA was a Luftwaffe officer attached to the OKW. However, the Bundespolizei suggested to MI5 in November 1947 that 'much of Roessler's intelligence for the Rote Drei derived from interrogations by the Swiss of German army deserters'. When challenged, Inspector Charles Knecht had asserted that Rachel Duenbendorfer had controlled the 'source in the German General Staff'.

As regards German participation, Pasche had revealed 'that the day following the arrest of Bolli and Hamel he received a telephone call from Hermann Haensel (Abt. IIIF KO Schweiz) with whom the Swiss police were at that time in contact, to the effect that he had discovered Bolli and Hamel to be Soviet agents from a document he had seen in the office of the German Consul in Constance'.

The KO developed a healthy respect for Masson's bureau which consistently rebuffed pleas for mutual exchanges of information, if not a full liaison relationship. Occasionally the tension between the two sides would escalate, as happened in 1943 when two accredited consular officials, Brunner and Moergeli, were arrested in Stuttgart. The Swiss had retaliated by detaining Sonderführer Geiger, a KO official in Zurich, and the resulting stand-off was settled by an exchange of prisoners. In 1944 the KO suffered another setback when two well-established III/F officers, Heberlein and Engelbrechten, were expelled on the accusation of seeking penetrate the Swiss army.

To avoid alienating the Swiss, Berlin banned collection by the KO against the Swiss in 1942, but the new arrangement was asymmetric as it was common knowledge that all Swiss consuls, worldwide and inside the Reich, collected information for the Intelligence Service, and that Swiss travellers were encouraged to maintain contact with their local consulates. Additionally, the Swiss were known to recruit agents among the deserters who had taken refuge in Switzerland and had agreed to complete short-term reconnaissance missions back across the frontier, Accordingly, Masson's agency was considered exceptionally well-informed and therefore a formidable threat to German interests, even after the threat of invasion had lifted because of the progress of the war.

Under interrogation at Camp 020 Meissner, a former torpedo officer on the *U-53* in the First World War who had also served on the battleship *Nassau*, had joined the Abwehr in 1935 and had been promoted to Berne from Alst Paris in March 1942. Previously he had served in Oslo before heading Ast Angers from March 1941 and then being posted to head Abt. III in Paris. He had opposed Berlin's policy of running operations in neutral Switzerland against the Swiss instead of concentrating on the enemy, and his view would prevail, but not before he learned that Ast Stuttgart had infiltrated three wireless agents into Switzerland:

> Towards the end of 1942 or the beginning of 1943, however, it was discovered that Ast Stuttgart was operating 3 transmitters in Switzerland itself. The matter was reported to Berlin, the stations were closed down, and the officers concerned were punished. Meissner states that he himself gave strict instructions that no agents were to be employed for the purpose of obtaining information about Switzerland.[50]

Initially, when questioned Meissner was resentful and reluctant to give anything away, especially the identity of agents, but he soon came to realise that almost all his colleagues had decided to talk to their captors. The proof of his new attitude was his perspective of various incidents in which he had been involved. For example, soon after the abduction by the SD of the two hapless SIS officers, Richard Stevens and Sigismund Payne Best, at Venlo in November 1939, he had, at Canaris's request, visited the prisoners at Oranienburg concentration camp.

> Admiral Canaris, General Pieckenbrock and other high ranking German officers were very angry of hearing of the trick which had been played. It appears that the SD, in order to make contact with the two officers, had told them that they represented officers desirous of ousting Hitler and making peace with Britain.[51]

Meissner recalled that both captives had been treated well, and he had found 'Stevens sympathetic. And they discussed India, horses and hunting. Meissner has a vague recollection that one of them suggested that he be allowed to give English classes to while away the time.' After their interrogation Best and Stevens, codenamed WOLF and FUCHS respectively, were transferred to Dachau.

Meissner also described an episode after he had been appointed Leiter Abt. III and deputy Leiter Ast Oslo in April 1940, and then promoted leiter after the removal of his predecessor, Colonel Bruck. In July, while away in Berlin, one of his subordinates, I/H's Hauptman Bernecke and I/M's Pusback engineered a scheme to exploit an agreement that had been made to allow an American vessel to visit Bergen and collect twenty-six bags of US State Department mail collected from various missions across Europe, On his own initiative Bernecke staged a robbery by 'anti-American Norwegians' who stopped the diplomatic convoy on the Oslo to Bergen road and stole the entire consignment which was delivered to the Abstelle. Horrified by this breach of protocol, Meissner claimed that upon his return he ordered the still-intact mailbags to be delivered to the American chargé d'affaires, Raymond E. Cox, at the legation immediately, thereby averting a major diplomatic incident. Soon afterwards Meissner had been replaced by Major Nowak and posted to France.

Meissner also described how, while heading Ast Angers, he had been initiated into double cross by a young French sailor who had surrendered himself, his transmitter, codes and transmitting schedule to the Abwehr in Nantes: He also gave

a complete list of names and addresses of all the members of the group for which he was working. In return for all this information all he was asked was to be allowed to return to his home in Alsace-Lorraine where his fiancée was waiting for him. The matter was reported to Ast Angers and III/F took it in hand. Meissner cannot give the name of the 'dirty Alsace-Lorraine traitor' but it transpired that his information was correct and the leader of the underground movement Lieutenant-Commander Count d'Orpes was arrested together with all the members of his organisation. Meissner states that Admiral Canaris tried to intervene on Count d'Orpes' behalf but in spite of this the latter was shot.

The French sailor was used for about 7 or 8 weeks as a double agent and contact was kept with London. Meissner thinks that this was the first case of its kind in France. Material for the telegrams sent was obtained from Berlin and included reports about the invasion of England; Production in France, and location of troops. Meissner quotes as on example: 'ships and materials concentrating not only in North Sea ports but also in the Baltic up to Lubeck.' At the end of about two months London ceased transmission and the Frenchman was allowed to return to his home town of Schlettstadt in Alsace-Lorraine.[52]

It would later be claimed by SIS that although the Nantes escape network run by MI9, designated NEMROD, had been betrayed by an agent, Alfred Gaessler, London had quickly detected the attempted play-back which had been supervised by III/F's Friedrich Denbach. But how quickly? According to Stella Lonsdale, who travelled to England soon after the debacle, Gaessler had named nine senior members of his group, all of whom had been arrested. Top of the list was Henri d'Estienne d'Orves, a former naval officer and Charles de Gaulle's first director of his Free French Deuxieme Bureau in London, who was executed, and is now celebrated as a national hero and one of the first martyrs of the Resistance. His mission was to coordinate all the earlier missions sent into the Occupied Zone, to collect military information about German strengths in the region, and provide a much-needed communications link. Having remained silent, he was sentenced to death in May 1941 and shot at the end of August, together with his companions, 39-year-old Lieutenant Maurice Barlier from the Vosges, and a Dutchman, Jan Doornik, at the Fort de Mont Valerien. Lonsdale claimed that she alerted MI9 in Marseilles to the double-cross in April 1941, which suggests it was operational for about three months.

Aged 20, Gaessler had accompanied d'Orves on a fishing boat, the *Marie-Louise*, from Newlyn in Cornwall to Plogoff in Brittany in December 1940, and, adopting the alias Georges Marty, transmitted from their base in Chanenay-sur-Loire. As a petty officer telegraphist who had served on the submarine *Le Trimophant*, he had been in France for less than a month when he approached the Abwehr and thus facilitated the very first major funkspiel of the war.

After the arrests of d'Orves and Barlier, Doornik had attempted to return to England on the *Marie-Louise*, renamed the *Louis Jules*, but his rendezvous in Quimper was also betrayed by Gaessler so he was arrested. Codenamed MILO, Dournik was persuaded to cooperate with his captors who learned his family was in Paris. As a consequence, several SIS ferries to Cornwall, among them *Aouan d'Amor* and *La Brise* were compromised, and a second radio operator, J-J Le Prince, sailed into a trap and was arrested on 14 February while still engaged in his clandestine infiltration off the Pointe-du-Raz, As MI5 later reported, 'Gessler was responsible for the arrest of some 16 to 18 British agents'.

MI5's understanding of the scale of the Abwehr's coup was dependent on a version of events supplied by Stella Lonsdale, a self-confessed spy and putative double agent whose loyalties were deeply suspect. Nevertheless, as well as supplying information about Gaessler, supposedly supplied by her German handler who she would only identify as 'Rene', she named four other deception channels: a Dutchman named van der Waller who had been dropped by parachute and his British companion THIOU, who had refused to cooperate with his captors, Maurice Duclos, a BCRA officer who had broken both legs on landing near Le Bugue in February 1941 and his partner Muellemann. Duclose was exfiltrated by air to England in March 1942 and survived to undertake further missions.

In April 1941 Meissner had been transferred at his request to Alst Paris to replace Kapitän Liebenschutz who had been posted to the Eastern Front. Based at the Hotel Lutetia, the Alst had a staff of nearly 30 officers with a larger number of support ancillaries. His intelligence priorities were:

a) Traffic between occupied and unoccupied France.
b) Evacuation of certain areas of the Channel coast.
c) Cooperation between Abt. III/C and Militarerabfahnden I/c (Colonel Crone).
d) Closer cooperation between the Leitstelle and the Asts.[53]

Meissner's appointment to Berne in March 1942 upon Colonel Knabbe's retirement marked a high point in the KO's ability to operate effectively. Shortly before, and just after, the 20 July putsch in 1944 two important Abwehr officers, Eduard Waetjen and Prince Karl Adolph Auersperg, contacted Meissner and submitted their resignation, leaving him to ponder if they were already in contact with the Allies and, if so, for how long they had been haemorrhaging the Abwehr's secrets. A lawyer from a prominent Berlin family with an American mother, Waetjen had been posted to the Zurich consulate, Sonderführer and in January 1944 had been in touch with OSS's Allen Dulles in Berne. Originally recommended and introduced by Hans Bernd Gisevius to act as an intermediary between himself and Dulles' secretary, Mary Bancroft, Waetjen was codenamed GORTER by OSS but submitted his resignation to Meissner only four months later. His temporary replacement, to act as courier, was Theodor Struenck, a pre-war director of a Frankfurt insurance company who had been recruited into the Abwehr to a junior post on Hans Oster's staff.

The second departure was I/L's Lieutenant-Colonel Prince Karl Auersperg, whose disaffection had dated back some months to when the Nazi minister Robert Ley had made disparaging public remarks about the aristocracy, describing them as 'blue-blooded swine'. Recalled to Berlin with Meissner in August, Auersperg declined to make the journey and remained in Berne with his wife and children but there was no direct evidence that, having been posted to Switzerland in April 1942, he had ever contacted the Allies.

A further blow to the KO was the mysterious disappearance in Berlin of Gisevius, a former Gestapo officer and Canaris's representative in

Lausanne. He would not escape from Germany until January 1945, but in the meantime the Swiss expelled his deputy, Hans Daufeldt of Amt VI, who had also been under consular cover.

It was probably inevitable that, as the tide of war turned against the Axis, conditions would prompt more desertions, and two followed quickly in France as the Allies moved closer to Paris. The first was 35-year-old Herbert Berthold, an Abwehr II NCO who surrendered to Allied intelligence officers as they took possession of the Abwehr offices in the Hotel Lutenia in Paris on 25 August 1944. Before the war he had owned a nightclub in Marseilles, and when he was posted to Paris he had acquired a French mistress and traded in the black market. His knowledge of the French underworld and his fluency in the language had made him indispensable. Later code-named JIGGER, Berthold described the Abwehr's stay-behind sabotage networks, based on his two years' experience in Paris, and accompanied Special Counter-Intelligence (SCI) personnel to various arms caches.

The next defector was Peter Schagen, a 42-year-old Abt. II officer who turned up unexpectedly at the US embassy in Madrid in September 1944 hoping to make his way to the United States with his 23-year-old French mistress, Janette Bertremieux. In fact, she had made the first approach to the Americans, through the US military attaché, without Schagen's knowledge. Initially she had met a Lieutenant-Colonel Clark, but had been rebuffed, so she then talked to a Lieutenant-Colonel Hoffman, who was more receptive and introduced Schagen to the military attaché, Colonel Sharp, and to a member of the British embassy calling himself 'Mr Simpson'. By negotiation it was agreed that Schagen would be taken to the British consulate in Seville before travelling to Gibraltar to catch a flight to London on 2 October for interrogation at Camp 020.[54]

Schagen was a familiar figure to the analysts who had studied the ISOS traffic, and they recognised him as the leader of a stay-behind sabotage organisation based in southern France. ISOS confirmed that he had crossed into Spain from France with six of his Trupp-262 (Graf Guidotto Henckel-Dohhmark, Johannes Hummel, Soesking, Konstantin von Massenbach, Josef Otten and Max Foeschler) and as instructed reported to the KOS which informed Berlin on 24 August. The group was ordered back to Berlin but the KOS pointed out that because of recent expulsions it might be some weeks before there were any seats available on Lufthansa. Schagen then fell ill with appendicitis but had recovered by the end of September when the KOS became alarmed because he had failed to catch his flight, although his colleagues were due to fly home on 28 September. Initially Madrid reported 'We are undertaking a search ourselves; It is not advisable to call in the police' but on 1 October stated that Schagen's girlfriend had been placed under surveillance and 'all circumstances thus arouse suspicion of previous plan to desert to the enemy'. On 10 October the KO's investigation had got no further:

> Everything possible in the way of searching is being arranged, also in [Barcelona]. We may certainly assume that the disappearance was intentional. Naturally the lady friend has been questioned without result.[55]

By the time the KOS was resigned to Schagen's disappearance, Sonderführer and likely defection to the Allies, he was actually at Camp 020 where he revealed, coincidentally, that he had worked at Alst Paris with Herbert Berthold in February and March 1944, mentioning that 'owing to his extraordinary knowledge of French and the country had always been retained after his previous chiefs had departed'. According to him, Berthold had received a large sum of money, perhaps 300,000 francs, to buy a house, just before he had vanished from the Hotel Lutetia.

Schagen described how he had emigrated to Brazil with his brother in 1921 where he had worked in a bank and acquired a considerable knowledge of Nazi influence over the local German community, and in 1938 returned to Germany. On the outbreak of war he had been recruited by the Abwehr and sent on a mission to Portugal, and in 1940 joined the Brandenburg Regiment which, in May 1940, sent him on a sabotage mission to Switzerland which ended in failure when several of his colleagues were arrested and imprisoned.

Posted to Libourne with Trupp-262, Schagen participated in a large operation to equip stay-behind networks with stockpiles of materiel, of which a thousand were planned across the country. Schagen was engaged in this preparatory work when he had been cut off by Allied troops and forced to retreat into Spain. His decision to defect had been influenced by the arrest to his friend and Abwehr II colleague Wolfgang Abshagen, to whom he had lent his flat in Berlin-Charlottenburg, on a charge of complicity in the 20 July plot. Understandably, Schagen told his interrogators that he feared potential 'complications' if he returned to Germany.

Schagen proved entirely cooperative, his statements having been compared to numerous ISOS references, and was then returned to the custody of OSS's X-2 branch in London in November 1944 and flown to France, where he helped uncover nineteen Abt. II arms caches hidden in anticipation of a stay-behind sabotage campaign. Over a period of two months at Camp 020 Schagen gave a detailed and comprehensive account of Abt. II's plans, identified its personnel, training camps and forward bases, and explained that 'HQ Abt. II was located in a Schloss at Baruth near Berlin, belonging to Fuerst Solms'. As MI5's Helenus Milmo observed, in the absence of detailed ISOS intercepts on the subject,

> Our information on German sabotage projects in France generally and Southern France in particular is meagre and it looks as though Schagen may be able to go some way towards filling the present gap.[56]

Schagen was particularly well informed as he had been briefed on a II staff conference held at the Hotel Lutetia in March 1944, chaired by Dr Ameln, at which detailed preparations were made:

> Plans were laid at the conference for the placing of about 1,000 dumps of sabotage material, all of English manufacture, was held in a dump at Chateau Roquencourt, near St Cloud, Paris. This material, which had been dropped by Allied aircraft and which was destined for the FFI had for some time past been collected by German troops, the SD, GFP, and assembled at the chateau. Some of it had been handed in by the French population, under penalty if they did not do so, when found in fields.[57]

The scheme, originally codenamed EASTER EGGS, selected targets such as 'railways, bridges, high tension cables, and port installations' so the sabotage materiel could be buried in special containers close by. This expedient obviated the need for the saboteurs to carry their equipment around the countryside, thereby increasing the risk of compromise. Schagen fully understood the strategy because he had also attended a training course at Roquencourt to learn how to handle the British explosives, using an instruction manual written for the FFI. He also explained that the final EASTER EGGS plan, complete with maps identifying the location of the individual caches, had been retained at Alst Paris, and then evacuated to Wiesbaden.

Significantly, Schagen's information possessed high value because of its immediate currency and contemporaneous nature, in contrast to the many Allied interrogations conducted after the German collapse. While Schagen was detained at Camp 020, and JIGGER was guiding OSS X-2 investigators across the French countryside, a third Abwehr source, Georg Kronberger, was providing valuable information from captivity in Egypt.[58] Born in Bilov in 1919, Kronberger's father had been a PoW in the First World War and then worked on the railways.

Georg trained in Vienna as an accountant and bookkeeper and joined a Waffen SS infantry regiment in Klagenfurt in May 1938 but the discovery of a heart condition brought a transfer in May 1941 to the SD in Munich where he handled information from agents in Hungary and Poland. In March 1943 he was posted to the SD's headquarters in Berlin and in September 1943 moved to Dienstelle 3000 at Athens, then headed by a sabotage expert, Otto Begus, to act as paymaster while supervising the organisation's management which appeared to be financed by the ownership of two local casinos.

Dienstelle 3000, paired with Dienstelle 2000 in Salonika, operated under commercial cover of a firm named Sandner in the Odos Santa Rosa, with a radio station located in a series of villas at Kephissya, then Thilothei, and finally Psychico. There was a permanent staff of eleven with an additional seven Greek recruiters and case officers, and one Italian SIM liaison officer. Some of these handlers, among them Colonel Bekes, allegedly ran up to fifteen individual agents, although schemes to initiate counter-intelligence operations against the British using play-back radios never materialised. With that objective, a direction-finding unit was deployed in Athens which, between February and June 1944, monitored the traffic of twenty-two separate British transmitters.

The Dienstelle's principal role was the suppression of the EDES Communist-backed guerilla movement, counter-intelligence and the preparation of a stay-behind sabotage network equipped with suitcases of explosives, with a mandate to destroy

(a) The Marathon Dam; (b) Electrical works in Athens and Piraeus; (c) Gas works at Athens and Piraeus; (d) Canalisation system; (e) Port; (f) British ships in port; (g) Wharf in Scaramanga Harbour; (h) Allied munitions and ordnance depots; (i) Railways; (j) Allied officers' quarters and soldiers' billets.

Plans were also made to shoot British officers.[59]

As well as engaging in widespread sabotage, the SD planned to develop a pro-German resistance campaign which would exacerbate the existing conflict between EDEs and ELAS, and have the virtue of tying down large quantities of Allied troops.

The resistance group, as distinct from the sabotage group, was formed about May 1943 under the Greek leader Panteloglou with the purpose of recruiting Germanophiles to spy and create havoc in Greece. The group was formed round OEDE and grew from a nucleus of 50-70 men to about 3,000. Out of this body of potential guerrillas, 150 specially suitable Greeks were selected to withdraw into the mountains as soon as the Allied occupation took place, and from there to do everything possible to hinder the progress of the Allied armies. Panteloglou himself, recently murdered by ELAS, was to have been the leader of this group, assisted by a Yugoslav named Kondjukanin alias Schmidt. The latter was also to have acted as paymaster, but is now held by this detachment. The group in the mountains was to have a W/T set operated by Hans Becker. Although 150 specially trained men were chosen to go up into the mountains, they were possibly to be accompanied by 500 – 600 other Greeks from OEDE who had become too well known in Athens. The remainder of the original 3,000 were simply told to disappear.[60]

Early in 1944 Kronberger was introduced to an 18-year-old Greek girl, Stephanie Marketou, an heiress and member of a prominent shipping family which was in touch with a Greek intelligence network. Having made discreet contact with an intermediary, Kronberger indicated in August his intention to defect, and when the German occupation forces began to withdraw in September he went into hiding, and on 3 October was taken by caique to Dinos and then sailed to Chios where the couple was picked up by a British warship and delivered to Cyprus. A few days later they reached Alexandria, and were received by SIME in Cairo on 10 October.

By the time Kronberger underwent interrogation, the SD had withdrawn from Greece to Vienna, but he nevertheless possessed an encyclopaedic knowledge of the local intelligence apparatus and its personalities, including staff officers and their agents. Many of the names were already familiar to ISOS analysts, but his information proved invaluable, especially as he was the first SD officer to switch sides and knew his organisation's post-liberation stay-behind plans. Specifically, he disclosed the details of the BERTRAM network, named after its German leader, August Ludewig, a former member of the French Foreign Legion who was arrested on 20 September. An SIS report drafted by the counter-intelligence chief for the region, Stephen Hill-Dillon, described the scale of the project which was intended to go into action once the Allies had completed the occupation.

In September 1944 Ludewig received from Berlin 3,000 gold pounds and 2,000 paper pounds to last him for 2-3 months, and a quantity of sabotage material. A small proportion of these funds and the whole of this material has now been recovered,

Krueger alias Kronberger was paymaster and quartermaster to Dienstelle 3000 Athens from September 1943. He was to have returned to Berlin before the invasion together with all the other Germans except

Ludewig. An agent of the ISLD however, engineered his defection and he was evacuated by them to Cairo with his Greek girlfriend on 10 October 1944. Ludewig was arrested on 20 October 1944 as a result of information received from two of his agents named Takis Demou and Sombola who had defected, These men were his two chief cut-outs, and their defection placed the other heads of the organisation in our hands, On the same day Ludewig's principal W/T operator Rualdi was also arrested with his set. 27 other agents were either arrested or gave themselves up.

Ludewig has prepared for us a chart (copy attached) giving his idea of the organisation of the Begus network.

Vienna was to have been the control centre. Kronberger, though he appears on the graph, was not intended to remain after the Allied invasion. Ludewig would have been left alone to control, through his cut-outs Demou and Sombola, two main sabotage groups. One of these was predominately Italian and controlled probably controlled by Rinaldi and Corvo, both W/T men; the other predominantly Greek controlled by Drossopoulos. Our information on the Greek section is scanty as we have made only two arrests, namely Nikolaos Verales and Anastasios Karastatines.

Ludewig had contact through Dimou and Sombola with the PANTELOGLOU organisation under Kondjikamin alias Schmidt, but it is doubtful whether he would have exerted any control over that group.

Details of Hans Becker's function are not available. It appears probable that he was to have been a link between the PANTELOGLOU group and Vienna, and that the penetration of that group by ELAS compelled him either to leave or to go still more deeply to ground.

Ludewig's chart shows a third sabotage group organised by Begus through his interpreter Max Kanakes (arrested). This was the West Coast sabotage group of which control was left entirely in the hands of Lavrontios Lavrentiades. The latter, an Athenian merchant of Levantine origin, received instructions in 1943 to organise a sabotage group on the west coast of Greece from Corfu to Patras. He left Athens in July 1944 with money and materials.

How the group was to communicate with Vienna or Athens is not known.

A report to hand suggests that Lavrentiades will have disposed his agents at Ioanina, Paramithia, Igoumenitsa, Arta, Preveza, Karpenissiagrinion, Mesolongi, Andirrion, Patras and Lidorikoni.

The members of the BERTRAM group to whom this account is intended to be an introduction are named -

August Ludewig alias BERTRAM; Giuseppe Della Bella, W/T operator; Luigi List; Antonio Mastrovi, W/T operator; Alberto Rinaldi; W/T operator; Marco Steffanelli; Asturoo Zolia; Michele

Cervo, W/T operator; Nikola Farinola; Josef Planetz, W/T operator.[61]

Kronberger's continued cooperation, even after he had been sent to an internment camp in the Sudan, was encouraged by his belief that he would eventually be allowed to marry his fiancée.

In May 1945 Dr Begus was arrested by the US CIC in the Tyrolean town of Nauders and taken to Rome for interrogation about his version of his experiences in Athens, followed by his subsequent sabotage-training appointments in Verona and the Villa Grazziano at Campalto. A graduate of Innsbruck University, Begus had fought in the First World War and then seen combat against the Italians in Abyssinia. Later he practised as a lawyer before joining the GFP in 1939 and serving first in the French and then Balkan campaigns. He was described as 'fiercely anti-Italian, an adventurer and now only a lukewarm Nazi'.[62]

Although Kronberger's information effectively neutralized Nazi plans to create chaos for the Allied liberation of Greece, the country would quickly descend into civil war which would last three years and in fact tied down British troops committed to preventing a Communist takeover.

* * *

The Abwehr was always exceptionally cautious in its dealings with the Swiss, and had some evidence that they would never become liaison partners or develop anything more than a language-based affinity. This stand-off, misunderstood by the Allies, became clear in 1943 when Colonel Cesare Ame of SIM reported to Berlin that they had uncovered a spy-ring in Rome, targeted against the German embassy. According to SIM, the network was headed by Robert von Steiger who passed his information to Kurt Sauer, a journalist with an office in the Swiss embassy, supervised by the Swiss military attaché, Colonel de Watteville. An investigation was conducted by Otto Helfferich, the Ast Rome Leiter since April 1939, who established that Sauer's principal source was an Italian named Fazio. Born in Trieste in June 1888, Helfferich, who habitually wore a monocle, had joined Ast Salzburg in 1938 and had established his reputation as an intelligence professional during the Spanish Civil War when he been appointed liaison officer with the Italian General Roatta in Guadlajara where he had run six radio-equipped reconnaissance vehicles with great success until he was wounded in April 1937. Reportedly he had learned his Spanish in Argentina, and his secretary was the wife of his SD counterpart, Herbert Kappler. At the end of 1941 he was promoted to head a newly-created KO Italy.

> The sole task was to ensure the security of all German armed forces in Italy, and in practice its main activities were the prevention of sabotage and espionage within the armed forces and, investigations into desertions, and the security of the shipping between Italy and Africa. The KO had no executive powers and all arrests were carried out by the GFP.

In fact, KO Italy was dissolved in March 1944. The surviving records suggest that the Abwehr, headed by Helfferich who lived with his wife in an apartment at Via Archimodo 128, maintained an office in the Italian Ministry of War building, and SIM only collaborated on one joint espionage case, which involved Renato Levi, an Italian playboy who had been recruited by a former fellow student, Clemens Rossetti, to work for the Germans. Having undertaken an apparently successful mission for III/F's Rossetti to Paris in 1940, Levi was sent to Egypt in 1941 to establish a wireless transmitter to communicate with an Abwehr station in Bari. Although ostensibly a SIM/Abwehr enterprise, supervised by Count Carlo Sircombo, Levi's assignment was complicated by the fact that he was also, from the very outset, a British agent working for SIS. As Levi progressed on his journey through Budapest, Sofia and Istanbul to reach Cairo, he reported in to the SIS stations en route and compromised his Abwehr handler, Otto Eisentrager, with whom he had held a rendezvous in Sofia, while simultaneously allowing the British to monitor his progress and contacts through ISOS. Having safely arrived in Cairo in September 1940, Levi made radio contact with Bari and set about recruiting a (notional) network codenamed CHEESE. He returned to Italy in August 1941 and was scheduled to go on a second mission to Cairo when he was unexpectedly arrested, accused of treachery involving a scheme perpetrated by Rossetti's secretary Elizabeth Tabo, and sentenced to five years' imprisonment in the penal colony of Tremito in the Adriatic. There Levi languished incommunicado until October 1943 when he was released from captivity by the advancing Allied troops and eventually managed to contact his SIME case officer in Cairo, Evan Simpson. Arrangements were made to bring Levi to Egypt where SIME deliberated on whether to risk re-engaging him as a double agent to support CHEESE, the network which had become the best Allied conduit for foisting deception on the Axis. It was at this point that James Robertson consulted his namesake in London, MI5's Tommy Robertson, about the hazards of re-establishing Levi. The head of B1(a) made his views known in a letter dated 3 June 1944:

Up till late 1941 Sonderfuhrer Rossetti was working in Italy as one of Helffrich's assistants. Subsequently he transferred to Athens and, so to speak, took the [Levi] case with him. We have received reliable information that from the outset the Italian Intelligence Service (SIM) had been at pains to keep themselves informed of Helfferich's activities and to penetrate his network. SIM is, in fact, described by [Herbert] Kappler, the German BdS in Rome, from whom this information ultimately derives, as having 'consciously mislead' Helfferich throughout his entire career. The two agents principally employed by SIM for this work were, curiously enough, Sonderfuhrer Rossetti and his secretary Elizabeth Tabo, alias Annabella. We have, therefore, the extraordinary situation that [Levi] was employed by you to deceive Rossetti at a time when Rossetti was himself employed by the Italians to deceive Helfferich. We have no evidence whether Rossetti's employment as an Italian agent continued after his departure for Athens or not. On the whole it seems probable that some link at any rate between Rossetti and SIM did continue.

With this information, and what [Levi] himself has said it is possible to construct a coherent story of what occurred in Italy. Presumably, when [Levi] returned from Egypt, Rossetti handed to SIM a full account of his story. I think we must assume that, on the basis of this story, SIM came to the conclusion, or at any rate a strong suspicion, that [Levi] was a British double-agent. They would not, I imagine, have objected to this in the circumstances in so far as it only meant that Helfferich was likely to receive false information from the transmitter in Cairo. They would, however, have objected for security reasons to the unrestricted presence in Italy of [Levi] when they knew, or believed him to be, a British agent. When it came to arresting or taking action against [Levi], they were obviously in a quandary. They could not openly arrest him on the basis of Rossetti's information without running a grave risk of compromising Rossetti with the Germans. They therefore took the middle course by attempting to obtain evidence against [Levi] through Alessi whom we know to have been one of their agents. Having failed, or more or less failed, in this attempt, the only course remaining to them was the one they took, i.e. to arrest [Levi] on the ostensible grounds that he had betrayed Italian official secrets.

I think it reasonable to assume that the full facts in the case will only have been known to SIM, Rossetti, and Elizabeth Tabo. Other Italian authorities and other Abwehr officers such as [Hans] Travaglio would only have been aware of the ostensible grounds for [Levi]'s arrest. This would account for the precautions which SIM took to prevent [Levi], while he was in prison, from communicating with Travaglio when they allowed him to communicate more or less freely with Rossetti. Clearly, if [Levi] had said anything to Travaglio about the charges against him or the manner in which the Italians had questioned him, there would have been a grave danger of revealing something which would have been the source of the Italians' information.

This reconstruction, even assuming it to be correct, does not bear very closely on the central problem of why CHEESE, having one been thoroughly blown, was able to re-instate himself successfully. The only suggestion I can make about that is that Rossetti was kept informed by SIM of the results of their interrogation of [Levi]. As these were negative, as SIM were to Rossetti's knowledge in possession of the full facts, Rossetti must have had not unreasonable grounds for supposing that [Levi] was, after all, genuine. The Italians had interrogated him on the assumption that he was a double-cross agent and had not succeeded in breaking him. Moreover, it is obvious that if Rossetti was willing to act as an Italian agent against his own masters, the Abwehr, he is unlikely to be very closely concerned about the accuracy or inaccuracy of the information which his own agents produce, provided that his personal position is not prejudiced thereby. There is, however, this point. As I mentioned above, our information in this matter ultimately derives from Kappler, the BdS in Rome since at any rate December last year, the SD has therefore been aware of Rossetti's shortcomings. What the further progress of the affair has been we do not know. It is obviously on the cards that the SD may succeed in convincing the Abwehr that Rossetti is unreliable and thereby secure his removal. This in itself would tend to weaken CHEESE. Moreover, it is possible that the Abwehr, when they hear of Rossetti's dealings with the Italians, may be tempted to assume very reasonably that agents recruited by Rossetti during that period are, ex hypotheses, unreliable.[63]

According to Levi, who remained puzzled by the reasons for his incarceration and apparent abandonment by Rossetti, he had been entrapped by Elizabeth Tabo and an Italian pilot, Luigi Alessi. Within days of Robertson's speculation, Alessi fell into British hands in Rome where he had been placed by his close friend Helfferich as a stay-behind agent. He revealed that he was actually a SIM officer who had been deployed *against* the Abwehr, so he was promptly enrolled as a double agent, codenamed ARMOUR, and continued to operate until the end of hostilities.

Despite the risks involved, which were very considerable if the Abwehr ever realised Levi had always been under British control, he re-joined his old network and proved himself a model double agent until the very last day of the war.

Much to Allied surprise, the Abwehr in Italy avoided running independent operations and instead relied on SIM to act as its surrogate partner, especially in North Africa. When Helferrich surrendered to the Allies in Merano in May 1945 he explained that he had enforced a ban on running German agents independently of their Axis partners. 'By arrangement with SIM, other German agents were not permitted to operate in Italy. Source tried to enforce this rule so far as was in his power. It occasionally happened that agents dispatched to Italy by Aussenstellen without the knowledge of Source were arrested by SIM.'

Of course, in retrospect, it can be seen to have been an asymmetrical relationship, and the Abwehr only entered the espionage field belatedly when it was obliged to recruit, train and insert stay-behind networks, and deploy agents on short-range missions to satisfy OKW demands for tactical intelligence. The Allied landings in North Africa in November 1942 came as a shock, and almost no preparation had been made for operations in Sicily or the mainland. In May 1944 an Allied appreciation, entitled *Enemy Intelligence Services in Italy*, described the situation:

(a) Abt. 1 (Espionage)

1. Espionage generally is directed from Rome. At the time of the Anzio landing a general move to Florence took place, but with the exception of the two agent's training schools, which are still in Florence, most of the directing Abt. 1 personnel and their principal recruiting agents have returned to the capital.

Agents in Rome come under the control of [Capt] Berger whose HQ is in the Pensione Flavia. Agents are subsequently despatched to Arpino for the West and Bussi or Nocciano for the Eastern Front.

2. Agents are usually young and with a good Fascist background, frequently junior officers or warrant officers either seconded from their units or earning a precarious living following desertion or disbandment of their units. The material chosen is not on the whole of a very high standard, though there have been notable exceptions. Southern Italians are preferred in view of the extra incentive given by the prospect of seeing their families again.

Short range agents are sometimes of a very poor type of down-and-out who grasps at the chance of good pay for little work in a romantic atmosphere.

Few of these agents give much thought to the ultimate consequences of their actions, and those that do harbour any qualms allow themselves to be persuaded by their friends or by the specious argument of the

Germans that the worst that may befall them is to be interned by the Allies.

3. The training given to agents is normally sketchy, though a tendency has been noticed for the Germans to become more thorough in this respect.

Photographs and drawings of Allied military equipment are shown to agents, who are expected to memorise them in the way that a German would do, and lectures and given, but attendance at Espionage schools does not appear to be taken as a very serious matter by the majority of trainees.

4. German security as applied to agents, which at one time was extremely slack, has recently improved. Attempts are now made to prevent agents knowing one another, hours of instruction in training schools are arranged so that individual instruction is possible, and agents are allowed to meet only the minimum of Abwehr officers.

5. The pay of agents is adequate and on occasions generous, judged by the poor standing of most of the recruits and the fair purchasing power of the lire in German occupied Italy. Agents crossing the Allied lines have been given various selections of Allied occupational Republican fascist, original Italian, British and US currency.

6. The espionage training at Florence is done in two schools, agents being lodged at the Hotel Berghielli in the Lung Arno, Albergo Marstoso and Albergo Patria. Instructions in military subjects and sometimes in W/T is given at 51 Via La Marmora, whilst the Scuolo di Addrestmaento, Via Dante di Castiglione is where training in W /T is given to prospective agents with little or no previous experience of the subject. W/T instruction consists of lessons in ciphering and deciphering, reception and transmission.

German personalities connected with the schools are

Lt Filippi, lives at 51 Via La Marmora – speaks some Italian and French – instructs in Allied Army organisation, weapons and methods, shipping and landing craft, etc., illustrating the lessons with photographs.

Lt Bauer, a Luftwaffe officer and a specialist in Air Intelligence stationed in Rome but who has visited the school on occasion, to instruct agents in the collection of information on airfields, landing grounds, types of planes and bombs, shipping and port installations.

<u>Baron Schumann</u> aged about 26 and speaks some Italian, French and Spanish. He is an expert W/T and cypher instructor, and directs the training of agents in these subjects. When he is personally satisfied with their performance he directs their practice transmissions with Merano and elsewhere. Schumann gives agents equipped with W/T their final briefing in codes, code numbers and names, hours of transmission and emergency systems.

<u>Lt Jaeger</u> instructs on recognition of Army units, shipping.

<u>Lt Valentini</u> (possibly a cover name). Lives at Hotel Baglioni, with his office at Via Giovanni Bovio 19, administrative officer to the organisation, attending to Agents' pay, lodgings, etc. Security has recently been tightened up at the schools, efforts are made to prevent agents meeting one another, and hours of instruction are changed daily. Recruiting and briefing other Germans connected with the school Cav. Rossetti; Ing. Siemens (W/T expert); Lt Horner, seen in Valentini's house); Nagde (W/T Instructor in Scuola dl Addestramento).

Agents' missions include: Location of formations by name or distinguishing sign, shoulder flashes and M /T markings; whereabouts of HQs and dumps; types and quantities of AFVs; airfields and aircraft; shipping information including embarkation arid disembarkations of troops; arrivals, departures and destinations of convoys; routes and contacts for subsequent agents; and details of the control in Allied occupied Italy.

1. <u>Addresses in Rome</u>
Pensione Flavia, HQ of Abt. 1.

Albergo Savoia – Living quarters.

Via Venti Septembre 4, School of Espionage.
Albergo Royale.

Via Venti Septembre 30 – Agent's lodgings.

Albergo Atlantico.

Via Cavour 23, Agent's lodgings.

Hotels Flora and Excelsior – other addresses connected with the Abwehr.

2. Personalities Abt. 1
Bauer, Lt – Luftwaffe officer. Expert in Air Intelligence.

Berger, Capt (Lilli B) – OC Abwehr Kommando.

Capillaro @ EMIL @ TINO ROSSI – Recruiting and despatch of agents.

Fillipi, Lt. (Lili B) – instructor in military subjects. Briefs short-term agents.

Graaf, Lt – Instructor at Rome. Possibly in command of W/T school.
Bodenberg, Baroness @ Mme Tabo @ ANNABELLA @ Elisabeth Peterl.
Associate of Rossetti (below).

Rossetti, Sdf. Emilio– probably a German/well known Abwehr
personality. Recruiter of agents, especially in the Balkans.

Schumann, Baron – Chief W/T instructor. Technical controller.

Valentini, Lt. (possibly an alias). Administrator of agents, instructor in
unarmed combat.

Zametin, Giovanni, probably Swiss. Associate of Rossetti for many years,
possibly employed as recruiter of agents.

'ROLF' – 55, height 1.75 m. slim but well-built; brown hair, dark
complexion. Does not speak Italian. Sometimes addressed as 'Dr'.

Painmann, Capt. von. OC Abwehr at Bussi.

Amt II (Sabotage)
1. Abt. II agents are chosen in the main from Italian shock force, the
principal recruiting-ground being the 10th MAS Flotilla (and from one
of its component parts, the San Marco Bn). Recruits are sent to Lesolo
for training and later are concentrated in a camp at Capena near Rome
for 'toughening' training and their final briefing usually takes place at
the Dienstelle Keiser at Atelli. The senior Abt. 11 officers usually seen
at Atelli are Major Count Thon von Rohenstein and Captain Hagleitner,
alias Keiser.

2. Abt. II agents drawn from 10th MAS Flotilla and kindred units are
of an entirely different type from those employed by Abt. 1. Their
specialist training in such subjects as land and marine sabotage,
swimming, parachuting and 'arditi' combat make them a reasonably

tough proposition, and they are far more liable than Abt. 1 recruits to be convinced of the cause they represent. We can expect consequently greater determination and dash in carrying out their missions.

Land parties of several men cross the lines by routes which are often difficult, carrying their own explosives (of which the delayed-action bomb is the favourite type) and their scope is consequently limited. The possibility however exists of larger parties being sent by sea with a consequently much greater supply of material.

3. PERSONALITIES

Hagleitner,_Lt. @ Keiser. Organiser of sabotage. OC Atelli station (Dienstelle Keiser).

Marowitsch, Sgt Major von – works under Hagleitner.

Thon von Hohenstein, Major Count – apparently Hagleitner's superior officer.

Della Pietro, Gennao – seen at Atelli operating W/T. Was assistant W/T instuctor at Florence.

Negroni, Adusto Bianconi – Recruiter for Hagleitner and SD, by whom principally employed.

Paoletti, Lucio – formulated draft sabotage plan for Hagleitner organisation· tall; facial distortion; protruding eyes; one front tooth missing; speaks English, French, Arabic; understands German.

Volzone, Camillo – was W /Γ instructor at Florence. Latterly at Atelli and Nocciano for W /Γ purposes. Age 22; height 5'6"; large build; dark chestnut wavy hair; delicate white complexion; speaks Neapolitan.

II. SD (SICHERHEITSDIENST)

The SD, as the Political Intelligence Service of the Nazi Party, would normally not be expected to undertake operational espionage in a theatre of war. This Service has, however, sponsored several missions with objectives akin to those normally undertaken by Abt. 1 and 11 of the Abwehr. Though this degree of rivalry has been noted, it is to be expected that the main efforts of the SD will be the recruiting and placing of agents. In both espionage and sabotage roles, for work which will only begin when the territory in which they are placed is occupied by the Allies.[64]

The information contained in this very detailed analysis was drawn from ISOS (known locally as PAIR) and, very significantly, from the interrogation of dozens of agents caught as they attempted to infiltrate the front lines, their missions often betrayed in the planning stage by COMINT.

Caught unawares by the speed of the Allied advance from Sicily, and the unexpected landings behind the lines at Salerno and Anzio, the Abwehr responded by creating smaller, dedicated units to operate tactically under the command of Hans Berger who took over the Albergo Venezia in Rovereto and made his own headquarters at the Villa Lagarina. Several were created under the umbrella of the Frontaufklärungskommando (FAK) 150 at Rovereto and included mobile forward intelligence units, Frontaufklärungstrupp (FAT) 150, 151, 152 and 153 which by June 1944, had withdrawn from Arpino to Florence.

In the absence of any aerial reconnaissance flights undertaken by the Luftwaffe, which was unable to fly because of the overwhelming Allied air superiority, the OKW came to rely on the FATs to supply intelligence about the enemy order-of-battle and dispositions. From the Allied perspective, subtle exploitation of ISOS meant that every stay-behind and line-crossing mission was doomed. Quite apart from the COMINT material, it became obvious from the German reaction to the Allied landings at Anzio and Salerno that they had no advance warning of the operations.

From January 1944 Allied counter-intelligence, headed by SIS's Stephen Hill-Dillon, formerly of the Royal Ulster Rifles and then MI5 (serving as the Port Security Officer in Hull in 1915), began circulating fortnightly summaries detailing the activities of the FATs. Six infiltrators, equipped with three transmitters, were caught in the first three weeks of the year, and by May some sixty spies had been apprehended, of whom fifty were sentenced to death. All were interrogated and most cooperated with their captors, providing detailed accounts of their background, recruitment, training and Abwehr personalities that they had encountered. The overall picture that emerged was of a massive German effort managed by Clemens Rossetti to develop a large chain of spy-schools that produced a stream of Italian volunteers. An SIS assessment dated June 1944 described the organisation, identifying four sites, with the personnel associated with them, starting with an apartment at Via Venti Settembre 4 in Rome, headed by the Abwehr's Leutnant Bauer, with a wireless school on the second floor at Via Marina Vechia 116 with a second entrance at Piazza Barbarina 120.

Reportedly the training course, attended by sixteen students who were assigned individual instructors, lasted ten days.

A third centre, at the Villa Flaminia in Circonvallazione Olodis 72, was thought to be Leutnant Bauer's home. The main headquarters was at the Villa Flavia in the Via Collins where graduate agents were briefed before being deployed to their dispatch areas. Next to the Villa Flavia was the Villa Medici which acted as a test facility to check the competence of radio operators, and give them a final briefing.

In Florence the school was at Via Alfonsa La Marnora 61 with other offices at Via Giovanni Bovio 10 and Via Cavour 86. In March 1944 a radio school was added at Via Dante da Castiglione 15. By the time the Allies entered Rome in June 1944 some 150 student agents had been logged in ISOS traffic. Two months later, ISOS revealed that there were at least twenty-five spies operational, and at the end of the year no less than eighty-two spies had faced court martials, of which twenty-nine had been shot, and an equal number imprisoned. Undeterred, the Abwehr deployed more agents in January 1945, of whom fifty-eight were captured.[65]

The impact of the stay-behind networks is hard to gauge, although captured German documents revealed post-war that just such an agent had been responsible in September 1944 for alerting the Luftwaffe to the departure from La Spezia of the Italian battleship *Roma*, on a voyage to join the Allies in Malta, which resulted in the aerial attack that sank her.

In November 1945 one of the principal FAK recruiters, Aldo Vannini, was arrested by an SCI unit in Turin and willingly provided OSS X-2's James Angleton with his version of the Abwehr's strategy of infiltrating line-crossers into Allied territory. He had been recruited in Florence's Excelsior Hotel as a radio operator by Elizabeth Petzel (alias Baroness von Hodenberg), who later became his mistress. Astonishingly, Vannini had kept records of the fifty agents he had recruited, estimating that about half had joined up 'in good faith', a further sixteen had been motivated by 'self-interest' while the remaining three may have cooperated for fear of German reprisals against their families. They performed poorly, he acknowledged, because of the lack of electricity in Allied territory where the agents found it impossible to use their mains-powered transmitters. When questioned, Petzel remarked that the Abwehr had made a mistake by choosing to train agents in a small town like Revereto where the visitors were more conspicuous than in Rome or Florence.

Chapter III

THE DEFECTORS

Wurmann is not the type of person I ever want to see again once the orange has been squeezed dry.

Klop Ustinov to Guy Liddell, March 1943[1]

The first the Anglo-American counter-intelligence branches learned of the Abwehr from the inside came on 8 November 1942 with the capture of Major Richard Wurmann at Birkadem, near Oujda in Morocco, by British troops as he attempted to flee by car to Tunis, accompanied by seven of his staff. Posing as a member of the Armistice Commission, heading a detachment known as the Verbindungkommando, Wurmann had headed Ast Algiers and had an intimate knowledge of the organisation. Having bluffed his way through several American military checkpoints Wurmann and his subordinates were detained by British soldiers guarding a crossroads 20 miles from the frontier. They had pretended to be French officers, but when challenged by a British lieutenant, they surrendered. As they were taken into custody, Wurmann was remarked that he and his men had been so taken by surprise at the US invasion that he had failed to pay his bill at the Hotel Aletti.

When the report of Wurmann's initial interrogation reached London in January 1943 an alert SIS officer, Charles Stuart, realised Wurmann's potential value and advised MI5 of the need to have his American captors separate him from his fellow prisoners and fly him to London urgently.

Codenamed HARLEQUIN, Wurmann was brought to London on 1 December for a month of interviews conducted initially at Major Scotland's MI19 cage in Kensington Palace Gardens, and then by

MI5's Victor Caroe and Klop Ustinov. To encourage his cooperation, Wurmann was freed from formal military custody to stay with Ustinov at his cottage in Burford, and was given a rented flat at 184 Chelsea Cloisters and a monthly retainer of £400. As he explained, the German Armistice Commission was an Abwehr front, and even shared its headquarters in Wiesbaden with the Abstelle in the Hotel Vier Jahreszeiten. More controversially, he was also promised British citizenship, alias documentation and an account at the Sloane Street branch of the Midland Bank as a Latvian nobleman, 'Count Heinrich Stembock'. This cultivation, which included dining at Claridge's, proved highly effective, despite Wurmann's conscience which occasionally caused him to suspend his collaboration for a few days.

HARLEQUIN's information was skilfully teased out by references to knowledge derived by Hugh Trevor-Roper from fourteen ISOS texts dating back to October 1940 when Wurmann, codenamed BLANCO and using the alias Schneider, was at the Nest Biarritz. MI5's task was also made easier by the carefully cross-referenced allusions to an Abwehr officer who had played a role in smuggling three Belgian spies across the Spanish frontier near Bayonne. The trio, Leon Jude, Jack Verlinden and Corneille Boehme, had ended up incarcerated at Camp 020 where they had made detailed confessions in January and March 1942 which had implicated Wurmann. Thus, when Wurmann began to act as a human 'reference library', much was known about him, or at least enough to persuade him not to mislead his interrogators. Indeed, Jude had accurately recalled the house occupied by Wurmann in Biarritz as 'opposite a large block of buildings near the corner of the Avenue de Londres and the Rue de Palaises'. This was a precise description of the Villa Alma Nove, a property confiscated by the Germans from a local resident, Georges Levy. Jude had spent six weeks in Biarritz in July 1941 at the Hotel Lefevre waiting for an exit permit, supervised by one 'Captain Weiss' whom he described as

> Age about 35; height about 5 ft. 3 – 4 ins; medium build; thin fair hair; big head; blue eyes; clean shaven; always wore plain clothes – blue and white check coat and grey flannels; spoke a little French; lived in a villa taken over by the Germans.[2]

Wurmann's unexpected defection, which had added value because it went unnoticed by the enemy, gave MI5 personnel the unprecedented opportunity to wine and dine him, and extract top-level information from a senior officer. Accordingly, Dick White, John Gwyer and Helenus Milmo were among the MI5 officers to meet him over a meal and ask their questions in a congenial social environment. Elaborate arrangements were taken to keep HARLEQUIN's reception a closely-guarded secret so neither Berlin nor his fellow captives should suspect a defection and be prompted to take countermeasures to mitigate the damage. The latter issue was considered especially important as Wurmann disclosed the existence of a secret Abwehr unit designated 'kgf' ('Kriegsgefangenen') dedicated to clandestine communication with German PoWs, a covert channel long suspected, but never proved, by the War Office. Among Wurmann's other revelations was the scale of the Kriegsmarine's B-Dienst, and the existence of a major signals intercept site in a villa located in Athens' northern suburb of Kifissia, which had achieved great success in monitoring Royal Navy traffic in the eastern Mediterranean. This particular item appeared to validate information extracted from an Afrika Korps PoW named Wiesskopf who had actually served there as a wireless operator between September 1941 and January 1942.

Wurmann also identified a source of information inside the British embassy in Madrid, and claimed Prince Max Hohenloe had been in private contact with the ambassador, Sir Samuel Hoare, regarding a peace initiative. Additionally, Wurmann recalled that the Abwehr's best source of information from within Hoare's embassy was the loquacious wife of Bryan Wallace, employed as an honorary attaché to persuade Spanish cinemas to show Movietone newsreels. While Wallace, the son of the novelist Edgar Wallace, was engaged on the distribution of propaganda, his indiscreet wife hosted regular tea salons for the expatriate British community in Madrid, events attended by one of Wurmann's principal assets, a White Russian prince.

During three months of intensive question-and-answer sessions Wurmann relied on his considerable experience to impart the Abwehr's secrets, which included details of twelve different secret inks, some of them completely new to MI5's scientist, Henry Briscoe, and the letter censors. Indeed, Wurmann's only blind spot was Abwehr activities in the Balkans, but his posting to Biarritz and then Algiers had given him insights into the Asts at Cologne, Bordeaux, Angers, Paris and Athens, so his expertise was considered invaluable.

Allied knowledge of the Abwehr moved from the theoretical to the factual and a report on the defector was drafted by Guy Liddell's assistant Anthony Blunt in April 1943 for submission to Winston Churchill.

HARLEQUIN was commissioned in the German Army in April 1914, and served with distinction in the war 1914–1918, being wounded on five occasions and being twice decorated, once with the Hohenzollern EK 1,1 and once with the Verdienstkreuz for bravery in the field. On leaving the Army he became a chartered accountant, and in 1933 became a member of the Nazi Party when the Stahlhelm, of which he was a member, was incorporated in the Party. In 1937 he was recalled to the Reserve and the following year was transferred to the Abwehr. From the outbreak of war until May of 1940 he was stationed at Cologne, and during the Battle of France was engaged upon the interrogation of British Prisoners of War. After Dunkirk he was sent to Biarritz to organise an Abwehrstelle and remained there until November of 1941. During this period his principal duty appears to have been the surreptitious slipping of German Secret Service agents and personnel across the Franco-Spanish frontier, with the assistance and collaboration of the Spanish authorities. In December 1941 he was transferred to Berlin, where he worked until March 1942. From Berlin he went to Paris and remained there for two months, after which he was transferred to Algiers as Head of the local Abwehrstelle.[3]

The information extracted from Wurmann resulted in a report drafted by Hugh Trevor Roper and circulated by SIS's Section V in January 1943.

One of Wurmann's motives for compromising dozens of German agents across France, Spain and North Africa was what Helenus Milmo described as his 'preoccupation with Admiral Canaris and a peace plan'. Wurmann recalled his former chief fondly as:

A very clever man with a rather biting sense of humour which shows itself in official discussions as well as in private. His subordinate officers respect his impartiality and fairness, and he is apparently well-liked by his close contacts (heads of Departments, friends, etc.). He is politically very reserved, but in his whole personality appears to be anti rather than pro-Nazi, which shows itelf in his marked refusal to adopt the Hitler salute. (In civilian clothes he greets his friends mainly by raising his hat). Further evidence of this is provided by the attitude, known to be anti-Nazi, of different people who are near to him (e.g., Oberst Rudolf, Paris and Oberst Mauer, Berlin).[4]

According to Milmo, Wurmann was 'obsessed with the idea of a compromise peace. He appears to suppose that this can be brought about by means of negotiations with Admiral Canaris, with himself, and possibly Prince Hohenloe acting as intermediaries. In view of the uncompromising terms in which HARLEQUIN recognises the necessity of the overthrow of the National Socialist Party as a precondition to peace, this Hessian line was felt to be decidedly out of place.'

HARLEQUIN's stated objective had been to get a message to Canaris so a private meeting could be arranged in a neutral country, probably Spain. However, if the media reports of his dismissal were true, the scheme was redundant, partly because of the difficulty in passing a message to the Admiral, but mainly because he would no longer be in a position to participate in a plot. The news was a bitter blow, but HARLEQUIN's MI5 dossier suggests that the Political Warfare Executive (PWE) representative Leonard Ingrams had been passed several of HARLEQUIN's reports by Caroe for his use, unattributably, as broadcast propaganda. In other words, it may have been MI5's over-ambitious efforts to exploit HARLEQUIN that led to his disappointment and decision to return to life as a PoW.

In May 1943, when HARLEQUIN's role as a source had been exhausted he opted to be returned to the PoW population, and was duly shipped to a camp in Canada in his own uniform, pretending that he had spent the past three months in St Mary's Hospital, Paddington, with a duodenal ulcer and appendix trouble. He was later transferred to Camp Trinidad, Colorado, and to Camp Ruston in Louisiana, before being repatriated to Cologne in June 1945.

Wurmann's decision to become a regular PoW had been prompted by a scheme created by the PWE to broadcast the news in April 1943 that Admiral Canaris had been dismissed from his post because of the Abwehr's failure to predict the TORCH landings the previous November and replaced by one of Himmler's nominees. This attempt at mischief-making had an unexpected impact on HARLEQUIN, as MI5's Helenus Milmo explained to his Section V counterpart, Major D. Stopford-Adams:

> For some time past HARLEQUIN has had little illusions about his own position, and has been satisfied that our interest in him, which has been dependent entirely upon the information with which he has been able to supply us, has greatly diminished, and has now got to the stage when it is scarcely existent. Matters came to a head when he read the other day in the press of the rumour – circulated I believe by PWE – that Canaris had been dismissed his post and had been succeeded by one of Himmler's nominees. On reading this news HARLEQUIN at once adopted the line that the whole structure of his contract with us had been undermined, since its principal object had been to enable him to proceed to a neutral country where he could meet Canaris personally and in that way act as an intermediary for the negotiation of a peace with the German Government which would supplant the Nazis. This proposition having been frustrated as a result of his departure, HARLEQUIN asserted that he could not reconcile it with his conscience to supply us with any further information since by so doing he would be acting purely as a traitor, and all the more so because he now realised, from reading the

British press, that when Germany was defeated the British people were
determined to impose the harshest terms upon her. He said that, rather
than feel at the moment of Germany's defeat and humiliation, he had
been in any way responsible for her downfall, he would prefer to return
to the status of a prisoner of war.

We regard this latest development as singularly fortuitous since it
releases us from a bargain in which we have received delivery of all but
an infinitesimal part of the goods for which we have only been called
upon to pay the first few installments.[5]

HARLEQUIN's decision to abandon his application for naturalisation
and resume his military status was considered fortuitous by MI5,
including Klop Ustinov who had completed a huge, 23-chapter
compendium of their conversations, and considered 'the orange has
been squeezed dry'. Nevertheless, MI5 was confident that it was in
Wurmann's interests to remain silent about his vast betrayal, and was
so trusted by MI5 that he was consulted about the only previous direct
contact there had been with the Abwehr, through a wily Yugoslav,
Mirko Rot, who himself had done nothing to engender any confidence
on the part of his SIS contacts in Lisbon.

* * *

Mirko Rot was a 27-year-old Yugoslav Jew, born in Hungary, who had
turned up in Lisbon in February 1943 seeking a visa for the United
Kingdom. Fluent in several languages, he had been educated in Vienna,
at St Margaret's School, Hampstead, and Swanley Horticultural
College: his three and a half-year-old son George was British-born.
Permission was duly granted, and he landed on 23 February 1943
accompanied by his wife Susanna. Under interrogation at Camp 020
Rot, who described himself as working in his father's drapery business,
revealed that his escape from Budapest had been sponsored by the
Abwehr, and he gave a detailed account of his recruitment in Budapest
and his involvement with the Ast Sofia from September to December
1942, and then his journey via Stuttgart to Portugal. According to Rot,
his mission was limited to reporting on morale in England and sending
messages to a postal address in Lisbon. However, having consulted
HARLEQUIN, MI5 concluded that Rot had been withholding
information, had probably met the Abwehr in Lisbon, and certainly
had not fully divulged all his financial transactions.[6]

Rot declared his willingness to act as a double agent, but there was
a significant complication as he had learned while in Sofia that the Ast

was running a spy inside the Soviet embassy, and that there was also a very large and productive spy-ring codenamed MAX active behind the Soviet front line. The issue for MI5 was the extent to which the Soviets were aware of these operations, and the possibility that there might be NKVD double agents involved. In reality Rot's lack of candour and the relatively low level of his Abwehr assignment ruled out any role as a double agent, so his true value was his detailed description of the two Abwehrstellen in Sofia, one of which was a KO, headed from 1941 to 2944 by Otto Wagner, alias Dr Delius. The other, on the other side of the city, was headed by Richard Kauder, alias Fritz Klatt, and was Ast Vienna's principal asset. He described Kauder as a Hungarian from Budapest, and a genius.

Under cross-examination in German by Section V's Henry Hudson-Williams, Rot identified every member of Ast Sofia, located in a corner villa at Boulevard Skobeleff 35, where Kauder lived with his mistress, and named Colonel Roland von Wahl-Welkrish as being in overall command, giving personality profiles of the staff, including the secretaries, wireless operators and support personnel. He also indicated the site of the Ast's radio station, five miles away in a suburb. According to the initial MI5 summary, Rot had mentioned that:

> At 0800 hours and 1500 hours each day a flood of wireless reports were received by the wireless station direct from Russia. The information in these reports was always very good operational information transmitted within a short time after the events had taken place. In recent months they had dealt exhaustively with operations in Stalingrad and were largely of Luftwaffe interest. There was excellent liaison between Sofia and the Luftwaffe as bombardment would start almost immediately on receipt of information. Rot was assured by his friends in the Abstelle that these wireless reports were responsible for vast Russian losses.
>
> Another source of information was an agent, a White Russian working actually in the Russian embassy in Sofia who had a brother or near relation on the Russian General Staff. This source in Sofia passes to the Abwehrstelle via IRA; Russian official dispatches and other documents which come to the embassy and also information leading to the arrest of Komintern agents in Bulgaria and Roumania.[7]

Rot also exposed Ast Sofia's other agents. For example, the Abwehr's best agent in Turkey, who sent daily radio reports of Turkish Army movements, was based in Ankara and was Getrud Placenza d'Alisma, a woman in possession of a Spanish passport but was 'a volksdeutsche from Galats'. Aged 35 and with 'a bad-tempered face' she signed her messages, written in French, 'Achmet'. Additional daily traffic which was 'quick and all of great operational importance' was relayed through Syria but originated in Egypt. Allegedly this material included advance warning of the Allied attack at El Alamein but it 'could not be frustrated because of insufficient forces'. MI5 noted that the source in Egypt 'was a British military officer, and from the nature of the information Rot thinks he must have been on the staff'.[8]

While MI5 and its regional subordinate organisation, Security Intelligence Middle East (SIME), may have been sanguine about the British spy in Egypt, who was recognised instantly as a locally-run double agent CHEESE, there was more concern about Rot's account of a hitherto unsuspected agent, Elie Haggar.

> An Egyptian student in Paris who was studying chemistry and who was recruited as an Abwehr agent by Dr Georg Busse, Sonderleiter of Ast Stuttgart, to go to Egypt. The inducement was money. Rot does not know his Christian name but states that he is the son of an officer in the Egyptian Police. Haggar was taken from Paris to Stuttgart and then travelled to Budapest with Rudolf Scholtz. He then went on to Sofia alone which he reached about 1 or 2 December 1942. Scholtz then took him on to Istanbul on about 15 December 1942. And Rot believes that Haggar arrived in Cairo in or about 20 December 1942
>
> His mission in Cairo was to send back military information in secret ink letters to an address in Turkey and also to stir up discontent locally. He was to live in Cairo and Rot believes that he was not equipped with W/T.[9]

Rot had first mentioned Haggar's name in Lisbon, presumably to establish his value to the British consular officials with whom he was negotiating a flight to England, but the authenticity of his information was quickly confirmed by SIME in Cairo where arrangements were made for Haggar, who had already been quizzed by an SIS officer as he arrived in Haifa on 16 December.

On 11 February Haggar, who was the son of the Egyptian Chief of Police Archimandrite C. Haggar, was arrested in Palestine, and part of the evidence against him, which he never saw, was a series of compromising references to him in ISOS, including a message to Sofia alerting KLATT that Haggar was to be paid through a contact at the Palace Hotel in Ankara. Under interrogation in a Cairo villa by SIME's psychological adviser, Major Kennedy, Haggar, codenamed GULL, proved to be cooperative and revealed at least a version of his mission. He explained that he had studied industrial chemistry at Lyons University in October 1938 but had failed his finals and had been recruited by the Abwehr in early 1942. The rest of his story neatly coincided with Rot's brief account, thereby serving to validate them.

While reluctant to make any incriminating admissions, despite having been drugged while under interrogation, Haggar's address book was found to be full of suspicious individuals who were already known to the security authorities, but one attracted SIME's attention. Haggar claimed that while in Budapest he had met a Hungarian cabaret artiste, Eta Barry, at a dance in the Ritz Hotel, who had been the mistress of a British naval officer, Lieutenant-Commander John Slater, then living at the Casino Hotel in Port Said. According to Haggar, Barry said she was working as a nurse and had provided him with a letter of introduction to her fiancé who would repay a loan Haggar gave her. Haggar would later make an appointment to meet Slater at Shepheard's Hotel in Cairo, but he declined to pay the debt. The Admiralty's Naval Intelligence Division confirmed that Slater, then aged 45, had retired from the Royal Navy in 1922 but had re-joined in 1939.

Haggar admitted to having been cultivated in France by unnamed German contacts who persuaded him to move from Lyons to Caen, and who had supplied him with high-value postage stamps, as well as a monthly retainer. When pressed on particular names, he feigned memory loss, leaving his principal CSDIC interrogator, Edmund Tilley, convinced he was protecting other agents.

Haggar would be detained for the remainder of hostilities, but his case demonstrated that Rot's information had been accurate. The investigation of Haggar would last for months, but in April 1943 SIME's James Robertson informed Dick White in London that it was 'an unsolved – and perhaps insoluble mystery', remarking that 'GULL's skilful technique as a liar does not appear to have been penetrated by the interrogators' who were military personnel attached to CSDIC and not intelligence professionals like himself and Desmond Doran, who had originally questioned him.[10] Nevertheless, despite these complaints, GULL did admit to having received in Stuttgart in secret ink a list of fifteen priorities on which he was to report fortnightly, to cover addresses in Sofia:

1. Lines of fortification around ALAMEIN.
2. Movement of troops in EGYPT.
3. Ammunition Dumps in EGYPT.
4. Aerodromes.
5. Whether horse-drawn vehicles were used by the British Army.
6. Condition of arms.

7. Size of tanks and calibre of guns.
8. Morale of troops.
9. If the Allied troops wore friendly towards each other.
10. Regiments in EGYPT (The badge to be described).
11. Arrival of ships (ALEXANDRIA-SUEZ – PORT SAID)
12. Location of HQ.
13. Types of automatic arms.
14. Treatment of PW.
15. Military details in SYRIA and PALESTINE.[11]

Haggar did identify one of his Abwehr contacts as Erich Popescu, a man who had already been described by Rot as 'a most important professional Abwehr officer of Ast Vienna' who travelled on a Hungarian passport but whose real name was Erich Werner. He drove a BMW sports saloon, was well-dressed, liked playing cards, and spoke Hungarian, Arabic, Turkish, French and German. MI5 noted that Werner

was the chief liaison officer between Ast Vienna and Turkey and is one of the cleverest spies in the Near East. He was in Syria in June or July 1942, and returned to Budapest at Christmas 1942 where Rot met him. On this occasion his reports which he had with him in writing concerned roads in Turkey, news from Basra, generally from Persia, news from Cyprus from which he stated it was difficult to get news except from soldiers. He had also reports of New Zealand troops in Damascus, etc. In Istanbul he met the agent Haggar who asked him for money. Werner reports to his chief Pachal in Vienna and in Christmas 1942 Pachal travelled to Budapest specially to meet Werner on his return.[12]

Rot would be released in March 1944 on the condition that he could not travel abroad, and all his correspondence would be subject to censorship. Accordingly, his case was left in suspension, but had linked HARLEQUIN and GULL thereby giving the two British agencies a distinct advantage, as it was hoped that the Germans remained unaware of Wurmann's defection, had no reason to believe that Rot had traded his information for his (relative) freedom, and that Haggar had been secretly detained in Palestine. Rot admitted that he had informed the Germans in Lisbon of his imminent departure by air for London, by a telegram addressed to Pachal on 20 February 1943, but there was no reason for them to believe that his subsequent silence indicated that he had been arrested. After his release Rot Anglicised his name to 'Michael Roth' and found a job with the Ministry of Finance in the royalist Yugoslav government-in-exile.

Chapter IV

THE 20 JULY PUTSCH

The general conclusion reached was that there was no evidence of a real
organisation in Germany likely to take action against the Nazis before
the military defeat of Germany.

Dick White to Guy Liddell, 1 June 1944[1]

The attempt on Hitler's life by Colonel Claus von Stauffenberg on
20 July 1944 would have immense consequences for the Abwehr and its
staff, and implicate some of its most senior personnel, including Hans
Oster, Georg Hansen and Hans von Dolnany. However, the question
that has puzzled historians has been the extent to which the Allies, and
specifically the British, were involved in the plot.

Schemes to remove Hitler and known to Whitehall had been
commonplace since 1938, but the Venlo incident had served to remind
SIS of the very considerable risks involved in making contact with
purported opponents of the regime. Nevertheless, there were several
channels of communication opened to the Allies through neutral
countries by self-styled anti-Nazis, and perhaps the most significant
was established in September 1942 when Hansen sent an emissary
to Madrid in September 1942 to make contact with the British. The
chosen intermediary, briefed by Hansen, was the Lufthansa lawyer
Otto John who met with Graham Maingot and Rita Winsor, based
at the British embassy in Lisbon, and Jack Ivens, then at the British
embassy in Madrid.

On 4 November 1944 MI5's Herbert Hart made an entry on Otto
John's Personal File declaring explicitly that John 'has been an SIS agent
for two years . . . ' which suggests that John had been enrolled as an SIS
agent and assigned the codename WHISKY in around November 1942,
which is consistent with his known meetings with Maingot, Winsor

and Ivens held between September 1942 and his exfiltration from Lisbon in November 1944.[2]

John had been called back to Berlin from Madrid on 19 July 1944 to participate in the putsch and, after its failure, returned to Spain on 24 July 1944. He was subsequently resettled in England under the protection of the British government, but not before he was obliged to undergo the required screening process conducted by MI5 at the Oratory School in Kensington which accommodated the London Reception Centre (LRC). The cross-examination was completed by a German linguist, Captain Basset, whose report established Prince Louis Ferdinand as a 'central figure in the conspiracy' who enjoyed 'close friendly relations' with John and intended to overthrow the regime and restore a constitutional monarchy on the British model.

According to the reconstructed narrative of events, John had flown to Madrid in 1942 with a letter of introduction from the prince to a Spanish Foreign Ministry official, Juan Terraza, who accompanied him to Lisbon to meet Maingot. John would be back again in Madrid in November to hold further 'exploratory talks' with the British representative he knew only as 'Graham'. Later, John made a fourth visit 'early in 1944' when he met Rita Winsor. He also travelled to Spain in February and April 1944, and was there on an eighth occasion when he was called back to Berlin on 19 July. He would escape from Germany on 24 July, and then meet Jack Ivens while a fugitive in Madrid.

Unbeknown to John, SIS had several other sources who had offered their opinions on the existence of a well-organised resistance movement in Germany. COLOMBINE, for example, denied that at the time of his defection any such conspiracy had existed. He was interviewed several times by MI5's Waldemar Caroe in September 1943 when an ISOS intercept appeared to reveal

> that there is a sort of secret organisation in German militarist and other circles which advocates the establishment of an independent politico-military body which will do its utmost to sustain the Eastern Front, but will seek peace with Britain and the USA. Should the latter prove impossible, the organisation will facilitate the entry into Germany of British and US forces but will on no account lightly forsake the Eastern Front, in order not to permit Communist influence to seep into the homeland.

When COLOMBINE was questioned on this topic, in a way intended to protect the ISOS source, he asserted that he does not think that when he left Germany any secret military organisation of this kind existed. A number of small circles with these ideas did exist, chiefly among the [Luftwaffe] officers. These circles are known as 'West Orientierung' and are largely composed of re-employed officers who had seen service in the last war, senior officers and Generals who are employed at the Luftfahrtsministerim.[3]

COLOMBINE went on to explain that 'he does not think that any organisation at present powerful enough to be of real organised assistance to the Allies in the event of a landing in the Balkans or anywhere else. He feels certain, however, that the Allies would very soon find German officers who had belonged to some anti-Hitler groups and who would be very anxious to assist them . . .'

It seems likely that an anti-Nazi group could become powerful enough to force the hand of the regime. There are many small groups in existence, all working for the overthrow of Hitler and all he stands for. They all, from time to time, hear of other groups but they do not trust each other as they never know whether the other group is not a 'plant' or whether it does not contain among others a representative of the SD or Gestapo. What these groups entirely lack is some central head whom they could all trust and to whom they could turn. If such a man were found they would soon all join together and become strong enough to stand against Himmler's power.[4]

In contrast Erich Vermehren, interviewed in London in May 1944, insisted he knew several members of a very determined plot.

Vermehren claims that a number of opposition groups exist in Germany, differing ln character according to their origins, e.g. those with local political aims, those with general political aims and those with ideological aims. Vermehren claims that his group belongs to the last category.

The fundamental belief of the group is that in National Socialism they are combatting not only the embodiment of political tyranny and ruthless imperialism, but also the implacable enemy of western culture and the Christian social order. The members of the group are only Democrats, Conservatives, Monarchists or particularists in the second place; they are firstly Central Europeans and Christians.

Vermehren claims that the conscious supporters of the groups in the ideological category include a large number of senior officials (State Councillors, Generals, Headmasters, Presidents of State Governments, Reich Bank Councillors), the majority of the Catholic and Protestant clergy, numerous men in the learned professions and economic life; senior employers and a large number of workers. Amongst other

139

unconscious supporters can be included the great majority of all active Catholics (including soldiers) and Protestants.

Vermehren can give no numbers for his group, since members are not registered. Its main strength, however, lies in the fact that it is in contact with various workers' groups, whose representatives assisted and joined up plans of action. It has secured the support of the Universities and high finance and industry are represented in the movement. Its followers are especially numerous in the Foreign Office, where the National Socialist principles of selection was applied less vigorously than elsewhere. Vermehren claims to know the identities of a number of leading personalities in the movement and also to be in possession of cover-addresses.

Vermehren says that his movement has no set internal political programme. Its aims are to remove the Nazi leaders and the war, prevent chaos with the assistance of the Allies and finally to take the initial steps towards organising a natural and healthy internal politics life. Whether it will then split up into different political parties or present itself to the people in its existing form as a Coalition Government for a further interim period will be decided later. The movement's political principles include, inter alia:

1 The restoration of individual liberty.
2 The protection of the Christian churches and other religious communities.
3 The reconstitution of a democratic system of government based on the recognition of the dignity of the individual.
4 The decentralisation of the administrative apparatus and the creation of autonomous cultural centres in keeping with the historic characters of the various provinces of the Reich.
5 The reorganisation of the educational system in Germany with the world-wide plans of the United Nations.
6 The independence of the courts.
7 Sanctity of private property and the safeguarding of private initiative.

The relations between the movement and the victorious powers would be fixed by the signatures of the movement's representatives of the Armistice and peace Treaty.

Vermehren says that he has neither instructions nor authority to act on behalf of his movement, whose leaders were unaware of his decision to go over to the Allies. He feels entitled, however, to act on his leaders' behalf since he knows that they recognise the necessity for establishing touch with the United Nations and more especially with Great Britain. He conceived it to be his task to carry out the necessary preliminary discussion, and subsequently to arrange for the establishment of contact.

Finally Vermehren claims that touch is maintained between his group and the senior commanders in the West. He hoped that, provided the outcome of negotiations between his movement and the representatives of the United Nations should prove satisfactory to both parties, certain of these commanders could be induced to make their military strategy conform to the changed political situation.[5]

Hans Ruser, the defector codenamed JUNIOR, also interviewed in London, averred that the resistance had been active at the time of his dismissal from the Abwehr in September 1942, and he had remained in touch with them until his exfiltration to England in November 1943. As MI5's J.C. Masterman reported on 1 June 1944, Ruser had held a meeting with a group of German generals 'interested in peace or at least armistice negotiations' shortly before his departure. He described how he had worked for SIS for the past 12 months, and the conference had taken place in August 1943 at a private home on the road between Biarritz and St Jean de Luz. The organiser, allegedly General Johannes Blaskowitz, had used Ruser as an intermediary with the British, in the form of the British military attaché in Madrid, Brigadier William Torr, but he was rebuffed with the response that London 'was not disposed to deal with any party or man as long as long as Hitler and his party were still in power'.[6]

Klop Ustinov was also in touch with another apparent strand of the anti-Nazi putsch, as recalled by Chantal Sabaret, a French woman who in 1937 had married an industrialist who, from 1939, was serving as a Wehrmacht officer. In December 1943, while living in Lyons, where he was attached to General Hermann Niehoff's staff, she had travelled to Lisbon on behalf of her husband's close friend, Claus von Stauffenberg, whom she had last seen in April. Reportedly, she attended a rendezvous in Lisbon railway station in December 1943 when she received certain documents from Ustinov, alias 'Captain Johnson'. As she described the encounter to an SCI Unit in December 1944, her husband had only narrowly escaped arrest after Niehoff had vouched for his loyalty to the regime. In her statement she claimed that 'shortly before the July plot her husband gave her to understand that the documents received contained directives from an important German émigré ([Otto] Strasser), and that there might be ramifications in Germany connected with the friends of Rudolf Hess'.

Actually, Ustinov had been in Lisbon to maintain contact, initially established in March 1943, with the influential *Kolnische Zeitung* correspondent Hermann Mariaux whom he had known in Brussels before the war. Significantly, Ustinov had cultivated the journalist since March and had visited his country home at Sao Pedro on 26 June 1944, less than a month before the planned attack, and reported back to London:

[Mariaux] has received a communication (I believe orally by someone who must have come over quite recently), which makes him think quite seriously that Hitler and the chief Nazis will be removed within a very short period of time. I am mentioning this opinion of [Mariaux] at a time when he is not yet ready to substantiate his views by facts owing to the great secrecy in which the whole thing seems to be clouded, only as a warning for possible developments which, in my view, will mean in fact that the organisation in question, after having got rid of Hitler and his gang, will want to get rid of 'unconditional surrender' too. I have of course thrust many questions at [Mariaux] and have received in view of the secrecy to which he seems to be pledged, countless evasive answers. I have however been able to form a somewhat incomplete picture of what might be brewing. It seems to me that the Generals Halder and Beck are after all the nerve centre of the plotters.

Two days later, Ustinov reported to London that Mariaux had said 'You can rest assured that whatever happens Hitler will be killed before any of you can do anything about it.' The two men had another meeting on 4 July, Mariaux having received a letter from his friend Major von Mutius who, he claimed,

is in the big plot aiming at the forcible removal of Hitler, that he, [Mariaux], informed him in the course of his last journey to Germany in March, that he was in touch with the British, but that he did not give Mutius my name. [Mariaux] says that Mutius's object in coming to Lisbon is certainly to take up contact with the British and that he would certainly want to see me with the object of meeting later a political figure on the British side with whom the ways of maintaining order in Germany by means of some 'conservative organisation' after the death of Hitler and the military collapse of Germany could be discussed. I understood from [Mariaux] that they are going ahead with their plans for the assassination of Hitler without any regard for what they might hear from us before the event or after; that they are in no way concerned with peace negotiations or peace conditions; that they are expecting the worst possible conditions but that notwithstanding everything they aspire, mainly if not solely with the help of the British at maintaining some sort of order after the breakdown so as to prevent the country sliding into complete anarchy or what they call Bolshevism. Though I personally cannot see the validity of the optimism of [Mariaux] and his friends in the question of the early removal of Hitler and his gang, I feel it my duty to put on record the full confidence of this particular group of conspirators that Hitler will die an unnatural death very soon or, as [Mariaux] puts it, Hitler's death is approaching with rapid steps.

Ustinov's discussions with Mariaux had 'not been taken entirely seriously' in London, but within days of the putsch it was realised by the Foreign Office that Mariaux had been in deadly earnest, as Peter Loxley acknowledged to Dick White on 27 July. 'It has now, however, become clear from [Ustinov's] latest reports and from what he himself told us when in London that Mariaux must have been in direct contact with those Germans who staged the recent attack on Hitler's life with a view to approaching the Allies with peace overtures.'

One of the few men who had an intimate knowledge of the Abwehr's top management, and its transformation into the Mil Amt, was Erwin Lahousen who, by sheer chance, was commanding a regiment on the Russian Front and had been wounded three days before the 20 July debacle, and therefore escaped all the consequences experienced by his colleagues. The son of an Austrian field marshal, Lahousen was born in Vienna in October 1897 and had served in the infantry during the First World War. Afterwards he remained in the military and in 1935 joined Austria's Nachrichtendienst, then headed by General Max Ronge, as a specialist on the Czech military. Evidently in that role he had impressed Admiral Canaris during an official visit to Vienna in 1937, as he was appointed to the Abwehr after the Anschluss, despite his older brother's well-known anti-Nazi credentials. He was promoted head of Abt. II in January 1939, and had used his position to obtain from the Brandenburg Regiment the explosives that were concealed in luggage placed aboard Hitler's aircraft on a flight from Smolensk to Rastenburg on 13 March 1943. The bomb failed to detonate, probably because the time-fuze had become too cold to function as intended.[7]

In January 1944 Lahousen requested a transfer to a combat command and was posted to the 41st Jäger Regiment of Army Group North on the Eastern Front, and was replaced in Abt. II by Wessel Baron von Freytag-Loringhoven, who would shoot himself on 26 July 1944 at Mauerwald, East Prussia, to avoid arrest by the Gestapo, having been implicated in the supply of the explosives.

Lahousen later heard that on 20 July 1944 the acting chief of the Mil Amt, Naumann zu Königsbrück, detained at gunpoint the Mil Amt's senior staff at their headquarters at the Schloss Baruth, and was in an armed confrontation with Sonderführer Witzel. The organisation was then headed by Dr Loos who completed the SD's purge.

Lahousen was still hospitalised when he was arrested by US forces in late April 1945, and underwent a lengthy interrogation. He would later appear as a prosecution witness before the International Military Tribunal in Nuremberg, and be released from custody in April 1947 to live in the Tyrol, where he died in February 1947.[8]

Under interrogation, Lahousen named several Abwehr colleagues as having plotted with Canaris to assassinate Hitler, among them Hans Oster (Abt. III), Helmuth Grosskurth (Abt. II), Graf Rudolf Magorna-Redwitz (Ast Vienna), Hans Piekenbrock (Abt. I) and Karl Fiedler (Abt. II). He had also appointed several Austrian anti-Nazis to the Abwehr, including Major Melzer von Orienburg and Major Gustav Fechner. Melzer, designated a 'non-Aryan', was married to a Swede and his brother had been imprisoned by the Nazis. He also recruited several co-conspirators, including his trusted secretary Hedde Voight and his adjutant, Wolfgang Abshagen, and he appointed Friedrich-Wilhelm Heinz to command a battalion of the Brandenburg Regiment. However, Lahousen could not re-assign his deputy, General Erwin Stolze, whom he distrusted as a Prussian Nazi.

As regards Canaris, Lahousen knew of his secret relationship with Halina Szymanska, the wife of the former Polish military attaché in Berlin, who had moved to Berne under the Admiral's sponsorship, describing her as 'a very wise, politically educated woman whom Canaris looked up regularly in Switzerland and whose family in Warsaw was protected and especially looked after by the Abwehr'. The fact that Lahousen knew about Szymanska, who was also managed by the British SIS station in Berne, and had his own contact with the Americans through Hans-Berndt Gisevius, an Abwehr officer under consular cover in Zurich, confirms his status as one of the chief's most trusted inner circle, and as an accomplice.[9]

* * *

The most positive evidence of British involvement in the putsch is through the Lufthansa lawyer and Abwehr I/L officer Otto John, originally of Ast Stettin, who is now known to have acted as a link between Georg Hansen and SIS. Born in 1909, John became a corporate lawyer for Lufthansa in 1936 and, because of his fluency in Spanish, which he had acquired while a student in Spain, he had been promoted by Lufthansa's pioneer, Freiherr von Gablenz. While in Madrid John became close to a Spanish diplomat, Juan Terrasa, and allegedly 'their friendship also found common ground in mutual homosexual tendencies'.[10]

According to Josef Ledebur, who was interrogated at Camp 020 in February 1945, John had been one of four trusted subordinates or contacts, including himself, whom Colonel Hansen had selected to open a dialogue with the Allies.[11] The other two were Eduard Waetjen in Switzerland and the banker Robbi von Mendelsohn in Sweden. Protection for them was provided by Hansen's colleagues, Kapitän Walther Wiebe of Ast Stettin, his ADC Prince Gunther Knipphausen and Kapitän Ludwig Gehre of Abt. III, who were assigned to a special unit, Sonder-Verbinungschef JOE, at Zossen. To preserve security, all internal communications were carried by dedicated KO couriers, and Ledebur's cover for his frequent visits to Madrid was the pretext of collecting intelligence reports from his French source, Pierre Bastide, and from John himself, codenamed JAEGER. Thus Hansen created his own compartmented organisation in which few of the membership knew each other as co-conspirators, but administratively enjoyed the full protection of the Abwehr's senior management to further the aims of the plot. However, Hansen confided to Ledebur, without apparently disclosing his true motives, that

> he had had great difficulty in protecting his confidants: 'He could no longer expose himself' for Gehre, Knipphausen or Mendelsohn. Waetjen and John were on a different plane; he wishes to keep them under any circumstances, and Ledebur was now to manage their affairs in full, including administrative arrangements. Communications with Waetjen were good, but he must have direct communication by radio with John in Spain; could Ledebur recommend an operator?[12]

Evidently Ledebur did suggest a KOS wireless operator, Bernard Rohe, to improve communications, but his trust would prove to be misplaced in the days following the attempted putsch.

On 19 July, which was the intended day of the coup, Hansen urgently recalled John to Berlin and, having arrived at very short notice, he was in the Reserve Army headquarters in the Bendlerstrassse the following day when the news broke that Hitler had survived Stauffenberg's attack. John promptly went into hiding for three days in his flat where he was completely isolated, dependent on radio news bulletins and unable to reach Hansen by telephone. He did call what he thought was the Abwehr's headquarters at Zossen, unaware that it had moved to the Schloss Baruth, codenamed BELINDE, two weeks earlier. He would be brought up to date by a co-conspirator, the diplomat Adam von Trott, and, having heard the details of the failure of the coup, he stayed at home until he could arrange a place for himself in the cockpit of a Lufthansa flight to Madrid, where he checked in to the Palace Hotel. John then described how he recontacted SIS through Jack Ivens, the Section V representative at the embassy's SIS station.

On reaching Madrid he got in touch with his friend Terraza, and through him with [Monsignor] Boyen-Maas. For about three weeks he lived at the Palace Hotel, where he had always stayed whenever he was in Madrid.[13]

John was continuously in touch with Terraza, who contacted Winsor, and furthermore, with Boyen-Maas, and through him with Ivens. There, in Madrid, he also encountered Ledebur, who was stunned to hear of Hansen's death;

John now broke down completely; in tears he confessed to Ledebur that Hansen was no longer alive; that Count Stauffenberg, to whom Hansen had personally handed the explosives, to be used in the attempt on Hitler's life, was also dead. And that he, John, has also been deeply implicated in the plot.[14]

Realising that he was 'walking around with a noose around my neck', Ledebur revealed that he was already in direct contact with the British. John refused Ledebur's offer to be put in touch with them, stating that he was already, though he would not name any particular person. The same evening, on seeing his own British contact, Ledebur disclosed the information which he had obtained from John.

Ledebur was placed in an SIS safe-house in Madrid in August 1944, an apparent defector, although there was a perceived ambiguity about his precise position. John suspected that Ledebur had been sent to Spain to track down the putsch conspirators, and ISOS showed that Ledebur was actively engaged in espionage as he was in touch with an Italian asset, Marco Pinci, and a French source, Pierre Bastide. Count Pinci was a director of the Bank of Indo-China and mining engineer and Bastide a mining engineer, and both were highly-rated as being well connected in the Vichy administration.

On the other hand, ISOS also suggested that John himself was running a spy codenamed PELIZAEUS in the Spanish capital, an item he had not mentioned to SIS. On 7 August SIS reported that information provided by Pinci and Bastide to Ledebur (consciously or unconsciously) was mostly 'worthless and appeared to have been fabricated'. When Ledebur had arrived in Madrid at the end of July he

expressed his willingness to work for us and gave certain information on German military potential in France. We have no direct evidence that previous to this visit the German Intelligence Services were suspicious of Ledebur, although this is not unlikely. On July 31 however, Ledebur was urgently summoned back to Berlin and it became clear in a few days that the German Intelligence Services in Madrid knew that he had made approaches to us. Moreover, they believed him to have been implicated along with Otto John, in the conspiracy against Hitler, and they appear to regard him still as a potential source of information to themselves, as of course to us, on the details of this conspiracy.[15]

In considering how to handle Ledebur, MI5's Tommy Robertson conferred with SIS's Desmond Pakenham because of the potentially damaging 'meal-ticket' Ledebur might disclose. One unanswered question was whether Ledebur had any knowledge relating to successful British double agents, such as GARBO. Once these issues had been resolved, by pretending that GARBO, in fear of exposure through Roberto Buenaga, a suspected leak in Spain, had gone into hiding, the way was open for SIS to formally receive Ledebur and bring him to London.

In fact, despite John's belief to the contrary, Georg Hansen was at that stage still alive, but had been arrested by the Gestapo and would survive until September when he was executed after a brief trial. While Ledebur and John wrestled with their future course of action, they lunched with Bernard Rohe and discussed the merits of defection to the Allies, a suggestion that Rohe later reported to his KO, as appeared in an ISOS text addressed to Berlin dated 4 August in which Rohe was referred to as ROSS;

Ledebur has gone over to the enemy. Wants to take the W/T operator with him. ROSS reported the matter in accordance with regulations. ROSS believes he will be able to extract from Ledebur yet more names of personnel implicated in the attempted assassination. So far it is established that member of Lufthansa, Dr John, who is at present here, is one of the principal persons implicated. If you sanction planting of ROSS against Lebedur and the English, please inform us whether ROSS may hand over to the English technical details of his W/T link to Hansen, or whether this would be harmful. ROSS will for the time being pretend to be undecided, we also request information at once by msg after you have consulted Hansen and Kuebart, of what they have told Ledebur about the GOLFPLATZ [British] link of FELIPE [George Lang].[16]

Having been advised by Ivens to go into hiding, John was taken to a safe-house run by a French woman, where he stayed for a further two weeks. Doubtless Ivens, with access to ISOS, had acted on good evidence of a Gestapo manhunt for the conspirators. After another fortnight as a fugitive, John was smuggled over the frontier near Vigo into Portugal and driven in a legation car from Oporto to the capital where he was accommodated at another safe-house in the city suburbs until 23 October when he was arrested by the PVDE during a routine anti-Communist sweep of the Spanish refugees in the neighbourhood. He was released from custody on 3 November at the British embassy's request, and stayed with another SIS officer, Gene Risso-Fill, at his home in Estoril until he was flown to England a few days later.

While undergoing his screening at the LRC, MI5 required John to make a lengthy statement describing his personal history and his political history. In it he explained that he had acted as an intermediary among various anti-Nazi groups to broker an agreement about a new constitution for a post-war Germany. All those involved had supported a restoration of the monarchy, but concluded that Prince Wilhelm was an unsuitable candidate, although his younger brother would be acceptable:

> Eventually, an agreement was reached in which John played an important part as an intermediary for the restoration of the monarchy – leaving the question of Wilhelm's successor in abeyance, perhaps in the hope that before the question became actual they would be in a position to approach the second son, Prince Louis Ferdinand, who was acceptable to all parties, not only as a statesman, but as the only member of the family, except Princess Cecilia, who had an unblemished record of opposition to the Nazi regime. The agreement to which all sections of the underground movement adhered was concluded shortly after the Polish campaign in 1939. At that time the matter was one of urgency, since the Army members of the Opposition Movement had planned an attempt on Hitler's life for November 1939.
>
> The plan had been prepared by Beck and his circle of Wehrmacht followers who, moreover, had at least the tacit support of Brauschitsch and Col.-General Halder, chief of the German General Staff. John blames Halder for the miscarriage of this plan, since everything was ready and it was Halder who drew back at the last moment, thereby losing an opportunity which did not recur for many years.[17]

John went on to describe how Prince Wilhelm's death opened the way for the opposition movement to coalesce around his brother:

> The death of Prince Wilhelm during the French campaign removed the most serious problem as far as internal unity was concerned. Louis Ferdinand became the successor and one of the central figures in their conspiracy. John's close friendly relations with Prince Louis Ferdinand

considerably strengthened his influence inside the Opposition Movement.[18]

Most importantly, John also recalled his first encounter with SIS in 1942, through Graham Maingot of the Lisbon station:

In April 1942, however, negotiations connected with the DLH's Iberian shareholding were to be opened in Madrid between Luz John, and Stauss, one of DLH's directors. This official journey was just the opportunity [Carl] Goerdeler [the former Mayor of Leipzig] wanted and John agreed to attempt to establish contacts with the Allies, through Terraza, who was known by Prince Louis Ferdinand to be friendly with us.

Once in Madrid John took Prince Louis' letter to Terraza and generally discussed with him the political situation in Germany, disclosing the existence of a large, well-organised movement in opposition to the Nazis. John gave Terraza to understand that he was an official delegate and quite readily accepted Terraza's suggestion that they should fly to Lisbon together, where Terraza would introduce him to an English friend, a man who at that time was known to him as 'TONY' and later as Mr Graham, of our embassy in Lisbon.

At that time Goerdeler and his group of industrialists and business men were convinced that they could secure a negotiated peace and that Germany had quite a lot of cards in her hands. John claims that he opposed this view, but that in his discussions with Graham he adhered to the line imposed upon him by Goerdeler – in other words, exploring the possibilities of obtaining conditions from the British for a successful overthrow of the Nazi regime. At Goerdeler's instructions no names were mentioned to Graham; indeed, names were never mentioned at any time until after the 20 July 1944. There were no negotiations with Graham, only an exchange of information which from Goerdeler's point of view was unsuccessful.[19]

As he described in his statement, John would be back in touch with Maingot the following year:

In July 1943 Terraza was invited to Berlin, where he lived in John's flat. Goerdeler had reached a fairly advanced stage in his plans and the project of sending John with a certain Captain Gehre to this country as a kind of delegation from Goerdeler's party in connection with our invasion preparations was, strange as it may seem, discussed, Terraza was doubtful about the whole proposition, but agreed to broach the subject with Graham. He was very early on a member of the Nazi Party. In about 1926 he withdrew, and in the course of time became anti-Nazi. He was a close friend of a certain Delbruck, Justus (son of the famous historian), a friend of [Hans] Dohnanyi, and later purchaser of the wholesale cloth business in which Harnack worked. When war broke out [Hans] Oster found Dohnanyi employment in the Abwehr, and Dohnanyi in his turn found employment for Gehre as a Sonderfuehrer. Later, when Dohnanyi was arrested, the Sonderfuehrers including Gehre were transferred to active service units. Gehre was a close friend of a certain Oberst-Leutnant Schradr, of the AHA attached to the Fuehrer's GHQ. Schradr was in the know as far as the military conspiracy was concerned and passed information from the Fuehrer's GHQ, including military plans and up-to-date appreciations of the military situation through to Gehre, who passed them on to Dohnanyi, through whom they found their way to [Friedrich] Olbricht and on to [Ludwig] Beck.

It was this channel which had made it possible for Beck to be so well informed about the military situation on the Eastern Front. Gehre was invaluable to Beck and to the military conspiracy as a whole and yet it was proposed that he and John should be sent on a mission to this country. Certainly Gehre's information about Peenemunde passed through Terraza brought the great Allied raid within about eight days, but there is no indication that John passed on to the Allies any of the other information which he claims was obtained by Gehre from Schradr.

In the autumn of 1943 Goerdeler and Beck once again were ready for an attempt on Hitler's life and of overthrowing the Nazi Party. General [Friedrich] Fromm, who was known to sympathise without being an active participator in the military plot, was Commander of the Ersatz Heer, and under him General Olbricht was Commander of the Algemeine Heeresamt, with Lt.-Col. von Tresskow as his Chief-of-Staff. This was the set-up which was to have made it possible to take over power in Berlin as soon as the attempt on Hitler's life had been successful.

By the autumn of 1943 Goerdeler, who was seeing John very often, told him that he was to get in touch with the English again to inform them that the attempt on Hitler's life would be made on the 15 September 1943. However, no names were to be given, and moreover, it was clear that Goerdeler still believed that he would succeed in negotiating with the British.

On the 15 October Tresskow was replaced by Colonel von Stauffenberg, who was also in sympathy with the plans of the military group, Meanwhile, however, the actual attempt on Hitler's life had been delayed over and over again. John emphasised to Goerdeler all along that any thought of negotiating with the British was out of the question and that moreover, any contacts with them were bound to be spoiled by continual delay over the attempt on Hitler's life.

By the autumn or early winter of 1943 Goerdeler had greatly improved his relations with the Trades Union through Kaiser and Leber. On the debit side of their balance-sheet was the arrest of Dohnanyi who, together with Oster, had been their main liaison member inside the

Abwehr. Dohnanyi's arrest, according to John, was the outcome of the arrest of a certain Abwehr officer attached to Ast Munich named Konsul Schmidthuber. This man, although a member of the Abwehr, was in fact wholly engaged carrying out the instructions of the Opposition groups' chief, Abwehr officers Oster and Dohnanyi. His cover activity seems to have been freelance work in Italy – whatever this may mean. He was a man of very considerable wealth and was arrested by the Gestapo in connection with smuggling of foreign exchange. Interrogation of Schmidthuber led to Dohnanyi's arrest and to the house arrest of General Oster – a serious blow for the military conspirators, who thereafter had to rely on Col. Hansen, head of the Abteilung Eins and one of Oster's closest friends and confidants.[20]

John's narrative then turned to events in Madrid:

In November 1943 John was back in Madrid, where he stayed until just before Christmas; once again his visit was ostensibly in connection with the DLH holding of Iberia shares. He got in touch with Terraza, who told him that Graham was no longer in Lisbon, but took him to Lisbon where he was introduced to Graham's secretary, Miss Winsor. Once again there was an exchange of information, but no change in John's attitude and no names mentioned. However, he took back a questionnaire to Madrid, filled it up there, and handed it to Terraza for transfer to Miss Winsor.

Early in 1944 he was back again in Madrid, again saw Miss Winsor in Lisbon. After his return this time to Berlin he insisted on a very much more businesslike attitude on everybody's part and emphasised his own view that there was nothing doing with the British unless they gave proof of their bona fides by disclosing at least some of the names of those playing leading parts in the Opposition Movement.

In the early part of 1944 John had many meetings with Goerdeler and Hansen, by then their principal Abwehr contact. Hansen told John that Ast Stettin had come under suspicion and that he would have to transfer him to the Central Amt to avoid any awkward investigations,

In the meantime he learned from Goerdeler and direct from Hansen that Hansen and Stauffenberg had the military side of the revolt well in hand and that they were all set for an attempt on Hitler's life in March 1944. In connection with these – at that time believed – final preparations, Goerdeler and Hansen decided to make one more attempt to advance peace proposals to the Allies, using John of course.

However, in view of the breakdown with the British it was decided this time to make peace proposals to Eisenhower, and in February 1944 John was again sent to Madrid, ostensibly by Hansen on an Abwehr mission, but in fact without an Abwehr mission at all and wholly in order to get in touch with the Americans.

While John received favourable treatment from SIS, and eventually from MI5 too, Ledebur was not so lucky and on 30 November was transferred from the LRC to Camp 020 where 'under interrogation he produced a wealth of most valuable information, the main report on his case consisting of some 86 pages of narrative and approximately a further 100 pages of appendices, every word of which has been of value'.[21]

Born in Vienna in February 1899, the third son of an Austrian nobleman, Graf von Ledebur-Wichein was commissioned into the Austro-Hungarian army in 1917 and after the war worked as an agricultural engineer in Europe and the United States until he joined the Abwehr in May 1941, having been recruited by Erich Pfeiffer at Alst Paris, who sought to exploit his business associate, Charles Bedaux.

In November 1943, having been appointed an aide to Georg Hansen, Ledebur visited the Madrid KO and while there was introduced by a mutual acquaintance to Michael Cresswell, the MI9 representative at the embassy. At a discreet meeting Ledebur gave 'a brief verbal report on conditions in Germany and other information concerning the Wehrmacht. The two agreed to meet again by arrangement on Ledebur's next visit.'[22]

Ledebur's frequent trips to Spain were predicated on a supposed need to manage his agents Pinci and Bastide who were, as SIS suspected, unwitting sources, and his alleged recruitment of Daniel d'Araoz, a close friend of General Luis Orgaz, the Spanish commander of the Pyrenees military district, was also notional. These supposed assets provided cover for Ledebur's fifth visit to Madrid, in April 1944, but when he attempted to re-establish his link with the British embassy he was informed that Cresswell 'had no authority to renew the contact'. Mystified by the British attitude, Ledebur asked Pinci to make discreet representations on his behalf. In reality, SIS feared that Ledebur's overt defection would undermine its stable of controlled double agents reporting through the Madrid KO, and no doubt compromise Otto John, over whom he exercised administrative control for Hansen.

In terms of agents, Ledebur knew of at least two in England. One was an I/L spy codenamed KILLIAN, trained and run by Emile Kliemann of Alst Paris about whom he had learned in the autumn of 1942 when Erich Pfeiffer had remarked to him that I/L 'were very proud of this bird who occasionally gave a peep which was really worth reading, though the present report was journalistic nonsense. Not long before KILLIAN had supplied a three-line radio report about port movements in Plymouth which was worth very much more than this ten-page story which had arrived in secret writing via Portugal.'[23]

The second spy mentioned by Ledebur was one he had learned about from Heinz Engelhorn at Zossen on 5 June 1944.

> Engelhorn told him that the most valuable reports on England for the past six months had been received from Kuhlenthal of KO Spanien, who had a 'most valuable agent in the UK.'[24]

According to another Abwehr officer, von Bohlen of I/H West, 'the agent was a Yugoslav with very good connections, but he declared that the Allied invasion must be imminent, as the reports from the agent during the last few weeks had stated that the landing operations had reached a stage that one could already call them the prelude to the coming sea-invasion'. However, another officer, I/M's Kapitän Humpert

> said that they were suspicious of the source of Kuhlenthal's information was much contested. He could only say that the agent was an active diplomat of the Yugoslavian Government, working in London but going regularly each quarter of the year to Lisbon and Madrid; he was a most expensive agent, 'costing £400 every month already for two years'.[25]

The day after D-Day, Ledebur was in hospital in Vienna undergoing a minor medical procedure and 'decided that he could safely desert to the Allies'. On 21 July he left Paris for Hendaye and crossed into Spain without difficulty, lodged with a friend, checking in with von Rohrscheidt at the KOS where he received orders to fly back to Berlin immediately. Meanwhile, Pinci had 'prepared the way' for a meeting with the British and arranged a rendezvous in the Calle Valdivia at which 'preliminary talks began'.[26]

As he procrastinated over his summons to Berlin, Ledebur received further instructions to catch a flight on 7 August, and was called in to the embassy by von Rohrscheidt to confirm his travel plans, which he did. However, 'shortly after the encounter, Ledebur left [his] house and was taken by the British into hiding, when he learned that the Gestapo and the Spanish police were already on his track. After several weeks' isolation in Madrid, Ledebur was finally transferred to the UK via Gibraltar on 17 November.

* * *

In June 1946 Kim Philby explained SIS's relationship with Otto John in answer to a routine query from MI5:

> Between 1942 and 1944 John was in touch with a contact of ours in Madrid and claimed to be a representative of the opposition groups. He also made contact with the Americans and asked to be put in touch with Dr Brunning, He returned to Germany on the eve of the attempt on Hitler's life and was in Berlin at the time that his colleagues were being arrested. However he managed to return to Madrid by the 24th July and reported to our representative on the attempted putsch.
>
> As a result of the 20th July plot John was immediately suspect to the Germans and believing his life to be in danger, he succeeded in escaping to Gibraltar whence he was evacuated to England by the British authorities.[27]

When John was brought to England in November 1944, MI5's Herbert Hart alerted the LRC to his imminent arrival, explaining that John 'has been an SIS agent for two years and whom the Germans are hotly pursuing on the footing that he was a party to the attempt on Hitler's life on July 20th'.[28] When John landed at Poole, with a British emergency travel certificate identifying him as 'John Collinson', he was taken straight to London to undergo a routine security screening, as agreed between SIS's Tim Milne and, with some reluctance, Guy Liddell. The latter's hesitancy was a consequence of SIS's reticence in acknowledging John's role as an SIS agent, but when this was revealed, MI5 immediately acknowledged the need for his resettlement, if not a commitment to a lifelong pension.

The key figure in the conspiracy, which centred around Carl Goerdeler, the former mayor of Leipzig, and Generals Beck and Olbricht, and the former ambassador to Rome, Ulrich von Hassell, was Hansen. A Wehrmacht officer who had joined the Abwehr in 1937, Hansen succeeded Hans Pieckenbrock as chief of Amt. I in 1943, and then was appointed Canaris's replacement in February 1944. By then he had already made one unsuccessful attempt on Hitler's life, with a bomb placed on the Führer's Condor aircraft in March 1943 on a flight from Smolensk to Rastenburg supported by a group of conspirators which included Otto John, Ludwig Gehre and Fabian von Schlabrendorff.

Hansen had made the final arrangements for the putsch, acquiring the explosives from Captain Herzmer, and moving the Abwehr's entire headquarters in the first four days of July 1944 from Zossen 15km to the Schloss Baruth, codenamed BELINDE. The first attempt was planned for Thursday, 15 July at the Führer HQ at Obersalzburg, but was abandoned when Heinrich Himmler failed to attend the planning conference where a bomb was to be detonated. The plotters, Hansen, Theodor Struenk and Stauffenberg, held a final meeting on 17 July at Struenk's home, when a new bomb, supplied by Abt. II which for years had accumulated enemy materiel, such as explosives, detonators and time-pencils, for use by Brandenburg Regiment saboteurs. The objective, for example in Spain and Portugal, was to stockpile these items so, if used, the blame would be misdirected. Accordingly, Colonel Heinz of the Construction and Training Company possessed a ready supply of bomb-making equipment that could be easily traced back to Allied sources, and one of his subordinates, Herzner, delivered samples to Hansen, despite not being a member of Abt. II, on the authority of Lahousen's deputy, Erwin Stolze, and Wolfgang Abshagen.

General Lahousen, the sceptic who had the good fortune to be transferred to the Russian Front in November 1943, later recalled a meeting attended by Oster and Herzner at which the subject of training the chosen assassin was raised:

> There ensued now a lengthier debate, during the course of which I made known that it would be very difficult for me – without taking in an extra person to get at the required explosives and the fuses and that it would be equally difficult to familiarise the perpetrators with the functioning of the fuses; since 1 myself understood nothing of that sort of thing.. and I didn't in the Abteilung know of anyone with whom I could discuss this subject . . . But perhaps he (Oster) could work the person in question into my Abteilung in such a way that, very unostentatiously – hence best as an agent he might by a simple course of instruction come to learn the handling of time-clock fuses.[29]

Although anti-Nazi, Lahousen knew from personal experience the ruthless nature of the SD as his brother-in-law was still serving a prison sentence for high treason. In short, he had little confidence in the conspirators or of their ability to pull off the coup.

The attack was postponed until Wednesday, 19 July, when Stauffenberg flew from the Rangsdorf aerodrome with his aide Werner von Haeften and the bomb to Rastenburg, but at the last moment Hitler cancelled the usual midday situation conference. On Thursday, 20 July von Stauffenberg made a further attempt, and half the bomb detonated, but failed to kill its principal target.

As the putsch got underway, the codeword VALKYRIE was circulated to signal the mobilisation of the Reserve Army, and the Schloss Baruth was sealed off under orders from Berlin given by Hansen's deputy

Wilhelm Kubert to Horst Engelhorn who isolated BELINDE. The senior officer present, Gunther Naumann zu Königsbrück, armed with a machine-pistol, ordered the arrest of the SD's Witzel, but at midnight, when Hitler made his radio broadcast, Engelhorn promptly declared his loyalty to the Führer and the emergency measures at Baruth were cancelled, allowing the SD's Major Dr Loos to take control of the compound.

The existence of BELINDE as an alternative command site to Zossen, which appeared in ISOS as ZEPPELIN, was known to Allied analysts although its exact location remained a mystery until Peter Schagen disclosed it in October 1944.[30] While Otto John knew of BELINDE's existence, he had never been there, and on the day of the putsch had telephoned Zossen for news, not realising the Abwehr's headquarters had relocated. The main building was then owned and still part lived in by Prince Friedrich Hermann zu Solms-Baruth, the Prussian noble who had inherited the title of Fürst at the age of 34 upon the death of his 67-year-old father in December 1920.

Baruth had been the family's ancestral home for some 500 years, and the main house had been expanded over the centuries in four sections totalling forty-five rooms and a hall, with the family living in the oldest part which was separated from the main house, connected only by a long passage on stilts. This semi-detached building contained the kitchen, administrative offices, Friedrich's private study, the dining room and a guest wing at the very back, which was occupied by BELINDE, camouflaged as an officers' mess. This part of the property was accessed by a separate entrance, out of sight from the courtyard, and Abwehr personnel travelled to the compound either by a special daily bus for commuters from Berlin, or by rail using Prince Friedrich's private station located a few hundred metres from the edge of the large park, discreetly covered by a densely tree-lined avenue, in an estate amounting to 40,000 acres.

While the Abwehr was in occupation Friedrich also remained in residence, together with his wife, Adelheid, his son Friedrich Wilhelm, youngest daughter Caroline Mathilda, and his second-oldest daughter, Feodora, and they retained a small staff to run the house and the estate. Prince Friedrich, who had been born at his family's other estate, Klitschdorf Castle in Silesia, would eventually be forced to accept the confiscation by the Gestapo's Willie Bruhn, acting on direct written orders from Heinrich Himmler, of all his property, amounting to some 40,000 hectares of land, in exchange for his life and those of his family.[31]

The Schloss Baruth would emerge as the epicentre of the 20 July plot, for as an Abwehr base it was a fully secure site, conveniently close to

Friedrich Baumeister, alias Colonel Rudolf, the head of Alst Paris and legendary intelligence professional who had run espionage operations in England before the war.

Hermann Giskes, the Abwehr counter-intelligence expert who had been wounded and taken prisoner in the First World War. Having rejoined the army in 1938 from his father's tobacco business, he was posted to Alst Paris before being transferred in November 1941 to the Netherlands where he masterminded the NORDPOL manipulation of SOE's radio networks. During his post-war interrogation at Camp 020 he was fully cooperative.

Heinrich Schubert. A dual national born in London but brought up in Germany, he was an important I/M recruiter attached to the KO Portugal in Lisbon where he specialised in recruiting agents destined for England.

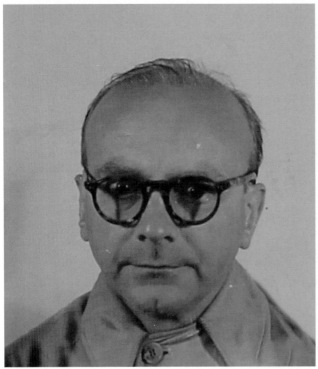

Gerhard Huntemann. The head of Abweher Truppe 367, Huntemann ran NORDPOL which gave the Germans almost complete control over the Dutch resistance organisation. Arrested after the war, he was cross-examined for three months at Camp 020 from June 1945. His interrogation reports made for uncomfortable reading at SOE, and their distribution was restricted to prevent circulation to Americans and French intelligence personnel.

VI/1	II/1206	
VI/2	II/13	**PFEIFFER, Freg. Kapt. Dr. Erich**
Old VI	II/26	@ WEKIL
II/360	XIV/28	@ CHEF GANZ : PETERSEN
II/8	II/56	
5B/678/OS	II/1A	
II/355	II/506	Born 1897 Altenkirchen.
II/120	II/57	CX.12799/592
N.2.	II/38	Passport No.871/43
II/3	II/1027	
II/351	XIV/6	1). Leiter Brest.
II/309	II/1026	2). Leiter III Paris.
II/380	II/523	3). Deputy Abt. Chef. I.M.
II/7	VII/89	(Berlin) 12.5.43.
XIV/39	XIV/100	4). Leiter KONO (12.5.44.)
II/56	5b/678/DEG	
N.1.	II/522	
II/141	II/511	
II/120	I/163	
II/1053	II/125	
II/347	II/310	
II/536	N.15	
XIV/105		

17.5.40. 0001	Message to Einsatz Kommando PFEIFFER from ABW. I.N.WEST. Re port security posts in Holland.
19.5.40. 0011	For Einsatzkommando PFEIFFER of Berlin ABW. I.M. WEST :- Is requested to be at German Embassy The HAGUE, on 20.5.40. for consultation with the Chief (CANARIS). The Chief and Chief of III (B ENTEBEGNI) with four other officers arriving at The HAGUE on 20.5.40. Is informed that suspect lists of FRANCE being passed on by Ast Wiesbaden to the Ic. A.O. of IV Army.
26.5.40. 0002	Is instructed that material forwarded should be checked before distributing for local Naval posts. Important material to go direct to the appropriate quarters, notifying ABW. I.M. FUNKER (W/T operator), ready to set out. In event of no decision to the contrary, will start 28/5.
27.5.40. 0037	For Einsatzkommando PFEIFFER:- Message from WICHMANN re wireless operator. Requests PFEIFFER to address to him (WICHMANN) personally all requirements concerning personnel and material for forwarding to Nest.
30.5.40. 0005	To Ast HAMBURG :- Ref. settling of route, Kptlt. CONRAD requests to await the return of PFEIFFER
4.6.40. 0006	To ABW.I. for I.M. PFEIFFER (Rotterdam) asks for an officer skilled in accountancy as Ast BELGIUM and HOLLAND cannot work with Einsatz-kommando in financial matters. Requests that independant management of accounts be arranged as long as the Einsatzkommando as acting as such.
4.6.40. 0007	To ABW.I. Reports all means of communication in Occupied FRANCE interrupted and N. lines (passage corrupt) and coast over loaded owing to own W/T messages of Coast Command. Asks for another AFU apparatus and 2 W/T.
10.6.40. 651	PFEIFFER, KRUMBHOLZ, SCHUCHMANN, UTHE at DUNKIRK. DIERKS at BRUSSELS for consultation.
15.6.40. 0016	To OKW. ABW. I.M. GF. PFEIFFER reports Kommissar FENDT interrogated 5 French Captains at DUNKIRK regarding their last voyages.
15.6.40. 0016	PFEIFFER, KRUMBHOLZ, SCHUCHMANN at LE HAVRE. UTHE...Boulogne. DIERKS....Antwerp. CONRAD...Rotterdam. WREDE....Amsterdam.
16.6.40. 0047	Forward to AMSTERDAM & ANTWERP. Following new arrangements:- PFEIFFER - to maintain traffic with M.K. CONRAD - ANTWERP as I.M. BELGIUM. DIERKS - from ANTWERP to BOULOGNE. ANZINGER - BOULOGNE. "AN ZINGER to bring our luggage from ROTTERDAM to BOULOGNE". Sgd. PFEIFFER. 7 men for Einsatzkommando being sent from WILHELMSHAVEN via COLOGNE - to be sent to BOULOGNE, Rue du Tetre.
16.6.40. 0017	To ABW. I.M. LILLE:- "Clerical staff of Einsatzkommando hitherto working ROTTERDAM will have to be given over to Ast LILLE for time being but to remain at disposal of E.Kdo., till E.Kdo. has found permanent place of work". Sgd. PFEIFFER.
17.6.40. 0018.	Einsatzkommando disbanded. Clerical staff to LILLE. Rest of office personnel with W/T operators will go to BOULOGNE tomorrow. Sgd. CONRAD.
24.6.40. 0019	PFEIFFER reports to OKW. ABW. I.M. that Liaison with A.O.K.4 and Heeresgruppe 3 established today by telephone. Reinforcements from

cont. over.

The first page of Erich Pfeiffer's ISOS file which amounted to sixteen pages, and logged his signal traffic from May 1940 to March 1945. This resource proved invaluable when he was interrogated post-war at Camp 020, and was typical of the dossiers developed by the comprehensive monitoring of Abwehr communications.

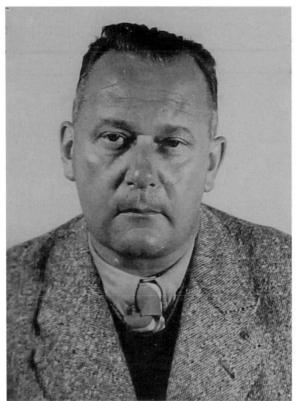

Erich Pfeiffer. The senior Abwehr I/M officer in Bremen before the war, where he ran several espionage networks in the United States, having recruited numerous crew members of transatlantic liners to act as couriers. In 1940 he was posted to Brest in occupied France, and then was promoted to head the KO in Istanbul.

Walter Simon. Arrested in England in March 1938 while on an espionage mission, Simon was later delivered by *U-38* in June 1940 to Ireland where he was interned. During his detention Simon believed he had opened a covert channel of communication with Berlin for his fellow prisoners through the German legation in Dublin, whereas in reality the correspondence was part of an elaborate deception stage-managed by the Irish G-2 intelligence service, acting in tandem with MI5.

Josef Ledebur. An Abwehr officer who defected to SIS in Madrid in August 1944, Ledebur was on the fringes of the 20 July plot to assassinate Hitler, but not entirely trusted by the other conspirators. A major complication materialised when Ledebur offered, as the price for his desertion, to expose the Abwehr's star spy in London, MI5's GARBO.

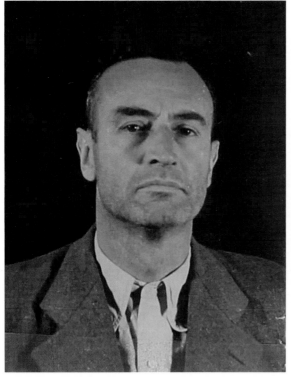

Otto Mayer. An Abwehr officer captured in November 1943 by partisans during an ambush in Dalmatia, Meyer was treated for his wounds in Brindisi and then brought to England for interrogation. His enthusiastic cooperation was motivated by his fear that he would be returned to Yugoslavia to face unspecified charges of war crimes.

Wilhelm Kuebart. One of the Abwehr's most senior 20 July conspirators, Kuebart was arrested by the Gestapo the day after the putsch failed. However, he resisted his interrogators and was absolved of any participation by Georg Hansen. He was acquitted at his trial on charges of treason but was dismissed from the Abwehr. After the war he was brought to Camp 020 to be questioned by MI5.

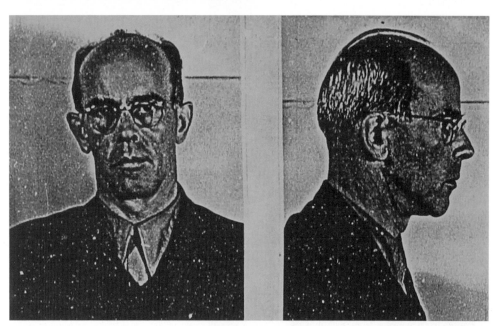

Thomas Ludwig. Codenamed ALADDIN, Ludwig was the Abwehr IIIF officer with a formidable reputation promoted to head the Istanbul KO following a series of damaging staff defections in 1944. A professed anti-Nazi, he had been posted to Turkey in April 1941. In May 1945 he was taken off the SS *Drottingholm* when the Swedish liner docked at Liverpool, while being repatriated to Germany and underwent a lengthy interrogation at Camp 020. Having previously served in Belgrade, Ludwig proved to be exceptionally well informed about Abwehr operations across the Balkans.

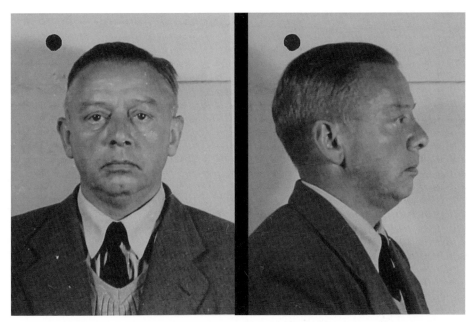

Friedrich Wolf. Germany's military adviser to the Argentine army since 1937, Wolf took on an intelligence role when he was appointed to Santiago in July 1940. In July 1943 he transferred by the SD to Buenos Aires to direct all the networks across South America. He was interrogated at Camp 020 from May to October 1945.

Friedrich Wolf's 28-year-old mistress, Adriana Barahona, whom he had met while serving as military attaché in Santiago before the war. She shared the apartment in Buenos Aires with Ernestina Arias, who was conducting an affair with the Japanese military attaché, Colonel Toshikazu Suzuki.

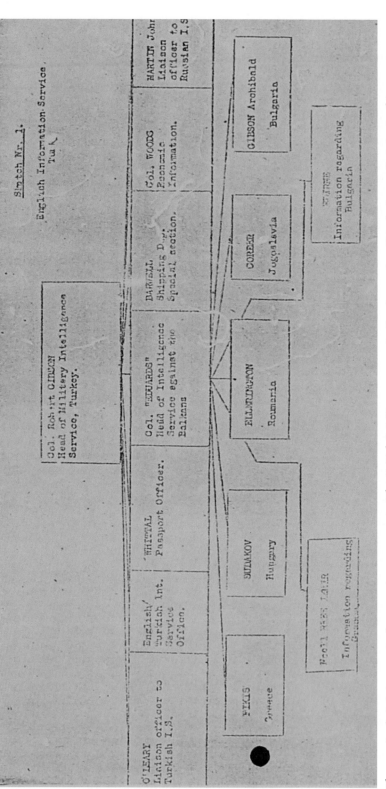

Thomas Ludwig's impressively accurate assessment of the British Intelligence organisation in wartime Istanbul, supplied during his interrogation at Camp 020 in August 1945.

Kuno Weltzien. An energetic and aggressive recruiter on the Lisbon docks, Weltzien operated under the commercial cover of his family business and rarely visited the KO Portugal. He was particularly adept at mounting operations designed to embarrass the local SIS station.

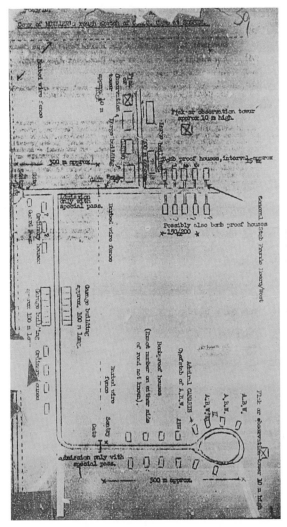

Zossen, as sketched by Gottfried Müller in August 1943. Codenamed ZEPPELIN, the site was located in a dense pine forest 40km south of the OKW's former headquarters in central Berlin.

Prince Friedrich Solms-Baruth, the German nobleman whose home, the Schloss Baruth, became the epicentre of the 20 July plot to assassinate Hitler. He provided cover for the conspirators to plan the attack and to install a constitutional monarchy. In the aftermath of the failed putsch Solms-Baruth was imprisoned and his lands were confiscated by Heinrich Himmler.

The Schloss Baruth, south of Berlin, which became the Abwehr's secret headquarters after key elements were evacuated from Zossen in November 1943. The estate was codenamed BELINDE and provided accommodation for the Mil Amt while some of the Solms-Baruth family remained in residence. During the attempted putsch senior Abwehr officers sealed off the building and arrested the SD component.

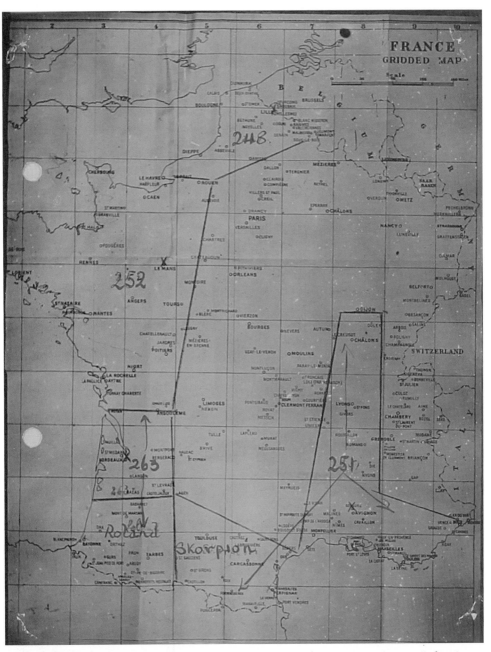

An Abwehr map marked with the locations of weapons caches prepared for stay-behind sabotage organisation following D-Day, as betrayed by Peter Schagen, an Abwehr II officer brought to London for interrogation.

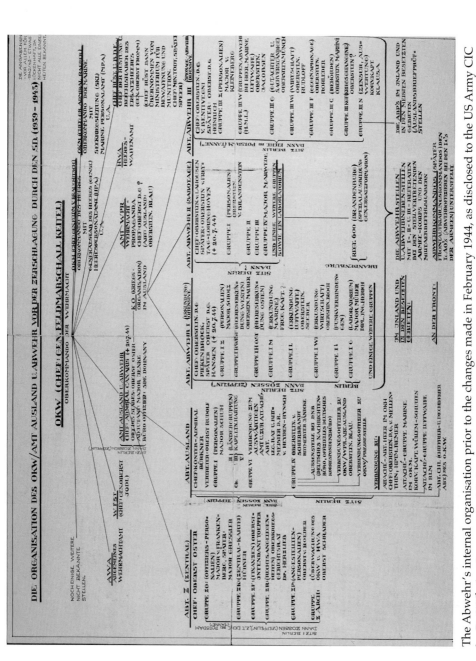

The Abwehr's internal organisation prior to the changes made in February 1944, as disclosed to the US Army CIC by Dr Wilhelm Grosse at Bad Sulza.

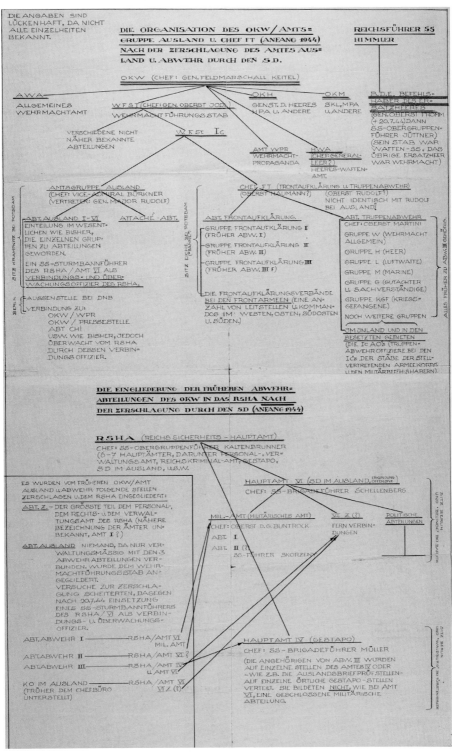

The Abwehr's internal organisation following the changes made in February 1944, as disclosed to the US Army CIC by Dr Wilhelm Grosse at Bad Sulza.

Otto John. Codenamed WHISKY by SIS when he was recruited in Madrid in September 1942, John was a Lufthansa lawyer who acted as an emissary for the Abwehr's Georg Hansen. John used his genuine credentials to fly to Spain after the failed 20 July putsch, and defected to the British. His clandestine role only emerged when SIS was obliged to reveal it to MI5 after his arrival in London.

General Anton Turkul, the White Russian officer who worked closely with the Abwehr's Richard Kauder at the KO Sofia and appeared to have access to several spy-rings reporting from behind the Soviet lines. The intercepted wireless traffic, designated MAX and MORITZ, would be scrutinised for years in the hope of determining whether the material was genuine, or evidence of a complex deception campaign supervised by Moscow. Turkul died in Munich in 1958, the mystery of his sources unsolved.

Colonel Georg Hansen. The Chief of Abwehr Abt. II, codenamed BRIZO SENIOR, Hansen was the principal conspirator and coordinator of the 20 July plot to assassinate Hitler. When arrested, he admitted his role but cleared his colleague Wilhelm Kuebart, thus saving his life. Unfortunately his indiscreet diaries served to implicate his chief, Admiral Canaris. This photograph, taken in 1940, shows Hansen with the rank of major.

Albert Meems. After the war MI5 researched Abwehr espionage operations that had been directed by Ast Hamburg and discovered that Albert Meems, a well-known dealer an exotic animals, had been a long-term agent who had frequently visited England, India and the United States. His wartime missions had been undetected and unsuspected. Born in Holland, Meems was arrested in Berlin in 1945 but acquitted in The Hague in 1949 of charges of collaboration.

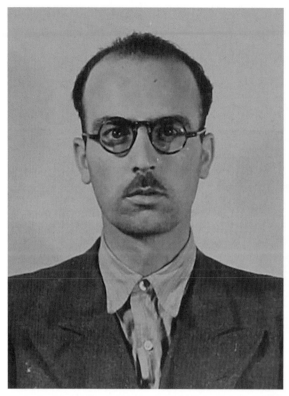

Hans Scharf. ISOS traces of DOEHRER from November 1941 revealed Scharf to be an Abwehr II V-Mann and wireless operator on a mission from Paris to Spain and South Africa. Captured in December 1944 in Algeria, he was interrogated at Camp 020 from July 1944 and then transferred to the French authorities. In 1939 he had been sentenced to life imprisonment for espionage, but had been liberated by the German invasion in 1940. Fluent in English, French, Spanish and German, he had been born to German parents in Lorraine and when questioned pretended he had not joined the Abwehr until 1940.

Peter Schagen, an Abwehr II officer who defected to the American embassy in Madrid in September 1944, accompanied by his 23-year-old French girlfriend, Janette Bertremieux. The following month he was taken to London for interrrogation where his true motives were revealed.

Berlin and to the Rangsdorf aerodrome, yet Prince Friedrich remained in the property and could gather his fellow conspirators together, sometimes for meetings on horseback in the park, with complete confidence and no danger of eavesdroppers. Among the aristocratic visitors to the schloss were those in the circle around General Ludwig von Beck, including Field Marshal Erwin von Witzleben, Generals Paul von Hase and Friedrich Fromm, Count Heinrich von Lehndorff-Steinart, Count Wilhem zu Lynar, Count von der Schulenburg, Carl-Hans Graf von Hardenberg, and the Prince's family lawyer Fabian von Schlabrendorff. These horseback conferences, conducted in the very extensive wooded grounds surrounding the schloss were given the appearance of entirely innocent social events by the inclusion of two of the Prince's children who were instructed to remain in the rear at a safe distance, just out of earshot.

Although the Gestapo never found any direct proof of his complicity, Prince Friedrich was arrested on 21 July and taken to the PrinzAlbrecht-strassee headquarters before being incarcerated in the Lehrterstrasse prison. On that day, immediately following the failure of the putsch, the SD and the Gestapo initiated a purge which resulted in the arrest of Hansen, who confessed his involvement in the plot, and Kuebart, who resisted his interrogators and was released from the Wilhelmstrasse dungeons 14 days later and transferred to the Lehrstrasse prison where he was detained until 17 September.[31] Among the other Abwehr prisoners he encountered in the prison were Engelhorn, Struenck, Alexis von Roenne and Graf von Schrader. Later, when Kuebart was questioned about these events at Camp 020, he acknowledged that his life had probably been saved by Hansen who had 'absolved him of all guilty knowledge of the plot'. At his trial, held in October, Kuebart was acquitted on charges of treason but dishonourably discharged from the Wehrmacht.[32]

The task of investigating the putsch fell to Horst Kopkow of Amt IV a 2 who had run the Sonderkommando Rote Kepelle so successfully. When he was interrogated in May 1945 at Bad Nenndorf Kopkow deliberately distanced himself from 'the political side of the matter' but described how, as a professional criminal investigator, he had visited the remains of Hitler's conference room on the same evening, and quickly determined the British origins of 'the English time-pencils' and the explosives. 'Altogether the explosives and fuses were obtained three different times since the autumn of 1943; twice from OKW stores (Amt Ausland – Abwehr II) and once from Engineer Park stores on the Eastern Front.'[33]

Because of the very widespread purge conducted in the aftermath of the failed putsch, and the savagely ruthless tactics adopted by Hitler's loyalists, what remained of the Abwehr's senior management was thrown into chaos, at the very moment, during the height of the Battle of Normandy, that the Wehrmacht should have been responding to the still-uncertain Allied advance. What effectively became the decapitation of the German intelligence machine, combined by an exacerbation of the hostility of the SD, served to distract the two rival cohorts of intelligence professionals and crucially undermine morale to the point where actual desertion replaced discreet defeatism among those senior officers with an informed view of the conflict.

Chapter V

MORE DEFECTORS

Turkey and the Turks have played a part which should not be underestimated in making the enemy's task of spying on the Middle East more difficult.

Guy Liddell, 24 September 1944

Whereas well-informed defectors are usually regarded in the intelligence business as a high value commodity, an extraordinary situation arose during the Second World War which militated against the Allies embracing, or even giving any encouragement to, line-crossers. Indeed, after the events of November 1939 when two British SIS officers had been abducted by the Sicherheitsdienst (SD) at Venlo, any direct encounter with the enemy was considered too dangerous and most probably a staged provocation. Since contact was likely to occur in neutral territory where the Allies were already at a disadvantage in a largely hostile security environment, an approach was regarded as potentially hazardous for all concerned. In addition, there was the powerful disincentive in the knowledge that there was a good chance that information offered in return for asylum might be embarrassingly counter-productive, especially if a putative deserter was in a position to compromise delicate operations involving agents already under control.

These circumstances would change in January 1944 with the acquisition of PRECIOUS, a senior I/H officer in the Istanbul KO. Dr Erich Vermehren, born in Lubeck in December 1919, was the son of a well-connected Hamburg lawyer whose wife was a correspondent for *Das Reich*.[1] After graduating with a law degree, his refusal to join the Hitler Youth movement had prevented him from taking up a Rhodes Scholarship at Oxford, and in 1939 he converted to Roman Catholicism after meeting his future wife, the Grafin Elisabeth von Plettenberg, an anti-Nazi activist six years his senior, who had been imprisoned briefly by the Gestapo for distributing subversive religious literature.

In late 1942, despite an exemption from military service because of a childhood injury, and thanks to the influence of his diplomat cousin, Adam von Trott, Vermehren joined the Abwehr and worked as an interpreter at Oflag VIB, a camp for British officer PoWs at Dossel. His transfer to Turkey came at the request of his father's friend Paul Leverkuehn, and he arrived in Istanbul in December 1942, ostensibly to negotiate the release of fifty Societé Francais de Navigation Danubienne tugs which, French-built and destined for use on the Danube, had been interned by the Turkish authorities. In reality, Vermehren was assisting in the management of KONO agents active in Iran and Iraq.

In the summer of 1942 Vermehren's request for permission to have his wife join him was refused by Berlin, as appeared in an ISOS text from Admiral Canaris addressed to Leverkuehn on 22 September 1943:

Ref letter KONO No 4/9/43 Secret of 1/9/43, Amtschef [Canaris] has rejected Vermehren's application for his wife to enter the country, bearing in mind the state of leave on the front.[2]

Undeterred, Vermehren had made another application while on home leave in November 1943 and obtained a passport for her through the intervention of Monsignor Angelo Roncalli, the Papal Nuncio in Istanbul. Then, following influence exercised by a family friend, Adolf Marschall von Bieberstein, she travelled to Sofia where she initially was refused an onward air passage to Turkey. However, on Christmas Day 1943 she completed her journey, despite Leverkuehn's disapproval, and was granted two weeks' sick leave by the ambassador, Franz von Papen, who happened to be her cousin. In January Vermehren approached the British assistant military attaché who put him in touch with Section V's Nicholas Elliott, and the two men met for the first time on Monday, 18 January.

Three days later, on Thursday, 21 January, Vermehren reported to his office that he was ill and would not return on Monday, also that he was moving to a new address in Istanbul. When he did not appear at his office on Monday, a messenger was sent to the new address, which could not be found with the aid of a deliberately misleading map supplied by Vermehren. Six days later, from the safety of Cairo, a jubilant SIS issued its first assessment, entitled *The German Secret Service in Turkey*:

1. A well placed and reliable source whose previous information has been substantiated by our records, has produced the following information on the organisation and personalities of the Abwehr station known as Kriegsorganisation Nahe Osten, the headquarters of which are situated in the German Embassy building in Istanbul. This organisation is usually known in Abwehr circles by the short title 'KO NO'.

2. The Dienstellenleiter Hptm Dr Paul Leverkuehn, who succeeded Major Shulze-Bennett, is responsible for coordinating the activities of the various Abwehr sections in KO NO and maintaining general supervision over them.

3. The staff directly under the control of Dr Leverkuehn consists of two sections known as the Aussendienst which might perhaps be described as an administrative section. The Aussendienst consists of Abw. I Heer officers and the Leiter I/H is Leverkuehn's deputy.

4. The other sections of KO NO, the Abw. I. Marine, Abw. I. Luft, Verwaltung, Abw. III and Abw. II, whilst under the general supervision and coordination of the Dienstellenleiter enjoy a very large measure of autonomy and receive their instructions direct to their own headquarter sections in the Abwehr Amt., and also render their reports direct to their own headquarter sections, only passing a copy to Leverkuehn for his information and not necessarily his approval.

5. W/T traffic between KO NO and the OKW is passed by the W/T station in the German Embassy building in Istanbul; the staff of which are under the command, for discipline and administration, of Vice Admiral von der Marwitz whose office is also situated in that building. All incoming and outgoing messages are decoded and encoded by the W/T staff and all messages are handled by the Naval Attaché's office which passes the enclair texts by special office servants (and not by consular officials) to the KO NO. OKW messages which include Abwehr messages are encoded by a special procedure. Messages for the Consulate General, however, are sent in the normal foreign office code which is kept in the safe of the Chancellor.

6. It is the general policy of the Abwehr to appoint the Leiters I/H, I/M, I/Luft to the posts of Assistant Military Attaché, Assistant Naval Attaché and Assistant Air Attaché, respectively. Source has produced a chart shown in Appendix 'D' which is largely self-explanatory. The German Foreign Office naturally provided the staff (diplomatic) for their Embassy in Ankara, Consulate General in Istanbul and various consulates in Turkey. The Attaché Department of the OKW naturally provided the service attachés who have their main offices in the Embassy in Ankara with the exception of the Naval Attaché whose office is situated in Istanbul. The Abwehr appoint officers for the I/H, I/M, and I/Luft to their respective attaché departments under which cover they work. In the case of Turkey the Abw. II representative works

under the cover of the 'Regierungs Rat'. The Abw. III representative works in Istanbul under the cover of 'Konsulats Sekretaer'.

7. Under the control of the Dienstellenleiter there are aussenstellen at Izmir, Ankara, Adana, Iskendeun and Trabzon, for details of which see Appendix 'C'.

8. Source states that the KO NO has the strictest instructions not on any account to engage in espionage against Turkey and that even if sources should offer them information on the Turkish armed forces they should refuse to handle it. Source adds that KO Bulgaria is responsible for espionage against Turkey and as far as the source is aware none of the KO NO representatives in Turkey hold German diplomatic cover.

9. At Appendix 'E' is attached a list of cover names supplied by the source and used by KO NO, Aussenstellen, and officers and at Appendix 'F' is a further list of various Abwehr cover names.[3]

Attached to this summary were four pages of diagrams created by Vermehren to illustrate the KONO's internal structure and its links to Berlin. The other appendices included some forty cover-names which, when delivered to the RSS cryptanalysts, opened up the accumulated and current ISOS traffic by identifying each individual referred to. He also listed five Abwehr officers active outside the KONO, headed by Willi Hamburger.

On 27 January, the same day that SIS circulated its first interrogation report based on an initial round of interviews with Vermehren, the III/F representative, Thomas Ludwig learned from an MIT (Turkish Intelligence Service) contact that Leverkuehn's subordinate had defected to the British, accompanied by his wife. He immediately reported the incident to Berlin and repeated that, as he had warned previously, he had grave suspicions about the loyalty and intentions of another Abwehr staff member, Willi Hamburger. Ludwig's cable resulted in the arrival of Hans Milo Freund from Berlin who spent two weeks investigating the circumstances of Vermehren's defection, and the subsequent disappearance of both Hamburger and two other III/F agents, Karl and Stella von Kleczkowski. While KONO was in the midst of this crisis, Ludwig Moyzisch's former secretary, Cornelia Kapp, whose father was a German diplomat, defected to the Americans in Ankara. Consequently, Leverkuehn was recalled to Berlin and replaced temporarily by Admiral von der Marwitz before the SD took over. In the Gestapo complaint against Leverkuehn he was accused of

having created an Anglo-Saxon atmosphere at the KO, giving too much freedom to his people to make uncontrolled contact with the enemy, and having strong homosexual tendencies.[4]

MI5 was unsure of Leverkuehn's fate, as there were rumours that 'he had been shot in Germany. Also reported to have been sent to the front as an ordinary soldier or appointed to an insignificant post at Dueberitz.'[5] However, according to Robert von Tarbuk of Amt V1/Z, who was arrested in Zweisel and interrogated by the US Third Army CIC in July 1945, 'Leverkuehn was cleared of suspicion' by Freund who 'later boasted that he had been able to effect Kolchevsky's arrest by convincing British Intelligence that he was still a German agent'.

Naturally Berlin was stunned by these events and in May 1944 Erich Pfeiffer was appointed to head KONO. Pfeiffer, of course, was a seasoned Abwehr officer whose naval career had begun as a gunnery officer on the battleship *König* at Jutland.[6] At the time, he was engaged in negotiating with the Reich Foreign Ministry about Abwehr representation at the embassy in Ankara, having more recently conducted the investigation of Osmar Hellmuth's arrest in Trinidad, which had been blamed on the Abwehr by the SD, and promoted to Georg Hansen's deputy at Amt. I.[7] In November 1943 he had conducted a brief four-day inspection tour of KONO at Hansen's request, because of concerns about Leverkuehn's leadership style. On that occasion

> he had set out from Zossen well primed with the results achieved in Turkey recently, and he impressed on Leverkuehn the need to apply himself exclusively to military intelligence work, pointing out also that he observed a certain lack of coordination in the work of the several sections. It appeared that only the I/H section took direct orders from Leverkuehn; I/M. I/L, II, III, and Vermultung enjoyed considerable independence and took their orders directly from headquarters. The few Aussenstellen worked in a haphazard fashion.[8]

Also summoned back were the KONO office manager, Leo von Koblensky, Gottfried Schenker-Augerer and Rosner. Even General Rohle was withdrawn briefly, for 'reorientation', before he was allowed to return to his attaché post in Ankara. According to the British-controlled double agent BLACKGUARD, who retained his access to KONO, the organisation was 'in pandemonium' with Kurt Zaehringer in particular apparently convinced that there was another traitor at large who had been responsible for the recent arrests of Fotuhi and KISS, threatening to exercise his own discipline and shoot Leverkuehn and Ludwig.

After lengthy interrogation Leverkuehn and Schenker-Angerer were dismissed from the Abwehr, Koblensky was posted to Denmark and Momm was returned to the Luftwaffe to serve in an anti-aircraft battery. Meanwhile, Vermehren was undergoing questioning by SIME professionals whose task was to extract maximum information from their prisoner without even hinting at their access to ISOS, or to knowledge gathered by the management of double agents. Any question or approach that might betray a degree of insight had to be attributed to another Abwehr prisoner, Otto Mayer, who had been wounded and captured by Partisans in an ambush near the Dalmatian coast in November 1943 and flown to Brindisi.[9] However, although the 40-year-old Mayer had undergone a preliminary interrogation by CSDIC in Bari, where a bullet was removed from a wound in his neck, he had not reached Camp 020, via Algiers and Prestwick, until *after* Vermehren had defected. It turned out that Mayer had also served in Istanbul, so information disclosed by Vermehren's interrogators gave the impression that they were seeking corroboration for his assertions, rather than material from infinitely more sensitive sources. Even better, the Abwehr (and Vermehren) were unaware of Mayer's exact fate, and had no idea he had been handed over to the British for questioning, thus setting the scene for a classic triangulation strategy, pitting Mayer against Vermehren and vice-versa. ISOS revealed that Ast Belgrade knew Mayer had been captured by Partisans, but planned to negotiate his release in a prisoner exchange, an event then not unusual in the Balkans.

In Mayer's case, the incentive to cooperate was his fear of being returned, as a British liaison officer had already agreed, to Tito's Partisans to face trial for unspecified war crimes, a fate he was understandably anxious to avoid. For Vermehren, the pressure came from an unwanted press statement released by Cairo declaring what purported to be his political motivation for opposing the Nazi regime. Both Abwehr officers were truly at the mercy of their hosts.

Based at Ast Belgrade as an I/H specialist in captured documents, Mayer had been posted to Istanbul for 14 months between May 1942 and July 1943 under commercial cover with the codename MURAT where he had run some agents with a colleague, Rudi Sterke. Originally from Karlsruhe, Mayer had fought as a subaltern with the 109th Infantry Regiment near Nancy in the First World War and later had emigrated to Yugoslavia, when the family's dairy farm was nationalised in 1935, to represent a pair of German refrigerator manufacturers, Stohrer AG and Suemax AG. Initially, when Mayer underwent questioning at Bari, and his full significance was not yet appreciated, he had not mentioned his involvement with KONO, and his interrogators had concentrated on what he had to say about the Abwehr's very considerable political links with the Chetniks loyal to Draza Mihailovic. While he was willing to discuss his duties for Major Lasser von Zollhaimb at I/H Ast Belgrade, and named the local Persian consul Abas Ali Khan as an agent, he avoided talking about his experiences in Turkey.

When asked about Mayer, Vermehren recalled his visits to Leverkuehn, and alleged that he had been withdrawn following his mismanagement of Abwehr funds. Mayer, on the other hand, claimed not to have heard of Vermehren until he reached Camp 020 where his name had been mentioned. Through their separate interlocutors Vermehren and Mayer each accused the other of lying, but the exercise served its purpose and encouraged both to disclose rather more than perhaps either had intended. Mayer gave up a detailed account of Ast Belgrade and Ast Zagreb, while Vermehren described KONO.

MI5 noted that 'an idea of the importance of Mayer's work in Turkey may be gathered from the considerable sums of money known to have been transmitted to him', concluding that Mayer was 'an obstinate liar' unconcerned about his future and reluctant to divulge much about his Turkish agents, one of whom was actually DOLEFUL who gave a rather different version of Mayer's active recruitments.[10]

During the summer of 1942, when Mayer had been staying at the Park Hotel in Istanbul, he had cultivated a fellow guest, a Yugoslav lawyer named Jankovic who was pro-German, with a German mother, and would become his talent-spotter constantly on the lookout for likely candidates. As Mayer eventually admitted:

I told him that I would be very interested to know what instructions the British had in relation to the Balkans and Turkey. I also told him that I would like to get news direct from Iraq and Syria and possibly Cairo of any preparations they might be making. Jankovic displayed great keenness and said that he was already in a position to do so and that he had contacts. I pointed out to him that a sleeping-car attendant would have great opportunities for seeing a lot on the way and, above, all, would be able to cross the frontiers in a proper fashion. Jankovic promised to let me know something in a short time. A few days later he visited me in the Park Hotel and said that he already knew someone who was going to Cairo. He then told me that he knew the courier of the Yugoslav consulate in Istanbul, Pesic, who he knew very well and was very much indebted to him because he had carried news to and from his wife in Belgrade. Pesic was ready to tell Jankovic, and Jankovic alone, what he had learnt in Cairo, if his wife in Belgrade received adequate financial aid so that she could live there in comfort and safety. I told him that that would present no difficulty at all.[11]

Accordingly, in April 1943 Mayer recruited Jankovic's nominee and supplied him with a questionnaire. Thereafter, his reports were forwarded to Belgrade, addressed to the Ast Belgrade leiter Colonel von Kohoutek, via the diplomatic pouch from the Istanbul consulate. Jankovic then introduced Mayer to AHMED, described as 'a sleeping-car attendant for the Wagon-lits who regularly travelled on the Baghdad and Tripoli routes'.

@AHMED explained that he travelled alternatively on the Istanbul – Baghdad route and the Istanbul – Ankara – Tripoli – Beirut route. Now and again he also travelled on the Turkish route Ankara – Izmir. I then asked him if he had opportunity on his journeys through Syria and Iraq to observe and report on conditions and changes in those countries. He immediately replied in the affirmative. He said he was a Turk and would never report anything, nor give away any secrets which concerned Turkey. But on the other hand he had no duty to any foreign power and what he saw and heard he could tell to someone else. As it was the cost of living had gone up in Turkey so much, while his pay had not gone up at all, that he had to try and improve his financial position. I asked him if he had already told anyone about his observations, to which he replied that he was answerable to no one, but if anybody asked him he would say no. I then asked him about his observations on his last journey. He gave some general but not very detailed information about the presence of English, Polish and Indian troops in Iraq. He said the Poles were being moved from a camp between Mosul and Baghdad (I have forgotten the name) which was very large and lay right beside the railway. He would find out their destination on his next trip. He had seen many American officers in Baghdad. Many supplies were moving by train from the Persian Gulf via Basra – Baghdad to Kirkuk and from there by road to Persia for the USSR. Near Mosul there was a large aerodrome on which there was heavy air traffic. There are always planes in the air there. I gave him to understand that these reports were all of such a general nature as to be of no use. I asked him to concentrate his observations onto actual details. Since he said that his next journey would take him via Tripoli – Beirut I gave him the same question I had already given Jankovic for Pesic.

(a) Repairs or improvements to railways or roads.
(b) Rail and road traffic north to south and south to north; movement of materiel and troops.
(c) Identification of troops on the ground or in transit. Special troop concentration areas, and whether there were any in the vicinity of the Turkish frontier.
(d) Shipping and supply movements in Tripoli and Beirut harbours.

(e) Conversations of officers, men or other persons, especially those about preparations for operations, intended landings, etc.

The reports were to be handed over personally by him on his return.[12]

Thus Mayer had unwittingly recruited DOLEFUL, a double agent run by SIME since November 1942. He had served in the Kaiser's army in 1918 and actually worked for the MIT which handed control over to the British. DOLEFUL, originally known as DOMINO, never reached his full potential, but eventually persuaded the Abwehr that he had successfully recruited Mosul's police chief as a spy.

According to his file maintained by SIME's B Section, DOLEFUL had been approached by Mayer on 4 January 1943, both men having been introduced by their real names, and tasked to find a radio operator in Syria to communicate with Belgrade. On his occasion Mayer had been insistent that the relationship should not be reported to KONO. Two days later Mayer asked him to recommend a Syrian to come to Istanbul for wireless training, and on 9 January gave him two letters for delivery to addresses in Beirut and Damascus. The first was for Sherif el Dabul, and the second was for Ziaeldine el Dardari, a retired army officer. At a further meeting on 20 February Mayer had reminded DOLEFUL of the need to find a wireless operator, and pressed the matter again on 15 May. Mayer, of course, could not be directly challenged about DOLEFUL without compromising his double agent role, but the episode demonstrated that Mayer was still seeking to protect his assets. He was also contradicted by ISOS messages which documented five of MURAT's missions to Istanbul and two examples demonstrated the pressure he was under to collect military information. On 20 January 1943 a text was transmitted from Sofia to KONO:

PANDORE [Sofia] to POLLUX [Leverkuehn] for MURAT [Mayer]. Photographic material urgently needed on fortifications, bridges, aerodromes, harbours, important road points and terrain in the Turkish THRACE area. 2. Check up on the reported concentration [corrupt] HADIMKOEY. 3. What is known about the reported setting-up of commandos in Turkey and landing exercises under English guidance. 4. What is known about the report building of roads and tracks near the frontier in THRACE. 5. It is said that the new HQs and troops have arrived in THRACE. Reconnaissance necessary.[13]

This intercept clearly showed MURAT's active involvement in espionage in 1943 while, a year later, he was insisting to his MI5 inquisitors that his visits to Turkey had been on refrigeration business exclusively. Furthermore, the message for MURAT had been sent via POLLUX which, according to Vermehren, was the Abwehr internal codename for Leverkuehn, the KONO chief. Another ISOS text, dated 28 April 1943, was quite specific about verification of intelligence, suggesting that Mayer was being deployed to double-check the validity of data already in the Abwehr's hands.

> Belgrade – Istanbul via Sofia. BERNHARD Leiter I to POLLUX [Leverkuehn] for MURAT [Mayer]. Confirmation necessary of: troop movements of Indian and Polish troops IRAQ-SYRIA-EGYPT; Allied troops SYRIA-EGYPT-TUNIS; troop movements [corrupt] DEIR ES ZUR –ALEPPO (heavy increase in W/T traffic between these two places); concentration of Greek troops in EGYPT and SYRIA; transfer of parts of the British 8th and 1st Armies from TUNISIA to the MIDDLE EAST; storage of equipment for leading or commando troops in Syrian, Palestinian and Cypriot harbours; USA transports from SYRIA and EGYPT to CYPRUS (air-landing or commando troops included); conference of senior officers of all arms of the service of Allied forces in the NEAR EAST also a representative of the Turkish armed forces on 27/4 in ALEPPO.[14]

Mayer's lengthy ISOS file disclosed that in the past he had appeared in the traffic as OSCAR and '264', but the central point was that he had consistently tried to play down his own status as a sonderführer in Yugoslavia and Turkey, unaware of the accumulated COMINT that contradicted him. The fact that he had held a meeting with Georg Hansen, the Abt. I chief, also suggested that Mayer was a big fish, and a rather better catch than he pretended.

While Mayer was gradually becoming more cooperative from the safety of Camp 020, where he remained until he was transferred to Diest in July 1945, Vermehren continued to haemorrhage KONO's most closely-held secrets, including details of German penetration of the US Office of War Information (OWI) in the person of Edgar Yolland, the 33-year-old son of Professor Arthur Yolland of Budapest's Royal University. A naturalised US citizen who had been a teacher at the American College, Yolland had been in touch with the Germans since at least January 1942 and had been handled by KONO's Helmuth Hohne and the SD's Georg Streiter, then under journalistic cover as the *Berlin Börsen-Zeitung* correspondent.

Vermehren's account of Yolland's espionage would be confirmed by his friend Willi Hamburger and several other sources. For example, when Willy Goetz was interviewed by SIME in November 1944 in Syria, he recalled his contacts with Yolland, and having received

> political information and also some military information on the Middle East (invasion losses, troop and ship concentrations in Tunis prior to the landing in the South of France, troop locations in the Middle East and India, etc.) Yolland apparently obtained his information by dint of pumping his many British and American acquaintances, and was especially successful in loosening the tongues of unwary Allied persons (e.g. the Rev. Hutchinson). Yolland's contacts in Turkey included Captain Eskenazi (who worked at a British W/T station in Istanbul), OWI officials, and the head of the Socony Vacuum Company.[15]

Although Yolland lost his access to the OWI premises in August 1943, he remained on the KONO payroll in receipt of a monthly retainer, as he acknowledged when he was interrogated by SIME in Syria in February 1945, having been expelled from Turkey. In a signed statement that amounted to a confession, Yolland admitted that he had received questionnaires from Kaydi, an attaché at the Hungarian embassy acting as an intermediary for Georg Streiter:

> He required information on the effects of V1 and V2 bombs in England and France; effect of the submarine warfare; tonnage losses, etc.; dates of convoys from American ports and types of ships and cargoes. I received several payments from Kaydi of sums varying from 300 – 500 Turkish Lira.[16]

As if to complete the circle, Yolland recalled his meetings with Vermehren, having been introduced by Streiter:

> From time to time he would ask me questions about persons I know in Istanbul, members of the OWI and their ideas and characters; and any news I received emanating from the Middle East. These questions I answered within my knowledge giving fictitious detail supplied from my imagination when I had no information. When Streiter went on leave I continued to contact his assistant Vermehren in Streiter's house. With him I discussed the possibilities of getting my relatives out of Hungary and it was Vermehren, during Streiter's absence, who first suggested directly that I could, with my contacts, supply information that would be of interest to them. During this period of Streiter's absence Vermehren gave me two questionnaires on which to endeavour to obtain information. One of these I answered on the spot. This was a questionnaire mainly dealing with American official and public reactions and sentiments. Some points that I can recollect are – American reaction

to British policy abroad, the labour situation and war effort in America, and American public sentiment toward the Polish question. The second questionnaire as far as I can remember dealt with figures of production and naval and air queries. I answered this questionnaire purely from my own imagination and made no effort to discover the correct answers from any source whatever. I was anxious to please them hoping that if satisfied they would help my family. I also supplied Vermehren with pictures, some of them unpublished, and news tips that I obtained from the OWI.

As well as acknowledging his links with Streiter and Vermehren, Yolland said that he had been coerced by the SD's Bruno Wolf who 'when he became aware of my background and family difficulties, began to put pressure on me to obtain him information'.

> He was particularly interested in the activities of Mr Earle, the US Naval Attaché at Istanbul. He wanted to know whether Earle was head of an organisation working against the Axis in the Balkans and whether he was contacting any Bulgarian, Rumanian or Greek nationals coming from Europe. I did not contact Earle or search for information on him and only gave haphazard replies to these queries.[17]

* * *

When Erich Pfeiffer arrived at Istanbul to take over KONO's management he undertook a survey of the staff and their assets, beginning with Kurt Zaehringer of I/M who was perceived to have failed in his attempts to run agents into the Caucasus, mainly because of early intervention by MIT, but nevertheless he enjoyed the approval of the naval attaché, Admiral von der Marwitz.

Zaehringer had always been one of KONO's key figures. His father had been an engineer on the Anatolian Railways and he had served as a petty officer in the First World War on the battlecruiser *Goeben*. Later he had fought with the Cossacks during the Russian Civil War. Although he had lived in Turkey for years and spoke the language fluently, Zaehringer's sole assets appeared to be a pair of Czech agents, codenamed MAHMOUD and SCHEMKET, and a Slav or Turk in Istanbul, whose reports were assessed as being 'so vague as to be practically useless'. Syria was covered by ARMEN 'which was probably an organisation rather than an individual'.[18] Pfeiffer suspected that ARMEN, which supplied information from the Lebanon too, was 'selling its wares indiscriminately to the Axis and to the Allies.'

Pfeiffer was especially unimpressed when he read a report referring to the arrival of a British cruiser in 'Cairo harbour'.[19]

Another I/M source was Mizra Khan, codenamed SHAROCK, who was a Persian linked to the Young Iranian Movement which published a weekly subversive anti-government pamphlet, and supplied political information, but offered no military intelligence.

Pfeiffer's audit of I/H was more encouraging. 'Walther Hinz had good links with Palestine, Iraq, Syria and Lebanon, the majority of the reports arriving in Istanbul through sleeping-car attendants and guards of the Taurus Express, among them three using the cover-names GOLD, SILBER and KUPFER. These men were controlled by Erich Lochner who also wrote up the reports from the various sources.'

> Other assistants of Hinz were Leutnant Helmuth Braun, whose main interest was in Iran, and Leutnant Robert Ulshofer who claimed to cover Persia, Iraq, Syria and Egypt. The latter, who had been a lecturer at Ankara University, had several agents, all of them trained by himself. The agents were not expensive, probably because Ulshofer was reputed to be very close-fisted; he paid only on results, and then parsimoniously.[20]

The nest at Tabriz, headed by Paul Passarge, was closed, with Passarge sent back to Germany, and Pfeiffer was also unimpressed by Clemens Rossetti, KONO's liaison with the Italians. In summary, Pfeiffer judged the I/H section as having produced several reports 'done with thoroughness but of little immediate operational value'.[21]

I/L, headed by Dr Wolfgang Dietze, was considered to be 'producing reasonably good results' although many of Schenker-Angerer's contacts had been dropped, including Jusuf Kuvvet, for whom the Abwehr had invested between T£14,000 and T£15,000 in his bar, in an effort to assist his intelligence collection 'with little result'. Furthermore, Ludwig suspected Kuvvet of being a double agent.[22]

Abt. I, under Dr Hans Lowe, 'had come to a standstill since the defection of Vermehren' so the section was refocused on protection duties for the cargos of chrome ore being shipped to Germany by the Donau line.

Gruppe III received good marks from Pfeiffer who approved of the internal security measures introduced by Ludwig following the period now tactfully referred to internally as 'the troubles', which included greater care over the protection of agent identities, and the preparation of a stay-behind organisation in the event of a suspension of diplomatic relations with Turkey, an event that took place in early August 1944, leading to the internment of KONO's entire staff.

In anticipation of the rupture, and the loss of KONO's wireless links, Pfeiffer had helped supervise the creation of a stay-behind organisation equipped with its own transmitters. Hinz arranged for a Franciscan monk, Father Karaklian from St Antoine's church, to take over a set for I/H and another station codenamed IGEL was established in an Istanbul suburb. In parallel Ast Sofia created its own network headed by Karl Schnick and Kurt Beigl, with two sets in Istanbul, one or two in Ankara, another at Kars or Erzurum, and at Diyartakum. In addition, a Turkish reserve officer, codenamed KIRGA, who had been trained as a radio operator in Berlin, was entrusted by Zaehringer with a set but, as Pfeiffer later recalled, 'nothing came of the whole affair; the agents either destroyed or sold the transmitter and shared the proceeds'.[23] He also blamed the collapse of the stay-behind structure on Beigl who, he claimed, had been injured when he had fallen from a train and found himself in hospital in central Anatolia. This event had prompted him to desert to the British, thereby compromising their entire organisation. In reality, Beigl, who had been a good friend of Vermehren's, was a defector who switched sides in August 1944, having negotiated his defection and that of his wife Hildegard with SIS's Nicholas Elliott by revealing the true identity of his chief Turkish agent Coskin, alias Bairandaraoglu Sali. A dealer based in Mersin, Coskin had been supplied with three suitcase transmitters which he had distributed to his network that was to be run by the KO Bucharest but communicated direct with Ast Vienna. In return, Elliott gave the couple British papers allowing them to travel to Aleppo, where they were taken into custody and escorted to Beirut and then Egypt.

An Austrian from Gratzen, born in July 1910 to a physician, Beigl had joined the Abwehr in 1937 and undergone training with the Brandenburg Regiment in February 1940. Then he had been posted to Ast Bucharest for Abt. II before being transferred under commercial cover for a firm selling car spare parts to Istanbul in February 1942. Under his 'long and severe' interrogation by SIME in Cairo he explained that when Vermehren defected he was warned by Leverkuehn to expect his imminent arrest, and instructed to move his transmitters. SIME concluded that Beigl 'saw that his ship was sinking and was unwilling to sink with it'. However, one mystery remained unresolved. Why did the Abwehr continue to have confidence in Beigl's stay-behind network if there was every reason to believe it had been compromised by Vermehren, and probably Hamburger too?

Pfeiffer's posting to Istanbul in May 1944 did not go unnoticed by the Allies, as he was on a mission to tighten security, improve morale and reinvigorate intelligence reporting, and in early June MI5 noted that he 'means to have a strong team'.

> Since Pfeiffer's arrival in Turkey there seems to have been a revival of reports from KONO agents. HELMUT, the Turkish controlled and perhaps notional, agent reports on military units in Syria. An informant of KONO reported on Polish units seen in Beirut and quoted statements of Polish officers. There is a time lag to twelve days between the date of report and its forwarding by KONO. The ROMEO network reports British order of battle in Syria. Here the time lag is about two weeks. ROMEO is almost certainly Mahmoud Hamada who in June 1942 arrived in Turkey from Italy where he had been broadcasting for the Axis from Bari. He is the cousin of Jawad Hamada who made an ill-fated submarine trip to Syria in August 1942. The Germans appear to be sceptical about the quality of his reports. Two KONO informants report British troop movements in Iraq, one from Baghdad, the other from Basra. The time lag in each case is between three and four weeks. Ostensibly all these reports are the observations of 'a man in the street' in Allied territory who has brought the information personally or sent it by courier to Turkey; the 'informant' as opposed to agents, may in some cases be unconscious sources, We are not at present in a position to assess how far these reports are conscious deception by (a) the agent himself for financial reasons, (b) Allied deceptionists for strategic reasons, or (c) the Turks for reasons best known to themselves. We do however know that in the past the Abwehr have been particularly susceptible to this sort of thing and it will be interesting to see if the Pfeiffer regime, which undoubtedly includes men of some ability, will enforce a higher standard of reporting.[24]

* * *

Following not long after the Vermehrens was Erich's good friend and fellow lawyer Willi Hamburger, who defected to the American OSS in Istanbul on 12 February as soon as he received orders summoning him back to Berlin, ostensibly for him to begin a tempting new posting in Paris. Hamburger was suspicious because his past behaviour had made him unpopular, especially with the SD which, back in April 1942, had accused him of being a British agent, and there had been considerable resentment concerning his very public affair, conducted until the summer of 1942, with the wife of a German journalist named Westedt.

Born in Vienna to a prominent Austrian merchant family, Hamburger, who joined the Nazi Party before the Anschluss, had studied law at university and gained a knowledge of Iraq and Syria from his fellow students while an undergraduate studying Turkish. His father was well respected, having served as a personal adviser to Emperor Franz Josef, and then a director of the Steyr-Daimler-Puch armaments manufacturer, and who also had been president of the Vienna Chamber of Commerce. After having been called up for training with the Luftwaffe in October 1940 he was posted to Ast Vienna in March 1941 and in August the following year was transferred to Istanbul under commercial cover as a representative of the Semperit rubber company. Later he would act as the manager for an import-export firm, Suedostrop AG, but was always under commercial cover and was formally not a KONO member, nor even subject to its code of discipline. He cultivated a very wide circle of friends and was rarely seen at German social gatherings or at the Teutinia Club, a venue popular with the expatriate community. When Vermehren was asked by his SIME interrogator about Hamburger, he predicted that the young man, who had gained a reputation as something of a playboy, would also defect. Hamburger made no attempt to conceal his anti-Nazi opinions and was widely thought to be a supporter of the nationalist Austrian Freedom Movement.

> In September or October 1943 Willi Hamburger was in touch with George Earle, the American naval attaché, through having stolen his mistress, and was trying to get information which he could take out to the British without hurting the Abwehr. He told PRECIOUS that he had heard that someone connected with the SD, that at the back of the PASCHA organisation was an Italian Jew connected with Marconi's office or shop in Cairo, and asked PRECIOUS for his name and further particulars. These PRECIOUS told him he could not give, because he did not have them.[25]

Thus, according to Vermehren, now codenamed PRECIOUS, the 27-year-old Hamburger had been contemplating a defection to the Allies for a considerable period, and had felt safe enough to confide in his colleague. Certainly there were rumours in circulation about his affair with Adrienne Molnar, a glamorous Hungarian who also enjoyed the company of several influential Americans, among them the US naval attaché.

Hamburger's Abwehr role had been disclosed to SIME by Walter Aberle and Waldemar Weber, and then by Gottfried Muller, Wilhelm Hoffmann and Georg Konieczny, two teams of Abt. II saboteurs, collectively codenamed THE LIBERATORS, who had been arrested

12 days after parachuting into Iraq near Mosul on 17 June 1943, on what became known as the MAMMUT Expedition, a mission to establish a local espionage and sabotage network among the Kurds. However, the three German officers, equipped with a transmitter and accompanied by an Iraqi interpreter, Nafi Rashid Ramzi, had been dropped some 200km from their planned landing zone and, having split up, had been spotted just east of Erbil and detained. Codenamed HARDY and TIGER, Hoffmann and Muller admitted that they had been directed to blow up the Trans-Iranian railway and interrupt the delivery of oil to the Allies. Although they had not brought explosives with them, the group was equipped with a new Luftwaffe VHF device which would facilitate further supply drops.

The planning for the mission had begun in October 1942 and Muller had been trained at the Abwehr's school at Quenz and at a laboratory at Tegel, which he described to his interrogators in considerable detail. He also revealed that once they had been established, a second team, codenamed MAMMUT II, would then be dropped to them by the Luftwaffe. SIME later established that the intended spies were Robert Baheshy and Louis Bakos, a pair of Iraqi students attending college in Istanbul.

During the summer of 1943 the Abwehr sent two parachute missions to Iraq and Persia, and both failed. The first, at the end of March, was FRANZ, led by Gunther Blume and consisting of Ernst Kondgen, Karl Korel, Werner Rockstroh, Hans Holzaptel and Georg Grille. All were captured and interrogated, with the exception of Korel who succumbed to typhus.

The second, dropped in July, was ANTON, an entirely SD sabotage team headed by Martin Kurmes, with two Waffen-SS wireless operators, Kurt Piwanko and Kurt Harbers. Their wireless malfunctioned in December 1943, so they were out of contact with their control station for the last three months of their mission, when they were betrayed to SIME by local tribesmen.

The interrogation of Muller in Baghdad in July 1943, supervised by MI5's Martin Forrest on secondment to SIME, was a classic example of triangulation, challenging his account by information derived from his companions, ISOS and other prisoner reports. While Ramzi, an Iraqi who had acted as an interpreter, turned out to be the least well-informed, having been recruited in Istanbul, Muller over-compensated for him and between 31 July and 22 August the Combined Intelligence Centre Iraq (CICI) in Baghdad generated a dozen formal interrogation reports. By September Muller, who had been moved to Cairo, was fully cooperative and, as Forrest remarked, 'has now described Zossen in detail' and sketched the entire site. He added that Abt. II's previous accommodation, on the top floor of the OKW building in Berlin, had been considered too tempting a target for the RAF. The son of a farmer in Oschwend, and a Nazi since 1932, Muller had travelled to Egypt, Palestine, Syria and Iraq before the war as a sales manager representing Braun Brothers. Under cross-examination, he also revealed his intelligence collection priorities:

(i) Allied troops, where, what units, where from, where to, what equipment and arms?
(ii) New aerodromes, where, type of construction, what buildings, etc.?
(iii) Where are the new Polish units which are supposed to have just been formed?
(iv) Indian troops, where, how many? Especially 7, 10 and 13 Divisions?
(v) Where are American units (Known to OKW Supreme Command that some are near Basra).
(vi) What tactical signs on British Motor Transport? (Divisional signs on MT).
(vii) For American MT, same as (vi).[26]

Muller's mission, codenamed MAMMUT, which landed near Mosul, was to stir up dissent with local Kurdish tribes, promise German support for a free Kurdistan, and encourage them to destroy railway bridges and oil installations. For this purpose they were equipped with two radios, a quantity of weapons and sabotage materiel, and could arrange for further air-drops. Allegedly 'without prompting', Muller volunteered details for a further planned operations that he was aware of. He also, when encouraged by questions founded in ISOS, acknowledged he had worked for Ast Vienna and had visited Istanbul on a short assignment to KONO. Between July 1941 and April 1942 he had undertaken various assignments which had involved travel to Vienna, Budapest, Sofia, Paris and Turkey, which he recalled in detail. His assignment to Istanbul on which he had been accompanied by a friend and colleague named Hagleitner, and stayed at the Tokatlyan Hotel, had been in preparation for despatching a pair of agents into eastern Turkey and Kurdistan, but the scheme failed when the Turkish authorities refused them visas, causing Muller to be recalled to Germany.

Upon his return Muller was told that his mission had been compromised by an Abwehr source, Josef Kuvett, who was suspected of being a British double agent, as indeed he was, for he had also been reporting to SIS under the codename MIMI. Kuvett had identified Muller as having adopted the alias 'Jean Gottfried Bartos', which neatly corroborated traces of that name in ISOS, linked to the codename BARTOSCH. Furthermore, BARTOSCH would later emerge in Willi Hamburger's interrogation, as did his companion Hagleitner, described, not entirely accurately, as:

> Both lieutenants in the German Air Force [*sic*]. In 1941 Hamburger was told by Vienna that these two men would work under him. Hagleitner was very poor and after two or three months was returned to Vienna. BARTOSCH was a w/t expert and worked with Yusuf Kuvvet. BARTOSCH is dangerous to the Germans because he talks too openly and is a bungler. He rented a house in the Ortakoy district and installed a transmitter, but his dog killed a child and subsequently the visit from the police caused BARTOSCH to bury his transmitter for a certain period. For a time BARTOSCH worked well, obtaining maps and plans from Persia, partly through Kuvvet. Finally, Hamburger heard that Kuvvet was an agent for the Turkish police, so decided, as BARTOSCH was always in trouble, to get rid of him. In April 1942, when he went to Vienna, he told the authorities that they must recall either himself or BARTOSCH. BARTOSCH returned to Vienna.[27]

One of the intelligence gems that enhanced Muller's value was his visit to the Abwehr's top-secret research laboratory at Tegel where new sabotage devices were under development. Obligingly, Muller sketched a map of the site and provided an explanation of the buildings and their functions. Muller's accumulated knowledge was considerable, extending across the region to North Africa, and was distilled into dozens of interim reports for circulation within MI5, SIS, RSS, the Delhi Intelligence Bureau (DIB) and the Indian Political Intelligence (IPI) in London until October 1943 when a consolidated report was drafted and sent to Section V by MI5's Middle East counter-intelligence expert, Alex Kellar. What makes this particular document so interesting is that the SIS officer who expressed a wish to learn more about the case was John Cairncross, who at that time was regularly passing classified information to his NKVD contacts in London. He acknowledged that the reports 'contain a great deal of background information which will be extremely useful to us in the future. We should be glad to have copies of any further statements that may be made by this or other parachute parties in the Middle East.' As SIME observed,

Muller has been very cooperative during interrogation. He has supplied a great deal of most valuable technical information concerning the workings of the German espionage and sabotage organisations. He has also supplied us with much concerning other expeditions which have been planned and in some cases actually undertaken.[28]

In preparing the final report on Muller, who had initially concealed much of his past, Martin Forrest acknowledged Alex Kellar's essential role in analysing the ISOS references, and 'all the conscientious beavering which you have undertaken in this case, and which has in fact made it possible to batter the truth out of Muller'.[29]

Muller's German deputy, Friedrich Hoffmann, was a Persian interpreter who pre-war had worked in the machine-tool industry for the Brown-Boveri engineering company before being posted by Siemens to Kabul in 1937 for four years. After joining the Wehrmacht he had been posted to Russia to inspect mechanical repair workshops, and then had attended a demolition course. MAMMUT's third German, Konieczny, was a doctor fluent in Farsi from Berlin where he had been a portrait painter and interior decorator. In 1936 he had spent a year in Azerbaijan and later worked in a glass factory in Tehran. Of the three, only Muller could be said to be an Abwehr professional. Three years later, when in November 1946 SIS researched Hoffmann's travel to the Afghan capital, it was Section IX's Kim Philby who revealed to MI5 that the German had visited Peshawar in June 1939.

As for Ramzi, he had arrived in Turkey in November 1942, only to discover that his diploma from the American University in Beirut was insufficient for acceptance at Istanbul's Rebert College. His dilemma was solved by an Abwehr recruiter who offered him a place at a college in Germany, in return for attending the Abt. II sabotage course at Quenz and then participating in MAMMUT.

Under interrogation by SIME, Muller identified Hamburger as his contact in Istanbul who in 1941 had supplied him with commercial cover as a representative of Suedostropa, seeking to invest in local flax and hemp cultivation. In the 11th CSDIC Interim Report, dated 20 August 1943, Muller described him as

No. 127. V-Mann Ast Vienna in Istanbul. Director of the commercial firm Suedoeuropa, Galicia, Minerva Pan (personal description available in Army No 1012, para. 6b). Speaks German and English. Learnt Turkish.[30]

178

Other agents also described their encounters with the young Dr Hamburger, and when his Abwehr codename RUST was disclosed, it appeared that he had left a lengthy ISOS trail.

Hamburger's conversation with Vermehren about the mysterious PASCHA was illuminating for SIME, which had failed to find any trace of such an individual or organisation in Cairo, as MI5's War Room acknowledged in April 1946:

The exact nature of the PASHA and REMO organisations is still one of the unexplained points in the Middle East; and it is only possible at the moment to indicate the broad lines of the available evidence. The leading personality was a certain Dr Reichert who was the Near East representative of the Deutsche Nachrichtenbuero in Cairo before the outbreak of war. Reichert was deported, as an undesirable alien, and from the end of 1940 continued his work in Turkey where he remained until the beginning of 1942. Through his connections with the DNB, Reichert was instrumental in building up a well-organised information service with sources probably in Cairo itself. The organisation was not directed either by Amt VI or by the Abwehr, but the information obtained by Reichert was made available to these two departments according to its nature. In addition Reichert also supplied information to the Embassy, the Propaganda Ministry, and the Foreign Office. His chief assistant journalist in this activity was a journalist named Zamboni.

The information supplied by Reichert's organisation, which went under the name PASHA in the Abwehr, and REMO in Amt VI, was of sufficiently high quality to make Schellenberg suspicious of its authenticity. It was for this reason that [Hauptsturmführer Robert] Mohr was sent to Istanbul in 1942 with the assignment of working with Reichert in order to establish whether or not the information obtained through those sources was genuine or smoke.

The sources of the PASHA and REMO organisation are still unknown, and unfortunately Reichert himself cannot supply the answer as he was killed in an accident early in 1943. Zamboni returned to Italy in July 1943 when the network ceased to operate. Zamboni himself was arrested in Rome and sent to Berlin for interrogation as the Germans themselves were still uncertain as to the reliability of Reichert's organisation.

Zamboni is now under interrogation at AFHQ, and the results of his interrogation may be instrumental in clearing up the outstanding points in the REMO organisation. The other personality who should be treated as a priority target in connection with this still outstanding problem is Mohr himself who returned to Germany some time in 1944, and was last reported in April 1945 at Reutor in Southern Germany.

Hamburger was interrogated in Cairo by SIME but given no indication that the British had run any double agents in the Middle East or that some of his own sources were controlled. He provided lengthy profiles of the Abwehr's staff and assets and on one occasion, while having breakfast with the Kleczkowskis in Cairo, remarked on an apparently important spy in Egypt, evidently unaware that the individual in question was CHEESE, SIME's prized channel. Hamburger had mentioned casually that 'the Italians had a W/T set operating in Cairo and playing back to Istanbul. They got messages on this W/T link up till the Italian Armistice and toe downfall of Mussolini in August – September 1943 when the set stopped transmitting.' This assertion attracted a note in Hamburger's SIME file.

> When Hamburger mentioned it, von Kleczkowksi said 'Yes, I know about that. But I always wondered whether the information we were getting though that set was true or whether in fact it was not being controlled and played back to us'. Hamburger then said 'Good heavens, no! The information we got from that set was absolutely first class and absolutely true. It was grand.'[31]

When Hamburger was asked about particular individuals, he identified Erich Lochner as 'the only efficient and dangerous member of Abt. I in Istanbul', describing him as 'a dangerous little devil' who was in charge of the wagon-lits agents, mentioning one

> whom they considered to be an absolutely first class agent; he did not know the conductor's real name as he was always referred to under his cover-name which was ARTHUR. ARTHUR's sole job was to report on the signs which he saw on Allied military vehicles, the numbers of such vehicles, where seen, whom driven by, etc. and apparently he did this job to Lochner's and the Abwehr's complete satisfaction. It should be mentioned that Lochner was the member of the Abwehr who ran and instructed ARTHUR.[32]

Naturally, Hamburger's escort resisted mentioning that ARTHUR was better known to SIME as their agent DOLEFUL, noting that Hamburger had gone on 'to describe how the Abwehr numbers of formations, etc. from being told about vehicle signs and also what the importance of the vehicle sign business was'.

Another colleague singled out by Hamburger was his fellow Austrian Gottfried Schenker-Angerer, assigned to I/L KONO in mid-1941 after

180

being wounded on the Eastern Front. The owner of the Schenker freight business, Schenker-Angerer was married to the Hungarian actress Margit von Rupp. According to Hamburger, Schenke-Angerer almost certainly would have defected too if his wife and daughter had not been in Budapest, potentially vulnerable as hostages.

The 'desertions', as the Germans referred to them, had the effect of inflicting carnage at KONO, and Allied observers watched in March 1944 as a purge was conducted among their social and professional contacts, noting the victims and their status as they were recalled:

> Reinhard Huber, member of the staff of the press attaché, Ankara, and author the book *Die Turkey* which was featured by German propaganda bookshops in Turkey in 1941.
> Ursula Hurtung, who arrived in Istanbul in February 1943 from Sofia and was subsequently reported as Jacob Liebl's Confidential Secretary.
> Soifa Maria Mathilde Henschel, wife of a German Embassy secretary.
> Heinz Franz Wilhelm Eugn, an embassy official, member of the German Military Attaché's office in Ankara. Abwehr official.
> Richard Erhard Wunsch, known to be an Abwehr agent.
> Werner Schuler, an embassy official and leading figure in the Abwehr.

While almost all of the personalities mentioned by Hamburger (and Vermehren and von Kleczkowski) were familiar to SIME, mystery surrounded the SD source codenamed PASCHA who passed information to an Italian journalist in Istanbul,

> who offered Leverkuehn information arriving by wireless from Cairo. The journalist had always refused to disclose the identity of the source of his information. The Italian was the journalist, Zamboni or Zaporetto by name, who had left Turkey with the Italian ambassador to Ankara to join the Badoglio Government when that ambassador became Badoglio's Foreign Minister. Zamboni was a protégé of Kleczkowski who had helped him get away. Hamburger had first heard that the Cairo source of the information was a Spanish Jew when Kleczkowski was telling him and Vermehren what he was doing to help Zamboni in October 1943. Since it had subsequently been common talk that the source was a Spanish Jew, he had passed on that information. It was certain that this Italian journalist was the Istanbul receiver of the PASCHA information because, since his departure shortly after Mussolini's fall, nothing further was heard of this organisation. Hamburger had the impression that Zamboni had some link to the SD because Kleczkowski once said that he had only one quarrel with the SD and that was in connection with Zamboni.[33]

181

In contrast to Mayer's intransigence, Vermehren became increasingly forthcoming about KONO's activities across the region and provided further detail about his spy-rings, the largest of which was in Egypt and centred on two nationalists, Prince Shahab and Prince Mansour Daoud, with Hassan Sirry communicating in secret ink to cover-addresses in Istanbul. Other supporters were an aide named Abubakr and the *kavas* (caretaker) of the Egyptian consulate codenamed HAZARD. Vermehren's KONO office was next to a room allocated to Robert Ulshofer and Schenker-Angerer, so he could also name some his colleague's agents, among them Dakhlia, Ahmet Saabet and, most significantly, the Radio Berlin propaganda broadcaster Hamdi Kaqqay who was working for the British under the codename BLACKGUARD. The I/M representative, Kurt Zahringer, was also named as an able recruiter, and Walther Hinz was identified as having handled Ali Shinar.

Vermehren's knowledge of agents seemed encyclopaedic, and he identified Hinz's best I/H source as Ali Shinar, and Ulshofer's as Abdul Karim. He also knew about some SD operations and identified Ahmet Saubet and Hassan el Bemhe as being handled by Waldemar Fast, the peacetime owner of two hotels in Beirut and Palestine.

The I/H networks were taken over by Colonel Ohletz who held the view that 'the I-network in all probability had been blown by the Vermehren case' but, surprisingly, Berlin did not assume that all Vermehren's agents had been compromised by him, as Walter Schellenberg later explained:

Of the 3 links prepared, and later even 5, continued to function as time went on. According to Ohletz, 3 of them were so suspect that he suppressed their messages for the most part or classed them as 'not definite, requiring check', and passed them on as such . . . Ohletz told me that the agents of the I-links were all Turks. Thus, if the Vermehren case had not done some harm, there was always the possibility that the Turks had contacted their own police and were being used by the police as double agents, even if the Vermehren case had done no harm.[34]

The Vermehren and Hamburger defections proved the catalyst in Berlin for a tumultuous series of events, beginning with the submission by Ernst Kaltenbrunner of a seven-page memorandum dated 7 February 1944 describing the recent events in Turkey and listing other 'urgent suspects', including Schenke-Angerer, Semperit's local representative named Herock, the company's Vienna executive Joseph Ridiger and the Deutsche Bank director Dr Barth. Specifically, the document charged

Vermehren with having passed information from Levekuehn's office to 'Major Elliot and Major Cripp of the British ND'.

During the following fortnight, despite some mutual personal antipathy, Kaltenbrunner and Schellenberg drafted a Führer directive giving the RSHA full authority over the Abwehr, which went into effect five days later, on 12 February, unifying the Reich's intelligence structure and passing its control to Heinrich Himmler. The precise circumstances of how the directive came into force would be disputed by the two men when they underwent Allied interrogation:

> Whilst Kaltenbrunner claimed that he was really responsible for Hitler's decision at the beginning of 1944 to dismiss Canaris and entrust Himmler with the Military Intelligence sector, Schellenberg states that this claim was completely unjustified. He says that quite apart from Hitler's declining regard for Canaris personally, this question had often been the subject of long discussions between Hitler and Himmler, mostly on account of the alleged and actual failures of the German Secret Service. The Vermehren incident in Turkey was only really the superficial reason for finally concluding matters which had been developing for a long time.[35]

According to Schellenberg, there had been several perceived failures that had undermined Canaris's reputation. Firstly, there had been the absence of any warning of the Allied landings in North Africa in November 1942. Then there had been the arrest in Trinidad of Osmar Hellmuth, an embarrassment that the Abwehr had been blamed for, albeit unjustly. On that occasion the Foreign Minister, Joachim Ribbentrop, had been especially vocal in his condemnation of Canaris and his organisation, as Erich Pfeiffer recalled:

> Admiral Canaris was away on business at the time and had to end his trip at once and was recalled to the Amt. Meanwhile, Ribbentrop had stated in a report to Adolf Hitler that the Abwehr was endangering his foreign policy in a big way; he represented the [Hans] Harnisch-Hellmuth affair as purely an Abwehr matter.
>
> Canaris, it appeared, was not believed when he denied it; a long report in writing had to be made by us and submitted to the Hauptquartier. I don't remember exactly what happened next; but those of us who were in close contact with Admiral Canaris had the feeling that the affair was exploited as an instrument to bring about his gradual downfall as he had already made enemies on many sides. We knew only too well that the SD intended to take over the Abwehr, and that the immediate objective, Abt. III, was practically won already; it was obvious also that

their claims went beyond 'Abwehr' work properly speaking, and that their eye was on the Nachrichtendienst sections.

These claims could be easily supported, for the Abwehr received little help from the OKW and the Wehrmachestellen. For this there were many reasons. I don't know whether Canaris and Keitel were on good terms, but I doubt it. All three sections of the Wehrmacht were in agreement on two points: their ignorance of the difficulties in the path of a Secret Intelligence Service in wartime; and their haste in blaming all military disasters on the Abwehr. It was easy enough, in those circumstances, for the SD to promise better service in the future.[36]

A SHAEF intelligence assessment of the Abwehr, circulated in April 1945, alleged another coincidental mishap, which supposedly reflected poorly on Canaris's reputation at this crucial moment. This was the cancellation of a visit to Biarritz planned for 10/11 February 1944 to confer with the Spanish intelligence chief General Carlos Martinez Campos. Despite being on cordial terms, the SHAEF report claimed that the Spanish had declined the invitation, an event interpreted as a sure sign of Canaris's diminishing influence on Francisco Franco's government. Canaris had enjoyed close links with Spain for many years, dating back to his nine months spent in Madrid from December 1915. Since the outbreak of war he had made eight visits to Spain, and his most recent trip had extended over four days in early October 1943. The timing had been inopportune because of a recent deterioration in bilateral relations caused by three unexpected events. One was the delivery to the Foreign Minister Francisco Jordana by the British embassy of a formal note protesting, and specifying, the number of German intelligence officers working under consular and diplomatic cover. The relevant ISOS text, dated 18 October, reported that:

> According to statement of VICTOR [General Vigon] English had handed Jordana a note of protest concerning activity of German personnel, giving names, in the Straits.[37]

The Abwehr's reaction to the British demarche had been explained to Jordana by Canaris, who sent Berlin a contemporaneous summary of their conversation:

> I declared that it was absolutely essential for our intelligence organisation in Spain to continue and that I should merely withdraw a few people from Algeciras and Tangier and carry out certain camouflage measures. I referred to the activities of our enemies in Spain who, according to our

information, were working on a large scale, especially in the Balearics. Jordana asked for our evidence in regard to this and then expressed his agreement to our being able to continue our activity in Spain as hitherto.[38]

Unfortunately for Canaris, the Allies maintained their pressure on the Spanish and submitted further complaints, citing the covert infra-red apparatus monitoring shipping through the Straits of Gibraltar and the existence of a sabotage organisation that was concealing time-bombs in crates of oranges and onions loaded onto British ships in Spanish ports.

Allied counter-intelligence staff with access to ISOS had been monitoring Canaris (referred in the intercepts as GUILLERMO) and the traffic suggested that the Spanish feared his visit would provoke a reaction from the Allies, and on 2 February the KOS signalled to Berlin:

> In a discussion with MC [Martinez Campos] a few days ago, before the political crisis here had reached its peak concerning GUILLERMO's intended journey, the former advised urgently against it in view of possible consequences to be expected from the Allies. He advised at most a meeting on French soil.[39]

The message went on to explain that VICTOR (General Vigon) would not be available to attend because of his ministerial commitments, and another colleague 'states the same opinion on GUILLERMO's presence here at the present time, as it would certainly be impossible to keep it secret from the Allies, who are just waiting for such an opportunity which would be exploited against Spain and also against our service ... Cover is not secure at the moment, as our service is shadowed to a very great extent and use of the few transport services which still remain available would be conspicuous.' Apparently undeterred, Berlin responded the same day:

> GUILLERMO intends to come to Madrid on 9 February with BRIZO SENIOR [Georg Hansen]. Itinerary as follows: Wednesday by plane from Berlin to Bordeaux Thursday journey from Bordeaux to frontier at San Sebastian, slipping through by Puente Thursday evening San Sebastian by sleeper . . . Prepare for continuation of discussion with VICTOR [General Vigon]. Cover is to be maintained in all circumstances. ELCANO [Wilhelm Leisner] is to be in San Sebastian on Thursday 10 February to meet GUILLERMO. Date not yet finally fixed. Further instructions follow.[40]

On the following day Berlin sent the KO a reminder, and a request to obtain the embassy's approval for what was intended by the Abwehr to be a routine conference.

> We request agreement of Kanzlerchef [ambassador] for discussion on afternoon of 10 February at the Spanish frontier on French soil in the presence of ELCANO [Wilhelm Leisner] Chef ROON attaches the greatest importance to this discussion. After discussion with Kanzlerchef state the place of the intended meeting.[41]

However, later the same day, the KOS reported a strong negative reaction from the embassy, which had apparently consulted the Foreign Ministry.

> Kanzlerchef requests urgently that the idea of a visit here to be abandoned for the time being in view of the strained political situation still prevailing, and endorses HEYDEN RYNSCH's reasons stated in yesterday's message. The Spaniards are still engaged in negotiations with the Allies, which necessitate extreme restraint on our part.[42]

Overnight, with Ribbentrop effectively vetoing the gathering, Berlin signalled Lisbon to alert the KOP Leiter, Cramer von Auenrode, that 'discussions will not take place in Bordeaux but in Biarritz on Friday 11 February at 0900'. Berlin then changed the arrangements again, moving the meeting's venue to Barcelona, and listing the attendees as Canaris, Leisner, von Auendrode and Friedrich Baumeister from Alst Paris.

Overshadowing this last-minute flurry of activity to interfere with Canaris's itinerary was, of course, the news from Istanbul on Monday, 25 January, that the Vermehrens had disappeared. This was another complication because, according to a further message from Berlin on 9 February, Vermehren had known about a source in Portugal named Bogomolez who, according to a leak locally, had alerted the Lisbon police, the British and the Americans, to a visit made to Madrid and Lisbon in early October 1943 by Canaris and Hansen.

* * *

The Istanbul catastrophe proved to be the last straw, with the ambitious Schellenberg seeing himself as the principal architect of the new organisation which would be entirely under the RSHA's umbrella:

The 'Geheime Meldedienst', the new name chosen by Schellenberg for the old designation 'Abwehr' which he thought had fallen into dispute owing to its inefficiency and the low intellectual and moral standard of most of its members, was the task entrusted to 'Amt VI', which was joined by the 'Mil Amt' when the incorporation of the Abwehr in the RSHA took place. The 'Geheime Meldedienst' in its present shape and composition represented by no means Schellenberg's ideal of a future German Secret Service. If Schellenberg had had his way and if defeat had not put an end to his grandiose, not so very megalomaniac, plans, which provided the participation of more or less the whole educated part of the nation in secret service work, he would have branched out in time into a social, cultural, economic, scientific and even artistic manifestations of German life at home and abroad in order to permeate them with 'collaborators' (honorary and paid) and 'runners' (Zuträger) of the 'Geheime Meldedienst'.[43]

At the end of the war Schellenberg fled to Sweden but then returned from Stockholm to occupied Frankfurt to face arrest and eventual confinement at Camp 020 where he underwent lengthy questioning. One of the contributions to his MI5 dossier was a ten-page character sketch provided on 12 July 1945 by his former Amt VIE subordinate, Dr Wilhelm Höttl, who made a curious comment, linking Hansen's 'England connections' and the 20 July putsch:

No doubt Schellenberg can claim major credit if, in the wake of the Vermehrren incident (desertion of Abwehr personnel in Turkey to the British), Kaltenbrunner was able to dethrone Canaris and annex the Abwehr. After all it was Schellenberg who had systematically gathered evidence to prove that close connections between the Abwehr and the enemy powers went beyond the experimental stage. Schellenberg never confided to the new chief of Amt III (the successor of the Abwehr), Oberst G. Hansen. He either must have known about Hansen's England connections or must have suspected their existence. His conduct, after the plot of 20 July blew up, was certainly not prompted by disapprobation. As one of the very few leading men in Germany Schellenberg clearly perceived that Germany's military fortunes were on the wane and would not have hesitated to act on that conviction and strike a bargain with his opposite numbers. Therefore his dominant reaction upon 20 July was one of petulance rather than of downright indignation. What irked him most was Hansen's double-cross and to have been accorded pride of place on the liquidation roster of the new government.[44]

As for Schellenberg himself, he played no part in the 20 July plot, although in retrospect he recalled having been sounded out for his opinions very tentatively a year earlier by the Wehrmacht's communications chief, General Fritz Thiele, an approach he had reported to Ernst Kaltenbrunner, who had ignored it.

> Since their close association Schellenberg and Hansen had taken frequent walks together discussing current problems. On one of these occasions at the beginning Hansen spoke of the great changes which would be taking place shortly in the German hierarchy since the whole Wehrmachtfuhrungsstab was no longer capable of controlling the military situation effectively. Hansen raised the question from a security angle of the foreign workers in Germany and then asked what Himmler's real attitude to Keitel was. He further asked as to whether Schellenberg's own peace proposals had received Himmler's approval, and as to the strength and reliability of the Ordnungspolizei. Towards the end of this particular discussion Hansen urged Schellenberg to remain calm in the near future when a better intelligence service would be set up, with the possibility of Schellenberg being appointed Ambassador in London. From this conversation Schellenberg was able to deduce for himself that some coup was being planned by the Wehrmacht apparently directed not against Himmler but against Hitler and the Wehrmachtfuhrungsstab. On receiving this information Schellenberg was careful to maintain a diplomatic silence.[45]

In the event, Hansen did not survive the Gestapo investigation into the attempted putsch. Five days later Schellenberg had summoned him and Karl-Heinz Engelhorn from BELINDE to his office in the Berknerstrasse where the spent two hours alone with Hansen. Engelhorn, who was accused of turning BELINDE into an armed camp in anticipation of a siege, was taken away by the Gestapo. Thereupon Schellenberg accompanied Hansen to Heinrich Müller's headquarters where he stated that he was convinced Hansen 'had nothing to do with the plot'. Schellenberg left the two men together but.

> alone with Hansen, Mueller announced that he had documentary proof of his guilt, producing in support of this a notebook found in [General Friedrich] Oblright's possession implicating Hansen, whereupon Hansen confessed his complicity and was arrested.[46]

Having detained Hansen, Müller ordered Schellenberg to search Hansen's office for further incriminating evidence, and nine days later, on the first Sunday in August, Müller ordered him to arrest Canaris and escort him to Fuerstenberg, the Sipo training school 60 miles north of Berlin.

Taking with him a former member of the Lehrregiment Brandenburg, a certain Hauptsturmbannfuhrer von Foelkesam, he drove to Canaris's house at Zaehlendorf in the Betazielostrasse. On their arrival Canaris was engaged with two visitors but these at once took their departure and Schellenberg was shown in. Foelkesam remained in the hall of the house, affording Schellenberg an opportunity to converse alone with Canaris. Canaris professed to have no reason for concern although he pressed Schellenberg for information as to whether 'that potty General Staff official, Hansen, had not been taking notes again in his niggling manner'. He then asked whether he, Schellenberg, had had anything to do with the affair or whether Himmler had played any part in connection with it, to which Schellenberg gave his assurances that this was not the case. They then drove to the Sipo School at Fuerstenberg, confining their conversation en route to mundane matters in the presence of the driver and Foelkesam.

Before leaving Canaris at Fuerstenberg, the latter requested Schellenberg to seek an interview for him with Himmler. To this Schellenberg answered that he would do all that lay in his power.

Some fortnight or three weeks later, Schellenberg did in fact have an opportunity to raise this matter with Himmler who answered that he wanted to help Canaris as far as he could, and that he would talk it over with Kaltenbrunner. What consequently transpired is not exactly known to Schellenberg and certainly effected no amelioration in Canaris's position, who continued to remain under detention. He did not however appear as a defendant in the proceedings later instituted by the Volksgericht, and in so far as Schellenberg is aware his case remained undecided. Schellenberg later understood that some documentary and incriminating evidence implicating him to some extent was found in Canaris's safe.[47]

* * *

Karl and Stella Kleczkowski were Austrians working for Abt. IIIF under *Volkischer Beobachter* journalistic cover who, earlier in their career, had run agents in the Skoda plant in Czechoslovakia. Their defection on 11 February to the Americans in Istanbul was prompted by their friendship with Willi Hamburger, and their subsequent summons to Berlin. As Stella Kleczkowski was half-Jewish, their fate had probably been sealed.

Allied newspapers reporting the event claimed on 12 February that the Kleczkowskis worked for a sinister Thomas Ludwig, codenamed ALADDIN, whose offices in Istanbul included a trapdoor in the floor 'to do away with undesirables' that had been offered a poisoned cigarette. The propaganda served to undermine KONA and utterly compromise Ludwig who remained bitter about the news coverage two years later.[48]

As the tide of war turned against the Axis, the 'front-line' Abwehr staff were in the best position to gauge their change in fortunes as neutral support in Portugal and Spain melted away. This deterioration was marked as the number of deserters increased, and was manifested in particular in August 1943 by a member of the KOS's I/M staff, Luipold Haffner, who approached the SIS station in Madrid offering information about BODDEN, an apparatus thought to be an infra-red sensor which monitored Allied night-time shipping movements through the Straits of Gibraltar. The existence of BODDEN had been known to the Admiralty's Naval Intelligence Division since May 1942 and was categorised as a collection priority, so the prospect of exfiltrating him to England generated considerable enthusiasm, as shown by Guy Liddell who noted at the end of August that 'the idea is to get him over here as soon as possible for interrogation. His information should prove extremely valuable and provide us with a stick with which to beat the Spaniards.'[49] The issue of Spanish connivance in the BODDEN project had been the subject of a formal demarche from Sir Samuel Hoare to Franco's government and, according to ISOS, the Germans had undertaken to dismantle and remove the offending equipment.

However, as the relevant ISOS intercepts showed, the KOS had learned of Haffner's absence and alerted the Spanish police to arrest him. Three days later Liddell remarked that

> certain ISOS messages indicate that the Germans have been making frantic efforts to get him arrested by the Spaniards. At the moment it looks as if the Spaniards have got hold of somebody whom they believe to be Haffner and who is alleged to have committed suicide. The probability is that they have got hold of the wrong man, since the latest SIS reports indicate that Haffner is still in hiding in the charge of our people.[50]

Nothing more is known of Haffner's fate, which suggests he probably did take his own life in Madrid, and certainly never reached England, despite SIS's commitment to his protection.

Another relatively early intelligence deserter was Fritz Lorenz, formerly of the SD, who surrendered in August 1944 to members of the Belgian resistance movement, the Brigade Blanche, at Ciney near Namur. Once employed in pre-war London by Joachim von Ribbentrop's dienststelle as a weekly courier, Lorenz proved to be an enthusiastic source of information and was conveyed to Camp 020 in October 1944, where he remained for the following ten months. Under interrogation Lorenz described his experiences which included a posting in 1941 to the Ukrainian front as a Waffen-SS war reporter where he was a witness to the murder of 5,000 Jews at Mariapol and 1,400 Jews at Taganrog, and 10,000 Soviet PoWs by the Adolf Hitler SS Panzer Division. Accordingly, he offered himself to the Allies as a witness in any war crimes trial, and as a broadcaster of anti-Nazi propaganda for the PWE. Serious consideration was given to this latter proposal, but it was eventually rejected.[51]

Born in January 1913 in Cuxhaven, Lorenz was a gifted linguist who spent five years as a merchant seaman. He joined the Nazi Party in 1931 and four years later was recruited as an intelligence agent while serving aboard the NordDeutscheLloyd steamer *Stuttgart*. Soon afterwards he was summoned to Berlin to join the Ribbentrop dienststelle, then a part of the Reich Foreign Ministry, headed by Hermann von Raumer, and after the outbreak of war went on an intelligence collection mission to Paris. Following the occupation in June, he stayed in France to help Dr Helmut Knochen establish the SD's local office at 78 Avenue Foch with a staff of twenty, and two provincial branches in Bordeaux and Dijon.

In June 1941 Lorenz resigned from the SD and was posted to the Eastern Front but in May 1942 was recalled to Ribbentrop's staff in Berlin and was assigned a mission to Spain to investigate allegations against Ambassador Eberhard von Stohrer's wife, Maria von Günther, which turned out to be groundless. By 1944 he was back in Paris, and, following the Allied invasion, was evacuated to Chaumont-Gistoux where he decided to desert, intending to surrender to British troops then entering Brussels. However, he was arrested by Americans who escorted him to Paris in preparation for his transfer to Camp 020.

Although never a senior officer, Lorenz's lengthy relationship with Ribbentrop made him a valuable intelligence resource, and his knowledge and willingness to cooperate proved boundless. One episode he recalled was the arrests on 20 July in Paris of the three most senior SD officers in the city, Carol Oberg, Herbert Hugen and Helmut Knochen, on orders issued by the military commander of France, Carl-Heinrich von Stuplnagel. On the following morning the orders were countermanded, and Stulpnagel was recalled to Berlin. En route, near Verdun, he shot himself with his service revolver, but only managed to blind himself. He was charged with treason and executed on 30 August.

Lorenz, who did not entirely convince all his interrogators regarding the claimed nobility of his motives for switching sides, nevertheless gave detailed accounts of the Foreign Ministry's top-secret codebreaking bureau, the Reichsforschungsamt, located in Berlin's Grunewald district. As his interrogator concluded, 'Lorenz is undoubtedly a man of exceptional ability. His memory is remarkable for names, dates, places, events, etc., and he has also an unusual gift for languages.'[52]

Taken together with the eleven other significant wartime intelligence defectors (Erich Vermehren, Hans Ruser, Paul Hamburger, Hans Zech-Nennwich, Georg Kronberger, Richard Wurmann, Otto John, Josef Ledebur, Herbert Berthold, Peter Schagen and Carl Marcus), the Allies accumulated a comprehensive grasp of the entire German intelligence structure, with all its complexities and unique characteristics which made is such a formidable adversary over such a long period.

Chapter VI

THE KLATT MYSTERY

Klatt after all is one of the great mystery men of the war and he would not have been able to retain this status for long if he had been in the habit of disclosing the inner secrets of his organisation.

Memorandum, RSS to MI5 March 1946[1]

The approach taken by the interrogator was that of a historian attempting to complete the picture of Abwehr activity during the war. One of the largest blank spaces in this picture was labelled Meldekofp KLATT.

John Heinig, 7707 Military Intelligence Service Centre, March 1947[2]

It is true that the MAX reports all came from my head. What interest did the Soviets have in giving MORITZ reports?

Ira Longin, interrogation by Klop Ustinov and Gilbert Ryle, 20 March 1947[3]

The great unresolved issue of the era, of course, was the problem of the MAX network in Soviet-held territory. Was this an elaborate NKVD deception campaign, or a costly, undetected spy-ring? Certainly the MAX material greatly enhanced the Abwehr's reputation and provided a large proportion of the information that was fed to General Reinhard Gehlen's Fremde Heere Ost at the Boyen Fortress, a heavily fortified Prussian hilltop citadel in north-east Poland built in 1865, which accommodated the military intelligence centre for the Russian Front.

The traffic had been spotted in December 1941, and thereafter had been followed assiduously because of the explosive nature of its content which implied a massive breach of security across the entire Middle East theatre, placing in jeopardy all the elaborate deception campaigns created in Cairo to mislead the enemy. The situation in January 1943 was summarised in a report sent to MI5 in London:

MORITZ reports began on 5/12/41, though they were not at first headed MORITZ. Up to 6/1/43 there have been 502 MORITZ reports, known to us. These represent a large fraction but certainly not the whole of those sent by Sofia to Vienna.

The majority of these reports have been received by Vienna within 24-48 hours of their dispatch from (?) Egypt and in most ascertainable cases within 48 hours of the happenings reported on. MORITZ reports are deemed reliable enough to be forwarded from Berlin to the Abwehr officer with Kesselring and sometimes to the Naval Intelligence officers of Sofia and Athens. They are known to be not always accurate, but Kesselring's Abwehr officer complains if the supply dries up.

The Spanish Minister Prat, who desired all Luftmeldekopf intelligence is, apparently, to be kept quiet with MORITZ and IBIS reports. MAX reports, for special reasons, are clearly not going to be given to him. so MORITZ is not thought to merit the highest degree of security.

MORITZ reports give military, naval and air force intelligence as well as some which is primarily political. About a quarter of the reports deal with air force matters, about a seventh with marine matters, the rest with military plus a few political matters. The air force and marine intelligence is as a rule much more detailed than are the reports on troop-movements etc. Airfield equipment and convoy compositions are described with an appearance of precision. Troop strengths are not estimated. MORITZ seldom if ever identifies military, naval or air force units, save in so far as he occasionally mentions their nationalities. Battle-order particulars are not given. The reports appear generally to issue from the visual observations of MORITZ or from hearsay and not from official documents or from questioning.

In one case MORITZ was to be instructed to keep the aerodrome of Burg el Arab under continuous observation for at least 10 days, reporting on the number of aircraft and mentioning the time of observation. He was not instructed to ask any questions. (There is no sign that he fulfilled this assignment).

MORITZ reports deal with the following areas: EGYPT, LIBYA, TRIPOLITANIA, SYRIA, PALESTINE, CYPRUS, IRAQ, IRAN, SUDAN, RED SEA, PERSIAN GULF. It is noteworthy that while about a third of his first hundred reports dealt with SYRIA and PALESTINE, only three or four of his last hundred do so. It is still more noteworthy that from about the middle of November MORITZ reports have dealt with LIBYA, CYRENAICA and TRIPOLITANIA, almost to the exclusion of anything else. TOBRUK, DERNA, BENGHASI, AGEDABIA, SIRTE, seem to be the successive origins of MORITZ reports over the last two months. MORITZ intelligence seems to hail from the area DERNA round 20/11/42, from area BENGHASI during the last ten days of November and early December, from area BENGHASI-AGEDABIA during second and third weeks of December, from AGEILA and area AGEILA-SIRTE during the first week of January. What is general knowledge in Alexandria and Cairo no longer features largely, as it had before, in MORITZ reports. The inference is that MORITZ has moved west with the Eighth Army, and that before this advance he had been at base in Egypt.

The 'hotness' of his reports proves that he must be in W/T contact with Sofia or with a permanent intermediate relaying-station working to Sofia. The former is the more economical supposition. In either case, if he is with the 8th Army, he must be either an authorised W/T operator or the controller of an authorised W/T station, doing Abwehr work on the side. He must also be able to encipher and decipher messages.

He must then communicate with Sofia (or an intermediate relaying-station) with a cipher and W/T procedure which resemble his normal authorised cipher and procedure. He must transmit nearly every day (one or two possibly significant gaps will be mentioned later).

On 16/3/42 Sofia passed a MORITZ message to Vienna at 1512 GMT. The report mentioned the arrival of an American Air Force Mission at SUEZ early on that same day. As Sofia could hardly receive, decipher, appreciate, perhaps rewrite and re-encipher the report in less than an hour, MORITZ must have transmitted from Egypt before say 1400 hours on that day. Similarly on 29/3/42 MORITZ must have sent his report before 1500 hours on that day. On 16/6 he must have transmitted before 1800 hours, and on the 17th before 1600 hours; on 17/8 before 1700 hours; on 27/8 before 1600 hours, on 16/9 before 1900 hours. This only proves that MORITZ sometimes transmits fairly early in the day. On an ordinary day MORITZ's transmission would take between 15 and 40 minutes. MORITZ's habit of giving detailed particulars about airfields, his BURG EL ARAB assignment and the fact that he works for I Luft suggest that he may have some connection with the RAF or some Allied air force. And he should have been at BURG EL ARAB in the latter half of August. (Of course MORITZ may stand for a collection of persons, in which case the man at BURG EL ARAB need not now be in TRIPOLITANIA).

There has been nothing to indicate in what language MORITZ's messages are originally written.

MORITZ's external sources

Until the middle of November, MORITZ would seem to have been in Egypt, probably based on Alexandria, though with some freedom of movement. During this period while the bulk of the intelligence secured dealt with what could have been observed or overheard in

Egypt, a considerable part consisted of reports, often 'hot', from SYRIA, PALESTINE, CYPRUS, IRAQ, IRAN and other remote places. How did MORITZ secure this intelligence?

It is clear that the intelligence was not sent from say, BEIRUT, HAIFA, CYPRUS, BAGHDAD, etc. direct to SOFIA, else it would not have dried up in the middle of November. Moreover, the tidings from, say, CYPRUS or BANDER SHAHPUR came at irregular intervals and often in splashes, which independent W/T services would have obviated. Somehow the intelligence came quickly to MORITZ, who sent it alongside of Egyptian and Libyan intelligence to Sofia.

There is nothing to show what these outside sources were or how they communicated the news to MORITZ (save that the time available rules out anything but W/T or land-line).

It is possible that MORITZ has informants in or visiting all or most of the localities from which these reports come. In this case they would, perhaps, communicate by sub-rosa use of an authorised transmitter. Alternatively the intelligence may come to MORITZ's office as to an official clearing-house, while MORITZ steals some of it for his private use. In this case MORITZ would have to be working for an intelligence organisation, such as the Staff of one of the Services. The intelligence itself seems not to be of any one restricted type, but political information, riots, morale, disaffection, etc., bulk rather largely.[4]

By November 1943 the MAX-MORITZ traffic had been the subject of interception, and conjecture, for almost two years, a period of insight which was summarised in a report drafted by Gilbert Ryle and Hugh Trevor-Roper of SIS's Radio Intelligence Section (the renamed Radio Security Service).

Recent information (mostly in the new Service 2/5265) about developments in the mysterious career of Richard Klatt's organisation gives interesting indications about his relations with other official bodies and about the attributes of some of the persons whom he employs or contacts. They throw, at present, little light upon the sources of his operational reports or on the way in which these reports reach him. We also know very little about Klatt's present distribution of his reports.

2. Klatt himself has moved to Budapest, where he has a W/T station named BULLY. This move was correctly predicted by Gyorgy except as regards the date. According to this story the move was ordered as a result of a conference in Sofia held shortly before July 25th, attended by Canaris, Graf Marogna-Redwitz, Leiter of Ast Vienna, Oberst Kittell, Ritter von Wahl, the German Air Attaché Sofia, the C-in-C of German troops in Bulgaria and Delius (head of KO Bulgaria). Klatt attended one meeting. The reason given for the move was that the position of German

stations in Bulgaria was precarious. It is true that there was a big conference in Sofia on 21/7 at which Canaris was present. And it is true that Graf Marogna-Redwitz, Ritter von Wahl, the German Air Attaché at Sofia (Oberst von Schoenebock) and Dr. Delius would all have been concerned in the question of the removal of the Luftmeldekopf.

The rest of the story cannot be checked by us, Certain indications collected below suggest that Klatt went to Budapest to avoid trouble from the Bulgarian Government and the Abwehr in Bulgaria, and not from anti-Axis elements in that country.

Klatt has left behind him in Sofia a party of unknown size with a W/T station – perhaps only a transmitting and receiving set.

This station is now called STROH instead of SCHWERT. It is managed by someone who signs as HANS, who may be identical with a Dr. Deutsch whom Gyorgy puts No. 1 on his list of Klatt's hand-picked staff. We know that HANS was organising the removal of some Russian interpreters from Sofia to Budapest and that Dr. Deutsch was to call on KO Bulgaria to make arrangements in connection with this. But an elderly man called Hanns Sturm (Senior), No. 2 on Gyorgy's list, is another candidate.

This Sofia station collects and forwards to BULLY (in ISOS form) the operational report which is like those which Klatt had previously sent to Oberst von Wahl (1 Lutft Ast Vienna) on Service 7/23. On 4/9 KO Bulgaria enquired whether it was true that these reports no longer go to von Wahl, adding that Klatt had refused to pass them to the Abwehr via KO Bulgaria and that the Air Attaché, Sofia, (Oberst von Schoenebock) was now off the distribution list.

1 Luft, Vienna (= von Wahl) is now again forwarding Luftmeldekopf reports to e.g. Salonika.

We also have a fairly recent case of the Abwehr station at Nikolaiken passing a batch of Russian front reports to a station on the Russian front for operational use there.

So Klatt has retained or renewed some way of passing his reports to Abwehr HQ.

On 28/7 BERNDT (Major von Lossow) who is in charge of Russian operational intelligence for Abwehr HQ (Mil.lntell. East-North) said 'as MAX, for reasons known, has dropped out . . . ', which suggests that Klatt's Russian reports had either ceased to be supplied to the Abwehr or had ceased to be credited. Yet we know that these Russian reports were in fact being sent on Service 7/23 to von Wahl till late in September. BERNDT may have been anticipating a cessation of reports, which did not in fact take place when he expected it.

2. Klatt's operational reports are no longer headed MAX, MORITZ, IBIS ANATOL, ANKER or VIGO. Nor do the later substitutes for MAX, namely OLAF, EDELWEISS and 5029, appear nowadays as message-headings.

Ordinarily pass-ons of Klatt's reports are merely headed BULLY, though Nikolaiken ascribed some Russian reports from Klatt to 'agent CHUR'.

3. There has clearly been some clash between Klatt and von Wahl, in which Klatt seems to have prevailed. HANS congratulated Klatt on his success, and von Wahl now requests KO Bulgaria to facilitate certain transactions for Klatt.

4. The old feud between Dr. Delius (head of KO Bulgaria) and Klatt seems to have flared up again. Delius, at the request of von Wahl, has had the Luftmeldekopf's Wehrmacht telephone connections suspended. When Klatt's W/T operator Hanns Sturm (Jnr) was apprehended for smuggling currency and furs across the Turkish frontier, he was kept in detention by KO Bulgaria until Berlin decided his destiny. KO Bulgaria was at pains to suggest that Sturm was also improperly avoiding military service. Sturm boldly referred to his connection with the Fuehrer's HQ through which he would be released in 24 hours.

The White Russian Spanish Press Attaché Welikotny, who had been a regular source of reports from Turkey for the Luftmeldekopf, was, by order of KO Bulgaria, to be carefully frisked on his entry into Bulgaria. KO Bulgaria is also empowered to control the issue of visas and passes to all members of Klatt's organisation.

It is also likely but not certain that Dr. Delius is the 'D' who has been an instigator of certain criminal proceedings taken by the Bulgarian Government with German backing against an underworld collaborator of Klatt named Baumruch. Financial irregularities of some sort were alleged but there are clear signs that other underground activities were also suspected. One Bach of Klatt's circle (identity unknown) was also interrogated and later proceeded against, and HANS himself had to answer searching questions about certain secret contacts and information which he had enjoyed. He pressed Klatt to instruct him what answers he should give. Baumruch is now in Budapest. Bach was cleared of the Bulgarian charges, but certain German charges were at a recent date still undecided.

Klatt has changed his cover-name to KARMANY, for some purposes. (For others he is styled RICHARD, which is his genuine Christian name.)

HANS warns Klatt that telephone conversations on the military lines are monitored by careful and unfriendly censors. Even courier-consignments between Sofia and Budapest undergo such a merciless scrutiny that sealed cases of cigarettes are broken open by the inspectors. We do not know if Klatt, on his frequent visits to Sofia, has to travel incognito.

Klatt's connection with the Bulgarian police chief Pawloff continues. Pawloff seems to have been implicated or nearly implicated in the Baumruch inquisition. HANS warned Klatt that D (? = Delius) wished to take proceedings against Pawloff and Klatt. Last April Dr. Delius reported to Abwehr HQ. – '1) It has been ascertained beyond doubt that the Chief of the Bulgarian State police Pawloff is informing Klatt of the Abwehr affairs of the KO. Months ago Pawloff was instructed by me at his own request that he should not confide to Klatt any more than was necessary within the bounds of Klatt's special tasks and of collaboration with Bulgarian police aw/T. 3) What has come to light concerning the liaison between Pawloff and Klatt proves, however, that Stelle Klatt probably by heavy bribes ... III ... Pawloff watched and ask that FLETT (head of Abt. III P 3) 'should visit this end as in my view the case is very serious end renders comprehensible a number of cases of failure in collaboration with the Bulgarian police which up to now have been inexplicable.' (2/13, 21.4.43)

5. One Dominik, described by Gyorgy as 'a typist and clerk who keeps the card-index', seems still to belong to the organisation, though he is clearly suspected by Klatt and HANS not only of financial dishonesty but also of conversational indiscretion or treachery. Even HANS has recently had occasion to protest with some rhetoric his unswerving and eternal loyalty to Klatt. It is obvious that Klatt thinks that some of his secrets have become known to his enemies, though we can only conjecture who these enemies are.

6. Ira Lang or Langner who has some connections with the Russian Legation, Sofia, is still in regular touch with HANS. He gets money from Klatt (1,500 dollars a month) and has or is to have a flat found for him in Budapest, During the Turkul crisis, (see below), both Klatt and Lang hastened off to Vienna and perhaps Rome to make sure that General Turkul should not betray his knowledge of the MAX organisation to the Italians or the British. They seem to have got the General safely to Budapest, It is possible that Lang has gone or is going to Budapest for good.

7. It now transpires that the Luftmeldekopf has been housing and presumably employing two Russian prisoners of war, described as 'interpreters'. They are now being transferred, with their bedding, etc, to Budapest. Von Wahl had to enlist the services of KO Bulgaria to effect their removal.

8. There seem for some time to have been close relations between the Luftmeldekopf (Klatt and HANS) and – a) Major Hatz, Hungarian Military Attaché at Sofia, who has Hungarian Intelligence Service connections, and b) perhaps Oberst Merkly, a Hungarian at Budapest who also has Intelligence Service activities. Hatz is prepared to convey

material for Klatt across frontiers with diplomatic immunity and there has been talk of some W/T collaboration as well. HANS seems to secure motor-tyres for Hatz. But an attempt to get an entry-visa to Hungary for (?) HANS on official Hungarian endorsement was resisted by another Hungarian official IKONE, which suggests that there is a bad diplomatic smell about Klatt's menage.

Klatt's station BULLY now has a W/T service (2/5380) to a second station in or near Sofia, which is in quick telephonic communication with STROH. The operators call this second station HAT, which is likely to be an abbreviation of 'Hatz'.

The hypothesis that Klatt is now providing the Hungarian Intelligence Service in Budapest with operational intelligence is tempting but unproved. We know that Klatt's mistress Iby was empowered to pass reports to one ALTISCHT, apparently in Budapest, but we know nothing of this recipient. (It is interesting to notice that she was at the same time forbidden to forward any reports to Vienna.)

NOTE: Klatt and Iby are both Hungarians; Baumruch is probably another, Gyorgy is another, and is apparently working both for the Abwehr and for the Hungarian Intelligence Service. Two Hungarian operators in Turkey, KAMARAS and MOLNAR, were working, with the knowledge of Hatz, both for the Hungarian Intelligence Service and for the Abwehr.

9. Klatt and HANS seem to have good relations with the German Police attaché at the German Legation, Sofia. He is an SD functionary. There are other hints of some sort of dealings between the Luftmeldekopf and the SD, and specifically Amt. VI, but these hints do not reveal whether the dealings were formal or informal, friendly or hostile. It is conceivable that Klatt has both come into bad odour with the Abwehr and discovered how to protect himself and his employees against Abwehr reprisals by establishing an understanding with the SD and so, perhaps, with the Fuehrer's HQ (the support of which was anticipated by Sturm); but the point is not yet decidable. Klatt's independence of ordinary Abwehr control and discipline, which has always been remarkable, would be easier to explain if he has in fact enjoyed such high-level protection. On 5/11 HANS says that one HOFMANN has arrived in Sofia and was greatly interested in the last report, on 20/10 he had mentioned an Obersturmbannfuhrer (?) HOFMANN in some connection with 'attaché GruppeReichssicherheitshauptamt, Berlin'. On the same day he had reported that the police attaché was away from Sofia at a conference in Berlin, A message on 13/17 of 10/5 mentions Police Attaché HOFMANN as concerned in some Sofia transaction, though it does not definitely locate him at Sofia.

The suggestion is therefore strong, but not conclusive, that Klatt's organisation has put the SD, via the Police Attaché Sofia, on the distribution-list of anyhow some of its intelligence reports. The possible connection between the Police Attaché, Klatt. Pawloff and the Bulgarian police W/T is interesting.

On three occasions in 1942 there are references to contacts between Russian individuals in German hands (who worked or might work for the Luftmeldekopf) and one '02'. Some anxiety was expressed lest certain of these Russians might have divulged something about '02'. There is an SD office at Sofia who signs as '02' (= 6902) who seems to be concerned with Bulgarian and German police matters. This may be a pure coincidence.

10. Klatt has a house or rooms in Boulevard Ferdinand, in Sofia. His Russian prisoners were ensconced there, according to Gyorgy. Klatt's offices were at 55 Boulevard Skobeleff. (A recent message refers to Skobeleff 55 and suggests that HANS and party are to move from this address presumably to the Boulevard Ferdinand.)

11. So far as we can tell, the only W/T link directly controlled by HANS with an intelligence source outside Bulgaria is the W/T service 7/62 (= ISLAM traffic) over which are sent now VIGO's (Willy Goetz) and formerly DALISMO's reports from Turkey. This service also passes a few reports signed SCHIN emanating from a new informant professor ALEXCHIN (= probably Professor Alexis Shenshin who seems to have contacts with both the Abwehr and the SD). It seems to be intended that this link will in future be switched to Klatt's station in Budapest, There are strong reasons for thinking that operational reports from Russia and the British Middle East (MAX, MORITZ, and IBIS) are radioed to some other receiving station in Sofia and not to STROH (formerly SCHWERT). As Dr Delius in his complaint of April 21, 1943 (see para. 4) clearly indicated his belief that Klatt's intelligence-service depended upon his known liaison with the Bulgarian police W/T system, we can infer with moderate confidence (what we had previously conjectured) that the reception of MAX, MORITZ and IBIS signals is done by a Bulgarian police W/T station in Sofia. The deciphering of them may be and the translation from Russian (of MAX reports anyhow) has presumably been done in the Boulevard Ferdinand.

If this is so, and if Klatt is, as appears likely, planning ultimately to sever his whole connection with Sofia, he will have to find a substitute for the Bulgarian Police W/T station to perform the same function in Budapest. Perhaps Hatz and Merkly are making such arrangements. Klatt's interest in the arrival in Hungary from Turkey of a Hungarian W/T operator KOVACS would square with this. This operator has long been known to us. He worked in the Hungarian Legation at Ankara, transmitting for both the Hungarian Intelligence Service and for Friede's Abwehr reporting service.

12. At the end of July there was considerable alarm about the danger of a White Russian émigré General Turkul falling into the wrong hands in Italy, and so compromising the secret of MAX reports.

Not only Klatt and Lang but also the head of Abwehr I Luft Obstlt. Kleyenstuber altered all their arrangements and hurried off to Vienna and Rome to extract Turkul (sometimes referred to as 'T(oni') from Italy. He was successfully got away to Budapest. General Turkul, who has a long record of espionage activities in connection with the intelligence services of various countries, seems to have worked with especial vehemence against the USSR.

We must presume that the MAX intelligence-system was built up either by friends of Turkul or at least with his cognisance and advice, in a message of 19/10/1943 (service 2/38) Abwehr HQ (Air Intell. South) forwards to Salonika a batch of operational reports under the heading Source BULLY. (Luftmeldekopf Suodoct TONI – formerly MAX) 'T(oni') likely to stand for 'Turkul'. On 26.11. 1943 messages (on 2/5265) show that Ira Lang vetoed a suggestion that TONI's address should be divulged to Shenshin.[5]

At this early stage in the MAX-MORITZ saga the complexities of the Sofia Dienstelle were somewhat underestimated, and little thought had been applied to the thorny problem of double agents, deception campaigns and Soviet mischief. The challenges, soon to emerge, would remain a puzzle for many years and be complicated by the fact that Kim Philby told his Soviet contacts in 1942 that the British were reading the Abwehr's Vienna–Sofia Enigma-encrypted traffic, a channel designated VERA-SCHWERT ('Sword'), and Anthony Blunt had kept Moscow informed about the arrest and interrogation of Mirko Rot.[6] When eventually two Section V handbooks on Ast Sofia and Ast Bucharest, edited by the head of the Balkan and Soviet section Major O'Brien, were supplied through the official liaison channel, the NKVD complained that both items were out of date, and contained nothing new. This was largely true, as the decision had been taken in London at a high level not to reveal what, as it turned out, were the cryptographic breakthroughs already divulged by Philby and Blunt.[7]

The question of who really controlled the MAX network became moot during the summer of 1943 when a highly suspicious source in Istanbul, Andre Gyorgy, claimed to SIS to have access to KLATT's organisation and in March 1943 offered to install two radio transmitters in Sofia. Too good to be true, Gyorgy was a Hungarian Jew and a professional smuggler whose real name was Andur Gross. Considered an agent-provocateur, his material appeared to mirror some of Ast Sofia's traffic. Furthermore, he was identified by some of his acquaintances as having been employed by Colonel Otto Hatz's Abt. III/F section in Stuttgart and Budapest.

Gyorgy's approach to the British had been to Hugh Whittall, a member of Harold Gibson's SIS station based at the consulate-general, who passed him on to Klop Ustinov, introduced as 'Captain Johnson'. Gyorgy's offer to work for the British was conditional on him having post-war employment with a British firm, preferably in London, but Johnson suggested he might be able to settle in Kenya. According to Gyorgy, he was acting as an intermediary for Klatt who wanted him 'to induce the British and the Americans to give him a radio and codes, which he proposed to work himself in secret contact with the Allies'. After consulting, Ustinov suggested Gyorgy should identify two or three of Klatt's network on Allied territory, and let SIS run them.[8]

In September 1943 Klatt moved his headquarters to Budapest where he set up an office under commercial cover, Mittermayer Export-Import, in Roszaucca, with another in Rakos Palati. He employed four wireless operators, including Ilya Long, who also acted as secretary to the White Russian head of the Eastern Front networks, Anton Turkul. In addition, Klatt trained an Estonian woman as an operator, and two Russian PoWs who were intended to undertake a mission into Soviet-held territory.

Gyorgy made seven trips to Turkey to see SIS as an intermediary for Klatt, but was arrested in June 1944 in Istanbul because of an irregularity over his papers, and deported to Aleppo where he was arrested and consigned to SIME.

Gyorgy's contact with SIS, known in the Middle East as the 'Inter-Services Liaison Department' (ISLD), revealed the personalities in Sofia and Budapest that had been so carefully logged by the cryptanalysts, and the growing picture would be enhanced by another Abwehr insider, Willy Goetz, a Hungarian journalist working for the *Brüsseler Zeitung* and engaged to a Jew. Goetz was Klatt's representative in Istanbul from July 1943 and in that role collected information which he passed to Sofia. Originally a III'/F agent from Ast Vienna, Goetz's principal source was a forestry expert, Professor Alexis Shenshin, formerly of Belgrade University, who was in contact with a large group of Hungarian émigrés. For communications, Goetz relied on ALFONSO, a wireless operator based in the chancery of the Spanish legation in Ankara, who was in daily contact with Arnoldo Dalisme, the Spanish assistant press attaché in Istanbul. Goetz was also instructed to pass information to Klatt via a second route, through Major Bartalits, the Hungarian military attaché in Istanbul and his wireless operator,

Lajos Konya, designated ISLAM, which followed a regular schedule, transmitting twice a day.

In November 1944, when Goetz was deported to Syria he cooperated with SIME and asserted that his information on 'political and military matters in Soviet Russia' came from Shenshin, codenamed ALESSY, who

> claimed to have obtained his material from diplomatic couriers who bought it from a secret group in Russia which was hostile to the Soviet regime and championed White Russian interests. The couriers took Shenshin to be a genuine White Russian who passed this information to General Turkul and the latter's secretary, [George] Romanov, in Budapest. According to Shenshin, the anti-Soviet group in Russia included some notable generals, such as [Marshal Konstantin] Rokossovsky, his cousin.
>
> Shenshin's information was, very broadly, of the following nature:-
>
> (a) Military situation reports from various Russian fronts.
> (b) Details of various Russian army groups and their commanders.
> (c) Details of a special Communist army in Siberia trained to 'communize' all Europe after the defeat of Germany.
> (d) Plans of the anti-Soviet group to conclude a secret treaty with the OKW Berlin.
> (e) Reports on Finnish-Russian negotiations etc., etc.[9]

Goetz also told his SIME interrogators that the Moscow-born Shenshin had been in contact with other sources, among them

> [Legationsekretar] Henschel, a German OKW officer to whom he gave information; with Velikotny, a Spaniard who worked for a host of German Dienstellen; with [Yascha] Loltitch, a Yugoslav in Belgrade who was in touch with the Germans; with certain employees of Schenken & Co.; with the secretary of the German naval attaché Seiler (?); Shenshin was previously in contact by letter with Turkul through [George] Romanov who used to be in Istanbul; Shenshin also knew a number of White Russians in Istanbul including Serfanov (?); the Yugoslav Consul Petkovits; Nureddin, a French professor in Istanbul University who used to work for Velikotny and Gyula Kovacs.[10]

To complicate matters further, Shenshin was also employed by an US assistant military attaché, Norman Armour, Jnr., to teach him Russian. He was also commissioned by the US assistant naval attaché George H. Earle to write a series of articles about the Soviet Union. Furthermore, in September 1943 he had visited SIS's Archie Gibson at the embassy, and volunteered to work for the British, but had been turned down. His rejection by SIS was based on the knowledge that his ISOS traces revealed his Abwehr links, and there was also a suspicion that he had been responsible for the recruitment in January 1943 of a double agent, codenamed CRUDE. A Turkish businessman resident in Iraq, CRUDE was controlled by SIS and communicated by letters written in secret ink, and Shenshin was implicated in the case.

When Shenshin was eventually interviewed by SIME following his deportation by the Turkish police to Syria, he described how twenty-one different couriers had visited him at his Istanbul apartment between March 1940 and August 1944, and offered a detailed account of their reports. This material, allegedly assembled by a network known as 'Glebov' (supposedly after the chief of staff in the Moscow military district), would be the catalyst for an endless, unresolved debate among analysts to detect whether the information provided was Soviet 'smoke' or the product of a genuine anti-Bolshevik resistance organisation.

There is a certain irony in the fact that Shenshin's SIME file was shared with MI5, in particular Roger Hollis and Anthony Blunt, and with SIS where Kim Philby took an interest in the investigation. All were canvassed for their opinions, which varied greatly as there appeared to be so many contradictions in the versions offered by Shenshin and Goetz.

Under pressure from four days of interrogation, Shenshin broke down and admitted having passed information to the Germans, but only, he claimed, because some of his family were being held hostage by the Gestapo. He was kept in Cairo until March 1945 when he was transferred to a detention camp in the Sudan. In December 1946 Michael Serpell's study of the Klatt case concluded that Shenshin 'in 1943 and 1944 passed to the Germans not only Soviet propaganda and "smoke" but obvious deception material'.[11]

In January 1945 Hugh Shillito, MI5's expert on international Communism, drafted a five-page analysis of Shenshin's interrogation reports, concluding that:

It would seem probable that the couriers actually visited Senshin but that they were operating on behalf of the Soviets, and that the 'Glebov organisation' does not exist.

It seems extremely improbable that no less than 21 couriers from the USSR should have reached Shenshin without the knowledge of the OGPU. Soviet diplomatic couriers normally travel in couples, are carefully chosen for their political reliability and would have been subject to close supervision by the OGPU representatives in Istanbul on arrival there. Shenshin's story therefore, if true, argues a powerful and efficient underground movement in the USSR. But the information which is alleged to have been sent out at the greatest risk by this organisation is in fact mainly trivial and much of it could have been found in the current newspapers. Now and then there are items which appear to be of high importance but it will be noted that such items are either impossible of verification or are qualified or contradicted in later reports.

Again, there are various items dealing with Soviet military strength and morale, which are generally described as high. Flaws in the military machine are soon ironed out and the net result is highly favourable to the USSR. It is interesting to follow the reports on the Soviet Air Force which from being 'seriously crippled' goes from strength to strength till it outnumbers the German. This all gives the impression that material adverse to the Soviets is there to add verisimilitude, while the residuum presents a picture of Soviet military and political strength and success.[12]

While Shenshin languished in the Sudan, Allied counter-intelligence analysts tracked down members of Ast Sofia to piece together the background to the Abwehr's greatest triumph, or most embarrassing humiliation. Opinions were divided, but all agreed that Klatt was a man of great charm and boundless powers of persuasion. One of his favourite ploys was to have a subordinate enter his office during a meeting and hand him a vital message. This would then prompt him to draw a black curtain from a large wall map bearing small red lights, apparently to indicate the location of his network's transmitters. This piece of theatre always left a lasting impression on visitors . . . until they compared experiences.

Otto Wagner, commander of the Sofia KO, who was always on bad terms with Klatt, surrendered to the French in Austria in May 1945 and under interrogation in Karlsruhe described how in 1940 he had been sent from his Abt. III post in Berlin to Bulgaria to develop networks in Greece and Romania, a process in which he established branches in Tirana, Skopje, Athens and Salonika, with a KO later opened in Istanbul under Paul Leverkuehn. Wagner, whose KO was accommodated in a private house at 57 rue Patrich Eftimie, a few blocks from the German legation, was transferred to Budapest in May 1944 but returned to Sofia in October.[13]

When questioned about Klatt, Wagner insisted that his scepticism of claims that he controlled a wireless network stretching across the Caucasus had resulted in rebukes from more senior personnel, including Canaris who had sent Georg Hansen to warn him against monitoring Klatt too closely. Wagner said several others shared his doubts, but Klatt repeated that his White Russian organisation was controlled by Ilya Lang.

Under interrogation in 1947 Wagner held the 'unshakeable conviction that Klatt had all along been a conscious agent of the Soviet intelligence service', and was in fact nothing more than a 'Nachrichtenschwindler'. Early in 1942 Wagner had assigned a III/F officer, Kleinhempel, to investigate the MAX source:

W/T stations in the Soviet Union supposedly beamed their transmissions to a receiving station in Samsun, Turkey, from which the messages were telephoned to Istanbul. In Istanbul they were turned over to a courier who took them by railroad to the Bulgarian border; thence they were forwarded, also by courier to Sofia. Kleinhempel again went to work and soon reached the conclusion that Klatt, in making up his story, had failed to take into account several important factors. To establish telephone connection between Samsun and Istanbul Kleinhempel determined would take about four weeks and the railroad from Istanbul to the Bulgarian border was not a feasible route, since an important railroad bridge in Turkish territory had been blown. Moreover, Klatt's claim that an average of six messages arrived dally indicated a truly remarkable performance if one accepted his version of how the MAX reports got to Sofia.[14]

Wagner later recalled how his suspicions about Klatt had hardened:

Klatt's account of his W/T contacts in the USSR only strengthened Wagner's belief that he was not on the level, Klatt's claim that W/T stations were operating all over the USSR and that his agents were members of White Russian organisations holding down staff positions and posts as heads of W/T schools in Russia. Wagner refused to credit simply because it would have been unrealistic for Soviet counter-espionage to have failed to neutralize so widely ramified a network of this type.

Wagner also discarded as utterly fantastic Klatt's assertion that the MAX messages originated from transmitters in a W/T school near Moscow headed by a Major Samoilov, who conveyed messages through lessons in the garb of training transmissions. Only then did it begin to occur to Wagner that Klatt might be working for a foreign intelligence service, and the question of whether it was a Soviet or an Allied service had to be left open. Wagner never actually obtained irrefutable evidence that it was the Soviet service for which Klatt worked, but the burden of proof pointed in that direction.

After having eliminated the possibility of W/T traffic from the USSR to a receiving station in Samsun, Turkey, or in Bulgaria proper,

Kleinhempel's field of inquiry narrowed down to the identification of Klatt's sources in Sofia. Several indications pointed to the NKVD representative in the Soviet legation, one Oesoekin (phon.) as Klatt's contact and probably the source of his reports. Kleinhempel found out that some of Klatt's intimate associates had been seen with Osoekin in a bar called Maxime's located in the basement of the Royal Theater in Sofia and reported that in 1943 IRA was seen leaving the Soviet legation. On the basis of Kleinhempel's investigations, Wagner came to the firm conclusion that both Klatt and IRA maintained connections with the Soviets through Oesoekin, particularly since Oesoekin was also known to be in daily contact with Klatt's girlfriend.

Wagner believes that Klatt's tie-up with the Soviet Intelligence Service was of a double agent nature. Klatt was in close personal contact with a number of ranking Abwehr officers and through them undoubtedly had access to classified information of great interest to the Russians. Wagner emphasized however, that his analysis is conjectural, for he had no direct evidence that Klatt actually gave information to the Russians. It is also possible that the Soviets used the Klatt Meldekopf to assist anti-German movements in Bulgaria. Wagner mentioned that in many instances local unrest where an opposition movement had formed was connected with the presence of Meldekopf members in the locality.

In determining the origin of Klatt's intelligence material Wagner suggested that the close relationship which he knew existed between Klatt and Otto Hatz, the Hungarian Military Attaché in Budapest (?) must be considered particularly significant. In 1942 Wagner obtained what he believed conclusive evidence that Hatz and Klatt were exchanging military information. (Hatz's brother was known to work for the Soviets but there had been no indication of a possible connection with Otto Hatz.) In May 1944 Hatz was recalled to Budapest and arrested on suspicion of having maintained connections with the Soviets while in Turkey (?). In order to satisfy himself of the exact nature of the relationship between Klatt and Hatz, Wagner prevailed on the Gestapo to release Hatz and took him under control with the assignment of collecting military information. In the further events Wagner obtained conclusive proof that the military information given him was also passed to Klatt. During May and June 1944 both Hatz and Klatt produced identical reports conveying the impression that the Soviet armies were on the verge of collapse and mentioning first one, then another front sector as the probable scene of an impending Soviet reverse. In Wagner's opinion, these reports were designed to promote a feeling of confidence in the German High Command and succeeded to the extent that some German army units were ordered to hold certain front sectors at all costs in anticipation of a Soviet retreat which of course never materialised. Wagner believes that these reports which were absolute nonsense contributed largely to the destruction of German armies in the East.[15]

Wagner's doubts about Sofia's alleged sources were manifest in March 1943, and showed up in the ISOS intercepts studied by British analysts. For example, the exchange of two highly sensitive messages illustrate Wagner's demand for further information, and Kauder's immediate refusal to disclose his sources, a reply signal transmitted within half an hour.

> 1596 VIENNA TO SOFIA at 1704 on 19/3
> 11 for KLATT.
> Reference message 87 of 6/31: From where did this reported 19 FRENCH pursuit planes originate, SYRIA or AFRICA? If possible, state the unit. Please give interim report. WAGNER

> 3006 SOFIA TO VIENNA at 1732 at 19/3
> Reference your number 11 enquiry cannot be answered from this end. According to report it does not concern planes which have arrived but planes stationed there. Inquiry at MORITZ's impossible as stated in the letter sent today.
> KLATT[16]

While Wagner harboured doubts, so did British intelligence analysts in the Middle East who, in February 1943, had undertaken a study to compare thirty-eight of MORITZ's recent messages with the known facts, a procedure known as a Veracity Report.

1. Out of these, 29 reports concerned the Eighth Army area directly, 14 of them being military and 15 air information.
2. Of the remaining nine reports, five reported naval convoy reports, as under:-

> (a) 2.2.43 from ALEXANDRIA to TRIPOLI.
> (b) 5.2.43 from BEIRUT to ISKENDERUN.
> (c) 11.2.43 arrivals In TRIPOLI from HAIFA.
> (d) 19.2.43 from TRIPOLI westwards.
> (e) 25.2.43 arrivals in TRIPOLI from ALEXANDRIA.

A report of February 1st gave a list of FRENCH formations en route from SYRIA to the TRIPOLI front on January 31st.

3. A report, transmitted on February 10th, stating that a goods-train with military deliveries for TURKEY had been blown up in JERUSALEM, was clearly nonsense.

4. A report transmitted on February 11[17] stated that a seaplane harbour had been constructed in CYPRUS for USA. This is incorrect.[17]

The RAF and Admiralty checked the relevant messages and were unimpressed. Fourteen texts were assessed as 'incorrect' and only one was 'generally correct'. Out of eleven checks by the RAF, four were 'incorrect' and one was 'generally correct'. The Navy judged MORITZ's reporting as 'almost 100% wrong'.

On 17 February 1943 SIME, MI5 and SIS held a high-level conference in Cairo to consider MAX, MORITZ and IBIS, and evaluated all the various options, dismissing the idea of a clandestine Vichy French transmitter or the interception of Allied cipher traffic, commenting 'no interception service would indiscriminately gather army, navy, air force, and political information over a large area, as MORITZ has done'. As for MAX, the gathering concluded that 'if it were intercept, hamchat or R/T, we should not expect the amount of spurious material to be so great'. However, the attendees were baffled by the absence of traffic going to Sofia, which raised the possibility that 'MAX is a Russian diplomatic cipher from Kuibishev to Sofia' or that the transmissions were hidden in an authorised channel which was not monitored. Whatever the explanation, it was noted that there was only a delay of a day between items being reported and then appearing in a decode, which was usually a strong indication of the original intelligence arriving at Sofia by wireless. Yet there was no such traffic on the airwaves. Another oddity was the absence of any relayed signals from Vienna to MAX via Sofia, apart from one directive for the Burg el-Arab aerodrome to be watched continuously by MORITZ for ten days. On that single occasion, the instruction was ignored.[18]

Despite Wagner's deep-seated reservations, the MAX reporting continued to be assessed as high value in Berlin, as recalled by an I/L officer from Ast Vienna, Horaczek, in November 1946:

> The reports were considered of extreme importance. And were termed as being quite essential and that they had repeatedly been confirmed as valid by subsequent events on the Russian front. From then on Klatt was given the special protection of Berlin and was granted all the assistance he requested.[19]

In June 1945 the MI5 War Room in London issued an assessment, while Klatt himself was in custody in Salzburg, noting that

Klatt had a number of agents, the majority of which were very bad. The most interesting were: (A) MORITZ who reported on the movements of the 8th Army during the summer of 1942 and early 1943, sometimes with considerable accuracy; (B) MAX who reported on Russia. Nature of information passed suggests he had w/t stations in the Rostov area, one near Moscow and one near Leningrad. Possible MAX himself was in Soviet legation in Sofia. (C) IBIS who reported on the Middle East.[20]

A contemporaneous study of the MORITZ traffic conducted by RSS's Professor Gilbert Ryle, the Christ Church, Oxford, academic who had been monitoring the traffic for the past three years from his office in Barnet, north London, concluded that they were 'to be regarded as inaccurate and of little importance'.[21]

Ryle's opinion on Klatt, and his advice to MI5, greatly outweighed the interrogation reports compiled by French and then American investigators who had little knowledge of the background to the case, or any understanding of its significance. However, there remained plenty of witnesses who held favourable opinions about the Klatt reporting, including Walter Schellenberg who was asked about Klatt while under interrogation at Camp 020 in July 1945. He recalled that he

worked in the first instance for military intelligence. His reports on Russian army matters were good and classed as 'important to the Wehrmacht (Heereswichtig)' and the General Staff (Fremde Heere Ost) thought highly of him. On air matters they were weak, and on political questions sometimes good and sometimes bad . . . KLATT ran his organisation very successfully; he had the advantage of working with Ast Vienna which supplied deception and play-back material. Finally he became too independent and started working with Hottle and Wanneck.[22]

When rumours reached Berlin about Klatt, Schellenberg had sent Colonel Ohletz, the head of Mil. C, to conduct an inspection of his 'shop' in Budapest. Dissatisfied with Ohletz who could not find anything suspicious, he

summoned Wiese from Vienna and asked him to investigate. The latter found out that the men who in reality provided intelligence for KLATT's racket were a Slovak lawyer and Prince Turkul. The latter had a White Russian line to Moscow. These lines also led to Istanbul and Bratislava. Weise arrested KLATT and twenty-eight small agents who formed a motley crowd containing all sorts of nationalities, and even a Gestapo man from Vienna. After only a few days it was possible to resume work

211

through KLATT's organisation, however, and although for the first week the intelligence declined in value, it gradually improved and in the end became excellent.[23]

Klatt's third network, IBIS, had been spotted in ISOS channels in March 1942 and over the next ten months some 143 messages had been intercepted. As MORITZ had been active between December 1941 and January 1943, when 502 messages had been copied, it appeared to be a separate, parallel organisation also reporting to Sofia. In total, an estimated 10,000 messages had been transmitted from Sofia to Vienna.

At the end of January 1943 MI5's Dick White, then Assistant Director, B Division, made a tour of inspection across the Middle East and remarked on how SIME had abandoned the KLATT material, noting in his highly critical report that

> the whole work of SIME in the counter-espionage field should be much improved. In particular, I believe that it is not necessary that problems, such as are presented by the MORITZ spy stuff in the Middle East, and the [PASHA], IBIS and ANKER rings, need not go unsolved. There is no doubt in my mind that SIME was not tackling counter-espionage work with sufficient understanding of its nature, nor had they the tools of the business.[24]

However, instead of explaining the challenge of dissecting and analysing the internal contradictions of the traffic in question, he suggested that SIS was to blame for a cultural reluctance to share information with the investigators, asserting that:

> Enquiries into such unsolved problems at the MORITZ network, the IBIS network, the Lisbon leakages and the case of the PASHA have, in my view, rather fallen between two stools. All these problems have been based on TRIANGLE. ISLD presumably kept a restraining hand on investigations. This should not and cannot be allowed. It is with SIME that the responsibility rests for neutralizing enemy intelligence organisations in the Middle East . . . [25]

An attempt in March 1946 to bring Klatt to London for interrogation failed when he tried to hang himself in Frankfurt. Accordingly, he was interrogated in Germany by Gilbert Ryle in July 1946, and on 13 August MI5's Joan Chenhalls sent a copy of Ryle's final report to Kim Philby, inviting his comments.

Dienstelle Klatt and the MAX-MORITZ Intelligence Reports.

<u>Foreword</u>.

From 1941 to 1945 Dienstelle Klatt in Sofia and later Budapest sent a daily supply of operational intelligence to the Abwehr in Vienna for the German Higher Command. These intelligence reports were of various types, the two main types being the so-called 'MAX Reports' and 'MORITZ Reports'. The MAX Reports dealt with Russian naval, military and air dispositions, chiefly between Sevomorsk and the Caucasus.

The MORITZ Reports dealt with Anglo-Saxon dispositions in the Mediterranean theatre and the British Middle East. Over 5,000 MAX and MORITZ reports were passed to the Germans in about 3 ½ years.

We were aware of the existence, nature and distribution of these reports from the end of 1941 but, though we knew a great deal about Klatt's Dienstelle, his staff, his agents in Turkey, and his W/T communications with Vienna, and with Turkey, we remained completely mystified by the following three problems:-

(1) By what channels and from what sources did MAX and MORITZ reports get to Klatt?
(2) What organisations, operating from what motives, collected and communicated the MAX and MORITZ intelligence (or misintelligence)?
(3) Was there a W/T leakage of operational intelligence (or misintelligence) from the British Mediterranean zone and if so how was it constituted or concealed from us?

As a result of my interrogation of Klatt on 17 July 1946, reinforced by study of the admirable results of the American interrogations of Klatt and others, I venture to think that a highly probable solution of these three puzzles can now be given.

I. <u>The Communications Puzzle</u>.

Although from late 1941 we had excellent reasons for supposing that the MAX and MORITZ reports were transmitted from their source or sources by W/T, the attempts of RSS to identify these transmissions were completely unsuccessful.

The following information given in or suggested by Klatt's interrogations may enable us to make a retrospective identification of them. It must be noticed that Klatt was shifty in his answers to several of the questions put to him on this matter, particularly when he began to realise their import, so some of the clues given may be false.

1. The first W/T communications from a source in Russia to Klatt in Bulgaria came between 18th to 23rd of June, 1941, i.e. just before or just after the outbreak of the Russo-German war. The source was a W/T operator in Tiflis. His signals were received and decoded by a Bulgarian police station in Burgas, whence they were forwarded to a Sofia police station, two functionaries of which were already in the pay of Klatt. Klatt passed these reports to Vienna first by telephone from the German Naval Command in Sofia and then by W/T from the Sofia police station to some corresponding W/T station in Vienna. Klatt's own W/T link with Ast Vienna did not function until November 1941.

Klatt thought that the messages were in Russian. He had not provided the Burgas police with cipher instructions but he thought that the cipher used was a figure-cipher, since the Burgas police complained of the difficulty of receiving figures as distinct from letters. This W/T link ceased to function in July or August 1941, allegedly because the Tiflis W/T operator became scared when follow-up queries were sent to him (presumably from Burgas) in connection with some report which he had sent.

(Klatt was vague or evasive in his replies to questions about the initial creation of this link and about the provisions of cipher and signals-plans for the Tiflis operator and the Burgas police. He spoke of a 'Macedonian organisation' or of a member of such an organisation as the creator of the link. The story of the decoding being entrusted to the Burgas police is implausible. However we have independent evidence that Klatt did have agents in Burgas in 1941 and that there was a Tiflis W/T operator who was an early source of Russian intelligence. A more plausible hypothesis will be suggested later to explain the cessation of the Tiflis transmissions.)

2. On 15 July 1941 Klatt's White Russian collaborator Ira Lang (@ Longin) came to Klatt with intelligence reports very similar to those of the Tiflis operator. From then until early in 1945 all the reports of the MAX and MORITZ categories came to Klatt from Lang. It was not until 1942 that the titles 'MAX' and 'MORITZ' were coined to distinguish the Russian from the Mediterranean intelligence.

So the problem is how and whence did Lang get his MAX and MORITZ messages.

The following (alleged) facts may help to identify the W/T traffic between Lang's source and Lang.

a) The cipher was a 'combined cipher', i.e. mixed letters and figures. (Klatt's story does not rule out the Tiflis operator's cipher from having also been a 'combined cipher'.)
b) The transmission time was some time between about midday and 3.30 p.m. (Central European Time). Klatt gave two discrepant accounts.

214

(2) In his <u>second</u> interrogation Klatt said that he thought that the transmission time was between midday and 1.0 p.m. 'since Lang would never come out to lunch'. Lang normally brought the reports by hand between 2.0 p.m. and 3.30 p.m. I believe this second story to be an attempt to lead us away from the real transmission time. There is an extra reason for thinking that this second story was an afterthought. When asked in another connection whether Lang was himself a W/T operator, Klatt denied it. Yet his second story assumes that Lang had to be present during the transmission time. If Lang had only to decipher messages and not himself to receive W/T signals, he could have postponed his decoding until after lunch.

3. MAX and MORITZ messages came every day of the week except Sundays. They were sent from 15 July 1941, to anyhow 12 February 1945.

4. Both MAX and MORITZ messages were brought round by Lang together. When in 1942 it was decided to head the reports 'MAX' and 'MORITZ', they were distinguished purely by their contents, i.e. from the geographical areas referred to in the texts of the messages. Both were in the Russian tongue. It follows that MAX and MORITZ messages issued from the same W/T source and were sent in the same transmission. We have a little evidence (not from Klatt's interrogation) that this W/T station was in the Novorossisk area.

5. There were nearly always exactly six MAX reports. Occasionally a seventh was added if of special importance. There were usually two or three MORITZ reports and sometimes none. When Klatt said that the cipher was a combined-cipher he volunteered the information that at a late stage in the war the German Funkabwehr was trying to identify the MAX-MORITZ transmissions. On hearing Klatt's suggestion that the cipher was a 'combined-cipher', the investigators were delighted and said that this confirmed their own hypothetical identification of the wanted traffic. Since Klatt volunteered this story, we should expect it to be false, unless he supposed that we had access to the Funkabwehr's records or had interrogated or could interrogate its officers. (Such an interrogation should be made, if possible.)

6. The deciphered texts were in Russian Schlegworter, i.e. in highly compressed 'headlinese'. These had to be translated into German and expanded into intelligible prose before Klatt could send them on to Vienna. That is, each MAX or MORITZ report in its original condensed form would consist of only plus or minus a dozen words. (This is my estimate. Klatt wrote out some typical specimens of the original messages

in their condensed form, together with their expanded renderings in German prose. These are appended.)

Note. Mirko Rot stated that he had overheard Klatt telephoning from Budapest to Sofia. Something was read out to him from Sofia which Klatt then construed out of his head. It is clear from what Roth said that Klatt was giving the German equivalents of certain code-expressions; he was not merely giving prose-expansions of 'headlinese' phrases.

Klatt was interrogated on this point. He admitted without hesitation that when he was away from Sofia he did often construe over the telephone MAX or MORITZ messages read out to him from his Sofia Dienststelle in their original condensed form. But he denied that any code-expressions were used. I think that he was lying. Any German-speaking clerk could have expanded into German prose the condensed messages described by Klatt without telephoning to Budapest for help. If this hypothesis is correct, then MAX and MORITZ messages as transmitted might have been very brief indeed, especially if, as may follow from Rot's story, the code expressions consisted of single or perhaps coupled letters or figures.

7. It was always possible for Klatt and Lang to put their own queries or those of, say, Luftflotte IV to the source or sources of MAX reports. Klatt thought that the need never arose over MORITZ reports. Replies to these queries never took less than 3-4 days to come back and often they took 8 days. This suggests but does not prove that

(1) MAX and MORITZ reports were transmitted 'blind', else anyhow some replies to merely textual questions would have been got within 24 hours.

(2) There was a W/T link available to Lang working to the source or sources of MAX-MORITZ reports, but a link which worked only once or twice a week. (These transmissions need not have been made from Sofia or even from Bulgaria. Lang had transactions, including cash transactions with Turkey and he said – so it is probably false – that he controlled a W/T station at Samsun. If so, the delay in getting replies may have been due to the slowness of Lang's communications with his transmitting station in Turkey.)

8. Klatt tried hard to sell us 'his own ideas' that Lang availed himself of the W/T facilities of a consulate (?Soviet) in Sofia and later in Budapest. But if the MAX-MORITZ transmissions were made 'blind', Lang need not have had daily access to a transmitter at all. He could have received the transmissions in his own home on an ordinary radio set. It cannot be supposed that Lang could have eluded for three years the vigilance

of the inquisitive Dr. Delius either in working a transmitter from his own residence or in making daily visits to some other establishment equipped with a transmitter.

9. There are tenuous reasons for thinking that the MAX-MORITZ transmissions were regularly intercepted in Rome as well as in Sofia or Budapest. If so, then either in Rome or in Sofia, or both, the transmissions were intercepted without the recipient being able to 'break in'. This suggests that the MAX-MORITZ signals were powerful. The same conclusion would follow from the assumption that the MAX-MORITZ transmissions were made 'blind'.

10. I think that there was only one W/T station involved in the transmission of MAX-MORITZ signals. Klatt said that though there were a few days on which nothing could be received, there were no days on which a half ration of MAX-MORITZ messages was received. Either these were the standard MAX messages plus the two or three MORITZ messages, or there were none. When transmission on one day did not occur, eight or nine MAX messages would be sent on the following day or two instead of the normal six.

II The ostensible roles of Lang and Turkul.

A Lang (Activities and their ostensible motive).

Lang was a former White Russian officer. In July 1940 he offered his services to his chief, then in Rome, and thus became a member of his chief's anti-Communist White Russian organisation. On the occasion of this visit to Rome he was given authority to collaborate with the German Abwehr. He was to create or exploit links with Russia, procure operational intelligence about Russian dispositions and convey his results to the Abwehr. He was not himself an Abwehr employee, and used Klatt, who was an Abwehr employee, as his middleman.

In 1940 and early 1941 Lang succeeded in inserting some bona-fide White Russians into Russian units; line-crossers were bringing back dispatches from these volunteer-agents before the outbreak of the Russo-German war. Against just this contingency Lang had, in March 1941, conveyed to these agents in Russia signals-plans and cipher instructions. On about 15 July 1941 his sources in Russia began to send their intelligence reports to Lang by W/T. Lang, 'who knew next to no German' and Klatt 'who knew only the Russian alphabet', collaborated in rendering the Russian texts of the messages into German. This they did with the aid of an ordinary Russian-German dictionary and a Russian-German military word book.

What came later to be designated as 'MAX reports' were headed in Lang's original Russian texts 'from R 1' or 'from R 2', 'from R 5' or from '03' or from '05'. 'R 1' 'R 2' etc., were outlying radio-agents; '03' '05' were their spy-bosses. '05' was a Captain Samilov (? Cover-name), who at one time ran a Russian Army Signals School in Kuibischev. Lang himself was known as '02'.

Lang spent most of his time in Sofia and even when Klatt removed to Budapest, Lang refused to do more than 'commute' between Sofia and Budapest. He had no trade or profession, but he had some authority over various circles of White Russians in Sofia and Bulgaria. His residence was 3 Sixth of September Street, Sofia. Lang had some White Russian agents working in Sofia, some of whom he had managed to insert into Dr. Delius' Ast Sofia.

For a long time Lang would not disclose the identity of his 'chief' in Rome, but soon after the entry of the USA into the war he revealed that he was General Turkul.

Lang firmly refused to become a member of the Abwehr and rigidly insisted that his contacts with that organisation were to go through the sole mediation of Klatt. His personal remuneration and the much larger payments for the upkeep of his organisation came through Klatt, and Klatt had to negotiate with the Abwehr on all questions of permits, passes etc. for Lang.

If Lang's remittances were delayed, he threatened to cut off his intelligence supplies; and any attempt by the Abwehr to investigate his methods, organisation, contacts etc. were successfully resisted by the threat that MAX and MORITZ reports would cease to be delivered. His and Turkul's White Russian Secret Service remained unpenetrated. It is not clear whether Lang was the head of Turkul's entire Secret Service or only of its Balkan and Russian wing. Lang's dominant motive was to destroy Bolshevism.

B Turkul (Activities and their ostensible motive).

General Turkul, who had fought under Denikin after the Bolshevik Revolution, was a prominent White Russian emigre in Western Europe between the two wars. He took an active part in helping to build up White Russian organisations in Paris and elsewhere and was particularly active in fostering a White Russian military elite. He was one of the most vigorous leaders of the movement to destroy communism in Russia, Spain or elsewhere and he had worked out for himself a sovereign position in the Russia that was to be restored.

Naturally there were feuds between different sections of the scattered White Russian community and Turkul was often involved in them. He had resided in Paris and Berlin before coming to Rome.

In empowering Lang to work the MAX-MORITZ intelligence system and to pass the results to the Abwehr, he had two motives, first to assist the Axis in its crusade against the Soviet regime and second to secure the funds necessary for the creation and maintenance of his White Russian organisation.

When the Germans encouraged General Vlassow to build up a fighting force of anti-Soviet Russians, Turkul tried to supplant Vlassow in the command of this force or at best to get an influential position on Vlassow's staff. Near the end of the war, Turkul was building up his own independent corps of White Russian warriors to help the Germans in their now unpromising fight against Stalinism.

Even after the collapse of Germany, Turkul would not give up the struggle. There was still a role for him and his corps, namely to assist the Anglo-Saxons to stem the tide of Communism in the Balkans. His private legion, which had not actually been committed in battle against the Russians, might yet be of service in quelling the EAM in Greece or curbing Tito in Yugoslavia.

C MAX and MORITZ. (Ostensible story).

Thus the MAX-MORITZ reports constituted a genuine leakage of operational intelligence; it was the White Russians' contribution to the Axis struggle against Communism

This whole picture was, at least for the greater part of the war, accepted by the Abwehr, the SD, the German High Command and probably by Klatt himself. Any doubts about its genuineness was allayed by the salient fact that the MAX intelligence (though not the MORITZ intelligence) was constantly corroborated by aerial observation and the results of operations in the field. The information was of direct tactical and strategic value. Minor inaccuracies were often detected but, during at least the greater part of the war, there was no trace of tactical or strategic deception.

The bona-fides of Turkul and Lang were proved by the veracity of the MAX intelligence. Enquiries into the Turkal-Lang organisation were vetoed on the score that it was duly laying its golden eggs.

III Arguments against the ostensible story.

The following points prove, in my opinion, that the ostensible story given above is false.

Klatt is eager to disclose everything he knows about the Abwehr, the SD, the Bulgarian police, his own agents and contacts in Turkey, etc. But when questioned about Lang and Turkul he lies, hesitates, 'forgets', steers the conversation away and looks uneasy. He has either much to hope or, more likely, much to fear from whatever organisation Lang and Turkul serve. He knows that Soviet agents attempted to kidnap him from the Americans and he has been overheard to say that when released he will work for the Russians. The inference is that he now identifies the Lang-Turkul secrets with Soviet secrets, and is right in doing so. I think that during the war he did not seriously suspect this. He would have been too much of a danger to Lang if he had had any good reasons for such suspicions.

Moreover Klatt was well aware of the military value to Germany of the MAX reports and, like everybody else, could not reconcile this fact with the notion that the MAX reports were Soviet controlled. Doubtless Lang, during his five-year intimacy with Klatt, was occasionally unguarded, so there may have been a number of minor clues which together with the kidnapping attempt now convince Klatt that Lang and therefore Turkul had all the time been Soviet agents. But before the kidnapping attempt Klatt probably swallowed the ostensible story and assumed that Lang's secrets were the secrets of a bona fide White Russian Secret Service.

2. In 1938 (?) the White Russian leader General Miller was kidnapped from Paris and smuggled away to Leningrad. The organisers of this exploit were one Skoblin and his wife. Skoblin immediately reported his success to Turkul, then in Berlin, who dropped everything and hastened to Paris. Skoblin got away. His wife was caught but died, conveniently, in a French prison before she could reveal anything. If this story is true, it almost proves that Turkul was not a bona fide White Russian loyalist, but a Soviet spy or *agent provocateur*, presumably an employee of the NKVD. If he was, then Lang was too.

I shall argue that the hypothesis that Turkul and Lang were – and are – agents of the NKVD explains every mystery in the MAX-MORITZ matter, including the biggest mystery of all, namely, the general veracity and military importance of the MAX reports.

3. When the Abwehr accepted the collaboration of Lang, the Hungarian Secret Police were astonished. They were convinced that their former gaol-bird Lang was a Soviet agent. We do not know what had convinced them. Dr. Delius had similar suspicions.

4. It is incredible on general grounds that a bona fide White Russian spy-network could have operated daily from July 1941 to February 1945 without the Russians discovering it. And we can be sure on special grounds that the Russians had some knowledge of the apparent leakage. Yet the Russians never stopped the leak and Lang never seems to have felt the qualms proper to a bona-fide White Russian lest the

intelligence which he was selling to the Germans might have become deception material.

5. The W/T procedure and the cipher-type of the MAX-MORITZ transmissions (according to our speculative reconstruction of them) are of fairly standard Russian secret service patterns. (Check with ME).

6. The cover nomenclature 'R.1' and '02' etc have a similar flavour. (Check)

7. Supposing that at least in the beginning the sources of MAX reports were bona-fide White Russians, working as spies from devotion to the anti-Communist cause, it is hard to explain the existence of MORITZ reports. For these reports were of poor quality and were fairly soon recognised by the Germans to be operationally worthless. Klatt was actually permitted to feed the Spanish Ambassador in Ankara, Prat, with MORITZ reports. Klatt himself volunteered in interrogation his belief that he denied ever having done so.

Now if the supposed bona-fide White Russian sources of these reports had no intelligence source in the British Middle East, they could have had no motive for concocting MORITZ reports. For they could not have wished Lang to receive or pass on misinformation. If on the other hand they had a source in, say Egypt, in W/T communication with themselves, this source would have been able and presumably anxious to send a fair amount of good information.

8. Turkul and Lang have never yet been the victims of kidnapping or liquidation attempts. They dwell apparently without qualms in the cauldron of 1946 Salzburg. These supposedly inveterate and active crusaders against Bolshevism enjoy charmed lives – or else unjeopardised lives.

9. For all his anti-Bolshevist fervour, Turkel never succeeded in getting his White Russian legionaries into actual battle against Soviet armies. True, he is said to have despatched three or four score White Russians to help the Spanish Falange against the Reds. They perished almost to a man.

IV The real story.

Turkul had for many years been an agent of the NKVD. Lang had been so at least since 1940. Both are still agents of that unostentatious organisation. The pre-war function of Turkul was to penetrate and steer

White Russian anti-Soviet organisations. He was more than a spy; he was an *agent provocateur*. He was probably in contact with, if not in control of, a bona-fide White Russian Secret Service, i.e. one for which convinced anti-Communists were ready to work. They certainly needed to secure themselves against penetration and treachery and there exist other grounds as well for thinking that they had a counter-espionage organisation. Besides this Turkul had an inner secret service of his own, the one which executed the wishes of the NKVD. Lang was high up in this inner service and was probably also high up in what may be called the official White Russian Secret Service.

The Russo-German war only slightly modified Turkul's assignments, though it considerably modified his methods.

He had still to supervise and hamstring the bona-fide White Russians, but as the Axis powers would inevitably try to mobilise White Russian sympathies, intelligence and perhaps battalions, Turkul would have not only to keep the confidence of the White Russians but also win the confidence of the Axis military and political leaders. He would have to gull Axis Secret Services as well as his fellow White Russians; to make himself seem indispensable to the Axis in order to be useful to the NKVD and Soviet Russia.

Moreover he would need money, the money which the NKVD could no longer get to him. (We may guess that Turkul's staunchness in continuing his work for the NKVD derived less from ideological sympathy than from love of money plus fear of ultimate reprisals.)

All these ends were achieved by one simple device. The NKVD supplied Turkul's subordinate Lang with copious and veracious operational intelligence from Russia and Lang sold it to the Abwehr. The more the German Higher Command liked the commodity, the more money, influence and immunity from investigation his organisation received for providing it.

It is quite possible that Lang really did insert bona-fide White Russians into the Russian forces in 1940-41 – and betrayed them to the NKVD as he did so. Indeed it is quite possible that the NKVD let them run, under covert supervision, during part or the whole of the war. So long as their intelligence was relayed through one central station controlled by the NKVD they would do no harm and might act as unconscious decoys for other malcontents or idealists who might come to assist their labours.

I guess that the early disappearance of the Tiflis W/T operation coincided with the installation by the NKVD of their controlled central station.

Were MAX reports 'smoke'?

It was no part of the concern of the NKVD to assist Russian generals to win battles or campaigns. Its business was to penetrate and tamper with anti-communist organisations. Its enemy was not the Axis powers but, *inter alia*, the White Russians. Consequently while the MAX-system was indeed a double-cross, it was not a method of leading the Axis General Staffs astray in tactical or strategic matters; it was a method of consolidating its agent Turkul's control over White Russian activities. It is conceivable that the NKVD did not at the start or perhaps ever take the Soviet military authorities into its confidence about the MAX-leakage. Doubtless care was taken that no obviously crucial military intelligence should be given in MAX reports; but the major consideration was that the MAX information should have a high reputation for truth – a reputation which it certainly got. It is also possible, though I think unlikely, that the NKVD did take on the extra non-commitment of penetrating Axis Secret Services. If so, Lang and perhaps Turkul had to be put into a strong enough position to find out what was wanted about the Abwehr etc. But my guess is that this duplication of tasks was not imposed on Lang and Turkul, save insofar as it would be expedient to know what knowledge the Abwehr etc. had of their secrets. Lang admitted to Klatt that he had agents planted in Ast Sofia, through whom he, Lang, had discovered what Dr. Delius was planning against himself. It is quite natural, therefore, that the most suspicious Germans never found a trace of strategic or tactical deception in the MAX reports. Had the NKVD allowed any grounds for such suspicions to appear in the MAX reports, the ostensible Lang-Turkul story would have been 'blown'. It is also quite compatible with the single-minded ruthlessness of the NKVD that it should deliberately have issued MAX reports which were likely to lead to the sinking of a Russian convoy, the bombing of a new airfield or the destruction of a Russian division. When Lang confessed to Klatt that he hated to think of the thousands of Russians whose death he had brought about, the explanation may be not that Lang was, as Klatt thought, beginning to swerve from his White Russian hatred of the Soviet regime but that he deplored the price paid by Russia for the build-up that the NKVD had given to him and Turkul.

What of MORITZ reports?

The MORITZ reports could have been fabricated in Russia. The actual incidents reported in them were generally fictitious, though the designations of the larger army and airforce units tended to be correct. On the basis of published communiques, war reporters' articles, and perhaps Military Attachés' appreciations, an intelligent student could have produced most of MORITZ without having a source of his own in the area. Some of his guesses would be correct.

Had there been a sensible eye-witness in the area, he could hardly have achieved such a high percentage of errors or maintained so high a level of vagueness. Moreover he would have found out how the English commanders' surnames are spelled. What motives could have led the source of MAX reports to concoct the MORITZ reports?

(a) Axis forces were engaged on more fronts than one. So the NKVD may have thought to secure more money and credit for Turkul's organisation by giving him Mediterranean intelligence to sell than he could get if restricted to intelligence from the Eastern Front.

(b) But a more likely hypothesis is this. Turkul himself was in Rome until just after Mussolini's fall. Perhaps Turkul was himself in receipt of MAX-MORITZ reports and was selling MORITZ and/or MAX reports to the Italians behind the backs of the Germans. There is some slender evidence to support this theory.

(1) Klatt volunteered the statement that on one occasion the German Military Attaché in Rome passed to Berlin three reports which turned out to be verbally identical with three MAX or MORITZ reports sent in by Klatt to Vienna on the same day. The Abwehr was suspicious but as usual dropped its investigation. If this story is true, it implies that someone in Rome was able both to intercept and decipher the MAX-MORITZ transmissions. This someone would have to be Turkul or one of his trusted staff. But Turkul's sole obvious motive for taking MAX-MORITZ reports would be that he could get something by doing so. He may therefore have been getting money and/or standing from Mussolini by selling to him what Lang was concurrently selling to the Abwehr. If so, he would have to have been selling his goods to a purchaser on a level higher than any at which intelligence exchanges took place between the Italians and the Germans.

(2) Immediately after Mussolini's fall, Klatt, at Lang's instigation, prevailed on Kleyenstubber to fly both of them from Sofia to Rome in order to extract Turkul from Italy. The pretext given to the Abwehr was that it was imperative to prevent the MAX-MORITZ secret from becoming known to the expected British and American invaders of Italy.

But this pretext is incredible. The Italian mainland was still uninvaded; German commands and Abwehr officers felt no fears about their present safety in Rome or their future withdrawal from it. Either, therefore, Lang was in an irrational panic or there was some immediate danger to Turkul quite other than the risk of Turkul falling into Anglo-Saxon hands. Perhaps it was not Anglo-Saxon landings but the fall of Mussolini that jeopardised Turkul and his work.

Klatt's own story unintentionally supports this theory. When he and Lang met Turkul, Turkul was vehemently opposed to the project of flying to Vienna. Either Budapest or nowhere was his attitude, and only with the greatest of difficulty was he persuaded to halt at Vienna, and under the strongest assurances that his further flight to Budapest would quickly follow. For some reason Turkul did not wish to be on German soil. The inference is that he did not wish to be where the Abwehr or the SD could get him, and that he expected them to wish to get him because Mussolini's fall was likely to result in the exposure of what had been literally his double-dealing. (No such exposure actually occurred.)

(3) Almost as soon as Turkul reached Budapest, the Abwehr had to pay more for their MAX-MORITZ reports, for 700 dollars per month had now to be found for Turkul himself. Who had subverted him before and for what return?

The suggestion is therefore that the NKVD concocted MORITZ reports so that Turkul should have something to sell to Mussolini in which Mussolini would be interested – and that Mussolini was interested enough to pay Turkul perhaps 700 dollars a month for them. Here again the NKVD would have had no motive for trying to make MORITZ messages the vehicles of strategic deception. It was probably regretted by the NKVD that the veracity-level of MORITZ reports was so low. Probably they consoled themselves with the reflection that the Italian Intelligence Service were unlikely to discover how low this level was.

Note 1. If this hypothesis is true, it confirms the theory that the MAX-MORITZ transmissions were made 'blind'. For either Turkul's or Lang's operator would have to be receiving 'blind' and if one could, both might. 2. The hypothesis would also explain why RSS was unable to detect any suitable unauthorised W/T transmissions taking place in the British Middle East. For according to the theory, no such transmissions occurred.

Some Corollaries.

The view put forward is that Turkul and Lang were agents of the NKVD with the primary assignment of penetrating and managing anti-Communist organisations in Europe, and particularly White Russian organisations. The MAX-MORITZ reports were maintained by their employers in order to secure for their employees money, influence and immunity from Axis investigation. The whole scheme required that at least the MAX reports should be generally true and of genuine operational utility to the Germans; and that the MORITZ reports should at least seem plausible to the Italians. No strategic or tactical deception was practised, for the object was not to inveigle German armies into Russian ambushes but to inveigle White Russians into Turkul's snares.

The NKVD deceived the White Russians and the Axis Secret Services about the true roles of Turkul and Lang by making them retailers of operational truths. It sacrificed Soviet soldiers in order to strengthen its own hold over anticommunists in the rest of Europe.

If this account is true, a new light is thrown upon Turkul's proffer of help to Mannerheim in Finland; his positive contribution to the Falangist cause in Spain; his attempt to oust General Vlassov from command of his White Russian Army and, failing that, to secure in it a staff appointment for himself; and his formation of his own independent Corps of White Russians; and his otherwise farcical offer of collaboration with the British or the Americans against Communism in the Balkans.

Even the Japanese were not deprived of the chance to benefit by his co-operation (check this). There is still time for the Government of India or the National Government in China to enlist this ardent crusader! Even if he becomes the target of vitriolic abuse in the Soviet press, his bones will remain unbroken and his work will go on.

Subsidiary points.

1. According to Klatt and to inherent probabilities Lang was the only person in Sofia or Budapest who could decipher the MAX-MORITZ signals. Yet when asked whether MAX and MORITZ reports ceased to be passed to Vienna on the occasions when Lang was away, e.g. on a visit to Rome, Klatt showed the greatest hesitation and uneasiness. He finally said that this was so and that on Lang's return back messages were deciphered and those that had not lost their utility were passed on to Vienna in addition to the current day's reports. (This suggests that Lang would not, or could not, tell the source of MAX and MORITZ transmissions to suspend traffic during his absences, which slightly corroborates the view that these transmissions were 'blind'.)

If Klatt's story is true it follows that Lang had at l.east one operator who could take the traffic in his, Lang's absence which in itself seems quite likely. But Klatt showed every [ ] of lying. The only reason I can think of for Klatt's embarrassment was that he, Klatt himself was able to decipher signals and did so when Lang was away, in which case he was very much more than he has said. I am, for other reasons, sure that he knows at least a little more than he has said.

For one thing, Klatt tripped up both in asserting that Lang knew next to no German and that he, Klatt, knew no Russian, save the alphabet. For, forgetting this assertion, he gave a circumstantial account of how he and Lang collaborated in translating the Russian texts into German – a collaboration which would be difficult on the "Jack Sprat' basis. Moreover when asked at another time in what language he and Lang conversed, Klatt unguardedly said 'German'. I am sure that in fact Klatt knew the Bulgarian language quite well and enough Russian at least to be able to read it. He also admitted that when he, Klatt, was away from Sofia, his W/T operator was able to deputise for him in producing the German text, though he (I think) knew no Russian or Hungarian. (The question whether there were gaps in the forwarding of reports to Vienna is one that we may be able to check for ourselves. If there were no such gaps, we shall have to assume that Lang allowed either Klatt or one of his own subordinates to decipher MAX-MORITZ signals. Klatt's embarrassment would then strongly indicate that he and Lang had taken the great risk of sharing a cardinal secret of the organisation for which Lang worked).

Klatt asserted that on nearly every day there were precisely six MAX reports, plus a very occasional seventh when of special importance. On subsequent reflection it occurs to me that the explanation for this fixed number may have been as follows. According to his own account the Max network consisted of 5 W/T spies known as 'R 1' – 'R 5'. I suggest that each of these sent in one report daily and that the boss of the central station, probably 'C5', added one of his own. It makes no difference whether this network was notional or real, or whether, if real, the W/T spies were bona-fide or were NKVD's pseudo spies. Klatt might be asked whether there was always one message per day for each of the 'R' sources.

There is a conflict of evidence about the date at which Lang entered Turkul's service. According to one account Lang went to Turkul in July 1940 only to get permission to collaborate with the Abwehr via Klatt: he had already been in Turkul's service for an unknown length of time. According to another account he first became a member of Turkul's organisation in July 1940. The former seems the more likely. The NKVD would hardly have given Lang such a delicate and important mission had they not tested his capacities and reliability over a lengthy period.

Klatt has fairly satisfactorily cleared up the question of the connections between his Dienstelle and the W/T system of the Bulgarian Police. From June 20 (approx) to August 1941, the Burgas police station received the signals of the Tiflis W/T operator, and forwarded them or the decodes of them to the Sofia Police W/T station, whence they were passed to Klatt. (I have doubts about parts of this story, namely about how the Tiflis-Burgos link was created and how the Burgos police got their W/T and cipher instructions). After August 1941 the Bulgarian Police had nothing directly to do with securing W/T traffic from Russia. They continued to assist Klatt, first by letting him pass his own messages to Vienna over their W/T link with some W/T station (? a police station) in Vienna, and later by letting him install his own W/T station 'Schwert' in police premises.

These arrangements have nothing to do with the MAX-MORITZ transmissions, not, as we might have expected, did Lang entrust any of his secrets to the venal Bulgarian police.

Klatt also explained satisfactorily the nature of his 'IBIS' reports. These were secured by the friendly and venal harbourmaster of Varna, one Sarapow, from a ship's captain who usually plied between Varna and Istanbul. Consequently IBIS reports tended to deal chiefly with Turkish coastal matters. This captain announced once that he had been chartered to sail from Istanbul to Aden and offered to send information by W/T to Varna while en route. It is not clear that he actually did so. Only one IBIS report was of any interest. It announced an impending landing at Dunkirk on the day on which that landing occurred.

Klatt confessed that he had been accused of heading as 'IBIS reports' what were really MORITZ reports, in order to get more cash for having found a new active source. He denied having done this.

6. Klatt first rented his house in Boulevard Ferdinand in July 1940. This suggests that preparations for his war-work were well advanced nearly a year before the German march into Russia. It also suggests that Lang's plans were ripening by this date. If so, he cannot have begun his espionage work only after his visit to Rome in July 1940.[26]

After Ustinov had reached his controversial conclusions, he was given an unexpected opportunity to revisit the KLATT mystery when Paul Blum of the US Special Services Unit traced Turkul's assistant, George Romanov, to Geneva, just days before he was due to emigrate permanently to Argentina, having taken holy orders as a Russian Orthodox priest.

The interrogation of Turkul and of IRA in London had not produced final and decisive evidence regarding the source of the MAX/MORITZ messages and the manner of their transmission to IRA. Every fragment of evidence was tediously collected. It did not suffice, however, to piece this tantalising puzzle resulting from the activities of the Abwehr during the war. The knowledge that certain Abwehr officers such as DELIUS, less gullible and more critically-minded than their colleagues and especially than the OKW, were doubtful about the MAX/MORITZ traffic and, what is more, that members of the 'Union' (this is Romanoff's name for Turkul's organisation) on the very fringe of this traffic, such as Romanoff himself, were so seriously perturbed by it that they resigned from the 'Union', offered no consolation for the lack of proof that the MAX/MORITZ reports were 'made in Soviet Russia'.

My journey to Geneva for the purpose of interrogating Romanoff was intended as a further contribution to a solution of the problem. It had, of course, become clear to me in the course of my interrogation of Turkul and IRA in London that Romanoff, although an important member of the 'Union', had been studiously kept away by IRA and Turkul from the

MAX/MORITZ traffic and that this very fact was the real reason for the ultimate break between Romanoff and the head of the 'Union'. I knew therefore that my only chance of contributing to the solution of the MAX/MORITZ enigma lay in concentrating the interrogation of Romanoff, in the limited time at my disposal, on points and phases closely connected with the MAX/MORITZ traffic and leaving less essential features to their fate. Apart from this main problem I laid considerable stress on the personality of Turkul in order to clear up the point whether he too, like IRA, was a Soviet agent or not.[27]

Romanov's MI5 dossier explained the context:

The main purpose of the interrogation of KLATT, TURKUL and IRA was to solve the war-time mystery-

1) From what ultimate source or sources did the Abwehr get its MAX and MORITZ messages?
2) From what motive were these messages provided?
3) By what channels were these messages communicated?

The latter stages of the interrogation were guided by the specific task of deciding for or against the hypothesis that the MAX-MORITZ messages were deliberately provided by some Soviet organisation with the intention of enabling certain of its agents to operate inside Axis-occupied Europe with the support of the Abwehr (and perhaps one or more other Axis Intelligence Services) – that, in short, the MAX-MORITZ messages were an up-to-date form of Trojan Horse.

Although neither KLATT nor Turkul nor IRA has been 'broken', all have been considerably 'bent', and what they have wittingly or unwittingly revealed has confirmed the hypothesis up to the hilt. There is no room for doubt that the NKVD (now MVD) supplied IRA with military intelligence of as high veracity as could be achieved in order that he might secure from the Abwehr in return for these golden eggs the funds, the immunity from surveillance, the communications and the travel-permits necessary for the prosecution of the covert-pro-Soviet operations of Turkul's organisation.[28]

This final verdict gained some traction with Ustinov's colleagues who had been so preoccupied with the puzzle.

The interrogators are in complete agreement about the principles of the solution of the MAX-MORITZ enigma. Some Soviet authority, presumably the NKVD (MVD), deliberately provided its agent Ira with military intelligence of as high veracity (but not necessarily strategic importance) as it could achieve, in order that he might sell it to the Abwehr for a good price. The price was the endowment of the Turkul organisation by the Abwehr with the funds, the immunity from surveillance and the communications facilities necessary to enable the Turkul organisation:-

1) To keep a watch on the activities of White Russians and other anti-Communists in Axis-controlled Europe;
2) At least in some degree to discourage or hamstring, these activities;
3) (Presumably) to keep that Soviet authority currently informed of the attitudes of these anti-Communists and of Axis exploitations of them.

The sole difference of opinion concerns the degree of complicity of Turkul in this operation. Neither of the interrogators accepts Turkul's story that he had, before his arrival in London, no idea that IRA was using the TURKUL organisation as an instrument of NKVD policy.

On one view Turkul was himself an NKVD agent, receiving (perhaps from 1936) remuneration and orders from the NKVD.

On the other view Turkul was never in receipt of money or instructions direct from the NKVD and can therefore say, with at least semi-honesty, that he has not been an NKVD agent. On this view, however, he was at least tolerantly conniving at Ira's work. He was a captain who allowed the pilot to decide the destinations of the ship. He was ready to enjoy the subsequent gratitude of Ira's employers, if they were victorious; and he was insured against at least the most extreme disfavour of the Axis powers (and even of the bona-fide White Russians) if the Axis should win the war. He could always prove that he had done his modest best to assist the victors, whoever these might be.[29]

In the absence of any definitive proof or a plausible explanation from anyone connected with Turkul for the myriad contradictions, MI5's experts agreed to disagree, leaving the case without any satisfactory conclusion.

So the question at issue really boils down to this. Did Ira and his employers rely on Turkul's (active or passive) collaboration because he was himself an agent of their organisation, or because they had some less official hold on him? And did Turkul help to steer the activities of his organisation in the directions wished by the NKVD or did he merely surrender the wheel to Ira? These questions do not affect the problem of the MAX-MORITZ pseudo-leakage. Nor would they greatly mitigate the judgment of bona-fide White Russians about Turkul's treachery to them.[30]

* * *

We now know, from NKVD files declassified in Moscow in 1998, that the Soviets had been equally intrigued by Klatt and the NKVD's military counter-intelligence service, known by its Russian acronym of SMERSH, had trawled the Balkans for information. After an investigation lasting two years a 61-page report, *Memorandum on the KLATT-MAX Case*, was submitted to Stalin in July 1947. The analysis found that only an insignificant amount of MAX's information was authentic, and a more detailed study of the MAX traffic between the middle of 1942 to January 1945 suggested that only 8 per cent was authentic.[31]

Having concluded that MAX was an invention, the NKVD was forced to rely on interviews with Klatt's former colleagues and his second wife Gerda Filitz, as he himself was in American custody in Austria. According to the report, Richard Kauder had been born in Vienna in 1900 to a Jewish family, but baptized a Catholic. At the age of 28 he had worked as a life insurance agent, and then had managed the estates of a local aristocrat, Baron Tavonat. Following the Anschluss in 1938 he had emigrated to Hungary where he had operated on the black market selling visas to Jewish refugees. Opinion about precisely when Kauder had been recruited by the Abwehr was divided. Some thought Hans Pieckenbrock of Abt. I had been responsible, while others through Klatt himself had approached the Ast Sofia in the summer of 1941, offering reports about the Soviet air force. However, Franz-Eccard von Bentivegni of Abt. III thought he had been recruited in 1939 in Budapest by Schmalschleger of III/F Vienna, and had worked on penetrating a channel of couriers run by the Polish intelligence service. Another version had Klatt hired in Vienna in 1940 by Wahl-Welskirch, who had gained his release from a prison sentence for currency offences. The NKVD investigators also pursued the issue of Klatt's sources. Early in 1945 Klatt had told a more senior Abwehr officer, Alfred Klausnitzer, that he had 'received intelligence information mainly from three sources: VIGO, alias Dr Willy Gotz in Istanbul; from his radio operator Arnold Dalisme in Ankara, and from IRA, alias Lang'.

Ilya F. Lang, alias Ira Longin, was a former Tsarist army officer who had emigrated in 1920 and was closely associated with General Turkul, a character well known to the NKVD as having been in the pay of the

Japanese and German intelligence services back in the early 1930s. As for the one-legged Captain Adrian Samoilov identified by SIS, it was determined that no such person existed.

Under interrogation Klatt's wife Gerda Filitz recalled that upon his return from Vienna her husband had been in low spirits and had told her that he 'had been reprimanded for the fact that Lang had passed dud information about the Soviet army and cheats'. Another member of the Klatt Bureau, Hanns Sturm-Schneider, said that on one occasion he had seen Lang dictate to a colleague, Eva Hamernik, while reading newspaper cuttings. Finally, Willy Goetz, said that before the war Lang had passed anti-Comintern information to Milan which he alleged had come from a White Russian intelligence organisation.

Although the overwhelming majority of Klatt's information seemed to be bogus, there was a small proportion that was authentic and the NKVD concluded that this material had been gleaned by Lang from Russian emigrés whom he had interviewed in the refugee camps on behalf of the Germans. It was also suspected that Klatt might have cultivated contacts inside foreign embassies in Sofia, and even the British thought it likely that the Swedish embassy might have relayed information from its embassy in Moscow. Finally, there was the strong possibility that Klatt had actually acquired some of his material from the Germans themselves, a technique that had been skilfully demonstrated by the White Russian emigré Vasilyev, who had worked entirely independently of Lang and Klatt and had bought material about the Soviet air force from a German intelligence officer named Brauner. He had then corrected it using newspaper articles and, using his own experience in the previous war and his imagination, he had fabricated a plausibly detailed report on Soviet plans for an invasion of the Crimea. When questioned, Vasilyev had remarked that the Germans had been snowed under with intelligence reports of varying reliability, so deceiving them was quite a safe undertaking. Although unconnected with Klatt, Vasilyev's ingenuity and enterprise had borne a strong resemblance to MAX's technique.

As for the British verdict, the official view espoused by MI14 in 1943, that MAX had been useful to the Germans, persuaded SIS to approach the Russians in October 1943 with a summary of the MAX traffic, but to their astonishment MAX continued in operation until February 1945. The post-war British interrogation of Klatt's surviving colleagues led SIS to conclude that the MAX reports were a Russian-controlled operation based on the penetration of the White Russian circles which purported to supply Klatt with his intelligence. Klatt's principal source, Shenshin, himself admitted that the MORITZ reports were 'pure smoke' concocted in Sofia as an additional lure for the Abwehr.

When Hans Pieckenbrock was questioned by the Soviets he explained that Klatt had come under suspicion several times for fabricating intelligence, but since the Luftwaffe never complained about his reliability, Klatt's reporting had not been the subject of any rigorous double-checks. Eventually suspicions about Klatt had strengthened, and he was arrested by the Abstelle Vienna in March 1945, together with some other members of his organisation, and questioned for six days in the Hotel Grande.

An Ast Vienna codist, Valja Deutsch, made a statement to the Soviets confirming that 'when, after my arrest in February 1945, I was interrogated by the Gestapo, they demanded evidence about Klatt's intelligence activity and told me that Klatt was an adventurer, a cheat who had cost Germany big money'. Nevertheless, Klatt's interrogator, Alfred Klaunitzer, was so impressed with him that he offered him a job as his head agent. After a lengthy study, he was persuaded that MAX had given genuine advance notice of no less than four separate Russian winter offensives.

When Walter Schellenberg was cross-examined, he asserted that the MAX network was run by 'a German Jew, and he conducted its activities in a manner that was unique'.

> The work of this man was really masterly. He was able to report large-scale strategic plans as well as details of troop movements, in some important cases down to divisional level; his reports usually came in two or three weeks ahead of events, so that our leaders could prepare suitable countermeasures – or, should I say, could have done so if Hitler had paid more attention to the information.[32]

Similarly, Reinhard Gehlen described MAX as 'the office controlling the Abwehr agents in Moscow' and characterised it as a source 'that must have been genuine'.

The MAX messages ceased on 13 February 1945, by which time Kauder's Dienstelle and its transmitters had moved to the Hungarian village of Csorna, 80 miles south-east of Vienna. At some point in the following three months he moved to Vienna where he was arrested by the US 42nd Division CIC on 24 May and held briefly in Kitzbuhel before being sent to Salzburg on 6 June for interrogation.

On 20 January 1946, following a failed abduction in Salzburg by the Soviets, and another attempt three days later to grab his mistress, Kauder was taken into a lengthy period of protective custody by the Americans at the Camp King interrogation centre at Oberursel, accompanied by Turkul and Lang. There the trio was cross-examined by Arnold Silver who also obtained testimony from Otto Wagner, then a prisoner of the French at Bad Widungen. According to Silver,

> Kauder eventually confessed that his principal source had been Joseph Schutz, an Austrian friend based in Vienna who had originally introduced him to General Turkul. Apparently Kauder had begun to suspect in 1941 that Schulz was himself operating under Soviet control, but had not dared share his opinion with either the Abwehr, in case he was handed over to the Gestapo, or after war, with his new American employers for fear that their supply of dollars might dry up.[33]

Kauder was also interrogated by Klop Ustinov, who accepted what appeared to be a confession given after the failure of his attempt to hang himself with his belt. Later Kauder would claim that he only pretended to 'break' and invented a non-existent recruiter, Josef Shulz, as his Soviet controller. The sessions with Ustinov were followed by the interviews with Professor Ryle, who questioned Turkul and Lang at the same facility. In November 1946 Turkul and Lang were brought to London for a detailed cross-examination, which elicited nothing apart from the fact that the Americans had employed Lang to run a network of sources for them. As was his practice, he had declined to explain who they were, and even went on a hunger strike to avoid being taken to England.

Kauder was questioned over two days in January 1947 on behalf of MI5 by Klop Ustinov who established from Kauder that shortly before the end of the war Schultz had confided that he had been a Soviet agent since 1939, and that the entire network had been a vast exercise in military deception, although neither Lang nor Turkul had realised the truth. The interrogation, conducted in German, generated a transcript covering twenty-nine pages.

By mid-1947 the Americans were convinced that Kauder had worked unwittingly as a wartime conduit for Soviet disinformation, and he was released with his two companions from Camp King in March 1947 and, reunited with his mistress Ibolya Kalman, settled in Salzburg where they were married in November 1955. They lived initially at the Old Fox Hotel in Salzburg, and then moved to a villa in the suburbs, where he died in July 1960.

In retrospect it is evident that the Anglo-American interest in MAX and MORITZ was partly self-interest, based on the potential for exploiting sources behind the post-war Iron Curtain, and secondly, from a counter-intelligence perspective, to plug any existing leaks.

As MI5 minuted in June 1945, Kauder had an 'apparent interest in undertakings which obviously appear to have been the ground-work for the penetration of the Allied services'.[34] MI5 retained a watching brief on the MAX-MORITZ riddle because of the possibility, articulated in February 1947 by Michael Serpell, that it was linked to the GRU's wartime ROTE DREI network in Switzerland. In that case the Soviet network's alleged sources in Germany were shrouded in mystery, despite having been investigated by the Funkabwehr's cryptographic expert, Dr Wilhem Flicke. Escapees from the Swiss organisation and the ROTE KAPELLE based in Brussels had been instructed to reach Sofia, but exactly how they had acquired top-level OKW material would baffle German investigators and those that followed in their wake.

On the Klatt story, however, we are now satisfied that the network of agents he claimed in the USSR did not exist and that his MAX information was a single line of Soviet directed material, intended perhaps to give MAX the status of a GARBO. There has been considerable speculation on the uses to which this grand deception was put and it seems just possible that Flicke's story of the ROTE DREI may provide the solution.

One of the uses of GARBO was the production of intelligence by reactions on outgoing material. A deliberate truth or untruth sent out by GARBO might stimulate an answer revealing German knowledge or ignorance; it might even be possible to provoke same sign of German intentions. The intelligence value of these reactions would increase according to the relative truthfulness and currency (in German eyes) of the outgoing material. In the case of MAX the Germans were in an infinitely better position to check information than they were in the case of GARBO, and we believe that the Russians took considerable risks, if they did not even make sacrifices, for the sake of building up German confidence in MAX as a source. So far as the OKW was concerned, it is known that the Russians were highly successful in this deception, and it does not seem unreasonable to suppose that OKW reactions to MAX information were rich and abundant. We knew, for example, that at one stage special sections of intelligence officers were formed by the Germans to handle MAX information in the field, and it seems probable that there was an extensive two-way traffic between the OKW and the field in this respect. In what size and shape these reactions were available to Klatt is at present uncertain. According to Klatt himself 'it was always possible for (him) and Lang (IRA) to put their own queries or those of, say, Luftflotte IV to the source or sources of MAX reports. Replies to these queries never took less than 3-4 days to come back and often they took 8 days.' But Klatt has been very secretive about his manipulation of MAX and during the war his main concern seems to have been to protect his pretended wireless links with the USSR as a 'private line'. We do not yet know the exact machinery by which Klatt received the MAX messages but if, as now seems probable, he himself was a conscious Soviet agent his environment of suspicious Abwehr colleagues would make him wary of any detectable commitment from himself to the USSR. All the MAX material, he professed, was obtained by his delicate handling of a White Russian organisation whose links with the USSR were originally established for political purposes and whose intelligence value would be lost if they were once taken under direct German control. It seems significant to find in this White Russian milieu a connection between Klatt and the ROTE DREI. If Klatt did receive regular supplies of OKW reactions on the MAX material, with a free hand to apply them to his White Russian sources, might they not be the basis of the most important Eastern Front material transmitted by the ROTE DREI to Moscow? As an intelligence operation the strategy seems practical; the MAX information stimulating the German reaction would, by the speed of wireless communication, still leave the Red Army with the initiative. The tactics also seem sound. The Germans might be expected to look for communications between the ROTE DREI and Germany or between Sofia (for Klatt) and Russia, but a link between KLATT and the ROTE DREI would not easily be suspected. It is noticeable that the ROTE DREI traffic abounds in cover-names, possibly intended to convey a multiplicity of sources to German interceptors. It must be added that the ROTE DREI intercepts available suggest the collection of information well outside the probable scope of Klatt. This is to be expected of a thriving concern like the ROTE DREI, but may also have been considered as cover for the single vital source.[35]

The connection between the Sofia Dienstelle and the ROTE DREI in Switzerland was through Ira Lang who was alleged to be closely associated with a group of White Russians led by Prince Konopkine, himself linked to Alexander Tscherniak, an academic based in Zurich and assessed by the KO Schweitz as the senior Soviet intelligence *rezident*.

The MAX and MORITZ mystery remained unsolved, and in 1954, when SIME closed down, the relevant files were passed to MI5 in London where the verdict was that Lang

> was almost certainly a Russian Intelligence Service agent and we are reasonably sure that the MAX reports were supplied to Lange by W/T from the Soviet Union as part of a Soviet deception operation. The source of the MORITZ reports which concerned military dispositions, supplies, etc. in the Middle East behind the British lines was never satisfactorily explained despite the interrogation of Kauder and Lange after the war. Generally speaking they were inaccurate though very plausible and it has been suggested that they were fabricated by Lange.[36]

Chapter VII

ENDGAME

The Germans are leaving behind both intelligence agents and saboteurs. Agents will have to be used to penetrate and round up these German organisations and also for deception.

The Running of Special Agents in the Field, Christopher Harmer, 27 May 1944[1]

Hans Ruser was arguably the first Abwehr officer to abandon the organisation. His background was cosmopolitan, in that his father, Kommodore Hans Ruser, who had died in April 1930, had been a universally respected HAPAG seaman and master of the *Vaterland* (later renamed the *Leviathan*). Six years later his son Hans would be sentenced to a suspended six months' imprisonment at Marienburg for homosexual conduct.

Kommodore Ruser, who had been decorated in 1904 by Kaiser Wilhelm II for his participation in the Glauss expedition to Antarctica, was one of Admiral Canaris's friends, and this may have been an influence on his son's decision to join the Abwehr in 1936. Ruser first surfaced in a wartime intelligence role in February 1941 when the double agent CELERY was driven from Lisbon to Madrid by Ruser whom he described as the Nazi economist Dr Hjalmar Schacht's nephew, but 'violently anti-Nazi. He is pro-British and pro-Hitler and Germany.' Ruser explained that he had spent nine years in the United States, from the age of five.[2] Ruser, who was then living with his mother, Paula, in Estoril, had entertained CELERY to dinner and had handed him a letter to post to what he claimed were his relatives in England. Significantly, CELERY disclosed to his MI5 debriefers that Ruser had expressed an interest in moving to England, and subsequently the Abwehr officer contacted SIS in Lisbon in

March 1942, with the Poles acting as intermediaries, as Guy Liddell noted at the end of the month:

> Kim Philby telephoned to me today to say that Hans Ruser had told the Poles in Lisbon that he was prepared to accept our offer to come to this country with his mother provided he could have a guarantee that he would not be interned and would be allowed later to go to America. Although Ruser is probably a time-server of the worst variety I think it may pay us to get him over. I think however he must satisfy us as to his *bona-fides* and that any guarantee as to his liberty will be on the assumption that we are satisfied that he is working 100 percent for us.[3]

On the basis of CELERY's recollection Ruser was then included in August 1942 in Jack Curry's 132-page analysis, *The German Secret Service*, for internal consumption only, and mentioned in the chapter on Lisbon, of course omitting any reference to the negotiations then underway for his defection:

> A German journalist named Hans Ruser who is in Lisbon and was in this country before the war, is believed to be working for Abteilung II. He is probably concerned with the propaganda and subversive side of the work.[4]

Evidently MI5 analysts kept an eye on any ISOS texts that were relevant to Ruser, and on 19 May 1942 Liddell remarked:

> There have been several indications recently that Dr Hans Ruser, who had been connected with German espionage work in Portugal at least since 1937, is now in disfavour with the German authorities. Recently there has been a suggestion that he was preparing to break away altogether from his German associates and attempt to seek refuge in this country. Subsequent to this information it has come to notice that the head of the German secret service in Portugal is making attempts to have Ruser called up for military service although his age group had not yet been reached.[5]

By 11 August ISOS revealed that Ruser had refused to cooperate with the Abwehr, and plans had been made by the KO for his return to Berlin.

> Lisbon has told Berlin that Ruser has come into the open and informed the Dienstelle that he can no longer collaborate with the Abwehr. This decision had followed a meeting of important Spanish and German

238

officials in Madrid. The Dienstelle had agreed to accept his decision but could only do so if he were released from his military obligations. Ruser agreed to go to Berlin and arrangements have been made to take him into safe custody as soon as he arrives.[6]

No doubt SIS found a way of discreetly warning Ruser of the danger he was in, for on 23 November 1943 Ruser had arrived in London from Gibraltar and been consigned to Camp 020 for three weeks, during which he wrote a lengthy account of his experiences. Six days after his release in December, Liddell recorded in his diary:

During the weekend I read the Hans Ruser report of ninety pages. It is extremely interesting since it was through Dr Kurt Johannsen of Hamburg that he first came into contact with the Abwehr. Before the war a number of journalists in this country, including Kurt Singer and Karl Abshagen, used to send reports to Johannsen on political and economic matters, marked 'Confidential and not for publication.' Ostensibly, Johannsen was dealing solely with the advertising of German import and export business. He was, however, financed by the Ministry of Propaganda and did a considerable amount of work for the German Ministry of Economic Warfare. Later Ruser worked in the Fremdedienst, a propaganda service which was set up for bear-leading visitors from this country and the United States to Germany. Ruser obtained this job through his shipping connections. His father had been employed by NordDeutscher Lloyd, had been captain of the *Leviathan*, and was interned in the United States. Ruser and his mother were at liberty and Ruser himself received most of his education in the United States. He eventually drifted to Spain and it was there that he became definitely connected with the Abwehr. There is no doubt that the Germans were giving assistance to General Franco in the very early stages of the revolution. The Ruser report shows how the KriegsOrganisation Spain and KO Portugal were gradually built up, through professional Abwehr officers making use of local business people. Ruser complains quite moderately that he never actually wished to leave Spain and that it was only on the insistence of Thompson that he did so. Definite promises were made to him that he would be given his liberty in this country. He thinks that he should still be of great use to us to Spain and Portugal owing to the number of contacts that he has there outside the Abwehr, and he is quite prepared to go back if we provide him with some sort of papers which will prevent him from being picked up by a junior member of the Spanish police and expelled from the country. The usual practice of the Gestapo in dealing with a recalcitrant German is to arrange that his passport should not be renewed. Immediately it expires the Spanish police arrest the man and push him over the frontier in conjunction with the Gestapo. Ruser thinks, however, that the tide in Spain is beginning to turn in our favour, and that certainly the junior Spanish officers would not now be prepared to act in this way.[7]

Although various promises were made to Ruser in Madrid, he was deposited at Camp 020 for interrogation when he reached England, an administrative error that was soon corrected. However Ruser, whose mother had remained in Madrid, expressed a willingness to go back to Spain in the Allied cause, an offer that created anxiety in London, not least because Ruser and his mother were friendly with Johnny Jebsen, who at that moment was himself in mortal danger, although he was the last to realise the gravity of his situation. A few days after Christmas, Liddell visited Ruser at his London safe-house.

> He was very pleasant and civil and I think of honest of purpose. There is no doubt to my mind that he is anxious to return to Spain and confident that he can get away with it. His proposal is to live somewhere just outside Madrid and to maintain contact with some six or eight agents who are rather on the fringe of the Abwehr. He would not have any contact with the regular officials of the Abwehr. He would move about only at night. He says that now that the Falange militia has been abolished, there is little danger from the Spanish police. He would like, if possible, to return with Costa Rican papers or, failing these, with Brazilian. I suggested to him that if he were going back it might be better for his mother to remain in Spain since people would consider it rather odd if she disappeared. He seemed to agree about this and thought that he would be able to gauge the situation better when he got back. He would in many ways prefer to see his mother in this country.[8]

Although MI5 was keen to accept Ruser's offer to rejoin his mother in Madrid, SIS was decidedly less enthusiastic because of the risk of capture, and the issue dragged on until February when Liddell noted Jebsen's concern:

> J.C. Masterman and Ronnie Reed came in to tell me about Hans Ruser. ARTIST does not want him to go back to Lisbon, and this view is supported by SIS. The argument is that the Germans are already looking for Ruser and his mother, and that if he were taken he might be forced to talk, and possibly to compromise ARTIST, although in fact he can have only a suspicion that ARTIST may be working for us. He knows that ARTIST offered his services, but thought they were turned down. I cannot help feeling that this case has been rather mishandled. There have been endless delays through [de Salis] in Lisbon not getting into

touch with ARTIST. Personally, I think, it is a pity that Ruser does not go back. He can only be an embarrassment to us here as we cannot give him anything to do.[9]

Ruser was 'very distressed' when the decision was given to him, and SIS then initiated hs mother's extraction. By June, this had been achieved, and Ruser asked to be allowed to travel to Argentina, but eventually he returned to Spain in 1946.

Codenamed ARTIST by SIS, and run in Lisbon by Section V's John de Salis, Jebsen had been recommended for recruitment by TRICYCLE on his own initiative, thereby placing all concerned in an unforeseen predicament. ARTIST himself wanted to defect, and in September 1943 approached Section V's Ken Benton in Madrid and offered his knowledge of Abwehr assets in England as what he supposed was a tempting 'meal-ticket' . . . TRICYCLE's identity. If SIS encouraged ARTIST's desertion, the Germans would consider their agents brulé and take the appropriate countermeasures, one of which would be a reassessment of their past performance, a process that would endanger several other controlled channels, including TATE, who had been operating a wireless link to Hamburg with apparent success since his arrival by parachute in September 1940, and GARBO's entire network, known to the Madrid KO as ARABEL.

In an unusual move, which indicated the gravity of the situation, an MI5 case officer, Ian Wilson, was flown to Portugal to help run Jebsen, who opposed the idea of Ruser's reappearance in Spain. Concern about Jebsen became academic in April 1944 when he was abducted in Lisbon by I/H's Dr Aloys Schreiber, driven across Spain and delivered to the German military authorities at Biarritz, to be questioned on charges of embezzlement. De Salis would later admit that ISOS had provided ample advance notice of the abduction plan, which also involved another victim, Jebsen's Abwehr friend Heinz Moldenhauer, who also was under suspicion of contemplating desertion. However, de Salis had been banned by SIS's Frank Foley from giving anything more than the vaguest warning to exercise the greatest care. Reportedly Georg Hansen himself flew to Biarritz to supervise Jebsen's arrest, which ended with his incarceration at Oranienburg concentration camp, where he would perish.

* * *

Following the D-Day landings and the first weeks of the Battle of Normandy, the Abwehr and SD had prepared extensive plans for stay-behind operations across France, Belgium and the Netherlands, and as the Allies advanced to Paris and beyond, the scale of the German networks became evident, partly through ISOS, the interrogation of prisoners, information from deserters such as JIGGER, and the manipulation of double agents. This latter source's value was the contemporaneous nature of the intelligence acquired, in contrast to the offerings of defectors whose 'meal-tickets' were inevitably diminished by the speed of military developments in the field. There were other complications too. Whereas hitherto MI5 and SIS had effectively sidelined the Americans in the management of double agents, and largely excluded the French, the convenient jurisdictional niceties and legal technicalities relied upon would not apply on the Continent, so the effective monopoly on double-cross operations would be impossible to impose in newly-liberated territory where the French would expect primacy and OSS would have to play a much larger role.

In anticipation of the challenges represented by a well-trained, well-concealed and well-equipped stay-behind enemy, MI5 and SIS created four mobile Special Counter-Intelligence (SCI) units and assembled them at Chelsea Barracks for deployment close to the Allied front lines to scoop up the German networks before they were activated. Each SCI was multi-national, with British, American and a few French personnel, all drawn from intelligence sections with recent experience of handling enemy agents. The planning for this unprecedented innovation, of deploying indoctrinated case officers into newly-liberated combat zones, had begun in March 1943 and, although considered controversial, it included provision for Americans who would be required to undergo six weeks' training. The final SCI charter was agreed in mid-January 1944.

Equipped with American jeeps and converted Dodge ambulances, the SCIs headed to Lord Rothschild's newly-established MI5 outpost in the rue Petrarque in Paris in August and then moved on to occupy offices in the Avenue Tervueren in Brussels. Each SCI, designated 101, 102, 103 and 104, was self-contained, with its own secure communications, and was supported by Camp 030 at Diest and an administration centre, a block of flats known as Wuthering Heights. Three of the SCIs operated from Brussels, with 102 SCI based at Antwerp. SIS's Section V(b), headed by Dick Brooman-White, collaborated closely with his MI5 counterparts but acted independently of the new local SIS station in Brussels. In September 1944 a new SCI, designated 106, was created of German-speaking officers and posted permanently to Paris, staffed by MI5's Peter Ramsbotham, Alan Day, Ronnie Reed and Basil Dykes.

As well as taking responsibility for dealing with the enemy networks, which posed an obvious threat in terms of intelligence collection and sabotage, the SCIs were also required to act as field representatives for B1(a) where current agents needed support on the Continent. This applied particularly to BRUTUS and SNIPER[10] who had been promised money and cached transmitters buried in anticipation of their arrival, the Abwehr having finally found a secure method of passing funds to their cash-starved agents. These locations, of course, were not entirely hazard-free, and MI5 was conscious that, for example, BRUTUS would be vulnerable to abduction if he visited the agreed location in person, unescorted.

By August 1944 DRAGOMAN, the Portuguese double agent run by OSS in Cherbourg, was the foundation upon which X-2 sought to develop a scenario replicating the experience in England, where the Allies had exercised a high degree of control over the enemy's espionage networks. At that stage DRAGOMAN, who was paid with money parachuted from aircraft originating in Jersey, was engaged in the relatively unambitious transmission of meteorological data and reports of troop movements, but was in contact with another (uncontrolled) agent in Grenoble. Further potential was offered by the arrest in August of a marine radio operator, Jean Senouque, codenamed SKULL, who also reported from Cherbourg and might be used to complement DRAGOMAN's messages but could not start transmitting until October. Later, SKULL would be redeployed to Brest, and was engaged as paymaster to pass funds to agents in Rouen and Le Havre.

DRAGOMAN became the pre-eminent channel for conveying deception, but also had a counter-espionage role, as in October, having received 62,000 francs, he was alerted to the imminent arrival of Albert Gabas, codenamed DESIRE by the Germans. Once apprehended by the CIC, Gabas, a former French naval officer and radio operator, appeared to comply with his captors and underwent interrogation at Camp 020.

Gabas proved to be an important catch, as he was already well known to ISOS analysts who had read more than fifty messages about him since September 1943. When entrapped in Cherbourg, attending a rendezvous with DRAGOMAN, he surrendered his transmitter, buried in his garden, and confessed to his recruitment by the Abwehr in Bordeaux in June 1943 and to undergoing a training course in Paris. After a short mission into Spain, which had generated much of his ISOS trail, Gabas had been briefed on an assignment to Cherbourg to pay

SKULL, DRAGOMAN and DRAGOMAN's sub-agent John Eikens, codenamed PANCHO. According to Gabas, his Abwehr I/M handler, Captain Michel Stockmann, had explained that

> before the war Frutos [DRAGOMAN] has been employed by the shipping company which owned the *Bremen*. Gabas was given to understand that Frutos was a respected and trusted agent who would keep his eye on Gabas. He was to give Frutos, who had two w/t sets, details of how to compose meteorological reports and were to share the same code.[11]

After his delivery to Camp 020 at the end of August Gabas provided a third version of his Abwehr activities that more approximated to ISOS and was corroborated by information extracted from another 020 prisoner, the defector Carl Eitel. Having already taken control of some fifteen stay-behind agents, the remaining issue was the question of how many Abwehr agents were still at liberty. Allied strategy was to achieve critical mass, being the point at which the Germans no longer felt the need to deploy new agents, but this information was not available from ISOS. Accordingly, a scheme was devised to lure SKULL's I/M handler, Friedrich Kaulen, into a trap, but the plan failed when he was accidentally shot at the rendezvous on the banks of the Gironde.

This mishap was not entirely unprofitable as Kaulen was found to be carrying a questionnaire for SKULL which, upon examination, seemed to suggest that the Abwehr was already very (and perhaps wholly) reliant on sources known to SHAEF. Nevertheless, the exploitation continued. Initially FAN, a French fascist, fell into Allied hands, and seemed a likely candidate, but the Germans failed to respond to his signals. However, the capture in Paris of an SD stay-behind, Jean Carrere, looked to be more promising as he was in possession of a questionnaire and his past traffic, and was codenamed KEEL. Unfortunately, the case was quickly thrown into doubt when, working as a waiter, KEEL was arrested by the French authorities. Upon his release contact was re-established and he answered a questionnaire about banknotes and ration cards in Paris. In March 1945 KEEL would become the lynchpin of PILLOW, a daring project in which Carrere suggested himself as an intermediary for contact between the Abwehr and 'certain members of the Allied Intelligence Services', a proposal in which 'the Germans were showing genuine interest' but eventually led nowhere.

Additionally, the French began their own double-cross with DAVIT in Paris and, following the liberation of Brussels, an SD stay-behind codenamed FRANK was started, together with DEMOCRAT (later renamed DEPUTY), based in Antwerp where he compromised a hitherto unsuspected Abwehr agent, DOMINANT, who would be imprisoned in November and then die a month later. DAVIT only lasted a couple of months, and after he had compromised two other agents, one in Paris and the other in Marseilles, he was closed down. Meanwhile DEPUTY, described as 'very intelligent and enterprising', was directed by his handler to supply information about V-2 strikes on Antwerp, using a map supplied by a new agent PAQUOT, and there followed a discussion about whether he should be paid via a parachute drop or through an address in Holland. The double-cross in Belgium would be increased in November by the acquisition of the SD's FLAME, and then by an SD line-crosser, MEADOW, although an administrative blunder meant he had to be terminated. Meanwhile, according to John Marriott on an inspection tour on behalf of the XX Committee, FRANK 'supplied an enormous amount of information about the SD in Belgium'.[12]

The enemy networks embedded in Belgium did not consist of Germans, and relied on Belgian nationals, such as Bayot who, though trained in radio, had not been equipped with a transmitter and had been instructed to collect one from van Meldert. The pair worked together thereafter, having surrendered to the liberators. Together with a third agent, de Coninx, these volunteers formed the basis of a very viable double-cross operation.

Christopher Harmer's 104 SCI in Belgium also took over DITCH and an SIS asset in Bruges, DERRICK, who had been considered reliable since he first became active for the British in 1940. However, having compromised four others, he was himself arrested by the Belgian Sureté in Ostend, and was obliged to reveal his true role in an effort to clear himself. Naturally, this extended his circle of secrecy and the wider indoctrination threatened to jeopardise his XX standing but he survived the experience.

In addition, by mid-September PENNANT in Paris, STANDARD in Rouen and BOILER had come under SCI control, but PENNANT failed to develop and STANDARD, suspected of a triple-cross because he never received a reply from the Germans, was sent to Camp 020 for interrogation.

As Allied troops moved up from the South of France several stay-behind networks were uncovered, and the French took five into custody, of whom PERCY agreed to be turned. Another, KELLER, had been instructed to collect his transmitter in Amiens, thus compromising another network and leading to the recruitment of MONUMENT who moved to Paris.

The best French channel was GILBERT, originally from Algiers, who had moved to Marseilles where GAOL was already operational. Both would travel to Paris in October, with GAOL notionally employed at Le Bourget. GILBERT was a French staff officer, Major André Latham, a St Cyr graduate and Abt. III stay-behind agent in Tunis who had been recruited in Paris by Oscar Reile[13] and equipped with a transmitter, designated ATLAS 1. However, upon the city's liberation in May Latham had surrendered to the Allies and was enrolled as a BCRA double agent transmitting to his Abwehr controller almost every day for 15 months, first from Tunis and, from November 1944, when he was based in Marseilles. His plausible cover-story, which made him valuable to the Germans, was that he was working on the staff of a French general and would later be posted to SHAEF's Civil Affairs branch in Paris.

FOREST, the distinguished French pilot Lucien Herviou recruited in 1943, began in Dragignan in October, as did ALTAZIN, apparently an I/L agent. ALTAZIN, later renamed MULETEER, proved to be too sensitive as he received very detailed questionnaires relating to airfields near Paris and troop movements from Brittany towards Brussels and Liège, which could not be answered. Then he was sent another questionnaire, about Paris airfields and two very specific Paris telephone exchanges, and this prompted his temporary withdrawal to England. An agent parachuted to deliver money to MULETEER was taken into custody when he called at his home to hand over the cash, which was to be shared with COSSACK. Evidence also emerged of a large stay-behind network in the south-west of France known as the Alder Organisation.

Two new cases, MONARCH and GLASS, were contemplated at the end of October, as were de Koenig and van Medeart. Others becoming active included LUC, an I/L agent and supporter of General Petain working a radio in Draguignan; JACQUES, an I/M agent in Marseilles; MARCHAND, I/H in Grenoble; GEORGE, I/L in Cannes; CABANON, I/H in Toulon; ADOLPHE, I/H in Marseilles; and JEANNOT, a woman trained by I/H.

With GIRRANT and PERRIER the Abwehr appeared to change tactics and parachuted them into the US 12th Army Group area, where they were quickly captured. Some agents had short-term missions, and the trick for the Allies was to extend the missions so as to justify the investment, as happened with WITCH and LEAGUE in

November 1944. MONARCH and GLASS could not make contact in October, and accordingly were dropped.

From a counter-intelligence perspective, a valued prize was George Speich, identified by several agents as having been their I/M controller. The objective was to manoeuvre Speich into endangering himself through personal contact with one of his agents, and then seize him. These plans, based on a tour of inspection to visit MONOPLANE, KEYNOTE and SKULL, came to naught.

Gradually, as the Allies tightened their grip on the surviving Abwehr networks, the 212 Committee overseeing the double-cross operations for SHAEF moved individual agents around to fill in perceived gaps in the Abwehr's intelligence picture, for example in January 1945 moving COSSACK to report on V-1 damage in Liège so as to deflect the enemy's aim. A Turk who had taken French citizenship, COSSACK had been arrested near Lille in November 1944. In counter-espionage terms, the Abwehr showed signs of increasing ingenuity, as was demonstrated by the arrest of MODEL who was found to be masquerading as a captain in the Canadian Army.

The 212 Committee, as a mirror-image of the XX Committee in London, would assemble fortnightly, often chaired by Dick White, mainly in the joint field headquarters rue Petrarque in Paris, to approve 'food-stuff' for passing to the enemy and protect really sensitive items, such as the location of vulnerable fuel pipelines. This was a fine balancing act to perform, with the intention of retaining the Abwehr's interest while simultaneously protecting really valuable secrets and political intentions. The Committee, consisting of British and American personnel only, also had an indirect liaison responsibility with the French and Belgian agencies which, for security reasons, were not allowed access to the Committee or its deliberations. Occasionally this would lead to 'ticklish' situations in which the relevant agencies would be required to take action without an explanation. More frequently, there was a duplication, such as the request to report on airborne troops, sent to the French-controlled GAT and to MULETEER almost simultaneously, thereby inviting contradictory replies. Only the tightest internal discipline prevented such potentially embarrassing incidents, and as GAT was notionally in command of nine sub-agents, such an incident could have had severely adverse consequences.

Although undertaking many of the procedures pioneered by the XX Committee, 212 was really its successor because much of its strategic activity was by now redundant, and by the end of 1944 there were only three transmitters still operating under control, being TATE, BRUTUS and GARBO. Supervision of the Belgian pilot SNIPER had already shifted to SHAEF as he was posted back to his own liberated country, where he had been supplied with a radio. In the post-D-Day era there were only a few deception schemes underway, such as the plan intended to identify non-existent minefields to the Kriegsmarine so as to deny U-boats entry to the English Channel from the Western Approaches. In the absence of any deception requirement, and in the words of the SHAEF Ops (B) deception planner Noel Wild addressing the SIS Committee held in Versailles in April 1945, the double-cross programme 'would now more than ever be concerned with the penetration and destruction of the German Intelligence Service'.[14]

By the New Year a combination of ISOS, defectors and double-cross had extended the Allied grasp of the Abwehr's intelligence collection and facilitated several counter-espionage operations and short-range deception campaigns, some of them involving LITIGANT and an Abt. III agent, LEGION. Counter-sabotage became a priority and a Flemish seaman, PIP, was interdicted and played back against his controller. Two Luftwaffe stay-behind operators, BLAZE and LAZY, were located by ISOS in München-Gladbach and turned, while the SD deployed FORGE. Other agents included CAMOUFLAGE, who reported on shipping movements, GOLDFLAKE in Marseilles and PENKNIFE. As the stable of double agents increased, the Germans experienced trouble in paying them. DERRICK was promised a visit from a seaborne courier, and FLAME complained about lack of funds.

On several occasions the Germans cancelled some potentially large-scale interventions, without explanation. FISH was instructed to establish a parachute reception area near Troyes, which was never used, and PIP was asked to receive a party of parachutists, but none materialised. If these were integrity tests, as had been set occasionally by the Abwehr, it was a technique that could be played by both sides. When Paul Jeannin, codenamed MONOPLANE, in Marseilles indicated that he was contemplating sailing as a radio operator on a ship bound for the United States, his controller reacted sharply, thereby underscoring his value. The threat was plausible because until his recruitment by I/M in March 1943, Jeannin had been a radio operator on the French transatlantic liner *Normandie*. In another example, a group of three agents codenamed FREELANCE were parachuted near Lyons with instructions to check on KEEL in Paris and pay him if convinced of his continuing loyalty.

Several cases, such as ROSIE and HOSTESS, failed to develop, and there was always the danger of a triple-cross, as seemed to have happened with HOST. He made radio contact with his German station in March 1945 and was promptly asked 'whether he was controlled and had answered no'. Evidently the Abwehr distrusted him so 'it was therefore proposed to run him as a triple-cross for as long a time as there appeared to be anything to be gained by the manoeuvre'.

As the endgame was played out, some desperate measures were taken. For example, in Kaiserslautern an Abwehr officer codenamed QUALITY surrendered himself and three transmitters, complete with their operators, and offered to continue operations under Allied supervision. Even at this late stage, the SD remained active, and MINT, one of two men dropped behind the Allied lines, had agreed to be doubled. He came from the same SD stable as DEPUTY and was promised more men would follow. Significantly, he was also entrusted with a codeword to indicate an imminent capitulation. According to MODEL, who crossed the lines for a second time, SD intelligence personnel were in disgrace because of their poor performance, and were being transferred to Waffen-SS units. He also reported that the celebrated Otto Skorzeny, who in September 1943 had led the daring mission to rescue Benito Mussolini from captivity, had been assigned the task of assassinating Field Marshal Montgomery and other Allied commanders.

Gradually the 212 Committee began to close down operations and turn some agents, such as the newly-developed VIOLET in Paris, over to the French, together with WITCH, LAZY, BLAZE and ATOM. But as they did so, many of the agents, having experienced communications problems because of electricity power cuts, lost all contact with their controllers who appeared to be withdrawing east, with some heading for the Bavarian Alps. The handover of agents to the French was further complicated by QUEASY who reportedly betrayed several other double agents based in eastern France. Nevertheless, in the midst of the chaos, members of new stay-behind groups were appearing, including three parachutists who were linked to the existing cases of FISH, FICKLE and GUN. One of the newcomers, LABBÉ, turned out to be a paymaster, well equipped with funds on an assignment to revive dormant agents and recruit new ones. Significantly, he had also been entrusted with two addresses, one in Switzerland and the other in Germany, for use only three months *after* the war had ended.

* * *

The Third Reich's ultimate collapse occurred without the intervention of the much-vaunted Werewolf resistance, and the German intelligence machine, with its tentacles across the globe, quickly evaporated. Staff who had dedicated their wartime service to promoting intelligence operations in support of the regime found it hard to adjust to the new reality of an Allied occupation, detention, interrogation and the voluntary disclosure of previously tightly-held information. Intelligence sources were named, cover-addresses compromised and operations forensically dissected, but none of those processed gained the slightest hint that their supposedly secure communications had been tapped, their agents turned on an industrial scale, or that the Allies had engaged in large-scale strategic deception so sophisticated that it had hoodwinked the most experienced of military analysts. Even three decades later, when the secrets of ISOS, double-cross and the D-Day cover-stories began to emerge, there was an inherent reluctance among the Abwehr veterans to accept that they had been so comprehensively misled. Some historians attributed the overall German intelligence failure to a combination of corruption and incompetence, and it is true that contemporaneous commentators were quick to find fault with their adversaries and ridicule them for some perceived obvious blunders in tradecraft, but the evidence of the immediate post-war reporting reveals a certain acknowledgment of the relative efficiency of Berlin's intelligence monolith, the skill of individual officers and the typically Teutonic administrative and organisational commitment that made Blitzkrieg possible, that enforced a crippling economic blockade on the British Isles and deployed legions of agents into critical theatres at very short notice. From a counter-intelligence perspective, the manipulation of the French Resistance, the control exercised over the Dutch underground, and the investigation of the Soviet GRU spy-rings across Western Europe, remain models of professionalism.

Outsiders relying on the partial memories of participants have tended to focus on internal dissent, emphasizing the ideological friction between the Abwehr and the SD, and it is certainly true that there were plenty of anti-Nazis within the Abwehr who schemed against Hitler and opposed his henchmen. But did any actively undermine the regime? Few of the defectors examined in these pages were little more than opportunists motivated to improve their own personal circumstances.

The 20 July plot can now be seen in its proper context as an Abwehr-inspired putsch to restore the monarchy, encouraged by SIS through a chain that linked specific officers in Lisbon to Otto John, Georg Hansen, Claus von Stauffenberg and to the tragically miscarried events at Rastenburg.

Appendix I

THE BAUMEISTER QUESTIONNAIRE

This MI5 translation of a 1931 Baumeister questionnaire[1] illustrates the problem of providing answers to very detailed queries and tasks. The nature of the nine-page document served to highlight German interest in tank warfare and the challenges presented by rivers and similar physical obstacles to a swift armoured advance, one of the pillars of the Blitzkrieg doctrine. From a counter-intelligence perspective, the issue was the inadvisability of sustaining a double-cross strategy to retain an adversary's interest at the cost of compromising authentic secrets. An added consideration, articulated by SIS's Valentine Vivian to MI5's Nigel Watson and Colonel W.A. Alexander, was the need to protect an SIS informant in Brussels who had been instrumental in revealing Baumeister's role as a spymaster. The dilemma of how to pass classified material to an enemy would not be resolved until the formation in January 1941 of the XX Committee which adjudicated the principles in each case.

Setting aside the merits of sustaining a double agent, with all the challenges and potential advantages involved, the successful management of a controlled enemy agent offers an opportunity to oversee, and maybe manipulate, an adversary's raw intelligence, and likely reduces the pressure to deploy additional, hitherto unknown spies, on the basis that if a particular source is performing satisfactorily, there is no need to go to the expense of duplicating the effort.

The significance of Friedrich Baumeister's directive is its value as evidence of early inter-war German intelligence collection priorities and techniques at a time when the British countermeasures were in their infancy.

The Inner Organisation of English Armoured Vehicles
Central and head organisation. London?
Military and civil establishments

I <u>Organisation</u>
(a) Now in Peace (b) In future – in war?

1) Independent Armoured Units.
>Tank or armoured car (Panzerkraftwagen) units?
2) Mixed mechanized units, also experimental units.
3) Army motor lorries Transport group.
4) Mechanised baggage, Supplies units
>How are the single units made up?
>Strengths of establishments.
>Are alterations or additions planned in existing establishments?
>What places outside London are used for tactical experiments and tactical development.

II <u>Stores and Equipment</u>
>Pictures, blueprints, plans, drawings giving exact organisation schemes.
>a) Equipment for Troops.
>b) Equipment for War.
>c) Equipment for Trials.

1) Armoured Fighting Cars (Armed for attack).
>a) Capable of being driven over any kind of country (including the crossing of ditches and the climbing of perpendicular obstacles, which is now only possible for track-chain driven vehicles, except the Italian Paveal Car.).
>b) Capable of being driven across country.
>c) Only for driving on roads.

2) Armoured motor-cycles.
Armoured motor-cars (for instance cars for reconnoitre on the field of battle).

3) Unarmoured cars and tractors (not armed or armed only for defence).
>a) for all cross-country driving.
>b) for cross-country driving.
>c) for roads only.

4) Special Vehicles
More details wanted

(I) Whether wheeled cars, caterpillar cars, [zwittèr?], wheeled caterpillars, or multi-wheeled cars with chains etc. Description of caterpillar and track-chains (photos and drawings).

II) Arming and supply of munitions (different kinds of munitions?)

III) Armour plating (different thickness, front, side, back, roof), thickness and kind of armour plating, for instance whether armour or overlaid layers of steel, rubber and lead plates reinforced, capable of resisting fire of what calibre & from what distance.

IV) Personnel and how disposed.

V) Weight (when equipped for action).

VI) Speed
      a) Maximium road speed.
      b) Average 200 km road speed.
      c) Maximum cross country.
      d) Average cross country.

VII) Maximum distance on one filling of petrol-tank.

VIII) Outside measurements (photo).

IX) Engine kind (benzin, heavy oil) 7 power. Water- or air-cooled mounting (front or back), special protection, bearings, position of and protection for fuel tank?

X) Climbing capacity.

XI) Destruction of wire entanglements.

XII) Fording or floating capacity.

XIII) Overthrowing trees.

XIV) How is strategic mobility arrived at?

XV) Is collective protection against gas provided? Details.

XVI) Means for Intelligence.

(a) Inside the vehicle.
(b) For liaison with the outside world.

XVII) Arrangements for observation.

XVIII) Capacity for crossing ditches and trenches.

XIX) What results of shooting in battle are known?

What places, towns, schools, etc. are devoted to technical trials and technical developments?

III Tactics
1) In what service publications (exact title) are the tactical operations laid down which are a guide for attack?
2) According to what Service Handbook are exercises held and troops trained?
3) What gunnery instructions are there?
4) Were important exercises in Army mechanization planned for the current year? Where? When? Object of the exercise. What units took part?
5) What schools, courses or other training possibilities exist or are planned in mechanical transport?
6) Is there a military junior training school in mechanical transport?

I. Infantry Rifles
1) Are Automatic rifles in use, or are trials in progress? Loading by gas pressure or recoil? Weight, length, calibre? How much ammunition does the magazine hold?
2) What kind of rifle grenades are used? How are they fired? What is the construction of the firing mechanism? Sight? Range? Effect?
3) How are troops equipped with rifle grenades in battle? How is supply effected? Quantity of ammunition?

II Granatwerfer
Are there other kinds of Granatwerfer (not trench mortars) besides Rifle Grenades?
What is the construction of the firing mechanism, sighting and loading?
Kinds of ammunition: (Brenn-Zunder) time-fuze (Aufachlag-Zunder) percussion fuze – smoke bomb – Gas? Range? effect?

III Hand Grenades
What kinds – time fuzes – percussion – smoke – gas?

Aspects to watch in foreign Intelligence systems

I Telephone apparatus
1) What armies have untappable telephone and telegraphs in use? (Descriptions, drawings and photos desired).
2) What field cable, especially double circuit is used? (dates of construction, range).
Also what statements regarding double-circuit cable not in use would be of value.
Samples of field cable, especially double circuit cable as supplied t all the great military states are asked for (if possible in lengths of at least 10m.)
3) What means are used for laying field cable, especially double circuit cable?
4) What cable-laying vehicles are in use, horse or mechanised? (pictures, etc, desired.)
5) What field telegraph apparatus is used by foreign armies? (Hughes telephone instrument, sounder, buzzer.)
6) Give details of cable drums and other apparatus (especially for use with horses and lorries) pictures, drawings, descriptions are of interest.
7) What Field Telephones and transmitting apparatus are in use. Description of inner construction desired.

II Wireless Apparatus
1) Does the English or French Army possess an apparatus for the front, working with beam wireless? What is meant here is the very smallest apparatus, working on waves of under 1m. What state has it reached (state of development; On trial by troops; adopted?) We should like to have one.
2) To what extent is short wave length apparatus used by the above-named armies for aeroplanes and tanks?
What efficiency, wave lengths, aerials, electric current do senders and receivers possess? Confirm types. Where is the apparatus manufactured, in Government factories or by firms?
3) Remarks on possibilities of interception of short wave messages, including range and exactitude.

III Interception Apparatus
Have the French and English introduced new Interception apparatus since the war? We should like samples.

IV Signalling Apparatus
Has an army of the above-named countries introduced telephone with visible beam with success? What are these armies doing in the lines of

telegraphy telephony with invisible beam (infra-red apparatus)? Sample of each apparatus desired.

Points of view to be examined with regard to foreign pioneer apparatus, R.E.
Any information interests us concerning:

Kinds of smoke-screen apparatus.
Are fuzes fired by pushing or pulling?
Kinds of fuze.
Portable entrenching tools.
Mine cable (either double or single).
Tank mines, construction and weight.
Is there electric lighting of fuzes by explosive charges?
Are river mines used?
Defence against mines?

All technical questions concerning military bridge-building with construction plans and exact figures regarding: measurements, carrying capacity; weights, transportation, trials and their results, developments in:

Pontoons.
Pontoon bridge apparatus.
Trestle gear.
Ferries.
Abutments.
Temporary bridges.
Collapsible Communications Bridges.
Portable ramps.
Folding boats, bridges for folding boats.
Raft building materials, and bridges for rafts.
Emergency bridge.
Any kind of emergency means of crossing.
Floating Pontoon Motor Lorries.
Pontoon and trestle wagons.
Make-up of bridging columns.
Motor boats and lorries for their transport.
Cable and ferry-cable apparatus.
Rocket rifles.
Distant control of stationary searchlights.
With what accuracy does distant control work?
Liaison with anti-aircraft.
Number and kind of site for the Defence of towns and important Industrial Centres.

Stone drills

Camouflage outfit, material, and method of use.

Types of parapet recesses.

Entanglements against tanks.

Emergency entanglements

Tools for tunnelling.

Gas protection in permanent buildings for instance, gas defence
     shelters by the Polish Air- and Gas-Defence League (Warsaw,
     Posen, Sonnowice), including material of specially reinforced
     cement – Ventilation, removal of air, oxygen generation apparatus.

Armour plating, especially that used in the field.

Machinery for speeding up of works for the construction of dug-outs.
     (Dredger, trench construction machinery, concrete mixer, portable
     stone drills, road cutting machinery, etc.)

I Light Machine Guns

1) What kinds are in use or in experimental stage? Exact descriptions of
hitherto unknown models, Drawings. What ammunition is used?

2) How are these light machine guns transported?
     a) by Infantry?
     b) by Cavalry?
     c) by other arms of the Service?

Transport on motor cycles? How? Photos, descriptions, reports on results.

3) What gun positions and methods of aims for firing at aeroplanes are
in use? Descriptions, drawings, reports on results.

II Heavy Machine Guns

1) What type are in use or in experimental sage? Exact descriptions of
hitherto unknown models, Drawings. What ammunition is used?

2) How are these heavy machine guns carried?
     a) by Infantry?
     b) by Cavalry?
     c) by other arms of the Service?

Carried on motor cycles? How? descriptions, drawings, reports
on results.

3) What positions and sighting control are used for air guns? Descriptions,
drawings, results of practice.

4) How is firing done from covered positions? Instructions on this
subject, also drawings, descriptions, photos, and plans of aiming
methods and instruments.

5) Is special ammunition used for shooting which renders easy the
observation of the hits?

6) Tracer bullets – samples.

III <u>Super-heavy Machine Guns</u>
1) What kinds are in use or in experimental stage? <u>Exact</u> descriptions of hitherto unknown models, Drawings. What ammunition is needed?
2) How are the Super-heavy Machine Guns transported?
    a) by Infantry?
    b) by Cavalry?
    c) by other arms of the Service?
Are they carried on motor cycles? How? Photos, description, reports on results.
3) What gun positions and methods of aim for firing at aeroplanes are in use? Descriptions, drawings, reports on results.
4) How is firing done from covered positions? Instructions on this subject, also drawings, descriptions, photos, and plans of aiming methods and instruments.
5) Are they employed against tanks? Special mechanism for this? Reports of results.
6) Are they used only against aeroplanes or against tanks or both? Reports of results.
7) What kind of ammunition is used? (shot, shell, sensitive fuze, tracer bullets). Photos, description, tests.
8) Special Command Posts for Super-heavy Machine Guns?

IV <u>Machine Guns in Aeroplanes</u>
1) What kinds are in use or in experimental stage? <u>Exact</u> descriptions of hitherto unknown models, Drawings. What ammunition is used?
2) How far are earth Machine Guns reconstructed for use in the air?

V   1) Rangefinders for aeroplanes. Are stereoscopic rangefinders in use for M.G. formations or in the experimental stage?
    2) Use of targets for training in anti aircraft defence.

<u>Points for enquiry concerning protection of the troops from air attack</u>

1) What method of alarm do the foreign military states use for the troops on the look-out for air attacks to employ to warn the troops elsewhere? Sirens, electric signals, bugles, signals?
How are the acoustic properties arranged for?
What arrangements for sending on the warning?
2) What regulations are there in the principal military countries for the introduction to and carrying of camouflage nets by the troops? Are special cars set apart for this? Are experiments being carried out for the carrying of the nets by the rank and file in battle, or has this matter been settled?

To what extent are the various arms of the service supplied with camouflage nets? Is the supply complete for troops on exercises, or only arranged for in case of war?

3) Table of equipment for the following flying formations in war:
    Two-seater fighter flight
    Night fighter flight
    Night bomber flight

What scale of reinforcements is arranged for in the Flying Units, and how many are kept within the Units themselves and how many at the aerodrome.

Quotation from Naval & Military Record

In the course of the year 1929 the English publication the *Naval & Military Record* and *The Naval Dockyard Gazette*, page 811, published the following in a report on French Artificial Clouds from Aeroplanes at Brest ('French Navy Notes'):

'A description of "artificial clouds" which are not blown away by wind and stay in the spot where they are wanted – do well in northern waters – look like ordinary fog – submarines can make them – or they can be made by bombs or gunfire.'

The apparent effect of the smoke-screen allows one to suppose that this is quite a new, unknown and a more effective smoke material than any that is known to us. Information is requested.

In the English journal *The Naval and Military Record*, page 811, under date 26 September 1929, the following report appears regarding the French system of smoke clouds from aeroplanes at Brest.

'Former artificial clouds were rather clumsy devices, being black, hanging over the water and rising skywards, and vary limited in the space they covered. They were local and temporary obstacles – an ordinary wind dispersed them, They delayed and hampered action, but did not render it impossible, as many war events go to prove. The "faits nouveaux" in the new, artificial clouds, that are the result of painstaking research and were first experimented upon in the huge Brest roadstead, reside in the tremendous space they are capable of covering, spreading by degree along the surface of the water, especially in windy or rainy weather, and in the long time during which their blinding or hazing effects last. A damp atmosphere prolongs their life. Very heavy weather is against them. They are best adapted for use in northern waters, and can be so easily produced at small cost that their advent is bound to totally alter former conditions of attack and defence, both for coasts and harbour and for ships. A few minutes after they have been emitted those new "images artificiels" assume the appearance of ordinary mists, which will lead, of course, to terrible surprises. Small vedettes, with "silencers", or, better still, submarines, can emit them and render impracticable to navigation for hours a wide surface of the sea, thereby hampering considerably the movements of an enemy. Bombs and shells by bursting can be made, of course, to produce similar clouds over a target.'

The working of the clouds, according to this account, makes one suspect that a quite new, unknown and much better system of artificial cloud is used than is known to us.

Information is requested.

Appendix II

MI5'S NORDPOL
INVESTIGATION[1]

Completed by Camp 020 staff in July 1945, based on the interrogation of Abwehr officers Hermann Giskes and Gerhard Huntemann conducted by Jack Hughes and Stephen Noakes based on questionnaires prepared by MI5's Ian Wilson and Laura Bingham, SOE's John Delaforce, and Section V's John Farmer.

1. General Situation in Ast Niederlande
In August 1941 Giskes was transferred from Ast Paris to Ast Niederlande with the rank of Oberstleutnant and appointment of Leiter Referat III. On taking up his new appointment he found that the entire section needed reorganisation as many of the officers were quite incapable and, in addition, many of the MSB members of the section were using their positions merely to terrorise their own nationals; moreover, Giskes had to reckon with the hostile attitude of the Sipo and the SD towards the Abwehr. This hostility became more acute every year until, as will be seen later, Giskes' life was even in danger.

As there was a German civil administration in Holland as opposed to a Wehrmacht administration in the other occupied countries, internal security was completely in the hands of the Hoehere SS und Polizeiführer, and, theoretically at least, the work of III/F was confined entirely to military matters and was not executive. The Abwehr had no powers of arrest and so in all cases where action was necessary it was taken by the Sipo.

For purely disciplinary matters Giskes found that he was subordinated to the leiter of Ast-Niederlande but, as regards his own activities, he was responsible to a certain Oberst Rohleders Abt. III, Berlin. While Giskes was still at Paris Rohleder had painted a gloomy

261

picture of the unsatisfactory state of affairs of III/F at The Hague, and had charged him with the task of reorganising the Referat.

On arrival Giskes made sweeping changes and restaffed his section with men recommended to him for their capabilities, amongst these being a certain Gerhard Huntemann.

2. British Activity in Holland in summer 1941

It was known through III/F, operated at that time by the Funk-Abwehr, that two enemy transmitting stations were active and there were constant rumours about sea communications between Holland and the UK. Prior to Giskes' arrival a seaplane had endeavoured to land off the Dutch coast and, in a brush with the German police, several of the latter had been killed. It is thus evident that at this stage British espionage and resistance activities in Holland were on a small scale, at least as far as III/F were aware.

3. Arrest of W/T Operators

At the beginning of September 1941, as a result of RDF, a W/T operator was arrested in the Bildhoven district and on him was found a series of messages, signed AC. The messages were of a purely intelligence nature. This matter was handled entirely by the SD and III/F were not told of the identity of the arrested agent, but Giskes thinks that he was a Dutch Naval cadet whose name may have been Ten Haak or Laak. A second operator, whose name Giskes believes was Van der Rkyden, was arrested probably in January 1942. This man agreed to act as a double agent but the attempt by the SD to play him back proved abortive. This case also was handled exclusively by the Sipo, and the Fu-B-Stelle-Orpo, who had replaced the Funk-Abwehr towards the end of 1941.

4. Arrest of EBENEZER

Amongst those handling counter-espionage and counter resistance agents in III/F was a certain Uffz. Kup who had been employed by the Referat since the German occupation of Holland in 1940. Sometime in the late summer or early autumn of 1941 a certain George Ridderhof @ Van Vliet, an agent of Kup, had been imprisoned in Amsterdam for illicit dealings in gold and diamonds. Whilst serving his term of imprisonment Ridderhof made the acquaintance of a man, name unknown to Giskes or Huntemann, who was apparently a member of an indigenous resistance group. When Ridderhof was released he was asked by the unknown to make contact with his wife and visit certain friends, whose addresses would be given by the wife. Ridderhof reported this to Kup who in turn informed Giskes. The latter then gave instructions that Ridderhof was to attempt to penetrate this group by contacting the addresses. In due course reports came in from Ridderhof as follows:

(a) About the beginning of December 1941 Ridderhof reported that a man with a motor-boat intended to make an escape to the UK and that he required petrol for the journey. Ridderhof was given 25 litres of petrol from III/F and the Sipo had the starting point watched. But nothing transpired and Ridderhof later reported that the man had departed from a point other than the one which had previously been decided upon. Enquiries were made at the man's home address, near the Abw-Stelle Scheveningen, on the corner of Larkweg and Hoogeweg, and it was established that the man's name was Maas and that he had been absent from home for three months,
(b) In January 1942 the broadcasting by London of the Wilhelminalied was to be the signal that a motor-boat would be arriving at Scheveningen to pick up certain members of the Dutch Resistance Movement, to take them to the UK. On the appointed day, plain-clothes police were on the beach and arrested Dutch patriots who were awaiting the motor-boat, which however failed to arrive.
(c) Later in January 1942, Riderhof reported that he was in touch with a certain Captain Van Den Berg, a Dutch Amy reserve officer, living at The Hague, who was connected with a resistance organisation at Vierlingsbeek, near Nijmegen. Reports on this organisation were to the effect that arms and explosives were hidden in churches and monasteries in the neighbourhood. A sub-agent, Graan, was charged with the surveillance of this group.

Again, later, Ridderhof reported that the organisation expected an aeroplane to arrive from the UK to drop sabotage material, who gave the locality but not the exact location of the dropping-ground. Upon hearing this Giskes, who at this time was sceptical, said to Kup: 'It is for this reason that the codename NORDPOL was given by III/F to cover the subsequent turning and playing-back of SOE agents.'

Huntemann, who had recently been discharged from hospital, was accordingly sent to Assen to keep observation. Towards the end of February 1942 a British 'plane was seen one night during the full moon period, circling in the vicinity and later it was learnt that in fact two containers had been dropped. On this occasion there was a genuine Dutch resistance reception committee headed by Captain Van Den Berg and a certain Sergeant Biermann. Only one container was found by the committee, which was taken to a warehouse nearby; Van Den Berg then went to Ridderhof, living at that time in The Hague, and asked him to arrange for the transport of the material to his (Ridderhof's) flat for safe keeping; Ridderhof obliged. This incident, when reported to Giskes, convinced him that there was a W/T operator in direct touch with the UK, especially as prior to this date the Fu-B-Stelle-Orpo had intercepted, but not deciphered, signals in The Hague area. Furthermore, Ridderhof had also given information, gleaned from Van Den Berg, to the effect that two British agents had been dropped, at the end of November 1941 in the area of Assen.

It was therefore decided by Giskes that intensive efforts would have to be made to locate and arrest the operator. Accordingly, the Fu-B-Stelle-Orpo was given this task as a first priority, and the area in which the operator was working was finally narrowed down to the vicinity of Laan Van Meerdevort, The Hague. A raid was organised in the district and one Hubertus Mattheus Gerardus Lauwers @ EBENEZER was arrested on 6 March 1942. He had evidently become aware that a raid was in progress and after throwing the W/T set into the garden, left the house with Teller, the proprietor.

Kup, who was taking part in the raid, had been furnished by Ridderhof with a personal description of EBENEZER, which had been obtained from Capt. Van Den Berg, and apprehended him in the street. Both men were conducted to Teller's house where the W/T set was found in the garden, and Giskes had a short interview with EBENEZER. The latter was then conveyed to the so-called Oranje Hotel, where Dutch patriots were imprisoned. At first he was confined in the SD section of the prison, but about a month afterwards, on Giskes' representation, he was transferred to the Wehrmacht section where conditions were better.

5. Implications of EBENEZER's arrest

Interrogation of EBENEZER by Krimrat. Schreiber, and to a lesser extent by Giskes himself, convinced the latter that if British intention were realised and numerous well equipped sabotage and resistance groups were created, an extremely dangerous military situation would arise, particularly if these measures succeeded simultaneously in all the Western occupied countries. For this reason, therefore, Giskes decided to concentrate the activities of his Referat on the hindering or prevention of any such plans.

6. Employment of Double Agents
An Abwehr Abt. Ill directive from Berlin, circulated during the early part of the war, laid down the objects to be achieved in playing back captured agents, as follows:

(a) To maintain contact with Allied espionage agents and their HQs in order to ascertain missions and enemy intentions.
(b) Deception (procedure is given in Annexure 1).
(c) The control of any Allied organisation and thus prevent the growth of a sister organisation unknown to the Germans.
(d) To penetrate organised escape routes (III/F were not interested in individuals who escaped haphazardly as these matters are handled by the Sipo).

7. The turning of EBENEZER
Shortly after EBENEZER's arrest Kup asked permission to visit him in prison, and on his return informed Giskes that EBENEZER was prepared to work for the Germans. Giskes maintains that no physical force was used to turn him. Giskes also personally visited him in prison, and with Schreiber guaranteed his life as well as the lives of any subsequent Allied agents who might fall into German hands through his treachery. EBENEZER, on accepting the proposal to work for the Germans, told both Giskes and Schreiber that he had been assured by a certain Colonel Blunt, before leaving the UK, that in the event of his arrest he was at liberty to accept any proposal put forward the Germans to save his life; for, at the most, it would be discovered within three weeks if he were working under control. Schreiber accordingly accepted the German proposal and, on 19 March 1942 sent his first message of German origin. This message requested further supplies and stated that the location of a previously agreed dropping point was too dangerous. Three further messages, all dated 15 March 1942 containing information about a ship's crew money and a reference to BRANDY, dealing with political and industrial information, and CXG 16 containing information about the position of the *Prinz Eugen* – all of which had been previously composed by EBENEZER and found on him after arrest, were allowed to go forward by the Germans.

The information as to the locality of the *Prinz Eugen* was found on reference to Referat I/M to be false, but Giskes denies that prior to this date false information had been passed to Resistance Groups for onward transmission. He declares that as far as he can remember

EBENEZER had received the information from his organiser, Thijs Taconis @ CATARRH, who in turn probably obtained it from Van Den Berg as the latter was believed to have certain sources among the Authorities and dockyard workers in Rotterdam.

8. Distribution of Functions

Giskes was responsible for the general policy of playing back EBENEZER and subsequent W/T operators captured, but the non-technical, detailed conduct of the traffic, i.e. preparing drafts of messages, seeing London signals received answers, keeping traffic on the right lines, and when necessary the notional killing of operators, etc., was the sole responsibility of Huntemann, who was struck off all other duties until the termination of the traffic on 1 April 1944. The messages were drafted by Huntemann and then taken to the Fu-B-Stelle of the Orpo which was always in close proximity to III/F.

The B Stelle was solely responsible for the enciphering and deciphering of all signals and for the actual transmission. In this connection it is interesting to note that only 2 SOE W/T operators ever actually transmitted, namely EBENEZER for about 3 months after capture, and TRUMPET (see below). All traffic with these exceptions was conducted by trained operators of the B Stelle.

The actual arrest and custody of the agents were entirely Sipo responsibilities, but of course both Giskes and Huntemann had access to them when necessary.

9. Arrest of CATARHH

About 15 March 1942 Thijs Taconis @ CATARHH was arrested by the Sipo at Arnhem whilst trying to effect the rescue of a member of his group who had been taken prisoner by the Germans. Neither Giskes nor Huntemann know much about the circumstances of the arrest as the entire affair was handled by the Sipo, but it appears that at the time of his arrest the Germans were unaware of his identity, and it was only at a later date that they realised the importance of their capture. Giskes had an interview with him at the prison at Scheveningen the day after he had tried to escape, but CATARHH refused to give details about himself, and it was only at a later date when he had been convinced that the whole organisation had been blown, that he could be induced to give details of his mission. As he was not a W/T operator he was not of much interest to Giskes and Huntemann, but Giskes expresses considerable respect for his steadfast and soldierly behaviour.

10. Arrest of WATERCRESS

On about 19 March 1942, SOE signal CG 21 UAJ 21 to EBENEZER advised that an independent agent was to be expected from 24 March 1942 onward, together with containers, with the result that Albert Arnold Baatsen @ ABOR @ WATERCRESS was received on 27 March near Steenwijjk by a Dutch reception committee working under SD control. Among those taking part in the reception were the Dutch subjects Schachter, Hoos and Ridderhof; the latter was drunk and his behaviour was such that his attendance on future occasions of this nature was forbidden by the Germans. The 'safe' arrival of WATERCRESS was acknowledged in EBENEZER's CXG 24 of 26 March to London.

WATERCRESS voluntarily offered his services to the Germans and was even prepared to undertake a mission abroad for the SD. He was used, however, by the Sipo for spying on his fellow prisoners at Haaren, to which all captured agents were sent after a short stay at Scheveningen prison.

11. Arrest of LETTUCE, TRUMPET and TURNIP

Early in April 1942 III/F was informed by the Feldgendarmerie that a dead parachutist had been found in a field north-west of Holten; it appeared that he had hit his head on a stone water-trough landing. From tracks in the neighbourhood of the body there were grounds for believing that other agents had landed at the same time. Early in May the Sipo, on information received from a certain Dr Stemkel of the Inkassen & Hypotheken Bank, Utrecht, arrested Goswigen Hendrik Gerard Rae @ LETTUCE and Johan Jordaan @ TRUMPET. The arrests were effected by the Sipo, and Giskes thinks that the informant acted unwittingly. About the same time the Sipo also arrested Leonardus Andringa @ TURNIP on information supplied by a woman (name unknown) in Utrecht. The informant is thought by Giskes to have acted unwittingly.

Interrogation of the three agents produced the full story of the dropping operation on 28th March and established the identity of the dead man, a W/T operator named John @ SWEDE. The latter's signal plan was found on TURNIP which enabled the Germans at a later date to operate a notional, locally-recruited operator named SWEDE. Moreover, under interrogation the three captured men gave the numbers of Dutch SOE agents who had completed their training and who could therefore be expected to be arriving in the not distant future. In addition, personal descriptions, aliases, an estimate of the capabilities, together with a description of their future roles, i.e. W/T operator, saboteur, clandestine press, organiser etc. were obtained. Thenceforward the Germans devoted a good part of the interrogation of captured agents to the obtaining of this type of information, with the result that they generally knew who to expect in the future; the information obtained enabled them to impress captured agents during interrogation with their seeming omniscience.

It must be remembered that towards the end of April, B-Stelle had been aware that clandestine transmissions were taking place, but they had been unable to decipher the messages.

The first controlled message on the TRUMPET link was transmitted on 5 May 1942 (CGX 14) proposing a new dropping point.

12. LEEK and W/T Operator

On 5 April 1942 Barend Kloos @ LEEK was dropped blind with his W/T operator Kendrik Sebes @ HECK @ LEEK. It appears that during the drop the W/T set was damaged and although these two agents were not, like the others, apprehended immediately, they were never able to get in touch with the UK. They were eventually arrested at a date unknown to Giskes and Huntemann. Huntemann recollects that after the arrest, London was asked for a replacement of the W/T set on another link, and this was furnished, The HECK transmitter was first operated on 22 August 1942 by the Germans, but HECK himself never operated.

13. Arrest of POTATO

On 19 April Johannes Henricus Man @ De Haas @ PYL @ POTATO arrived in Holland by a sea-operation. On 24 April TRUMPET in CXG 7 reported to London that he was in touch with POTATO, contact having been established through TURNIP, but that he could not contact EBENEZER. At this date TRUMPET had not been arrested although his signals had been intercepted by the B-Stelle. On TRUMPET's arrest, in early May, the Germans were able to decipher the TRUMPET messages that they had intercepted, and it is probable, according to Giskes and Huntemann, that POTATO's arrest by the Sipo was due to information furnished by TRUMPET. The first POTATO message sent, CGX 14 on the 5 May 1942, refers to a dropping point.

14. Meeting of CARROT and TURNIP

On 15 May London, in CGX 17, advised TRUMPET of a meeting-place where he was to contact GEORGE @ CARROT who had arrived in Holland on 27 February 1942. The name of the rendezvous was sent in an elaborately coded message, but was decoded by the B-Stelle and found to be The Bodega, Leidsche Poort, Leidache Flein, Amsterdam.

For some reason unknown to Giskes and Huntemann, the Sipo decided to send TURNIP, not TRUMPET to the rendezvous and TURNIP was able to warn CARROT that his two companions were members of the Sipo. CARROT thus succeeded in escaping through a lavatory, eventually arriving in the UK on 2 September 1943.

15. The Situation in May 1942

It had, at this period, become evident to Giskes from interrogation of captured agents that SOE was trying to build up a well-organised sabotage organisation capable of operating throughout Holland. Groups were to be formed by the various organisers by recruitment among NCOs of the Dutch Army, railwaymen and dockyard hands, for sabotage of railways, harbour installations, dockyards, shipbuilding yards, docks and in addition instruction had been given in sabotage, and missions had been allotted as follows:

CATARRH	Provinces of North and South Holland and Gelderland.
WATERCRESS	Special mission not to be divulged by SD to III/F.
LETTUCE	Utrecht area.
LEEK	Oberjessel area.
POTATO	Establishment of sea communication between Holland and UK. Suitable landing places were to be reconnoitred and the area of Katwijk and later Egmond-am-See.

Giskes gave consideration to the possibility of using the organisers already arrested, for forming German controlled Resistance Groups; this would have ensured that the best and most resistant elements in the population would be known and could, therefore, be arrested at any time when it was thought necessary, but he decided that such action was too great a risk to the security of his controlled links.

16. BEETROOT and W/T Operation

On 1 July 1942 London advised EBENEZER in message No. 56 of the impending arrival of two agents and on 29 May Herman Parlevliet @ BEETROOT and his W/T operator Antonius Vansteen were both dropped to the customary SD reception near Steinwijk.

GIIJKES describes these two men as being excellent agents and it was only at a much later stage that they divulged, under interrogation, that they were Eureka instructors; in addition they were to be assistants to WATERCRESS.

17. PARSNIP and SPINACH

On 15 June 1942 London advised TRUMPET (Message No. 28) of the impending arrival of two further agents and accordingly on 22 June, John Jacob Van Rietsschoten @ TURNIP and his W/T operator Johannes Jan Buitzer @ SPINACH were dropped to a German reception near Holten. Interrogations showed that PARSNIP had an independent liaison in North Holland whilst SPINACH was to act as W/T operator, not only to PARSNIP, but also to POTATO who had notionally been using EBENEZER, as London apparently feared that too much traffic on the EBENEZER link might endanger the latter who, of course, had been arrested on 6 March 1942.

Huntemann deduced from this that London regarded EBENEZER as being the best operator.

The 'safe' arrival of PARSNIP and SPINACH was notified to London on 24 June 1942 in TRUMPET 77.

18. MARROW and W/T Operation

On 15 June London No. CXG 61 to EBENEZER advised the field to stand-by from the night of 26 June onwards to receive bodies with the result that on the night of 26 June, George Louis Jambroes @ MARROW and his W/T operator Joseph Bukkens (Bakkers) @ SMIT @ MARROW were duly arrested, near Wezep. EBENEZER acknowledged the 'success' of the operation on 27 June 1942 adding 'SMIT staying with us some time.'

19. The six main links

Although during the NORDPOL affair the Germans operated many links (at one time they were operating 15) the six main links over which fresh arrivals were as follows: – EBENEZER, MARROW, TRUMPET, HECK, SWEDE, SPINACH, accounts of whose arrests have been given above.

At a conference at which SOE and MI5 were represented it was decided that it was unnecessary to give an account of the arrests of subsequent agents as they present little interest, the procedure being notoriously identical with that already described, i.e., London advising departure to the Germans with the resultant SD reception.

SOE, however, put forward a written questionnaire and, at a subsequent conference, a verbal questionnaire to fix a basis for future interrogations.

20. Reasons for closing the NORDPOL

At the end of August 1943, two of the captured SOE agents, Pieter Dourlein @ SPROUT and Johan Bernard Ubbink @ CHIVE, escaped from Haaren and eventually reached the UK via Switzerland.

Then, in October 1943, London intimated that Holland could expect no further deliveries owing to commitments elsewhere. Giskes was certain that these two men had either reached the UK or had in some way conveyed to London the information that the entire SOE organisation in Holland was German controlled. During the next, two months the traffic from London was of a non-committal character and Giskes concluded that the NORDPOL possibilities were at an end. Confirmation that SOE were aware of what had happened came through the arrest at the beginning of 1943 of the HEINTJE Group which took place in Amsterdam through RDF of one of the W/T operators. (It is interesting to note that at this period relations between the SD and the Abwehr were so strained that III/F were only informed of this group after the arrest, and the subsequent attempt to play it back was entirely handled by the SD.)

The HEINTJE Group had been sent by the Dutch Secret Intelligence Service in London aid had been briefed for an espionage mission by Major Solehn. According to Giskes and Huntemann, this group had received towards the end of November 1943 a W/T signal from London that the sister organisation, i.e. the SOE Resistance Movement, was completely under German control and further, that two agents who had been at Haaren had reached London. This information of course only became available in early 1944 when the group was arrested and the intercepted traffic could be deciphered. Giskes wanted to close the NORDPOL affair down immediately, with a message to London, giving the news that all those agents who had been notionally killed were in reality still alive. However, Abt. III/F Berlin refused permission for this and sent orders that the closing message must breath a spirit of confidence in the final victory for German arms, and in the certitude of repelling any Allied invasion of Holland. Accordingly, the closing signal to this effect was transmitted to London, not inappropriately, on 1 April 1944 thus ending the NORDPOL affair, which had lasted a little over two years.

Appendix III

THE HISTORY OF THE ROTE KAPELLE

By Heinz Paulsen, codenamed CARETINA, completed in July 1959 and annotated by the CIA's Munich base following his release from Soviet imprisonment in January 1956.[1] Accompanying the document was an explanatory memorandum outlining the background:

CARETINA was an official of Ast IV, sub-section 2A of the RHSA, which in effect means he was a Gestapo officer. His efforts to portray Amt IV, the Gestapo, in a more favourable light are obvious. At the same time he lectures against the use of 'executive' measures, i.e. police measures, as being less effective than counter-espionage operations. He obviously does not wish to recognise the fact that the RSHA was primarily a police security force, dependent on police power to carry out its security responsibility, and this same police power enabled him to run the large and complicated counter-espionage operations known as the Rote Kapelle.

CARETINA, as many of the former German Army officers and security police officials, is very emotional over the post-war effort to describe the Soviet agents working in the Rote Kapelle complex as 'anti-Nazi resistance fighters'. CARETINA is obsessed with making the record clear that these people were traitors, spying against their native land on behalf of an enemy power. We have not pointed out to him that most Western intelligence services know the Rote Kapelle complex to have been a complex of Soviet espionage nets and have no illusion about the 'resistance' claims of the members. This would have involved revealing too much of our own knowledge of the Rote Kapelle complex.

CARETINA considers himself, even today, as a professional counter-espionage officer and counter-espionage operations are his dominating passion. His conclusions to the report include his apologia for running complicated double-agent and radio play-back operations as opposed to arresting and imprisoning spies. Here again he reveals that he was aware of the Gestapo methods in spite of his efforts to whitewash the German security police. He has not admitted yet that he was able to mount an operation the size of the German control and playback of the Soviet principal agents because he had the complete support of the German military and security police organs in France and the Low Countries. He still think in terms of an intelligence service that has absolute power and, so far, refuses to take into consideration the fact that the only services with that power today are the Soviet services and some of the satellite services in their individual countries. He has also refused to recognise the other fact contributing to his large and successful counter-espionage operations which is the wartime conditions and the German D/F'ing created an ideal situation for mounting the extensive play-back and penetration operations which the Sonderkommando Rote Kapelle directed.

Anyone who has read the British Rote Kapelle Study will be immediately struck by CARETINA's assumption that his Sonderkommando had almost complete control of all Soviet and Communist espionage/underground nets in France and the Low Countries. The British advance a fairly positive theory that the two Soviet principal agents, Trepper and KENT, played back against the GRU headquarters in Moscow by the Germans, were able to notify Moscow through French CP communication channels, unknown to the Germans, of the German control of the Soviet espionage networks. CARETINA has not been interrogated directly on such a possibility but his report makes it fairly clear that he believes that his Sonderkommando, through the German D/F'ing and monitoring facilities, had at least located most, if not all, of the secret transmitters and through his penetration of the French CP, the transmitters were controlled. He does state in the report that his greatest concern was the possibility of a French CP clandestine transmitter establishing contact with Moscow before the Germans could make certain of controlling it. If CARETINA's information on the depth of the German penetration of the French communist nets and resistance groups is accurate, the British theory is weakened. CARETINA's description of how the Germans attempted to neutralize and seal off Trepper after his escape also bears on this question. CARETINA believes that they were successful in their effort to plant in Moscow's mind the suspicion that Trepper was being used by the Germans as provocation after his arrest because of the message the Moscow Head-quarters sent the French CP to have nothing to do with Trepper and warning against German provocation.

CARETINA is firmly convinced that KENT was not practicing a triple-play when he was under German control. The British may have more information than given in the Study Part II to substantiate their theory because the whole matter of the German penetration and control of the French CP nets and French resistance is touched on very briefly in the study. The British may not have wished to reveal how deeply the Germans had penetrated the resistance because of the reflection on their own operations in the field.

CARETINA believes that counter-espionage operations should be of a positive, aggressive nature and yield positive results. As he states, he wished to achieve more than the negative results of simply monitoring the activities of the Soviet nets and feeding the answers to the Direktor permitted by the German military command. His ultimate goal was to split the USSR from her Western Allies because he was convinced that any hope for Germany to survive as a nation lay in a quarrel between the two dominating elements of the Alliance, the East and the West. He used his radio play-backs to achieve this goal by feeding the USSR both factual and coloured reports on the activities of the Western Allies. His goal and his efforts to achieve it, all led to the trip to Moscow with KENT.

Having warned his headquarters in Washington, D.C. that Paulsen/CARETINA was not exactly a disinterested party, he provided a copy of his report, complete with helpful annotations referring to the earlier account of the ROTE KAPELLE compiled by MI5 from the documents recovered from Henri Robinson's Paris apartment and copied to Ast Brussels in the Avenue Louise where they were retrieved by the British Army.

HISTORICAL ACCOUNT OF THE ROTE KAPELLE

1. The name 'Rote Kapelle' (Red Orchestra) was selected by the Security Police (German RSHA) during WW II to designate a specific sector of Soviet espionage. The transmittal of espionage material during the war was done primarily by radio, i.e. on the air. The concert on the air had its conductor in Moscow in the 'Director'. Therefore, the name 'Rote Kapelle' came into being. The name was extraordinarily appropriate for the functions it covered and, thus, was much more extensively used to indicate, quite simply, Soviet espionage after the war. It is unmitigated nonsense to attribute other motives to the selection of this name as did

274

the journalist Margret Boveri in her book, *Treason in the 20th Century*. She wrote (on page 56) 'The name "Rote Kapelle" was a derogatory, collective term adopted by the Gestapo. The term "Rote Kapelle" was used so that all the people involved in the trials of 1942/43 could be thrown into one pot and sentenced in toto.' It appears almost as though the reader is advised to regard the poor members of the Rote Kapelle as pitiful victims of the Gestapo. The political police under a dictator always possessed enough power to avoid using such cheap tricks.

2. I am forced to mention this point because post-war publications have publicized individuals who were direct collaborators with the Soviet intelligence service and treated the traitorous nature of their espionage activities very casually, if touching on that aspect at all. Guenther Weisenborn, a leading member of the Nordwestdeutschen Rundfunk (Northwest German Broadcasting System) who moves around West Germany as a cultural representative, wrote that the work of the Rote Kapelle was resistance work against the Nazi regime. To equate high treason with illegal resistance is asking too much of the current younger generation who again must carry arms. A bad education in the free expression of private opinion is underway if the government ignores such Babylonian confusion in the understanding of high treason and does not firmly oppose this type of publication. Until now little has been done about this in the Federal Republic. The young citizen now bearing arms is again asked to take an oath. The judge before whom he would come must look only at the facts and the young citizen cannot justify himself by stating that he was confused by various publications which he read. More important is the fact that the damage already done may have a fatal effect on the nation and its allies. The warm reception given Guenther Weisenborn during his post-war trip to Moscow is evidence that Moscow is pleased with publications of this type.

Roll-Up of the Rote Kapelle During the War

3. Admiral Canaris, Abwehr (German military intelligence in WW II) was initially responsible for this area of operations. Amt IV E of the RSHA had the executive power to bring such cases before the courts. The Abwehr controlled the Direction Finding companies (DF'ing) which only during the war were developed into technically good, and smooth operating units. As far as I can recall the first enemy radio transmitter was 'fixed' by a motorised D/F'ing unit in 1940 at the very beginning of the French campaign. Previously D/F'ing had been performed with

some degree of success but there were always difficulties. The Abwehr had the upper hand because the most important agent groups always used radio communication during the war. Canaris himself asked the Security Police to play a bigger role in this work. Within the RSHA, Amt IV A 2 was selected as the central office instead of Amt IV E. This was done because IV A 2 was responsible for sabotage, acts of terror and assassinations which were practical results of agent activity. I do not know whether there were any personal reasons, such as resentment against the chief of IV E, involved. The D/F'ing companies had detected many transmitters, mostly in the German sovereign area and therefore undoubtedly belonging to the enemy. We knew the radio peculiarities and style of the English radio transmitters and thus deduced that the new radio transmitters must be working for Moscow. The unknown radio links were monitored and the messages recorded without, in the beginning, being able to decode them.

4. The first penetration of the Rote Kapelle complex occurred in Brussels. Quite by chance the German military police walked into the Rote Kapelle complex in the course of investigation of a black market group but the true nature of the Rote Kapelle elements were not recognised. Trepper, the 'Grand Chef', who accidentally entered the apartment, immediately grasped the situation and was able to escape arrest by a very clever performance. A short time after that the D/F'ing companies successfully fixed some of the Rote Kapelle transmitters and through this captured the 'Professor', Wenzel. (Station Comment: The British RK Study states on page 36 that Makarov, Sukolov's radio operator, and Dakarov, assistant to Makarov, were both arrested in December 1941. On page 42, the British Study states that Wenzel. Johannes or Hans Wenzel, @ HERMANN, PROFESSOR, CHARLES and possibly HEGENBARTH, was arrested on 30 June 1942 while transmitting for Effremov. The British Study says that Trepper visited the house where the Germans had seized the transmitter and was taken by the Germans. 'But his acting and his cover were good enough to secure his release and he was able to warn Sukolov before further damage was done.' CARETINA's account of Trepper having been picked up during the black market raid appears more plausible because had the Germans seized Trepper when they raided Makarov's and Danilov's radio transmission, it is unlikely that they would have released him without further investigation.) With Wenzel's arrest and the capture of the radio transmitter and operators, voluminous material and many persons fell into the hands of the Security Police and now, possessing

the codebook, the radio messages, previously recorded but not decoded, could be read.

5. Among the messages were messages from the Director to KENT, ordering the latter to use his German connection with the Organisation Todt and the Wehrmacht to arrange a trip to Berlin where he was to look up certain addresses. The addresses were given clearly and were those of Adam Kuckhoff and Harro Schultze-Boysen. He was given instructions how to carry out his mission, and to pick up the material in Berlin and forward it to Moscow via Brussels. If the radio silence of the Berlin group signified that that transmission could not be made from there, KENT was to establish a courier route between Berlin and Brussels (Station Comment: In order to bring the Berlin reports for transmission over the Brussels transmitters.) The Director was forced to reactivate the important apparat in Berlin which suddenly had gone off the air because the Berlin agents were occupying much too important positions within the German government. The Director, through his handling, dropped the entire Berlin apparatus into our hands; he had not even instructed KENT after his trip to Berlin, to destroy the codebook and select a new book. Such complete success had never been achieved before by means of D/F'ing. During my imprisonment in Moscow, the GPU/MGB wanted complete information on this coup. They wanted to know, 'Who was to blame for the total destruction of the German rezidentura?' I am certain the Director suffered the consequences of my report which was fair because he was responsible.

The Berlin Rezidentura

6. The decoded material led to the arrest of the entire rezidentura in September 1942. (Station Comment: The British Study states, page 49, 'The arrest of the Schutze-Boysen and Harnack groups in August 1942 seems to have been largely the result of Wenzel's betrayal of his cypher and the consequent reading of traffic intercepted between Belgium and Moscow for some time back.') All the Germans working for the Soviets in Berlin were separated and had no contact with each other. KENT's firm (Station Comment: SIMEXCO) was in close contact with the German military administrative offices and from the orders he received from the Germans had made profits of several million Reichsmarks. KENT's trip to Berlin was approved and sponsored by the Germans en route to visiting the Leipzig and Prague Fairs on official business. During his visit to Berlin he visited various members of the Berlin rezidentura (of the Rote Kapelle) but was careful to keep

each member separate from the others. Moscow also planned to have von Scheliha's intelligence reports from the German Foreign Office transmitted on a special link with an individual code which KENT was to arrange.

7. Harro Schultze-Boysen, cryptonym CORO, was a 1st lieutenant in the Luftfahrtsministerium (Air Ministry). The other leaders of the Berlin groups were Arvid Harnack, Oberregierunsrat in the Economics Ministry and his wife (Mildred Elizabeth Harnack nee Fish); the author Adam Kuckhoff and his wife (Grete Kuckhoff). All of the latter were identified and arrested by means of the decoded messages and subsequent telephone taps, surveillance, etc. What was not uncovered by the latter means was revealed by Schultze-Boysen's wife, Libertas Schultze-Boysen.

8. I will not go into detail about every member of these groups because enough has been reported about them by others who are perhaps better informed than I. I was in no way involved in the Berlin roll-up. The group had five transmitter/receiver sets at its disposal. This number was later increased by parachute agents. Originally the transmitters were located with: Adam Kuckhoff; Arvid Harnack; Kurt Schulze; Hans Coppi; Behrens (Karl Behrens or Behrends). Safe-houses were located at the residences of the following women: Erika von Brockdorff; Oda Schottmieller; Ros Schlosessinger. (Station Comment: The above names all appear in the British Study and the information agrees except that Schlosessinger is listed as a courier between Harnack and Coppi.)

9. Regarding the Communist history of the members of the rezidentura, not all of them were old-time Communists. The break-down of their political backgrounds is as follows:

A. Group who were members of the Communist Party prior to 1933: Schumacher, Sculptor (Station Comment: Kurt Schumacher in British Study. Schumacher is German spelling of name.) Kuckhoff, Adam, author Schulze, Kurt, in the German Navy, also one of the clandestine radio operators Schabbel, Klara, Harry Robinson's mistress Schottmueller, Oda, Schumacher's mistress and Communist only through association with him; not a Party member Huebner (Emil Huebner)

Husemann, (Walter Husemann), Communist through his father Wesolek, Huebner's son-in-law (<u>Station Comment</u>: British Study gives name as Wesselock, husband of Frieda Wesselock and son-in-law of Emil Huebner.)
Harnack, Arvid, Oberregierungsrat
Rittmeister, Dr. (Dr. Johann Rittmeister), psychotherapist
Sieg, Johann, journalist on the Berlin newspaper, *Rote Fahne*
Graudenz, Johann, journalist
Guddorf, Wilhelm, journalist on the Berlin newspaper, *Rote Fahne*
Kuechenmeister, Walter, publisher of Communist newspaper
Kummerow, Heinrich

B. Communist after 1933:
Schulze-Boysen, Harro
Coppi, Hans
Coppi, Hilde
Harnack, Mildred nee Fish
Cunneen, Ingeborg
Stoebe, Ilse, von Scheliha's secretary and mistress of Herrnstadt. The latter is active in the East Zone today
Behrens (Karl Behrens/Behrends)
Kuckhoff, Greta

C. Those whose political history is unclear:
Grime, Adolf, former Minister of Culture
Weissemborn, Guenther, author
Kraus, Professor Dr. (Prof. Werner Kraus/Krauss), currently reported in Leipzig
Gehrts, Erwin, Colonel

The above listing is in no way complete because I cannot remember every name. It can be seen from the list that all of the above whose Communist history and sympathies were known to the government's counterintelligence organs had complete freedom of movement and some even were working in high government and military positions of considerable sensitivity. Following the big break between the German governmental leaders and the Communist Party in 1933/34, (i.e. when the CP was declared illegal), a lax attitude developed and Communism was not regarded as a great danger in spite of the fact that a Communist counterintelligence section was established to combat Communism and considerable experience had been gained in the fight against Communism. Everything went along so calmly during that period that one could almost believe that the Communists had become obedient citizens and members of society, which was actually true in the majority of the cases of Communists. Unquestionably one fact was completely disregarded which was that as long as a pact between Germany and the Soviet Union existed, the German Communists would be ordered by Moscow to remain quiet and would only dare to become active upon Moscow's express order. If an attack on the Soviet Union was planned, the political and other background of all persons holding important positions should have been reviewed. If such a careless performance could occur in an anti-Communist dictatorship, how much more easily it can occur in a free and powerful democracy. The great espionage cases of Sorge in Japan, Harnack, von Scheliha, and Schultze-Boysen would not have occurred if the proper precautionary measures had been taken.

10. Although the German Communist Party no longer existed, in theory, after 1933, the Soviets had a long list of people, overtly Communists prior to 1933 and still under Soviet influence, who could be used later. This was very negligent on the part of the Germans. In the list were:

A. Kumerow, Heinrich, working for Moscow long before 1933, actually as early as the 1920s, in the field of economic espionage. Due to the fact that he was a very capable engineer, he had access to extremely valuable information and provided the Soviets with all of it.
B. Graudenz, Johann, Communist journalist and a correspondent for American newspapers in Moscow. He had been expelled from Ireland for Communist activity. After that he had lived in various parts of the world.
C. Sieg, Johann, born in the USA and working on the Communist newspaper *Rote Fahne* in Berlin.
D. Guddorf, Wilhelm, also employed as a journalist on the *Rote Fahne*.
E. Rittmeister, Dr. (Johann), worked as a psychotherapist in the Berlin institute headed by Professor Goering, the uncle of Reichsmarschall Goering. Rittmeister had been expelled from Switzerland because he was too leftist in his politics.
F. Kuecenmeister, Walter, publisher of Communist newspapers in the Ruhr and Rhineland areas. As early as 1918 he had been involved in the Communist-inspired revolt among the sailors of the German Navy.

G. Schultze-Boysen (Harro), he had, as had the atomic spy Klaus Fuchs, founded a radical, left-wing group in 1933 while he was in the university. He actually made no secret of his political sympathies.

The above is an indication what the German government knew prior to the round-up of the Rote Kapelle.

The Actual Roll-Up

11. The majority of the meetings with all the agents/sources were held in the homes of Schulze-Boysen, Harnack and Kuckhoff. Licentious parties were held during which feminine charms were not only displayed but exploited. I am today still acquainted with a family, the husband and wife of which had participated in such celebrations. Libertas Schultze-Boysen used every wile she knew to win the confidence of the husband who was working in radio counterintelligence during the war. Frau Schultze-Boysen was a very passionate woman and her action caused a quarrel between the two husbands which, in the long run, probably averted an even greater misfortune. (Station Comment: Source will be asked to provide the name of the family with whom he is still acquainted.) The clothing the women wore to these parties was even scantier than those worn by models modelling bathing-suits. Gefreiter (Lance-Corporal) Horst Heimann, who was employed in Radio Counterintelligence Cryptographic Section, was Frau Libertas Schultze-Boysen's complete slave sexually. Schultze-Boysen through his uninhibited and spirited enjoyment of life could captivate, not only his own wife, but other women which he did in the case of the dancer Oda Schottmueller and Countess Erika von Brockdorff.

12. Professional 'conspiratorial' methods were ignored by this group and, therefore, they were not respected or seriously considered by the long-time, dedicated Communists. The latter were extremely sceptical of the activities of the Schultze-Boysen, etc. groups insofar as they were aware of the activities. The parlor-pinks were driven by completely negative motivation. They wanted as much freedom as possible to enjoy their lives and they wanted power. Some wanted power more than others. I shall attempt to describe from memory some of the individuals in more detail because these people are typical of the intelligentsia, capable of, and inclined towards treason, whom one encounters repeatedly as traitors. It would be very useful to give an honest account of the human, in fact all too human, aspects of the

281

events to those completely different circles attempting to make heroes of the members of the Rote Kapelle.

13. Harro Schultze-Boysen: He was an intellectually stimulating and very temperamental young man who easily won over other people and induced them to follow him. He had sought his 'great calling' in various types of jobs but had not found it. He was interested in everything but pursued no interest to the end. The current talk that he was on the threshold of a brilliant career in the Reichsluftfahrtministerium has no factual basis except in the post-war efforts to glorify the 'heroes' of the Rote Kapelle. Certainly nothing was known of his possibly brilliant future during the war. His handsome wife, Libertas, was the one who obtained an increase in salary for him which enabled them to marry. She was working as an Arbeitsdienstführerin (work supervisor) in Karin Hall, Goering's representational country estate outside of Berlin, when Goering asked her, jokingly, if it weren't almost time for her to get married. She retorted immediately that Goering himself was to blame because her fiancé earned so little in the Reichsluftfahrtministerium that he could not support a family. Goering made a note of the name and shortly thereafter Schultze-Boysen was promoted with an increase in pay and so they were married.

14. Schultze-Boysen, because of his burning ambition, bitterly resented his slow and insignificant rise. His pride caused him to place the blame on others. By others he meant the Nazis at the time, before that it had been the Weimar Republic and if it were possible, it would have been the monarchy. Had this man ever lived under the Soviet regime, he would have been hung! Schultze-Boysen was clever enough not to express such ideas too openly but his ambition found another means of expressing itself. He was the identical type of many young careerists in the National Socialist State except that they sought success in their own country and found it – which, after all, did not lead to a happy end in their cases either. Schultze-Boysen was never trained in Communist ideology nor was he an idealist as his father claimed or as has been read into some of his statements and letters. He was, quite simply, a dictator by virtue of his character and entire personality. Any means were justified in his eyes to overthrow the existing order and put himself in power. The only thing he really recognised was 'I'. All of his work for the Soviet Union was, in the final analysis, for 'ME'; the constant effort to satisfy his egocentric drive was evident in everything he did including his private life, his sexual life, etc. The work for Moscow offered him the only opportunity to overcome the barriers

of his immediate and hated environment and with one jump gain a position on the very top. He wrote in his farewell letter, 'A death which befits me'. He did not recognise law, conscience, guilt, or any need for justification. None of these were necessary in his world. He was most exalted by the feeling that he was master of life and death. Typical of the romantic intoxication in which he lived was his insistence on standing guard, wearing his uniform, while the illegal posters were put up, posters which had been written as a result of heated debates. He was completely a child of his time, a political dreamer armed only with his intense egotism and like so many of the young people of that time. Schultze-Boysen, however, chose the side of the enemy, anticipating a faster rise by this method. His ambition was to be Minister of War in the German Soviet Republic.

15. The yearning for recognition and power, albeit of a different type, was also possessed by Arvid Harnack, Oberregierungsrat in the Wirtschaftsministerium. Harnack was very much Schultze-Boysen's intellectual superior. He was a cool thinker but suffered from hot-headed arrogance and an intellectual thirst for power. Even his cohorts in the Rote Kapelle complained about him. He indulged in such biting irony during an argument that he drove his opponent out of the discussion by sheer weight of argument. He was described generally as an intellectual snob. He studied in the United States where he met his wife, Mildred nee Fish, I believe, at the University of Wisconsin.

16. He made many contacts in Moscow during his visit to Russia. He was shown more esteem while in Russia than he had ever dreamed of receiving in Germany. His connections with the Soviet Embassy in Berlin and his serious political discussion in both Moscow and the Soviet Embassy in Berlin were very flattering during his young, impressionable years. This is a dangerous weapon the Russians employ. Young ambitious scientists, journalists, and visitors from all countries receive a welcome in Russia accorded them nowhere else in the world. The Government is directly interested in such visits and government leaders take a personal interest. The visitors experience only kindness and enticing dreams of the tremendous possibilities offered by this enormous Russia result. It goes without saying that representatives of the Soviet Intelligence Service are always present and working on tightening the connection. Harnack was well schooled in ideology. He wrote a short tract for the cause on capitalistic monopolies, containing nothing new inasmuch as Lenin had covered this ground thoroughly. Harnack's tract outlined the path for Germany very clearly, as he

conceived it, which was primarily to become the German Soviet Republic following the Soviet pattern. He wanted to hold the post of Economic Minister in his future German Soviet Republic but he desired to attain this position through his espionage on Moscow's behalf and not by means of Communist Party work. His personal 'I' was foremost in his case in spite of his ideological training. The dream of power and position dominated him.

17. Libertas Schultze-Boysen, nee Haas-Heye, wife of CORO (Soviet cryptonym for Harro Schultze-Boysen), played a very important role in the work. She played her biggest role, however, when, during the roll-up of the Rote Kapelle, she betrayed to the last person her fellow collaborators. She was an interesting and beautiful woman. Above all, she was a woman with an enormous sexual appetite which was never satisfied. She was always the aggressor and she had success, as much as she wanted. She used her sexual weapons frequently in carrying out the work of the Rote Kapelle. Several men were recruited into the net because she enslaved them. The work in the Rote Kapelle fascinated her with its promise of wild, stormy adventure accompanied by desire. She came from an aristocratic family and had had no political training. There was not the slightest trace of ideological motivation in this woman. It is difficult to judge whether she tried to save her life while she was in prison by all her sexual advances. She did, however, betray her friends because of a sexual experience. She entered into Lesbian relations with her fellow women prisoners. When the judge/prosecutor, Dr. Roeder (Dr. Manfred Roeder) was questioning her, she said, very sweetly to him, that although the Gestapo had searched her apartment they had not found everything. At her instigation, Dr. Roeder ordered the officials to check the panel of her bedroom door. They found there a packet containing hundreds of pictures of Libertas in the nude, etc. One wonders what her purpose was in introducing the pictures into the trial and why she wanted Dr. Roeder to see them. The primary fact regarding this woman was that her dynamic sexuality was the driving force behind everything she did.

18. I have described the above three types to show something of what the situation was viewed from the period when it occurred. This is the reality and not as it is so often described today. There were, naturally, other dedicated people who used their great intellectual powers in the service of their own convictions and were destroyed through treason. There were wives who unquestioningly followed their husbands, Frau Harnack being one example.

19. KENT reported to the Director after his return from Berlin and suggested that the Director establish direct communications with Berlin. This was attempted by the Director with several agents, parachuted into Germany, who were taken in by Erika von Brockdorff and the Coppi family. The agents were German Communists who had emigrated. One was named Albert Hoessler. The third drop brought Heinrich Koenen, the son of a former Communist Reichstag Deputy. As instructed, Koenen looked up Ilse Stoebe who at the time had been in prison for more than two weeks. Moscow was not well informed. Koenen had in his possession money and a receipt for more than $6,000 signed by von Scheliha of the Foreign Office before the war in Warsaw. The journalist Rudolf Herrnstadt had used von Scheliha's financial difficulties while in Warsaw to recruit him for the Soviet Intelligence Service. Later Herrnstadt had placed his mistress Ilse Stoebe as von Scheliha's secretary and this operation was running very well. Herrnstadt is reported to be the head of an institute in the East Zone today and is probably involved in intelligence work. Von Scheliha was one of the Director's highest paid agents, having once received more than 30,000 RM. His group was completely separate from the CORO net.

20. Agents were being parachuted into all parts of Germany by Moscow up to the very end of the war. They were seized almost 100%. I believe not one of them escaped. The English Airforce also dropped some of Moscow's German agents occasionally which astounded us. Veterans from the Red forces in Spain during the Civil War were in the majority. These men always enjoyed a special trust in Moscow. They must be carefully watched now and in the future. Many of them work today in official or semi-official jobs in the Federal Republic. In my opinion they are always vulnerable to an approach by Moscow. It should not be forgotten that the younger of these men are today only forty years old.

21. The roll-up of the Rote Kapelle was quite thorough which resulted in an impression in the RSHA that all active elements had been destroyed at the time. Kriminaldirektor (Horst) Kopkow, the specialist in IV A 2, told me after the assassination attempt on Hitler of 20 July 1944, that the investigation of the Rote Kapelle in 1942 should have been more extensive than it was. I do not know whether this statement was based on facts discovered during the investigation of the assassination attempt. We had no time than to discuss this in detail. The Rote

Kapelle members who received sentences, as far as I can remember and I cannot remember all, were:

Schultze-Boysen, Harro, death sentence
Schultze-Boysen, Libertas
Harnack, Arvid
Harnack, Mildred
Kuckhoff, Adam
Kuckhoff, Greta, was pardoned
Gems (Col. Erwin)
Coppi, Hans
Coppi, Hilde
Schulze, Kurt
Hebrew, Karl
Schottmeuller, Oda
Brockdorff, Erika von
Schloiessinger, Rosa
Sieg, Johann
Guddorf, Johann (believe CARETINA intends Wilhelm Guddorp)
Rittmeister, Dr. (Johann)
Kuechenmeister, Walter
Paul, Dr. Elfriede, Kuechenmeister's mistress who received a prison sentence and was released by the Soviets in 1945; reportedly Minister of Health in Lower Saxony as of 1945
Schuhmacher, Kurt
Schuhmacher, Elisabeth
Schabbel, Klara
Husemann, Walter
Huebner, (Emil)
Wesolek (Wesselock)
Gollnow, Herbert
Hetimann, Horst
Graudenz, Johann
Krause, Frau (Kraus, Anna)
Kummerow, Heinrich
Kummerow, Ingeborg
Scheliha (Rudolf von SCHLEIHA)
Stoebe, Use
Koenen, Heinrich
Hoessler, Albert
Weissenborn, Guenther, received a prison term
Grimw, Adolf, received a prison term

(Station Comment: According to the British Study all of the above were executed with the exception of: Greta Kuckhoff was noted by CARETINA: Rosa Schlessinger; Karl Behrens; Walter Schuemeister, Dr. Elfriede Paul, was noted by CARETINA; Emil Huebner; Herbert Gollnow about whom there is some doubt; Heinrich Kunnerow, also some doubt; Heinrich Koenen; Guenther Weisenborn and Adolf Grime as noted by source. Regarding Ilse Stoebe, the British Study says she was 'almost certainly executed.' Ingeborg Kummerow does not appear in the British Study. UPSWING has mentioned an Albrecht and Grete Kummerow in UJ/DRIZZLY discussions, presumably connected in some way with Heinrich Kummerow.)

22. The entire Soviet apparat in Germany was relatively unimportant but very successful when it is considered that it was a small apparat. The disadvantages for the Soviets resulting from the anti-Soviet measures instituted in Germany after 1933 prevented the Soviets from working on the very broad basis to which they were accustomed. They were very lucky with their improvised apparat in Germany. We were unlucky. Their operations could have been nipped in the bud, as I was once able to do. If the radio communications of the CORO group had been successful in the beginning, they would certainly have been located very early and neutralized. The most important intelligence could scarcely have reached Moscow because KENT was responsible for relaying the reports (Station Comment: Source means that KENT had not had sufficient time to forward the information from Brussels before the Germans seized him.) No emergency or secondary channel of communication for passing intelligence in case the radio communication failed was provided. All of the technical equipment of the Rezidentura had been supplied in great haste. Looking back over the impressive Soviet intelligence history prior to 1933, the German territory was, in any case, relatively immune to a large scale Soviet intelligence attack from Moscow. France and Belgium, where the Communist Party was not outlawed and where the Party could work as it wished, are examples of this. From this it is clear that a law declaring the Communist-Bolshevik activity illegal does reward any country.

France – Belgium – Holland

23. I have reported first only on the German section. The first penetration of the Rote Kapelle was in Brussels by means of D/F'ing as I have already mentioned. The first radio transmitter which was detected did not bring extensive results. It was only after the seizure of the

'Professor's', the German Comintern agent Wenzel's, radio transmitter that the codebook was available and with this the roll-up in Germany. Although everything started later in Berlin, it was possible to take immediate action and practically neutralize everything in Berlin. The clean-up operations could not progress as rapidly in Belgium, not only because this was a foreign country which had some bearing on the work, but primarily because in the West Moscow-trained agents were working and they used clean, conspiratorial (operational) techniques and made no mistakes. There was no comparison with Berlin with its non-homogenous and insanely mixed working teams. No one in the West broke the rules for conspiratorial (operational) work, except possibly the leaders themselves who frequently could not conceal in their overt lives their Soviet origin and Soviet mentality. This was primarily Moscow's fault. The selection of agents was very good and suited the purpose. The only fault was that many Jews were among the agents and the latter were always in danger because of anti-Semitism and they, in turn, could threaten their handlers. This makes it even more astonishing that this group could obtain so much from German military and civilian offices.

24. Another factor contributing to the difficulties encountered in the roll-up in the West was the extensive and continuous help given the espionage nets by the members of the Communist Parties of the various countries. The difficulties encountered were the disappearance and concealment of agents, the rapid and frequent changes in couriers, the many safe-houses available for radio transmitters, etc. It should be noted that KENT was well informed on the possibility of D/F'ing long before his own group was 'fixed'. Some agents were spread thinly through the Communist circles and certainly had no contact with the overt, known representatives of Moscow because of the excellent compartmentalization. For this reason the first penetration of the espionage apparat depended on monitoring and decoding radio messages.

25. OTTO (Leopold Trepper), 'Le Grand Chef', had had years of experience in the West which enabled him to carry out conspiratorial work to the best advantage. (Station Comment: CARETINA uses OTTO throughout the report for Leopold Trepper because OTTO was the name by which Trepper was known in the Sonderkommando. We have substituted Trepper for purposes of clarity.) No matter how much training in operational techniques the other Moscow agents had had in Moscow, they often made serious errors when first arriving in

the West. They were much more likely to err because of their lack of Western experience than the Western agents placed under them. I have reported elsewhere on this, for example, how KENT had been trained in Moscow along the lines of the official propaganda of the Soviet CP in what to expect in the West and had believed what he was taught. (Station Comment: CARETINA has written separate reports on both KENT and Trepper which will be forwarded as soon as possible.) He stocked up to the point of making himself ludicrous on leather shoes and cigarettes when he first arrived in the West because he was convinced that these articles were available only on the day he saw them in a store. This was a typical Soviet reaction, i.e. to buy as much as possible when the wares were available, which I experienced personally as late as 1956 in the Soviet Union. Even the trained intelligence officer, destined for a mission in the West, was not told at the time he left Moscow on his mission that there was a difference between the domestic Soviet propaganda and the facts in the outside world. KENT himself said, in commenting on the naive and, in his case, dangerous behaviour of Soviet Russian intelligence officers, that this stemmed from the general mistrust to be found in the Soviet Union. If, for example, an instructor in operational techniques had explained the difference and KENT had reported this, the instructor would have been sentenced according to Article 58-10. No MGB investigating official looking into the case would have known the truth because they believed implicitly what they were taught. For his own security, a man would not contradict official statements even though the success of the work in which he was engaged was at stake. It probably should be noted that the Soviets no longer make basic mistakes today. (Mistakes of behaviour in the West.) KENT's incredible capacity, unbelievable for so small a man, to eat and drink derived from his Soviet background. It was amazing to see the waiters in restaurants and bars always recognise him even though he had been in the place only once or twice because his enormous orders of food and drink were so conspicuous. He ordered the meat course two and three times. He ordered and drank Vodka and other highly alcoholic drinks by the half bottles or more. Some of the other young Soviet officers behaved in exactly the same way. It was reminiscent of accounts of the lives led by the owners of the large Russian estates long ago. A normal stomach could not have digested such masses of food and drink but a Soviet coming from a simple background, which almost all did, rarely had concentrated nourishment and had to stay alive by consuming masses of soup, sohi, a type of porridge, kascha, and black bread. I never ceased to be amazed while in the Soviet prisons at the quantity of this type of food a Soviet stomach could handle. Accustomed to food of this type, the Soviet agents in the West stuffed themselves with the same quantity of Western food – naturally many suffered from heart and stomach disorders. Details such as this are not unimportant in intelligence operations and I mention them to point out what should be noted on both sides.

26. KENT's legend in Belgium, that of a Uruguayan national, caused him some difficulties also. He himself found the legend unfortunate and thought that Moscow had taken the easy way out. It occurred once that the new Consul for Uruguay in Brussels moved into his pension and the well intentioned female owner of the pension wanted to introduce the two 'Uruguayans' to each other KENT almost had to flee from the pension because he was not prepared to converse with a consul or any other citizen of his alleged, native country. He was not satisfied that he had not attracted attention to himself through this incident. When I discussed this with KENT, he said that Moscow had good connections with Uruguay for obtaining original passports and had, therefore, sent him out with the Uruguayan legend. I thought to myself that from a counter-intelligence point of view it would be very advantageous to arrange for Moscow to obtain original passports from a few selected countries. (Station Comment: CARETINA, a confirmed counter-intelligence and espionage operator, cannot resist making operational suggestions. He is suggesting that for a service working against the Soviet Intelligence Service planting original passports for Soviet Intelligence Service use would assist in the identification of Soviet agents.) When the first traces of KENT's intelligence group were picked up in Brussels through D/F'ing about the beginning of 1942 and he had to leave Brussels immediately, it was not easy for him to travel via Paris and other French cities to Marseilles with a Uruguayan passport. KENT was not the only 'Uruguayan', Makarov also had a Uruguayan passport under the name of Carlos Alamo.

27. Returning to the identification and neutralization of the Soviet nets, the first group identified in Brussels toward the end of 1941 or early 1942 was KENT's headquarters. In the headquarters were the following:

KENT, himself
Trepper (Leopold)
Arbouldt, Rita, German Jewess and long-time Communist (Rita Bloch nee Arnold/Arnould)
Springer, Isador, Arnould's lover, German Jew, old Comintern agent (British Study states that Flora van Vliet was Springer's mistress)

Posnanska, Sophie, alias Anna Verlinden, Polish Jewess, long-time
Communist (Poznenska or Poznanska are spellings in British Study)
Raichmann (Rajchmann), Abraham, Polish Jew and expert in
producing false identity papers.
Gruber, Malvina, Raichmann s mistress
Grossvogel, Leo
Makarov (Micheal or Michel)
Danilov (Anton)
Etc.

Although all the members of the headquarters group were not
accustomed to visiting the house which had been fixed through D/F'ing
many of them knew each other. In spite of the fact that the group was
acquainted among themselves, the German counterintelligence organs'
coup was feeble because the group had followed the rules for clandestine
operations very strictly. KENT was the primary disciplinary force in
demanding obedience to operational security. The first arrests did not
produce a key to the code which left the long messages still uncoded.
KENT had decoded almost everything himself for this group. KENT
and Trepper fled immediately to Paris when the first arrests were
made. Most of the information came from Rita Arnould and Sophie
Posnanska. This slowed down our progress because the two women
simply did not have important information. Physical descriptions with
aliases which we obtained were not very useful.

28. The second group was detected and identified in Brussels about
the middle of 1942. This was the group of the old Comintern agent
Wenzel. Johann Wenzel, also called HERMANN or 'The Professor',
had fled from Germany in 1933. Prior to 1939 he headed a Communist
underground group in Belgium which was assigned special missions.
Belonging to Wenzel's group were Germaine Schneider, Wenzel's
mistress; her former husband Franz Schneider; and Franz Raichmann
(Station Comment: Whether this is a mistake for Abraham or whether
another Raichmann is involved will have to be ascertained from source.
We have no previous record of a Franz Raichmann). Jernstroem, the
alleged Finnish student whose true name was Effremov (Konstantin
Jefremov, with aliases Erland Jernstroem, HOFMANN, PAUL,
PASCAL, BORDO and possibly MANOLO) took over the leadership
of Wenzel's group following the capture of the first group. Effremov
was a Soviet officer from the technical section of Soviet intelligence
(probably GRU). All of the above and many others were arrested
when the German counter-intelligence organs made the second raid.

Encoded and decoded messages fell into German hands during the raid due to the fact that the transmitter had been fixed and raided while still transmitting. The agents had no choice but to hand over the codebook. For the first time the Germans had the information necessary for successful round-up of the entire apparat. The Berlin net was identified through the decoded messages. The number of arrests increased and the interrogations could be compared, one prisoner being played off against another.

29. The next group neutralized was that of Anton Winttrick (name given as Tino Winterrink in British Study) in Holland. The couriers between Brussels and Holland, including Maurice Peper, were in German hands as a result of the arrests in Brussels. About this time an outline or indication of the commercial cover used by the Soviet intelligence service began to emerge. The 'Grand Chef', Trepper, whose true name was not yet known, had together with his friend Leo Grossvogel, also a Polish Jew as was Trepper, founded a textile import and export firm in 1940 under the name of 'Au Roi de Caoutchow,' or 'Foreign Excellente Trenchcoats'. Trepper, under an alias, and Grossvogel were the owners. KENT had been trained in Moscow to sew microphotographs into textiles. The textiles were then exported to other countries where they were examined for content. When the microphotograph messages were recovered they were taken to the 'legal' (i.e. legal rezidentura) headquarters in the local Soviet Embassy and the latter forwarded the messages via diplomatic channels to the Director in Moscow. In some instances the goods were exported directly to Moscow but such goods could contain agent reports only with the approval of the highest authority in Moscow. The company was established and was to have branches in Copenhagen, Oslo, Stockholm and Czechoslovakia. The plan was to sell trenchcoats containing intelligence material in one of the neutral Scandinavian countries. The branch of the main company in the neutral company was then responsible for the next step in forwarding the intelligence reports. This plan was never put into operation. The company served, however, very well as a channel to official German offices. At the beginning of 1941, before the outbreak of the German-Russian war, Moscow ordered an expansion of the contacts with official German representatives in Holland, Belgium and France. A new firm was established for this purpose and the new firm was SIMEXCO.

30. SIMEXCO as a company had shareholders who were both Belgians and from neutral countries. The 'Grand Chef' remained

in the background as the founder. SIMEXCO was incorporated as a procurement company for construction supplies. The German organisations, especially the Organisation Todt, gladly accepted bids on procurement of supplies from companies of this type because a large quantity of supplies was being concealed in the occupied countries which were needed and would be requisitioned if found. The Soviet intelligence company, SIMEXCO, served German interests very well in performing this mission. SIMEXCO earned a good reputation, made a good profit, and naturally received from the Germans all support necessary to insure 'freedom of movement' inasmuch as travel was necessary to ferret out the necessary materials. Under SIMEXCO auspices, KENT was able to travel undisturbed to Berlin, Leipzig and Prague, provided with German papers from German military administrative offices – enabling him to assess German achievement as shown at the fairs along with his other work.

31. Due to the success SIMEXCO had, Moscow ordered Trepper to establish a similar company in Paris just at the time hostilities started between Germany and the Soviet Union. I am jumping ahead in the chronology of the history of the roll-up of the Rote Kapelle but Trepper's achievement should be mentioned here. Whereas SIMEXCO made possible for Moscow KENT's freedom of movement and thus enabled KENT to pass on the extremely valuable intelligence CONO's (Schultze-Boysen's) group had collected in Berlin, Trepper through his firm in Paris was successful in penetrating the headquarters of the German military commander of France. The firm in Paris was SIMEX, founded in late summer or fall of 1941. The company director was Alfred Corbin, a Belgian. The business manager was GILBERT, alias for the 'Grand Chef' (Trepper), and the secretary was DUBOIS, alias for Hillel Katz. A branch of SIMEX was opened in Marseilles with Jules JASPAR, a Belgian, as head. They had learned not to place exposed foreigners and Jews at the head of the concern and its branches because the anti-Semitic trend in the German Government would only result in unnecessary risks. JASPAR was the brother of a former Belgian Minister President. The history and motivation of JASPAR's connection with Moscow was never really clarified. We had noted an unusual thing among the Belgians which was that one side of the family would have Western sympathies and the other was inclined toward Moscow. This was a form of re-insurance for the family.

32. We found that the trail of those who had fled the Low Countries led to Paris. The bulk of the messages were going via Paris. In this case

D/F'ing was again responsible for the real penetration of the Moscow Director's Paris net. We had also made more progress through the usual criminal detective methods. The investigation developed faster primarily because the agents had to turn over their reports for radio transmittal which enabled us to maintain indirect contact with the agents through their radio stations.

33. The first radio station which fell into our hands in Paris was that of the Sokol couple, Dr. Herz Sokol, a Czech Jew, and his wife Miriam Sokol. Dr. Sokol had been interned by the French at the beginning of the war. He came in contact with Trepper through the Russian emigre Maximovich (Basil Pavlovich Maximovich) who was also interned. Thus Sokol became an agent for Moscow's Intelligence Service. The question would logically be asked whether Moscow did not have a previously established net in Paris. The emphasis had been on Brussels where everything had gone very well. In Paris Trepper had to start building a net through his own efforts. He was successful. Not only did he establish the radio station of Dr. Sokol but the radio station in Le Pecq near Paris in the residence of 'Robert' and 'Lucie', aliases for Pierre and Lucienne Giraud, (Station Comment: British Study gives names as Leon and Suzanne Giraud, with aliases 'ROBERT' and 'LUCY'), as well, where a young Spanish radio operator worked. Trepper accomplished all of this on his own without help from Moscow shortly before the war started with the Soviet Union. The Sokol couple were close friends of Madame Claude Spaak, wife of Claude Spaak. She supported the Sokols financially, knowing that they were Moscow agents which we did not know at the time.

34. The second radio station in Paris, Le Pecq, was also detected by D/F'ing. The Spanish radio operator escaped and we were never able to find him. We did not know his name which in any case would have been an alias. He never cooperated with the Germans as [David] Dallin claims in his book [*Soviet Espionage*], a book which contains a great many historical misstatements and false information. (Station Comment: According to the British Study, the Spanish radio operator was Valentin Escudero or Escudo who was working under Trepper's direction. Prior to the fall of 1942 when he was assigned to the Giraud transmitter at Le Pecq, he had been working in Grossvogel's communication set-up. His cover job was driver for the Wehrmacht and he was on this job when the Girauds were arrested by the Germans. The British Study confirms CARETINA's statement inasmuch as it says 'he is believed to have escaped'.)

35. The identification and neutralization of the radio stations did not suddenly provide us with an easy means of reaching the whole apparat. Progress was made only by careful, detailed and thorough work. It is difficult today to recall each step and perhaps also not important. The fact was that some of the interrogations in Brussels, later confirmed by the interrogation of Madame Sokol, revealed the cover names of the leaders of the net. Everything pointed, naturally, to the 'Grand Chef' and KENT because those two had the entire picture and not just one conspiratorial cell. It was very evident to the German counter-intelligence organs working in the different countries which of the prisoners possessed valuable knowledge and which did not. The Soviet net had carefully obeyed the conspiratorial rule of 'the need-to-know'.

36. Dallin's book is maliciously slanted in that he points up at every opportunity the Gestapo torture methods which drove the poor spy to confessing. Dallin and other reporters of these events continuously differentiate between the Abwehr (German Military Intelligence in WW II) and the Gestapo (RSHA Amt 1V). The entire investigation was the responsibility of the RSHA's Sonderkommando Rote Kapelle. All other units came under the command of the Gestapo whether Abwehr officers or other RSHA officers were included in the units; every one reported to the chief of the Sonderkommando. For the most part the men involved in the investigation were experienced, specially chosen, counter-espionage officials of the Gestapo who carried out their jobs and who were not at all as the tabloids have painted them. The only requirement for the minor members of the Moscow apparat was that they write what they could remember and describe those individuals known to them. Generally they knew relatively little. The professional criminal detective investigation progressed by piecing together the small bits of information. Trepper was caught by means of pedantic, dull, detective work and not through the use of terror or some chance piece of luck.

37. Trepper was too cunning to have a notebook in which he noted such things as dental appointments. One of his agents remembered that he was receiving dental treatment but knew nothing about the dentist, location of office, etc. We had obtained from other sources a list of possible dentists who might be handling Trepper's dental work. Thus through extensive surveillance, elimination of other suspects, the building and dentist were pinned down. All patients were watched

during a pertinent period of time. Trepper arrived. The dentist knew that the arrest was to occur although he had no concept of Trepper's importance. When Trepper sat down in the dentist's chair, the German officials appeared. Trepper looked them over, sized up the situation very calmly, and said in his heavily accented German: 'You have done some good work.' (Station Comment: The British Study states that it was Alfred Corbin who provided Trepper with the name of a dentist: 'Corbin seems to have been reduced by interrogation to a state of mind in which he was anxious to tell the Germans anything he knew about Trepper. The most he was able to produce, however, was a probable indication of Trepper's dentist, Trepper having been unwise enough to ask for Corbin's advice on a dentist, and – as the Germans discovered – to take it.' (Page 43 of Part II British Rote Kapelle Study).)

38. From the moment Trepper was in our hands, the roll-up of the remaining Rote Kapelle was assured. Trepper was much too clever to wish to die for a 'lost cause'. It was made clear to him that even during a war men of his stature and importance did not need to be tried and die although law throughout the world condemned such men to death. Trepper did not need time to think over the proposition. He knew immediately what he wanted to do and, perhaps, what he had to do. Without hesitation he betrayed one colleague after the other. He made meeting arrangements so that we could pick them up. While he was meeting them he would then order his people to tell us everything and they obeyed him, telling us all that they knew up to that point we were very successful. The Rote Kapelle could have continued to function without Trepper because we had not penetrated too deeply.

We would have mad to work on one section at a time. Trepper, however, changed the whole situation with one blow. The apparat lay completely exposed, totally paralyzed, because Trepper agreed to cooperate in a radio play-back against Moscow. No acts of violence were necessary, contrary to the reporting of our unsolicited historians. Whoever has actually engaged in this type of operation knows that it is not possible to engage in such a complicated operation as a radio play-back with a man who has been badly treated and bad treatment includes an unfriendly attitude toward the potential double-agent during the very first conversation. Those laymen who think always in terms of flogging, etc, should have seen, just once, the willingness with which the spies, so pitied by them, cooperated with us. Trepper told us much more than we ever hoped and much more than was necessary under the circumstances. The reason for his betrayal must be discussed separately. What Trepper had not betrayed, for example cells in the internal French Communist Party network about which he probably was not informed, was revealed to us through the play-back against Moscow.

39. Trepper betrayed all: Hillel Katz, Trepper's most trusted man; Robinson's entire group which was totally unknown to us; the brother and sister Maximovich and their group which included Voelkner, Podsiadic, Annemarie Hoffmann-Scholz, etc. (Station Comment: Basil Pavlovich Maximovich, Anna Pavlovna Maximovich, Kaethe Voelkner, Johann Podsiadic.) The picture of his activity before and during the war emerged more and more clearly but there was simply not enough time to concern ourselves exclusively with Trepper and his past. What was not relevant to our wartime investigation was not pursued. There were too few officials and too much work. Himmler ordered Trepper bound hand and foot – the criminal officers in charge of him and Trepper himself laughed at this order. We freed him after a short, token period from the ridiculous restrictions. Those 'on top' thought of the 'Grand Chef' as a wild animal requiring caretakers such as are necessary in a zoo and as described today in adventure stories in illustrated magazines. It was very difficult to convince those on top that the counter-intelligence officers handling such a really great spy must treat him as an officer and man of honor. Our relationships with both Trepper and KENT were the best possible.

40. We pursued those lines of Trepper's activities which had originated prior to the war and continued during the war. The Maximovich brother and sister were from one of the best Russian families of the Czarist period. They were emigrés and had been educated and raised with the help of Catholic Church organisations. The brother was an engineer and the sister a doctor. They were well known in Paris émigré circles. Because of the typical Russian homesickness for 'Little Mother Russia', they had contacted the Soviets in Paris and it all led, eventually, to Trepper. They had been interned by the French at the beginning of the war because of suspicion concerning their involvement in émigré support societies. They met Dr. Sokol during internment. With the help of high-ranking German officers they were released. German officers always have a weakness for aristocrats and the two were employed by the German occupation as interpreters. When this occurred Trepper moved in directly and Sokol was withdrawn as a cut-out. The Maximovichs were approved by the Director and recruited as full-time Soviet spies. The subsequent comedy played by the Russian aristocrats, the Maximovichs, and the German, monarch-

loving officers would have to be played on a stage and cannot be described. All of the exclusive, blue-blooded society of former aristocrats wanted nothing to do with Hitler while simultaneously carrying out his orders most obediently. They would have preferred, naturally, to have a 'beloved' monarch as a ruler because they would have played a much bigger role. The sanatorium of the woman doctor Maximovich proved the perfect atmosphere for German officers of the latter type to meet. Madame Maximovich was very distinguished; she complained with them about the common, plebeian atmosphere of the present; and they, in their discussions, betrayed, quite unwittingly, all their professional and military secrets. Trepper received a wealth of intelligence from that circle. A secretary, recruited through her lover for intelligence work, was found (Station Comment: Kaethe Voelkner, secretary in the German Kommandatura in Paris, recruited through Johann Podsiadlo). The charming brother Maximovich, working as an interpreter, was very successful with women and the woman Hoffmann-Scholz sacrificed her professional and patriotic honor for this happiness which she found late in life (Station Comment: Anne Margarete Hoffman-Schulz, British spelling, was employed in the Militaerbefehlshaber of the German occupation in Paris). I am certain that many of these conceited gentlemen of German officer clique used the subsequent events arrest of the Soviet spies as an excuse to adorn themselves with the halos of long-suffering resistance fighters who were persecuted for being anti-Nazi. It could have been a very good joke on the German military hierarchy if there had not been a bitter war in progress in which soldiers were dying on the front lines. This type of conceit (speaking of the snobbism of the German officers) is generally stronger than any service regulation or normal, human intelligence. Such conceit is found not only among the military. All foreigners employed in the German official headquarters, whether during the war or currently, should be screened by counter-intelligence organs but frequently the German officials employing foreigners are too proud to allow such screening. Regulations covering this were not always mandatory although they were certainly needed. The success a hostile intelligence service achieves can often be attributed to the faults within one's own ranks.

The Robinson Group

41. The Robinson group did not have a professional or operational link with Trepper before the war. The Robinson group had been working for years for the Comintern and Robinson was one of the latter's most

courageous and outstanding workers who had devoted his entire life to serving the Comintern. He had never married, officially, his mistress Schabbel (Klara Schabeel) in Berlin although she had a child by him, simply because he never had time for marriage. He was the same ardent revolutionary in 1942 that he had been for the past twenty years. Only the unusual circumstances of the war forced Trepper and Robinson to contact each other in the interest of espionage operations. Trepper had built a new net, the 'silent net' (sleeper net), which was to be activated only in an emergency. The 'silent net' was not permitted to have any contact whatsoever with groups or individuals who in the past or in the present had been identified as pro-Soviet, for example, the Communist Party and its various front organisations. The intelligence material from the 'silent net' was needed but there could be no connection between Trepper's net and the 'official and unofficial' (Communist) organisations except at the very top and through only one contact. The single point of contact was Robinson, one of the most successful and accomplished conspirators. I cannot describe his extensive connections in France and the rest of Europe because they are too numerous. Three of his closer co-workers were: Louis Mourier; a document expert whose name I have forgotten; and the most important, the Swiss engineer Maurice Aenis-Haenslin who placed his Swiss neutrality and his large apartment at the disposal of the service. (Station Comment: The 'document expert' is possibly Marcel Alphonse Charles Rouge, stated in the Personality Index of the British Study to have been an agent of Henri Robinson in France, probably concerned with the fabrication of identity documents and passes; apparently escaped arrest during the general round-up of Trepper's and Robinson's groups in 1942-43. Medardo Griotto is also listed in the British Study as an Italian printer and engraver who provided both Robinson and Trepper with false papers and stamps.)

Aenis-Haenslin's apartment was equipped with innumerable secret concealment places which were built into the wall, the floor and into every possible piece of furniture. There were secret documents practically everywhere, including financial accounts, reports, raw material collected together, etc. The eight to ten room apartment of Aenis-Haenslin was used by us as a safe-house, meeting place, etc. One of our penetration agents lived in the apartment for several weeks. During the latter's idle time he searched for new concealment places and found as many as we had in our original search. The secret drawers were so cleverly constructed that all of the furniture would have had to be taken entirely apart in order to find all of them. Our agent would casually and accidently rest his hand on a spot and a secret drawer would shoot out of the piece of furniture or wall. He would report this immediately and then start feverishly hunting for more hiding-places. This showed clearly that when working against a professional conspiratorial net, nothing is too small for careful investigation. Unfortunately during the war we lacked the necessary manpower for this type of careful investigation and we often had to be satisfied with only the larger aspects.

42. Aenis-Haenslin was sentenced to death but Switzerland protested and demanded his release. I do not know whether there was ever an exchange but I would think not because Aenis-Haenslin would have represented much too great a danger for German interests and for the success of the radio play-back if he had been in Switzerland. It is certainly possible that he survived the war in spite of the death sentence. He was used for innumerable courier trips and, therefore, knew a large part of the Soviet apparatus in Switzerland. Inasmuch as there were discussions later in Karlsruhe between the Swiss and German police concerning the ROTE DREI, it is probable that the Swiss intervened again on Aenis-Haenslin's account. Participants in these discussions certainly still are available and would know the outcome. (Station Comment: The British Study reported Aenis-Haenslin in Switzerland as of 1948. An UPSWING report, MGL- A-73036 of 17 August 1950, reported him to be connected with a Swiss firm, UNIPECTINE, as of August 1950.) I will cover the fate of the other, above-mentioned persons later because they were partially involved in the playbacks.

Other Radio Stations in Paris

43. The other radio stations in Paris had not been activated, although technically equipped to go on the air. Hillel Katz, Trepper's secretary, had immediately, when ordered to do so by Trepper, turned over all the hidden radio equipment. Trepper was actually not informed of all the equipment. It was only from Moscow, in the course of the play-back, that we learned about the supply of radio equipment held by the French Communist Party and through the French CP we learned of the latter's planned internal radio net of seven lines inside of France. Through this almost two truckloads of technical equipment fell into our hands. Later the equipment belonging to [General Waldemar] Ozols and his radio station, not yet activated, fell into our hands. Still later, fall of 1943, the last line was located by means of D/F'ing as contact with Moscow was being made. This was the last radio link which made its existence known to us and we did not have enough information to

move in on it. The details on the radio stations are mentioned here as a general explanation of the situation in the Paris area.

Lyon Radio Station

44. The Lyon radio station was seized while it was transmitting. The radio station had been established by an agent of the Soviet Military Attaché in Paris. The agent's name was something similar to Schreiber (Station Comment: Hesekil Schreiber with aliases Georges Kiefer, CAMILLE, and GEORGES). Schumacher, with alias ROGER (Otto Schumacher, spelling in British Study), and Isidor Springer from Brussels had fled to Lyon when the apparat in Brussels collapsed and they were working with the Lyon station. When the station was fixed by means of D/F'ing and raided, one member of the station was killed during the resistance offered by members of the station. I think, if my memory is correct, that the man killed was Schreiber. Isidor Springer committed suicide in the Lyon prison by jumping from a top floor. Schumacher was taken into custody.

Marseilles Radio Station

45. The radio station in Marseilles had been set up well in advance and was intended to become active after KENT fled from Brussels and Paris to Marseilles. Aside from necessary groundwork, little else was accomplished by this station. Margarete Marivet (Madame Marguerite Marivet with aliases Madame Madeleine Matenot or Matelot) and Jules Jaspar were not really suited or trained for the work. KENT, somehow, seems to have resigned himself. He later told me that his situation there had been such a contrast to his extremely active work in Brussels that he was unhappy and that in his heart he had already broken with Moscow. He would have preferred to withdraw with Barcza (Marguerite Barcza, KENT's mistress) and lead a quiet life. Only the fact that Moscow, i.e. the Director, was so irresponsible in directing his agents, asking everything from the agents and providing no support, had made him dissatisfied with matters as they were. He had never trusted Trepper, also, and was convinced that in case of danger Trepper would think only of himself and desert all the others – which he did.

46. We had received reports of KENT's presence in Marseilles. Kriminaldirektor Boemelburg (Obersturmführer Karl Boemelburg or Boemmelburg) in the company of some other officials went to

301

Marseilles which was in unoccupied France at the time. Boemelburg arrested KENT, his mistress Margarete Barcza, and her child. I do not know to what extent the French police were involved in the arrest but they participated to some degree. Barcza and KENT travelled with the German officials from Marseilles to Paris. The two slept in the same hotel room with an official so that their connubial life was never interrupted. The statement in various publicized stories that Barcza was arrested later is false. The landlord and neighbours where KENT and Barcza lived in Marseilles never learned that the two were arrested but believed that they had fled hurriedly to avoid arrest. The other members of the Marseilles group were also arrested and brought to Paris, later taken to Berlin. The role of the brother of the former Belgian Minister President, Jules Jaspar, as a Moscow agent, was never clarified (as mentioned above).

The Radio Play-Backs

47. Trepper's as well as KENT's agreement to cooperate in a German-controlled radio play-back against Moscow was obtained in the very beginning. The radio traffic was immediately resumed on all radio links which had been detected by D/F'ing and were under German control. There were no technical problems. The 'handwriting' of the original Soviet agent operator had generally been recorded on tape so that our German operator could quickly practice and reproduce the rhythm of the Soviet operator's 'handwriting'. This enabled us to substitute German operators almost immediately. Some of the Soviet operators continued to work on their sets under our strict control. As I recall Winterinck, Wenzel and Makarov did this. Using the original Soviet operator was done only for a short time because the danger of a control sign which could be sent to Moscow was always present. Actually this danger was not too serious because every Soviet agent realised that the death sentence, an automatic sentence for espionage conducted on behalf of the enemy during the war, had been waived only as long as the agent was willing to cooperate. Some of the leaders of the Soviet rezidentura, including Trepper and KENT, were not even on record as being charged with espionage before a military court.

48. In the beginning the controlled radio sets were played back against Moscow for the purpose of feeding the enemy effective deception as rapidly as possible and with the secondary purpose of identifying other members of the Red rezidentura in order to eliminate the entire Rezidentura. The officers of the military and security police counter-

intelligence organs were so fascinated by the hunt for Red agents that they were incapable of conceiving a long-term operational plan. The radio links under our control which the enemy, the Director, was able to spot as German-controlled, were immediately discontinued and a new play-back started from the reserves of captured sets and agents. Our counter-intelligence was able to provide a continuous supply of new agents for this purpose – all of the Soviet agents thus used had done sufficient damage to the German cause to warrant their arrest.

49. As a result of my experience in the investigation of the Heydrich assassination, I had made some far-reaching proposals regarding a completely new plan for exploitation of captured enemy radio sets to neutralize and paralyze resistance movements. In order that my proposals could be understood, even could be considered, the top officials to 'whom they were presented had to discard the habitual executive type of thinking. (Station Comment: Source used the word 'executive' throughout this report in the sense of police and legal action, i.e. executive action means arrests, passing sentence, imprisonment, execution, etc.) Mueller, Chief of Amt IV of the RSHA (Gruppenführer u. Generalmajor der Polizei Heinrich Mueller), had pigeon-holed my proposals because of the internal struggle for power within the RSHA. A new security chief had not been appointed since Heydrich's death. Mueller did not want to take the entire responsibility for such a radical and extensive change without a superior to back him. He realised very well that, due to the great shortage of professionally trained men, the stage would rapidly be reached whereby the constantly renewed and increasing resistance strength infiltrated by the enemy into occupied territories could not be combatted by executive methods. If, on the other hand, it was desirable to penetrate and paralyze the enemy's organisation in order to eliminate danger from that quarter, radio play-backs and double agent operations, necessary to accomplish this goal, would require intelligence, factual information and not deception, in order to build up the enemy's faith in his 'real' success. To accomplish this an entirely new approach and type of thinking was required and no one had even dared consider such an approach until then. In short, the enemy would have to be given as factual, credible, and ample information as possible, without endangering ourselves. The enemy had to be given truthful information which would interest him and was not dangerous to us. To accomplish this during the war required the highest authority because everyone engaged in the war had, until then, considered every soldier as an item of secret information.

50. When the new chief for the Security Police was appointed, Mueller returned to my proposal regarding long-term and extensive double operations because Mueller would no longer have to take full responsibility for the decision. I was asked by Mueller to take charge of the controlled radio play-backs instituted with the captured Rote Kapelle members in Paris in line with my early proposals. During the period when I was reading into the operation, I was shocked to see how the play-backs had been directed. It was amazing that the Director in Moscow continued the radio contact and had not long before discovered that they were German controlled. Before various nets were rolled up, a distinctive, alive and bubbling character was evident in all the work. The various nets had emphasized military intelligence as one could read from the decoded messages. After the roll-up the reporting was lifeless, dull, and limited to insignificant details which the Germans were willing to release. The reporting resembled the work of a journalist who wants to stretch his article out for the maximum number of words. The 'officials' lacked the initiative and courage to assume any responsibility and everything used in the play-backs had to be approved by the highest authority to avoid any 'flaps'. I obtained in Berlin the necessary authority to act freely and independently.

51. Trepper and KENT accompanied by Madame Barcza were living in a villa in Paris in which Kriminaldirektor Boemelburg resided and in which were housed the so-called 'noble prisoners'. The latter were prominent politicians, military leaders, espionage agents and resistance leaders. Trepper had a well-furnished room and private bath, a radio, his own shaving equipment, good food and many other comforts. He could walk in the large park belonging to the villa although under guard when he did. KENT and Barcza had a large room with the same comforts. Hillel Katz and Schumacher @ ROGER were also housed in the villa although both had received the death sentence. The latters' sentences had been commuted on the basis of Trepper's cooperation. Katz and Schumacher's sentences would never have been carried out if Trepper by his escape had not caused Berlin to decide that the two were no longer necessary and ordered them turned over to the proper authorities for execution. Katz and Schumacher had never really been needed to mount the radio play-back but the commutation of their sentence was a gesture of goodwill toward Trepper. Trepper certainly was not bothered by such considerations in his own actions.

52. I had many discussions with Trepper about the Rote Drei in Switzerland because this net originally came under my jurisdiction.

I had been told to do the ground work in Paris in preparation for the neutralization of the Rote Drei. The Kommando, headed before my arrival by Kriminalrat (Karl) Giering, was concerned primarily with Trepper as the most valuable agent. KENT had never been activated in a double play. It was obvious from the careless handling of his radio links that he was of little interest. KENT's link, EIFFEL, had to be operated on a much larger scale because the link was based in Marseilles where the radio transmitter was located. If the transmissions were not made from Marseilles, the problem was faced of how to prevent Moscow spotting, by means of the Soviet Direction-Finding equipment, that the transmissions did not originate in Marseilles.

The Kommando had a unit in Marseilles which would have enabled the operation to be run much better than it was. Trepper and KENT, the two chiefs, were not exactly flattering in their remarks about each other and the Kommando was inclined to side with Trepper. In addition Trepper had shown himself more willing to give information on the Swiss net which would assist us to determine at which point we could penetrate the net. This was not his own idea but he agreed without resistance. The neutralization of the French CP illegal radio repair and workshops was also in progress. Most of the French members had fled and had not been found. As I recall, information concerning the repair shops and store houses used by the French CP in Paris for radio equipment was obtained over Trepper's radio link by requesting from Moscow technical assistance for the rezidentura's radio set. There was a great deal of work for the numerically small Kommando and it was superficial work because we could not, then, dig any deeper.

Trepper's Escape

53. I had made a habit of sharing a bottle of wine with Trepper every few days but during September 1943 had had to neglect him because of the pressure of work. On 15 September 1943, Trepper asked that a medical prescription provided by a German doctor for his heart trouble be renewed. He had a heart ailment somewhat similar to angina pectoris. His prescription was obtained from a druggist in a large apothecary store of several floors located in the St. Lazare Station. I was absent, by chance, when Trepper made the request so Trepper's guard asked Kriminalkommissar (Heinrich Josef) Reiser, my deputy, for permission to drive Trepper to the apothecary shop. Reiser granted permission. When Kriminalobersekretaer Willie Berg was notified that he was to accompany Trepper, Berg called Reiser's attention to the fact that Berg and the chauffeur would have to go alone with

Trepper because no other officials were free. Reiser reportedly agreed in any case. Whether Reiser did approve or not has never been known because after the fact no one wanted to take the blame. I returned from my official conference and shortly thereafter Berg came to my office and told me that Trepper had escaped. Berg was so upset that I immediately asked some of the officers to keep an eye on him to prevent any attempt at suicide. Trepper's escape caused a sensation, naturally, because he was regarded as the 'Grand Chef' of Western Europe, excluding Spain and Portugal.

54. The entire area in which he escaped was immediately searched with no success. Berg provided the following report on the events of the escape:

> Berg and Trepper went by car to the large drug store in the St. Lazare Station. The chauffeur remained in the car before the entrance where they entered. The store had several flights of very narrow, winding stairs leading from the ground floor to the first (European) floor where the prescription was to be filled. Berg and Trepper climbed the stairs to the first floor. The stairs were so narrow that only one person could go up or down at a time. While the saleswoman was taking care of the prescription, Berg stood next to Trepper sunk in very deep thought. Berg's only daughter who had died quite some time prior would have had her birthday on that day. Berg's wife was very ill and also very depressed by the daughter's death. Berg was reflecting on his private troubles although, he said, only for a few seconds. Trepper disappeared down one of the winding stairs and out a street entrance other than the one before which the car was standing. The store was on a corner and had two entrances on two different streets so the chauffeur saw nothing.

Reconstructing the escape at the place it occurred confirmed Berg's account. Any attempt to follow Trepper in the crowded streets of Paris was hopeless. It should be added that Berg had from the beginning trusted Trepper, presumably too much.

55. The great question which was never answered as far as I was concerned was what really happened. I had been chief of the Kommando only a short time. The former chief, Kriminalrat Giering, had withdrawn because of his health. His close, 'per du' friend was Berg and both were on 'per du' terms with Kriminaldirektor Boemelburg. All three had very good relations and personal contact with Gruppenfuehrer Mueller, chief of Amt IV. In fact Berg was Mueller's cigar procurer during the war. Berg never made an official

trip to Berlin that he did not talk to Mueller personally, probably passing on local gossip from Paris. Berg was known to gossip and his personal honesty was not the highest. The question I asked myself was: Was it not possible that an operation had been planned, timed to coincide with the arrival of the new chief (source) so that it would go unnoticed? Investigation and careful observation, however, revealed nothing to support my suspicion. Berg was honestly very upset by the escape and his emotional state was not assumed. Mueller's reaction from Berlin was also authentic and a typical 'desk' reaction. (Station Comment: The British Study views Trepper's escape as possibly linked with Trepper's Intelligence Service 'triple-play', a British theory that Trepper although ostensibly submitting to German control in the double operation had somehow managed to notify or maintain contact with the Soviets. The British Study (page 44 of Part II), describes a visit to 'a shop' made by Trepper shortly after his arrest in December 1942. The Study states that Trepper told Spaak after his, Trepper's, escape that he had such a good understanding with his captors that he was allowed to visit a shop while meeting his agents on German orders and his German guards watched from a distance. During the visit to the shop he had passed a report to a woman agent whom he had not betrayed to the Germans. On page 57 the Study states that 'Trepper, practicing much the same ruse as he had used in smuggling out his 1942 report, escaped from the custody of his German guard.' In view of the British theory, the woman who prepared Trepper's prescription may have been the agent Trepper claimed to Spaak he had not betrayed to the Germans. Trepper may also have been building a cover story to protect himself against the time when he returned to the USSR. There is insufficient space here to comment on the complicated French CP communication link which the British Study suggests may have been used by Trepper while the latter was still in German custody.)

56. Berlin, apparently in a state of shock, completely forgot to answer my urgent teletype message concerning the escape which I sent to the RSHA Headquarters. There were at least five minutes of total silence before the biggest and most worrisome question came back: 'How are we going to tell Himmler?' I replied to say nothing which was their reaction after they had recovered from the initial shock. Later hundreds of questions and requests for the most minute detail arrived. We had to give the smallest bit of information; Berg was to be imprisoned on Mueller's personal order. Mueller sent his personal message on the teletype which was: 'How could anyone leave the side of a criminal?' We had tried to indoctrinate him with the basic principle that it was

impossible to run a double operation of long-term value and treat the enemy officers who were risking their lives as criminals. The storm centre finally became the practical means to be used to track down and find Trepper. I then clearly told Berlin that no trained man, including Berg, could be spared and that Berlin should send trained, competent replacements. Furthermore, I said that imprisoning the Kommando officers and staff would have a very bad psychological consequence. All individuals initiative would be killed if the men thought that in a dangerous undertaking failure would be blamed on an individual's carelessness, they would relapse into bureaucrats of the worst type. Omelettes cannot be made without breaking eggs. The crisis regarding the confidence and trust in my subordinates was relieved after a few days and none of the participants suffered afterward. Six weeks later the mood in the RSHA Berlin had so completely reversed that they were then of the opinion that Trepper's escape was actually a benefit inasmuch as the measures taken as a result of his escape produced more information than would have been uncovered otherwise.

57. During my years of interrogation later in Moscow, Trepper's escape was covered in the smallest detail at least ten times. I could never discover any clue to support the suspicion that a previously prepared plan had been made for the escape. In the beginning the Soviets took the point of view of interrogating me that Trepper had escaped with our connivance in order that he could penetrate the cadre of the French CP for us. The Soviets regarded his escape as provocation. Next the Soviets attempted to convince me that Willi Berg was a close, trusted friend of Trepper and a Moscow agent. The interrogators did not make much progress with the theory that Berg arranged Trepper's escape on Moscow orders. The whole purpose of that attack was too obvious, i.e. to provoke me and possibly make me tell something in anger. They also told me, in connection with trying to provoke me regarding Berg, everything which Berg, allegedly their man, had reported about me after the war. Such stupid statements were made at that time that they could not possibly have originated with Berg.

Search For Trepper

58. The RSHA Berlin was convinced at first that the radio play-backs were finished because Trepper needed only to go to the French CP and Moscow would have the report via some courier or other means of communication. The RSHA Headquarters was of the opinion that all the play-backs should be stopped. Orders came at the same time

to turn Hillel Katz and Schumacher over to the police officials for immediate imprisonment.

59. I had to tell KENT about the seriousness of the situation because he was also in danger. I would say KENT was at his weakest and most depressed state during that time. He obviously expected the worst would happen. I did not take such a gloomy view and made it very clear to KENT that everything depended on keeping the radio play-backs alive. I asked KENT to write a report, based on his knowledge of the workings of the minds in Moscow, on what he thought Moscow's reaction would be if Trepper suddenly announced that he had escaped from the custody of German counterintelligence. KENT produced a brilliant and comprehensive report for me. In his answer, he described the thinking, the mistrust, and the entire internal structure of the Soviet organisation. I later realised, after years in a Soviet prison, that KENT had put down the irrefutable truth. From his report I obtained a good background in the Soviet organisation and its peculiar mental processes which served me well during my experience in the Soviet Union.

60. The tactical lines of the comprehensive search for Trepper were determined by circumstances and what knowledge we could obtain. The outside would knew nothing of the police investigation. Trepper, 'le Grand Chef', was unknown to the general public. Newspaper announcements and placards bearing his photo were posted in the larger railway stations and in all border stations of France only. He was described only as an escaped enemy agent whose capture would bring a big reward. Simultaneously KENT announced on his radio link to the Director that he had seen Trepper's picture on placards stating that the Germans were looking for Trepper. KENT asked for instructions as to what he should do and what all of this meant. The Director answered promptly, as we expected, that KENT was to break off all contacts and not assist Trepper in any way; the French CP should be warned because this was all probably provocation. The Director now emphasized KENT's work. We allowed Trepper's radio link to die after two or three messages so that Moscow's suspicion of provocation would be strengthened. Later Moscow itself warned the French CP over 'ANDRE's' link in very strong terms against Trepper. Trepper was completely isolated by these acts within three days. No one would touch him. The French CP was no longer concerned with him and the Party representatives did not even appear for the regular meetings which Trepper had arranged. Trepper had continued meeting with the Party people every fourteen days in a Catholic Church as an

emergency measure. They frequently used the confessional booth for their discussions.

61. The entire Trepper complex was thoroughly and rapidly reviewed by the Kommando to detect any loopholes. Many of Trepper's contacts and many of his known meeting places were not, however, investigated due to lack of time and personnel. Very important among those overlooked was Trepper's mistress, de Winter (Georgina de Winter), who certainly should have been thoroughly investigated long before. It was very difficult to locate a person, recently arrived, through the Paris residence registry. Nevertheless, de Winter was quickly located working in a children's home. Her first husband was reportedly an American. Up to that time it had not been known that she had a child by Trepper, a son born about 1940. The old question, 'Ou est la femme?' was also pertinent in Trepper's case. He had gone directly from the apothecary shop to de Winter in the children's home and a half-hour later was in a deserted villa on the outskirts of Paris. His flight was followed step by step. Trepper was in luck because we arrived at each place about twenty to thirty minutes after he had left. Quite often the beds in which the two had slept were still warm. The trail led after several days to Madame Spaak, the wife of Claude Spaak. She had not kept them in her house overnight but had turned them over to a church worker who sheltered them for a short time. Madame Spaak also played another role in Trepper's escape; she was responsible for a large sum of money which Trepper had held in reserve. The key, a sentence containing the word 'parapluie' (umbrella), was sufficient for de Winter to collect the several hundred thousand francs which Madame Spaak had left with the Belgian representative of the Red Cross in Paris. This man, a Belgian count, had apparently carried out other missions for Madame Spaak because he appeared shortly thereafter at the Claude Spaak apartment which we had taken over. Before entering he asked the concierge whether everything was all right with Madame Spaak. The 'concierge' was one of our men. When the count entered the Spaak apartment, he was greeted by the German police and asked to produce his identity papers. He was allowed to leave and promptly berated the 'concierge' for not having told him that the Spaak apartment was occupied by German police. Madame Spaak mobilised all possible help for Trepper. This included Antonia Lyon-Smith, the daughter of an English general, and French groups who had radio contact with London and with the Belgian government-in-exile, headed by Paul Henri Spaak.

62. All of Georgina de Winter's contacts were traced and questioned. Most of them had fled and in that case we placed our people in the empty apartments. Among those who had fled was a sixty-five year old widow, Madame May, whose husband, a poet, had been dead for twenty-five years. May's apartment was occupied by French police officers who were assigned to help us in the search. While in the apartment the French police found a cache of weapons. Madame May returned finally to her apartment on a Sunday. She was immediately taken into custody and questioned. She admitted that she had come from Trepper's hiding-place and that another meeting as well as emergency meetings with Trepper were arranged. Madame May was a very resolute and energetic woman and a fanatical French chauvinist. In spite of the promises we made to her, she did not want to reveal anything. She screamed at us, kicked me quite vigorously in the leg and hit me over the head with the handle of her umbrella. Finally she gave us the information. Although we took every precaution, we were unable to catch Trepper. He was much too much of a specialist in clandestine meeting arrangements to allow himself to be taken by surprise. We realised that again we had missed him. Again he sought refuge in a home for old people and children. When we questioned the people in the home, we obtained a lead to de Winter's and Trepper's child who was hidden in the Maquis area of Correze and Limoges. The woman, charged with the care of the child, was brought to Paris under the cover of investigating a kidnapping in order to conceal the German interest in the child. Working from this lead, we located de Winter working as a farmer's helper on a farm about 150 kilometers from Paris. She and Trepper had been forced to separate when Madame May was arrested. De Winter was arrested in the late evening to avoid attracting attention in the area. The Kommando, not having had an opportunity to eat anything during the day, stopped about midnight, after arresting de Winter at a small cafe fairly near the place of arrest. Having drunk a large quantity of wine, de Winter asked to go to the toilet. Two women from a nearby German unit were summoned to accompany her to the toilet and search her. A complete and thorough body search was made. In the course of the search, 100,000 French francs and a letter was found on her body. The letter was written, apparently, by a French woman and contained instructions and a plea for help directed to an address in Grenoble and one or two addresses on the Swiss border. The people asked to help were told that an important individual was fleeing from the Germans and needed shelter for a night or should be passed on to other persons who could shelter him. The important individual would identify himself by a certain name. The writer of

the letter was later identified as Antonia Lyon-Smith. Her father was reported to be an English artillery general with Montgomery's army in North Africa and later in Italy. She had been staying with relatives (in France) at the beginning of the war but was not interned because she was not yet eighteen years old. When she had her eighteenth birthday, her relatives arranged for false French identity papers to protect her. Through her friendship with Madame Spaak, she was approached with a request to assist French nationals who were escaping from the Germans by introducing them to people she knew. As the daughter of an English general, she could scarcely refuse to help.

63. Lyon-Smith was a young, proud, and very honest girl who made such a good impression on us that I arranged to stop the court trial and prison sentence which would have resulted from her actions. More should be written about her because my former colleagues have stated that the English counter-intelligence officers who interrogated them spoke of her in a very derogatory manner, as if she had been working for either Moscow or the Germans which in both cases is complete nonsense.

64. De Winter's arrest led to the arrest of Madame Spaak and many other people. De Winter talked about Trepper's personal habits, their intimate relationship, their private jokes, etc. I decided to place another announcement in the newspapers. Trepper had, as a matter of fact, written me a letter on the second day of his escape, apologizing for his action. His letter read like an adventure novel. He claimed that a control agent sent directly from Moscow had shadowed him in the apothecary shop and commanded him to escape if he did not want to be shot: I thanked him for the letter by means of a newspaper announcement and asked him to call me on the telephone, all of this in disguised language which he would understand. After my newspaper announcement I talked to him on the telephone four or five times but never for more than two minutes. He would not remain on the line for more than two minutes and two minutes were not sufficient in Paris to track a telephone call. He claimed, in his telephone conversations and in two letters, that he wanted to maintain our cordial relationship no matter what happened. When we ran the newspaper announcement written in the intimate language he and de Winter used between each other and stating that the boy and she were with us, he phoned again. He implied in his telephone conversation that he would like nothing better than to return but for unstated reasons could not.

65. Madame Spaak, her husband and their two children had fled from their French residence. She was captured by German officials in Belgium but only she was found. She talked openly and freely, withholding nothing in the belief that we already knew too much. Her testimony agreed with the facts as we knew them. What we did not know and learned from her was that she had supported the Sokols, she claimed, out of pity. She had sent a message through her contacts to her brother-in-law (Paul Henri Spaak) concerning Trepper and had arranged with Trepper to use this channel of escape. Her contact man was arrested. He insisted that he had never assisted Trepper at Madame Spaak's behest and although he was confronted with her, they both stuck to their original statements. We never were able to obtain the facts. While I was in prison in Moscow, I obtained some information which leads me to believe that Madame Spaak was telling the truth. The contact man had stuck to his original statement with iron nerves, insisting that he was innocent. An examination of the literature in his apartment had revealed that he was a sincere admirer of Hitler. At the time of the interrogation, I had considered the possibility that Madame Spaak was possibly taking revenge on the man. I had the impression that there had been a very close relationship between the man and Madame Spaak at one time.

66. In spite of her involvement with Trepper, Madame Spaak was a very likeable woman who made an unforgettable impression. She was a serious, calm woman who looked at everyone with her large, protruding eyes in a composed fashion. Obviously she had followed her parlor-pink sympathies. She regarded all of her actions as an intellectual game and could never bring herself to sacrifice her comfortable living to become an effective and active worker for any cause. She was above all an artist with very modern taste in painting which the pictures, painted by her and hung in her apartment, indicated. Although we felt a great pity for her, she was too deeply involved for us to help her. She and Madame May were brought to court with the others and sentenced to death. Madame May actually received two death sentences, one for aiding the enemy and the other for concealing weapons. An order existed at that time that Hitler must review every death sentence passed by the courts against foreign women. He changed Madame May's death sentences into 10 years in prison but let the death sentence remain for Madame Spaak. It was evident to us that his action resulted from the fact that Paul Henri Spaak was leader of the Belgian Government in exile in London. I personally petitioned Berlin to have the sentence commuted on the grounds that Madame Spaak

was needed in the search for her husband, the brother of the Minister President. My petition was immediately approved. I proposed to Berlin that Madame Spaak be asked to assist in the search for her husband with the promise that the death sentence would never be carried out if her husband was found and both of them remained in prison for the remainder of the war. Berlin agreed clearly and unequivocally to this proposal. Madame Spaak was in the military prison of Paris-Fresnes in which the security police kept all their prisoners but which was administered by the military authorities. The only exception to the rule were the 'noble prisoners', security police prisoners who were housed in Boemelburg's villa and those prisoners, KENT, Barcza, and Lyon-Smith, housed in my villa. I proposed to Madame Spaak that she send her husband a letter through her children in which she outlined the German offer. She had asked the prison officials prior to writing the letter whether we would and could keep our word. The officials arranged for her to talk with me once more. I once more wrote Berlin asking for reassurance and emphasizing that in this case I had to keep my word. I received a firm positive answer that the promise would be kept. After the second assurance, Madame Spaak wrote the letter as instructed and enclosed two small dolls which she had made out of her own hair for her children. The children, who were living with their grandmother in Brussels, received the letter. The father must have learned of the contents of the letter but he had not appeared as of the time we withdrew from Paris. At the time of the German withdrawal from Paris, the transportation of the Paris-Fresnes prisoners was handled by the military prison administration. I know positively that the commutation of the death sentence into a prison sentence in Madame. Spaak's case was never revoked. I had always believed that she was taken to a prison in Germany. This belief was supported by the fact that towards the end of the war, in April 1945, I received a radio message from Kriminaldirektor Kopkow of the RSHA while I was in Heiligenberg on Lake Constance asking my opinion of an exchange of Madame Spaak for German prisoners. Inasmuch as I had no particular opinions, I did not express myself one way or the other but from this letter I had always assumed that Madame Spaak had been exchanged before the end of the war. I was confronted in Moscow with the accusation that Madame Spaak had been executed while still in Paris-Fresnes. I simply did not believe this. Since I returned from the Soviet Union, however, I have heard that she was reportedly executed. If that is a fact, a horrible mistake occurred somewhere because as far as my Kommando and the Security Police were concerned, the change of death sentence to prison sentence had never been reversed.

314

The responsibility can only lie with the administrative offices of the prison where the commuted death sentence may have been overlooked in the files. It was neither possible for, nor the responsibility of my Kommando to supervise the prison transport from Paris during the final hectic days of the withdrawal. It is most regrettable that all of our efforts to save this woman's life were in vain because of a stupid and horrible administrative mistake. (Station Comment: The British Study places all emphasis on Claude Spaak as Trepper's assistant. The Personality Index of the Study under Claude Spaak has the following: 'The confidence which Trepper reposed in Spaak suggests that he was a well-known and well-tried friend of the USSR if not of the GRU'. It then outlines the various steps by which Claude Spaak assisted Trepper and de Winter after Trepper's escape from the Gestapo. There is relatively little mention of Suzanne, Madame Claude Spaak, except: 'Suzanne was arrested in the Ardennes, interned in Fresnes Prison until her execution on 12 July 1944.' Ruth PETERS, who was living with Claude Spaak, became Madame Claude Spaak No. 2 and was working with him in assisting Trepper during the time Suzanne Spaak was in prison according to the Study. Horst Kopkow, mentioned by source above as having written regarding the possible exchange of Suzanne Spaak for German prisoners in April 1945, worked very closely with the British at the end of the war. It should also be noted that in the body of the British Study Part II appears the statement: 'Trepper told Spaak etc;' 'Trepper himself, after his escape, gave Spaak an instance of, etc.' which would indicate that the British either questioned Claude Spaak himself or obtained his story through his brother Paul Henri Spaak. From the two sources, Claude Spaak and Kopkow, the British should have fairly positive information regarding Suzanne Spaak's execution unless Claude Spaak, wanting Suzanne out of the way in order to marry Ruth Peters, and Kopkow, to protect himself, did not give the facts.)

67. From that time on the search for Trepper was unsuccessful. Many new contacts were revealed, however. Arrests were made and much new information obtained. The families living on the Swiss border to whom Antonia Lyon-Smith had written the letter found on de Winter were arrested. They were all Belgians who were living illegally on the French border after having fled when the Germans marched into Belgium. Antonia had spent a vacation there one summer at the recommendation of Madame Spaak. Antonia knew all of the people personally. They were for the most part former Belgian government heads and were transported back to Belgium via Paris. None of them

were connected in any way with the Rote Kapelle. The search after Trepper was so extensive that innumerable persons were involved whose names I cannot remember. I shall try to name the more prominent.

68. The third of the Spaak brothers (Charles Spaak according to the British Study) was imprisoned with his mistress for a few days. His mistress was pregnant so we cleared up as soon as possible the extent of their involvement in the Rote Kapelle complex. He and his mistress were released after a few days. He was very grateful for this completely humane treatment which was normal in the Kommando in any case but he thought he had seen given special treatment. After the war he interceded for members of the Kommando. While the latter were being interrogated he helped them with favourable statements and sent them food packages in prison.

69. Antonia Lyon-Smith lived in my villa with the Kommando, sharing a room with one of the secretaries, for more than three months. I did not allow her to be brought to court, as stated above, because she would have received a fairly severe sentence for helping the enemy. Purely humane motives led me to arrange this, without Berlin's knowledge but with the approval of the head of the military court which was handling all Rote Kapelle cases. My actions were inspired neither by an effort to obtain Lyon-Smith's collaboration in an espionage operation nor by a sexual interest in her. She had become involved in the war machine through an unfortunate series of circumstances and as the daughter of an English general, she simply could not refuse to do whatever was asked of her to assist, allegedly, the Allied cause. Her relatives in Paris with whom she lived were extremely bitter and filled with hatred (presumably against the Germans). She, on the other hand, did not share their bitterness although they did not conceal their feelings from her. She ate breakfast every morning with me and those of my staff who worked most closely with me. I undertook various psychological tests to determine exactly what her attitude and feeling toward Moscow was. By instinct she was definitely hostile to the Soviets. She had never known the true nature of the group she met through Madame Spaak. I once offered, joking but pretending to be very serious, to have her put over the Spanish border so that she could report to the English Consul in Spain who would arrange for her transportation back to England. She begged me not to do this because, she said, she would immediately be imprisoned in England as a German spy; no one would believe the truth. I then asked her if she would report what good treatment she had received in my Kommando. She replied that she would certainly not

make any such report during the first three years because she would be imprisoned if she did. I released her to her relatives toward the end of 1943 or early 1944 on her word of honor that she would not leave Paris. We checked on her regularly and I know that she kept her word. She had made such a good impression on me that I had never doubted that she would keep her word. We left her in Paris when we withdrew. She is reported to have been treated much worse by her own people than by us, the enemy. There were various indications of this. Later in Berlin I explained the entire case and was never reprimanded for my actions.

70. De Winter was also kept in Boemelburg's villa as one of the 'noble prisoners'. She was transported to RSHA custody in Berlin a few weeks before the withdrawal from Paris. I have never learned what happened to her. One of the Russian officers, I think it was Makarov but am not certain, was taken to the RSHA in Berlin at the same time. The latter had been with my Kommando in Paris before the withdrawal. Kriminalobersekretaer Willi Berg headed the transport. (Station Comment: The British Study states that Michel Makarov was executed after being taken to Germany. Unfortunately the last pages of the Personality Index, attachment to the British Study, are missing from Munich Base 1 copy so the final British information on Georgina de Winter is not available in Munich.)

The Radio Play-Backs, 'Funkspiele'

71. After Trepper's escape the radio double operations against Moscow were concentrated on KENT's radio links. Moscow had reacted as we hoped and ordered all contact with Trepper to be dropped. KENT received instructions from Moscow to contact SOLYA, true name General Osols (Waldemar Ozols with aliases SOLJA, Sokol, 'The General', 'Z', 'Marianne'). SOLYA was ordered to put at KENT's disposal radio equipment which SOLYA had concealed. Moscow's orders were carried out exactly and the operation was successful. SOLYA did not have a large net in Paris but his connections in the rest of France were excellent. Most of his connections scattered around the country were well suited for intelligence work although not at all suited to sabotage or terror activity, which was perfect for our needs. KENT's official headquarters, as far as the Director was concerned, was Marseilles but this was inconvenient for us. At this time KENT received orders from Moscow to move to Paris in order to step up the active work in that area. The move made the radio communication much easier for

us because we could place the emphasis on intelligence originating in Paris itself without making this conspicuous in Moscow's eyes.

72. I had finally achieved, after long negotiations with different military and political headquarters in Paris, permission to send only true and interesting material on our controlled radio transmitters. The sources of the intelligence which we sent to Moscow were the following:

a. I C Oberbefehlshaber West (G 2 of the Supreme Western Command)
b. BdS, Dr. Knochen (Chief of the Security Forces, Standartenfuehrer u. Oberst der Polizei Dr. Helmut Knochen)
c. Hoeher SS und Polizeifuehrer SS Gruppenfuehrer Oberg (Generalleutnant der Polizei Karl Albrecht Oberg)
d. Bickler, chief of Abteilung VI. beim BdS (SS-Standartenfuehrer Hermann Bickler)
e. The German Embassy in Paris
f. The German Trade Mission in Paris
g. French Ministers, through direct contact
h. German officers interrogating PoWs, especially Luftwaffe officers
i. Personal interviews with wounded PoWs in hospitals
j. Catholic Church and Jesuits, through direct channels
k. RSHA Berlin, information obtained from German Ministries.

In addition to the above, we used journalists, diplomats, propaganda organs, etc. Very few of the above, maximum four or five, had any knowledge of the use made of the material they provided. Every day I received a copy of the secret monitoring report of the enemy radios. There were only three copies of this report in Paris. Using all of the material available to us, we would study, evaluate, and edit the reports collected by the authentic Moscow agents reporting to the principal agents under our control. The intelligence from the authentic Moscow agents was included only when it had been carefully evaluated and judged in terms of the material we had on hand. Most of the Moscow agent reports were destroyed because they were too dangerous for us. We also put SOLYA on a firm financial basis so that he could travel and pay his agents.

Finances

73. Finances were the cause, naturally, of constant complaints to the Director. We had been successful in obtaining $10,000 from Moscow which the Director arranged through Switzerland. We had also had

a large sum of money placed at our disposal through a complicated arrangement with the Soviet Ambassador in Sofia. The latter transaction was carried out by an alleged merchant who could travel in Bulgaria and had arranged letter drops and clandestine meetings. When, however, the companies founded by Trepper and KENT (i.e. Foreign Excellent Raincoat Company; SIMEXCO; SIMEX) had been dissolved, Moscow's suspicions could be aroused by a report which might slip by our monitoring system. The first thing to do, obviously, was to start black market operations and establish another company which would provide an authentic source of funds for KENT. Agents, working under SOLYA and latter under Legendre (Paul Victor Legendre @ GOUPIL), were infiltrated as employees into a trading company in Paris. Their mission was to ascertain the black market possibilities while working as regular employees. I often had occasion to deal with SOLYA myself under the cover of an army purchasing agent interested in purchasing technical oils, fats, cocoa beans. (Station Comment: SOLYA had no knowledge of the German control of KENT so was completely ignorant of source's intelligence activities.) The trading company in Paris in which SOLYA and Legendre's agents were working was too restricted for our purposes. We, therefore, founded a firm, Helvetia Handelsgesellschaft, in Monte Carlo during December 1943 and opened branches in Paris, Madrid and Geneva. The fact that the home office was in Monte Carlo was indication enough that very slippery businessmen were involved. The firm in Monte Carlo was placed in contact with one of the kings of the black market along the French and Italian Riviera, a Corsican. This was accomplished through Italians in Paris and Madrid. The firm did not open its branch in Geneva as planned because the RSHA suddenly took action against the 'Rote Drei', a most unfortunate move done entirely on Headquarters' initiative. The RSHA in Berlin took action for some whimsical reason and completely without my knowledge although the 'Rote Drei' had clearly been included in my field of responsibility.

74. The branch of our firm in Madrid had to have Spaniards primarily, at least as the front men. Italians and French were in the background, of course, and behind all of them was the Sonderkommando. The brother of the head of Franco's bodyguard was one of the Madrid stockholders. The firm used a bank, one of the directors of which was an enemy national. This particular man, the bank director, said, in regard to the black market activities, that when it is a question of making money such things as nationality and patriotism do not matter. Through the bank we obtained connections with all enemy countries abroad.

The money which Moscow transferred for our use could be forwarded through the latter channels. Before our commercial organisation could be properly exploited, the invasion of France occurred. Our agents were able, however, to work under the cover of the firm and the finances for the controlled Soviet nets could be logically explained by the firm. None of the company's founders and members knew, naturally, the true purpose of the firm. The control and direction of the company did not represent extra work for the Kommando because the company ran itself. The simple desire to make money was the driving force of the business and was sufficient to make it successful. I received, early in 1944, an offer of a large wolfram delivery from Madrid through the channels of the company. This was, of course, illegal, but it was a sizeable offer concerning sixty-seventy tons per month to be delivered to the free harbour of Bayonne. As far as I was concerned, a transaction of this type was a by-product of the main purpose of the firm but Berlin was very interested in the wolfram. I had to go to Madrid, begin negotiations and obtain samples for Berlin. Our chiefs in the Armaments Ministry were very happy with the whole deal and wanted to complete it – but it was already April (1944). The invasion began in June and I assume that no deliveries were made. This is only an example of the small by-products which developed from the entire work on the Rote Kapelle complex. (Station Comment: The British Study, page 64, contains the following: 'In April 1944 (CARETINA), leader of the Sonderkommando controlling the penetration and deception service against the GRU in France, paid a visit to Spain. The purpose of this visit is unknown, but it is possible that he was following, up some lead into Russian intelligence: see, for example, Trepper's story of a Russian agent passing through France to the Iberian Peninsula in June 1941, etc.' We found no mention of the Helvetia Handelsgesellschaft in the British Study and assume from this that, at the time the English prepared Part II of the Rote Kapelle Study, the existence of the German-controlled firm was unknown, at least the German control and purpose behind the firm was unknown.)

75. The danger that Moscow would learn of the true situation of its rezidentura haunted me night and day. Trepper had escaped. We had to take precautions against the possibility that the French CP would seize the initiative and institute independent radio communication with Moscow. During the search for Trepper, a radio transmitter of which we were aware but had not touched went on the air. The transmitter was literally in our hands within three days. Action had to be taken as fast as possible. I would have preferred to wait a little

longer before seizing the transmitter but through a misunderstanding, the transmitter was seized almost as soon as the D/F'ing had definitely fixed the location. The radio operator ANDRE, who was caught in the act of transmitting, managed to cut the veins in his wrist and neck before he could be stopped. He was rushed to the hospital, streaming blood, but his life was saved. His neck and hands were put into plaster casts so that he would not again attempt suicide. We had to question him in this condition. His messages were quickly decoded. We found the first query to the Director from the French CP concerning Trepper and the reply from the Director, instructing the French CF to have absolutely nothing to do with Trepper because he probably had been doubled by the Germans. This was exactly the reaction we wanted from Moscow. We could not find the agents who were connected with the transmitter and consequently did not locate Trepper.

76. ANDRE was afraid of us at first but when the officials put a cigarette in his mouth and lit it for him, fed him as though he were a small child, he became talkative. His life story was typical of a Soviet agent in France. He said to us, 'You are humans. If I had known that I would not have cut my veins. You will understand why I acted as I did after you have heard my history.' ANDRE was by profession an electrician, if I remember correctly, and he had lived in the provinces where he was a dedicated Communist. The Party had great confidence in him and had given him some delicate missions to perform. One day a man, whom he did not know, visited him. The unknown man told ANDRE that as a trusted comrade he was to perform a special mission. He was first ordered to go to another village from where he would be passed along, step by step, to the Belgium border. He would be taken over the border and put aboard a Soviet freighter in one of the Belgium harbors. This occurred and he sailed to Leningrad. He had not been allowed to say farewell to his family before leaving. From Leningrad he was sent on to Moscow where he was well received and asked, as a comrade of the proletarian class, whether he was willing to undertake a special mission to which great honor would be attached. For a year he was trained in almost all operational techniques of intelligence work. Before departing he was given recognition signals, promised that a radio set would be brought to him which must be concealed, and finally was ordered to break all connections with the Communist Party. He had been thoroughly impressed during his training with the idea that if he should fall 'into the hands of the enemy, the class enemy,' he would be tortured in the most horrible fashion. Believing this, he had cut his veins when he was captured. In addition Moscow

had demanded of him that he not allow himself to be captured by the enemy alive in order that he not talk. He was returned to France as he had left ship to Belgium and then passed from village to village into France. When he arrived the CP had already started a press campaign against him. He was expelled from the Party as a traitor and none of his former friends would even look at him. He, of course, was waiting for the visitor who would give him the recognition signal and the radio set. After several years had passed the visitor came. ANDRE received his radio equipment and went to work. (Station Comment: A rather hasty examination of the entire Personality Index attached to the British Study did not provide further identification of ANDRE. The only remotely possible identification we could make was: EVE, radio operator for Henry Robinson's organisation in France in May 1941. French national. Born in 1904. Communist sympathiser but not a Party member. Radio-electrician by occupation; served in heavy artillery regiment of French Army; apprenticed to and subsequently employed by Pathe.)

77. We continued the transmission on ANDRE's transmitter but nothing came of it. We had guessed that Moscow would notice the interruption in ANDRE's transmission and would become suspicious. ANDRE did not appear before a military court because he was being held for possible future use. His was the last radio transmitter we detected. From then on the danger that a French CP transmitter would become active was ever present. It was true at this time that the leading cadres of the French CP were distracted because they were completely occupied in strengthening the Party's position in the Maquis in preparation for 'X' day when they wanted to be certain they would play a decisive role. The Party was working with all groups of the Maquis in an effort to infiltrate their men into the top positions of the Maquis. Their penetration efforts were done under the cover of French nationalism. Complete groups of the Maquis were composed only of Communists who were provided with weapons and organised into cadres in preparation for a civil, or in their terms 'class' war. We were well informed on the Party's activities along this line and did not fear the leading cadres. It was obvious to us that something had to be done for the benefit of the Party leaders who, in turn, would pass the news on to the intelligence section. It was thus we hoped to silence the latter section.

78. The elimination of the French CP radio links was actually a disadvantage for our planning. I decided, therefore, to rebuild radio

communication, not to serve the Party cadres but as a support for the Soviet intelligence work. The radio link would be available, through our plan, to the French CP if the latter wanted to send an emergency message. We undertook our enormous task.

79. Waldemar Osols (Ozols), alias SOLYA (SOLJA), allegedly a Lithuanian general, had been working for the Soviets in Paris since the Spanish Civil War when he had won Soviet confidence by his efforts for the Red side. KENT claimed to have known Osols in Spain but I doubt this. The two did not know each other when they met for the first time. SOLYA had a contact with the Soviet Military Attaché in Paris (when the Soviet MA was still in Paris) and with Trepper. He was supposedly working independently after the war started but he did not have a radio operator. During the entire time we were in Paris Osols was ignorant of the German control behind his work for Soviet intelligence. At the end of the war when KENT and I were in the Soviet Headquarters in Paris, Osols still knew nothing of the role the Germans played in KENT's operations. I was told during my interrogation in Moscow that Osols had been brought to Moscow to report. This may be but I have no proof of it.

80. Capitaine Paul Legendres had been the head of a resistance group, operating in the south and center of France, which the German security police had partially destroyed. A number of his people were seized including his wife. She was at the time (when Legendre came into Source's controlled group) in the Ravensbrueck concentration camp. He himself was being sought and his name was on all wanted lists. He hid in Marseilles and had begun to work again in a small way. The connection with Legendre was through SOLYA. Legendre was helped financially (by the Germans) and offered a radio operator because, allegedly, his reports were important enough to transmit by radio. He was grateful and honored by the offer. It was soon evident that he was a good Communist and had excellent connections with the Party. All of these attributes made him ideally suited for our purposes. He was allowed to continue believing that he was working for Moscow. Being an intelligent man with some concept of the entire situation, he realised himself that the emphasis should be on intelligence work. Consequently, he directed his espionage activities toward the harbors and shipyards in Toulon working for the Germans. The security weaknesses of the latter were quickly revealed to us by his reporting. We would intercede, however, only if a real threat existed. We stopped sabotage proposals from his group with the excuse

that Moscow's approval must first be obtained, nothing without the Director's approval. As a former soldier, he understood this type of discipline. The answer given him, allegedly coming from Moscow, was: 'Intelligence work is more important at the moment and should under no circumstances be endangered. Sabotage must be approved by us before any action is taken.' We finally summoned Legendre to Paris because we needed his excellent connections with the French CP and to prove to him that the 'Soviet rezidentura' was supporting him. The group in Marseilles continued to function for a long time. Our radio operator, JOY, working with the group, was responsible for the radio traffic with the central headquarters in Paris and so everything went as we wished.

81. In order to make absolutely certain of Legendre's allegiance to KENT and prove to Legendre that KENT was a very important man, it was arranged that Mrs. Legendre should be released from the Ravensbrueck concentration camp, allegedly by means of bribes and KENT's well-placed contacts in Germany. The result of this was that Legendre had complete confidence in KENT although his wife's release was not an unmixed blessing for Legendre because it offered certain obstacles to his love affair with his secretary. Legendre generally received instructions from SOLYA but occasionally directly from KENT. Reliable and rapid communication with the provinces which would enable the intelligence material to be brought to Paris for rapid transmission to Moscow was lacking. Beside his connections in the provinces which had already been activated, Legendre was given the task of finding young Communists with proper qualifications whom we could train as radio operators and simultaneously in clandestine operational techniques. We were very strict in our 'conspiratorial' techniques. Any member who made the smallest mistake was severely reprimanded by KENT. KENT's rigid discipline was respected by old soldiers such as SOLYA and Legendre and made them always stand at attention in his presence. Our own security was served to the best advantage by careful observance of 'conspiratorial' methods as taught in the Soviet training courses and practiced in Soviet clandestine operations.

82. Legendre found among the young French Communists both trained radio operators who could be put to work almost immediately and young men whom we trained ourselves. Although they were all Communists, they were under very strict orders not to reveal their Party affiliation to avoid arousing mistrust among the non-Communist members of the resistance organisations. As far as these young

Communists knew, they were working as radio operators for the Allies and the ultimate destination of their messages was London. Not all of them was told that Moscow was behind the entire operation. The only information given them was that the men who contacted them and served as cut-outs were members of the French CP and for the rest the 'conspiratorial' discipline served to keep them in line. After completing the training and with a minimum knowledge of their organisation, the young Communists were assigned to a radio station which we had detected and were monitoring and frequently told to develop their own contacts and sources of intelligence. The radio communication and the whole operation worked magnificently. I had, during the period when this operation was at its peak, hundreds of reports from the Communist penetrations of the resistance passing over my desk every day. The number of agents whom we were controlling increased and, most important, not one of them knew of the German control behind the entire network. Neither Legendre or SOLYA ever knew that the Germans were controlling their nets. They were played until the last day. I can't remember the exact number of principal agents but there were more than thirty. They were all well paid, by the Germans naturally, and all believed that they were being paid by either 'Moscow' or 'London'.

83. In my report on the 'Internal French Net' (Station Comment: To be forwarded as soon as possible), I have already described how we handled this network, how the radio operators controlled by us agreed to continue reporting on the Allied landings after the invasion. If a personal account of how we controlled the underground is desired, the American Air Force Captain (Station Comment: Major M. J. Gateswood) can be consulted. He was shot down, found shelter in the French resistance and thereby came in contact with the organisation controlled by our Kommando. He was brought to Paris and eventually put over the Spanish border, all arranged through radio communication controlled by us. This occurred shortly before our withdrawal from France. We passed the American flyer through the very heart of the territory occupied and ruled by the Maquis. Gateswood, as a result of his own experience, can give the best description of how securely and confidently my people moved among the ranks of the resistance.

84. The organisation controlled by our Kommando within the resistance groups was so extensive that we ourselves did not know all details and names. The basic skeleton was composed of more than two hundred people, all of whom were sources of intelligence. There were seven

radio stations. In spite of the size of the organisation, we maintained a very strict centralised control. The whole organisation obeyed and no one acted without prior approval or against orders. Occasionally we had to condone some action because disapproval would have aroused suspicion and caused the central directing powers to be accused of 'cowardice'. Such action occurred generally among the youth groups. The directing, controlling cadre was pyramidal in shape with KENT at the top and nets radiating from every member of the leading cadre, hanging from each man like bunches of grapes. The agent or working level had, naturally, no knowledge of the leaders because the exact same system as used in Communist 'conspiratorial' operations was used. All of the functions of the internal net are described in detail in my report on this subject.

Intelligence Material Passed on the Radio Links to Moscow

85. The information which we passed to Moscow was already touched on briefly but it was a very important aspect of the entire operation. When I first took over the Kommando, the level of reporting had to be built up again to the factual and current reporting, typical of the Soviet nets before we assumed control, in order that Moscow's suspicions not be aroused. The basic principle on which we compiled our intelligence for Moscow was to send interesting intelligence, not obviously deception, which would keep Moscow interested but would not enable the Director to detect the German origin. At the same time, we were seeking positive gains for ourselves through the two-way radio traffic. We hoped to learn, on one hand, of Moscow's continuing interests or targets in both the political and military fields and, on the other hand, to be able to direct Moscow's interest to areas of knowledge wherein we ran no risks and in which Moscow was not previously interested. For example, a report that the German Foreign Office in Berlin had made contact with the Western Allies brought an immediate reaction from Moscow. This report was followed with a report that Ribbentrop personally was handling the negotiations and reactions in the Soviet press were forthcoming from the two reports which we fed Moscow. Our first task was to whet Moscow's appetite for intelligence on the political situation, the Church, and in the world of business. Too much emphasis had been laid, during the first period of the radio play-backs, on military intelligence. During the early days the Kommando had been satisfied with answering the Director's queries and requirements. They also had to avoid passing too much military intelligence and as a delaying tactic, they had larded the military reports with

miscellaneous intelligence. A complete change of policy and direction occurred (Station Comment: Source implies when he took command of the Kommando). The replies to the Director's queries became the smallest part of the messages and we succeeded in eliciting questions from the Director based on intelligence we had volunteered. Within two or three months we knew exactly where the Director's interest lay and what the Director's targets were. We often inserted material which a member of the Kommando had suggested and which appeared to be a good idea even though we risked having the Director reply that there was no interest or that the report was nonsense. At the appropriate time, i.e. when we felt we had a clear picture of the Director's attitude, KENT sent a message that he would like to know whether he and his apparat had been successful, had contributed to driving out the Nazi occupation from our 'Rodinu' (native land) in conjunction, naturally, with the victorious Red Army; and furthermore, only the Director with a worldwide picture of events could decide which intelligence sent by KENT and his apparat was of real interest. This type of flattery with a mild overtone of reprimand was loved by the Director and generally such a message was immediately acknowledged.

86. The Soviets naturally were interested, within the field of military intelligence, in all technical information on weapons, all intelligence on troop units brought from the Eastern Front to France for rest and rehabilitation, on all new troop units destined for the Eastern Front, and all information on dates of transfers and changes in the command structure of the German Army. We received questions on the coastal fortifications along clearly defined stretches of the Atlantic Coast and canals. The latter questions seemed strange and inexplicable. Queries of this type were seldom and were limited generally to only one village. If we received a query of the latter type we sent, for example, the following reply:

> All guard posts are held primarily by Russian volunteers. It is surprising that the guards are all armed with the English Sten machine pistol, a weapon which is cheap and easily assembled. An informant has said that Germany purchased the Stens through a neutral source with a promise that the weapons would not be used on the Eastern Front.

This type of message brought an immediate reaction because, although not stated, it was clearly implied that the weapon, allegedly in the hands of the guards, had been sold with English knowledge. If the Russians had asked the English how the Sten machine pistol came to be in the hands of German guards, England could not and would not have been able to explain, both for reasons of prestige as well as lack of knowledge. The Sten machine pistols had been 'played out' of England in an English play-back operation, allegedly, for mass delivery to resistance groups and in reality for us (the Germans had then given them to the Russian volunteer guards under German command). Through such operations, we could compile our messages for Moscow, covering all fields of interest, and the information was 90% true, i.e. true at the time of the radio transmission or for a few days before or after the transmission. Frequently the Director would find the intelligence sent over the radio transmission confirmed in the press a few days or weeks later. The Director was shown time and again that his apparat in France had access to high-level sources who were reliable and authentic

87. The Director was very distrustful of his Western Allies because the Director regarded as quite normal and practical from the standpoint of the Western Allies the possibility that the Western Allies would join forces on European soil and attack the USSR. The Bolsheviks smelled the misalliance between the Western Allies and the USSR. I recounted before the story told me by the Red Army Political officer while I was in a Soviet prison, Kaganovich had gone to the front when the Soviet Caucasian Front was collapsing to try to bolster morale; the Soviet officers asked Kaganovich what was delaying the Second Front and he answered, 'You want a Second Front? We are happy that they (Western Allies) are not shooting at us!' – which should have been obvious to all. (Station Comment: Source is referring to the inevitable, in his opinion, hostility between the USSR and the Western Allies.) The inner relationship of the entire Alliance was certainly revealed by the query about the landing strength of the Western Allies. I did not dare to reply on my own responsibility and forwarded the query to Berlin. Berlin forwarded the decision to the Fuehrer's Headquarters. The Fuehrer and Commander-in-Chief (Hitler) answered eventually himself and gave a figure for the landing strength which was considerably less than the actual figure. After we sent the answer to the Director, the latter replied with another question: Was this really an invasion or only a feint? and this question must be answered definitively and exactly.

88. Toward the end of 1943, I sent a long, detailed, political report about the internal political situation in Germany; the dissatisfaction with the Nazi leadership; the unexpressed hopes of the military, financial, big industrial circles, and the clergy for the future; and in short a cross-

section of opinion of all classes in Germany. Before transmitting the message, I showed Dr. Knochen, the Commander of the Security Forces in France, the entire report. Knochen was so astonished that he said, 'My friend, that is all accurate. If I had such a report on England, I would pay 100,000 marks for it. How can you pass such intelligence?' A well travelled journalist, working in my Kommando, who had helped compile the report, said that I would never receive permission froth Berlin to transmit the report to the Director. I was convinced that Berlin, rather the RSHA, would approve it and bet six bottles of champagne which I won within twelve hours. The report was sent by the RSHA in a circular letter to all officials involved in radio play-back operations as an example and training for their work. How could such a thing occur? This was a typical example of how a dictatorship operates. Within the RSHA the officials could not grasp the fact that the report was true. The RSHA officials automatically assumed that the report was a very sophisticated deception. The government officials had swallowed the propaganda believed by the 'faithful' for so long that they were oblivious of the intellectual and emotional trends within the German people which were obvious to anyone with a brain. What was more important was that the moneyed, propertied classes who were losing more and more of their possessions would rather lose the war to the West than see everything they owned disappear in dust and ashes. The same propertied classes were violently opposed to the East and were afraid that Bolshevism would automatically accompany complete collapse. For this reason I could transmit to Moscow a message which was true but which would not harm my country and fellow Germans. If Moscow wished, Moscow could have seen clearly that although the Soviets were shedding their blood in the common cause of the Alliance, the German people were 100% pro-Western and had no love for the Bolshevik experiment of which they had seen enough on the Eastern Front. The Director reacted angrily, as we expected, with an ideological tirade, the only one we received on the radio link, against Nazi Germany. The RSHA simply could not comprehend the significance of the exchange of messages. The opinion in the RSHA was that we could safely feed such material to the East but never could send it to the Western Allies because the latter would exploit the information. The report was sent to the Chief of the play-back operations against the West along with the other counterintelligence officers.

89. The typical bureaucratic official and thick-headed military officer, both are worthless for operations such as our radio play-backs which demand a feeling and understanding of human beings. The man

for this type of work must be a man with an active and intelligent understanding of the political situation, not a Party politician but an intelligent political analyst. I mention these details because even in Moscow I was asked during my interrogation how it happened that permission was given to send the message containing the report. After the war the Soviets realised that the report was 100% true which they would never have recognised or admitted to recognising during the war because of the ideological blinders they wear. The gentlemen in the RSHA in Berlin were the same. If the Soviets had seriously considered the information in our radio message concerning the orientation of the German people toward the West, they would have been angry at the German people for blocking the progress of Communism in Germany. Had this occurred, the Soviets would probably have made much took heavy demands on the Western Powers which the latter, simply to keep face, would have had to refuse. We saw far reaching consequences from our radio message, much farther reaching than Berlin saw. We were not wrong in our estimate of the East but on the other hand we were far off in our estimate of the West. The idea of a trip to Moscow (on Source's part) developed subsequently out of this general train of thought and the problem of the trip was solved, in any case, by an invitation from Moscow. (Station Comment: Source's trip to Moscow resulted from messages sent to the Director concerning KENT's alleged German, anti-Nazi co-workers and was apparently a joint plan of Source and KENT.)

Results and Successes of the Radio Play-Back Operations Against Moscow

90. The Director had not found it necessary for the two and a half years (life of the radio play-back operation) to strengthen our area (France) or to call in reserves. Even a visit from a controller, a common practice for Soviet espionage nets, had not occurred although we had urged the Director to send one. When Trepper was still in our hands, Moscow had announced that a controller would visit the apparat. We had requested the visit under various pretexts, first on Trepper's radio links and then on KENT's link. Over KENT's radio link we had justified our need for consultation with the controller by the desirability for the controller to see with his own eyes how much the work had expanded and confirm the fact that financial assistance was necessary to support the expanded activities. Moscow assured us that money would be forthcoming via an American bank but we were asked to arrange the necessary channels. We had accomplished this by founding our

international firm, Helvetia Handelsgesellschaft. Unfortunately the military developments intervened and a transmittal of funds was impossible. Moscow was firmly convinced that everything would go as planned. We had covered all eventualities in our planning for the controller's visit and had no fears about his visit. About this time we wanted to start our biggest 'coup' which was to introduce the 'German resistance members'. The exact steps to be taken to accomplish this were not planned in advance because so much depended on the personality of the controller. As far as Berlin was concerned I had almost complete freedom of action.

91. As stated above, Moscow's interests and intentions had been completely revealed to us through the radio play-backs. Not only Moscow's tactics regarding the military situation but Moscow's plans for the internal French situation were known. We had provoked Moscow with such demands as 'A very reliable comrade, presently the head of one of the larger Maquis organisations in which a strong right element is present, would be most useful in our work. May we take him away from his present job?' Moscow replied: 'No, he is not to leave his present mission because he can exercise great influence where he is. You (KENT) are not to touch him or compromise him. You will find other workers who are free to help.' Through such exploitation of the radio operations we were able to ferret out all of Moscow's technical reserves and co-workers.

92. We were successful in guiding Moscow's interest toward targets which we had selected by means of harmless reports, unsolicited from Moscow. Through this channel we could, therefore, exercise some influence, thanks to the peculiar mentality of Moscow.

<u>Controlled Internal French Radio Traffic</u>

93. We had an exact knowledge of our own security weaknesses as a result of the detailed reporting on the invasion area, a very important area for us, and on the Supreme Western Headquarters. We knew that in certain French villages everyone from the mayor to the goat-herder was working against us along intelligence lines, a situation which made it impossible to maintain any secrecy. The best example of this was Rommel's Headquarters. He had an official Headquarters in which he did not live and an unofficial Headquarters in which he did live. I had received a radio message giving all details accurately of his two Headquarters. I warned the Headquarters to be somewhat more careful.

331

A certain Major Brink was in the I C (G-2) and Brink in civilian life had been an ossified district judge. He was angry because he had not been in on the work on the Rote Kapelle. In the absence of his commander, he issued an order to me to arrest the entire French group within twenty-four hours and submit a complete report to him. The justification for the order was that the French group was too dangerous to be allowed to remain free. The order was signed by Generalfeldmarschall von Rundstedt who, of course, had no information on the significance or background of the command. If I did not carry out the order within twenty-four hours I could be brought before a military court because we were at war in France and the Supreme Commander West was the highest authority. This ridiculous command stemmed entirely from stupid resentment which Brink had disguised under a command. I would have had to arrest more than 180 people in the area. This was impossible for practical reasons and would have ruined our entire operation. It was also morally reprehensible because in building up our operations and also to identify the honest and intensely nationalistic Frenchmen who might be driven to action, we had encouraged the latter to become active. Such nationalistic Frenchmen might have, in the course of events, become active against us but we had certainly pushed them toward action. It was so simple for a high-ranking general to sign an order to be executed within twenty-four hours, the order was then issued from a Wehrmacht desk and if not obeyed, we were the miscreants. To execute this particular command the entire population of a village would have had to be arrested. With the support of SS and Polizeifuehrer Oberg, still imprisoned in France today, and all the influence and strength I could muster, I fought the command. Oberg personally phoned Himmler and the RSHA Headquarters in Berlin turned to Himmler. I contacted Jodl in the Fuehrer's Headquarters. When the command went to von Rundstedt to withdraw the order, it originated in the Fuehrer's Headquarters. All that Rommel's staff would have needed to do when our warning was received was to set up a flying Headquarters for Rommel who, in any case, was always on the move. No matter what they did, the French would have continued to report on every new Headquarters and pass the information along to their cut-outs. The only real danger was that the reports might not reach our Kommando but it is hopeless to try to explain such complicated counter-intelligence support to a rank-conscious officer who assumes from habit that he only needs to think of a command and it will be executed.

94. Proposed acts of sabotage had to receive prior approval in our well-disciplined organisation and they were disapproved almost 100%. In cases where we could not securely disapprove the proposal, we sent our own special cadres to carry out the sabotage. Some type of sabotage was performed for purposes of cover and deception but visual evidence was the only evidence. In this way we got away with our alleged sabotage.

95. One of the positive products of our internal French network was an expansion of our knowledge of the French 'underground organisation.

96. We located many persons who were on the wanted list. For the most part they remained hidden and undertook no action. They generally were frightened into hiding by the fact that they were being looked for by the 'Gestapo'. This was due to the reputation of the Gestapo. The Allied broadcasts were largely responsible for spreading the reputation of the Gestapo, and thereby paralyzing the work of many people. (Station Comment: Source, as a former Amt IV Gestapo official, is naturally implying that the Gestapo did not earn its 'reputation', the 'reputation' was the result of Allied broadcasts!) We found this quite helpful at times because people on the wanted list remained in hiding and presented no problems. Some of them worked in organisations controlled by us, preparing 'political opinions' for the orientation of Moscow or London, depending on the case. We found appropriate work for all of them which chained them to their hiding places. In order to impress a man who looked worthwhile to us, we would have him warned that the Germans were going to search a village on such and such a day and that he should disappear for the day. The search would actually be made including his original hiding place and he would be very impressed with the organisation which warned him. The most prominent man in this category was a former Vice-Governor or some such former high official from the French African Colonies, also of course, a delegate of the French Parliament, who gave the impression of being very pro-Soviet.

97. We received considerable scientific intelligence, new inventions and improvements. Some of the intelligence was collected for Moscow and some for London. All reports went, naturally, to Berlin and from the reports several valuable items were obtained according to the German Scientific Institute.

98. Hidden stores of weapons, explosives, and fuel were located by us and for tactical reasons we moved them to other storage areas, mostly our own. We also gave trusted agents the mission of finding weapon caches and storing them until they were needed. We financed the buying of weapons and paid bonuses for each weapon procured. One of the most astonishing results was a delivery of German machine pistols which had been missing from a German weapons store for six months. In order to uncover the source of the German weapons, we ordered, through our controlled agent, more weapons and then put the storage area under observation. The Germans selling the weapons were seized. The Italians were so generous in selling their weapons that they could be purchased from at least half the men in any unit.

99. One of the more insane problems we faced was that of the mayor or prefect of the towns and villages. Most of them belonged to resistance groups and were, therefore, under our control. Such officials were dangerous because they had authority and were obeyed by the people. They could make very stupid mistakes. We were forced to withdraw some of them from their official and legal contact with the German officials to avoid trouble. The excuse used for such an order was that the French mayor or prefect was too valuable and would be needed later for important work. They should, therefore, under no circumstance expose themselves in short-term, active work. They were ordered to remain quiet, put on a friendly face for the Germans and allow no suspicion to be attached to themselves. This system worked perfectly.

100. The many-sided nature of the activities in which we became involved is too voluminous to cover here. Only a few examples are cited above to show the variety of operations in which we were involved. The most satisfactory result of all our operations was that executive measures (i.e. arrests, imprisonment, executions, etc.) were avoided and no court sentences or bloodshed resulted.

Conclusions

101. It is impossible to list accurately the manpower we saved with our organisation because the organisation ran itself. The conspiratorial system demanded a peak to the pyramid where everything finally was pulled together and which was unknown and unseen by the lower echelons. In spite of the variety of operations, the entire operation was a success. For example we were involved in the case of five millions of German 'soldier marks' which had been smuggled out of Rumania

into France by our firm, Helvetia Handelsgesellschaft; we had to keep a close watch on all underground activities; we obtained quinine which the German Army desperately needed and other such articles which were unobtainable in Germany because of the bottle-necks in production, etc. Our Kommando was sufficiently strong in manpower to direct our operations but if emergency action was necessary other agencies had to assist us. Unfortunately French agents and police officials were assigned to us for emergency measures such as surveillance, occupation of apartments, etc. because we did not have the manpower. The French were not at all hesitant to plunder and in a state of war nothing could be done to prevent plundering.

102. The technical side of the operations, the radio traffic, demanded many technicians on duty day and night to maintain the radio operations. Four to five radio operators were needed for the direct traffic and at the same time we were training illegal radio operators to be infiltrated into the various Soviet nets. I have reported previously about the unfortunate betrayal we experienced during the latter days in Paris. That report also describes the behaviour of the radio operators, how they continued to transmit after the Allies had rolled over them (Station Comment: This is contained in the report on the French Internal Network, not yet transmitted to Headquarters). We were both impressed and depressed by the young Frenchmen in their early 20's who obeyed Moscow's orders with no hesitation, much better than they obeyed the orders of their native country, France.

103. When we left Paris, we left the entire French internal radio net intact with SOLYA and Legendre as the heads. This does not mean either of the two knew every unit or member of the organisation. They certainly knew most of the organisation because much came under their direct supervision. Quite a number of stations had radio operators whom we had placed. The latter stations continued in operation and their work was neither influenced or controlled by SOLYA and Legendre. At the very last we gave SOLYA a complete transmitting/receiving set and a signal plan which was intended for future use. The plan could not be realised because when the Allies moved into Paris, a Soviet representation accompanied them. A radio link between us and SOLYA would have had no sense, as far as Moscow was concerned, when SOLYA had direct access to Soviet officials. KENT and, therefore obviously, my radio communication with France was broken in order that our radio communication with the Director would not be endangered after our withdrawal from Paris.

Double Operations as Opposed to Executive Measures

104. In weighing the relative values of executive measures versus double-agent, play-back operations, our experience showed that there is no question as to which is the most valuable. Executive measures (i.e. police measures), perforce, lead to violent measures, to the use of suppressive power. In any case Moscow wanted and promoted the exercise of force (by the Germans) because Moscow knew only too well that, violence always produces martyrs and martyrs are the best seed for the dragon's teeth, i.e. the most dedicated fighters for Moscow's cause and the most effective and enduring symbols for Moscow's cause spring from the seeds of violence. The punishment which the executive organs inflicted forced a man, threatened with such punishment, into a dead-end street. Having no escape, a man in this position was forced to fight to death and that was exactly what Moscow desired and demanded. If such a man survives imprisonment which alone is martyrdom for many spies, he will spend the rest of his life as a fanatic working for the cause for which he was imprisoned. He has no choice except to do this because he must make his suffering pay off; he must reap some reward for his suffering. The stiffening and delineation of the front between the two camps (East and West) is increasing. For this reason double operations should always be used although it means great determination and expenditure of intellectual effort. Only if the enemy has no opportunity to make martyrs of his followers, if it is possible to choose any other path than that of inflicting punishment, then all other paths remain open and the possibility of converting, perhaps recruiting, the enemy remains. If it was possible for us to achieve so much through double operations during the war, how much more can be done in peacetime. The professional handling of double operations to achieve the maximum results must, however, be the life career of a small circle of capable, counter-intelligence men.

SOURCE NOTES

All MI5 files are available at the National Archives, Kew.

Introduction
1. Richard Wurmann's MI5 PF at KV2/268.
2. Keith Jeffery, *MI6: The History of the Secret Intelligence Service 1909-49* (London: Penguin, 2010).
3. Ibid.
4. Ibid.
5. Ibid.

Chapter I: Naval Intelligence
1. *EttandienOrganisation der Kriegsmaine*, 30 July 1946.
2. Horst von Pflugk-Hartturg, GFM/33/2111/4764.
3. Ibid.
4. Ibid.
5. Ibid.
6. Heinrich Ahlrichs' MI5 PF at KV2/1173.
7. Fritz Scharpf's MI5 PF at KV2/3438.
8. *EttandienOrganisation der Kriegsmaine*, 30 July 1946.
9. Ibid.
10. Heinrich Schubert's MI5 PF at KV2/3438.
11. Army Security Agency: *European Axis Signal Intelligence in World War II as Revealed by TICOM Investigations*, 1 May 1946, Vol. 3.
12. Ibid.
13. Ibid.
14. Ibid.
15. Ibid.

Chapter II: Wartime Operations
1. Friedrich Baumeister's MI5 PF at KV2/266.
2. HARLEQUIN's MI5 PF at KV2/268.

3. Karl Abshagen's MI5 PF at KV2/388.
4. Friedrich Baumeister's MI5 PF KV2/266.
5. Ibid.
6. Ibid.
7. *The Abwehr in France* at KV2/153.
8. Ibid.
9. Ibid.
10. Oscar Reile's MI5 PF at KV2/3016.
11. Hans Rudolf's MI5 PF at KB3/410.
12. Hermann Giskes' MI5 PF at KV2/962.
13. Gerhard Huntemann's MI5 PF at KV2/967.
14. *German Penetration of SOE* at KV3/75.
15. Ibid.
16. Ibid.
17. Ibid.
18. Ibid.
19. Ibid.
20. Ibid.
21. Ibid.
22. Ibid.
23. Ibid.
24. Hermann Giskes' MI5 PF at KV2/962.
25. Freddie Kraus' MI5 PF at KV2/1727.
26. Ibid.
27. Ibid.
28. *The Real Enemy* by Pierre d'Harcourt (London: Longmans, 1967).
29. Freddie Kraus' MI5 PF at KV2/1727.
30. Ibid.
31. Ibid.
32. Herman Giskes' MI5 PF at KV2/962.
33. *The Rote Kapelle* by Michael Serpell and Robert Hembys-Scales (MI5 1949).
34. *The Rote Kapelle: The CIA's History of Soviet Intelligence and Espionage Networks in Western Europe 1936-1945* by Donovan Pratt and James Olson (Frederick, MD: University Publications of America, 1979).
35. Host Kopkow's MI5 PF at KV2/1500.
36. Heinz Panwitz's (alias Hans Paulsen) MI5 PF at KV2/1971.
37. Ibid.
38. Friedrich Sartorius' MI5 PF at KV2/1739.
39. Rudolf Rathke's MI5 PF at KV2/44.
40. Karl Meissner's MI5 PF at KV2/1368.
41. Peter Schagen's MI5 PF at KV2/161.

42. *The Abwehr in Switzerland* at KV3/245.
43. Karl Meissner's MI5 PF at KV2/1368.
44. Ibid.
45. Alan Foote's MI5 PF at KV2/1616.
46. Ibid.
47. *RHSA Investigations* at KV3/109.
48. Alan Foote's MI5 PF at KV2/1616.
49. Willy Piert's MI5 PF at KV2/1329.
50. Karl Meissner's MI5 PF at KV2/1368.
51. Ibid.
52. Stella Lonsdale's MI5 PF at KV2/733.
53. Karl Meissner's MI5 PF at KV2/1368.
54. Peter Schagen's MI5 PF at KV2/161.
55. Ibid.
56. Ibid.
57. Ibid.
58. George Kronberger's MI5 PF at KV2/163
59. Ibid.
60. Ibid.
61. Ibid.
62. Otto Begus' MI5 PF at KV2/527.
63. James Robertson to T.A. Robertson, 3 June 1944 at KV2/1133.
64. *Enemy Intelligence Services in Italy* at KV3/85.
65. Ibid.

Chapter III: The Defectors

1. HARLEQUIN's MI5 PF at KV2/268.
2. Ibid.
3. MI5 Report to the Prime Minister at KV4/83.
4. HARLEQUIN's MI5 PF at KV2/268.
5. Ibid.
6. Mirko Rot's MI5 PF at KV2/1922.
7. Ibid.
8. Ibid.
9. Ibid.
10. Ibid.
11. Ibid.
12. Ibid.

Chapter IV: The 20th July Putsch

1. Otto John's MI5 PF at KV2/2465.
2. Ibid.

3. COLOMBINE's MI5 PF at KV2/395.
4. Ibid.
5. Erich Vermehren's MI5 PF at KV2/956.
6. Although Hans Ruser's MI5 PF has not been declassified, his Home Office file is at HO 382/556 and his mother's is at HO 334/868/893.
7. Erwin Lahousen's MI5 PF at KV2/175.
8. Ibid.
9. See also *To the Bitter End* by Hans Bernd Gisevius (Boston, MA: Houghton Mifflin, 1947).
10. Otto John's MI5 PF at KV2/2465.
11. Josef Ledebur's MI5 PF at KV2/159.
12. Ibid.
13. Otto John's MI5 PF at KV2/2465.
14. Josef Ledebur's MI5 PF at KV2/159.
15. Ibid.
16. Ibid.
17. Otto John's MI5 PF at KV2/2465.
18. Ibid.
19. Ibid.
20. Ibid.
21. Josef Ledebur's MI5 PF at KV2/159.
22. Ibid.
23. Ibid.
24. Ibid.
25. Ibid.
26. Ibid.
27. Otto John's MI5 PF at KV2/2465.
28. Ibid.
29. Erwin Lahousen's MI5 PF at KV2/173.
30. Peter Schagen's MI5 PF at KV2/161.
31. Wilhelm Kuebart's MI5 PF at KV2/410.
32. Ibid.
33. Horst Kopkow's MI5 PF at KV2/1500

Chapter V: More Defectors

1. Erich Vermehren's MI5 PF at KV2/956.
2. Ibid.
3. Ibid.
4. Ibid.
5. Ludwig Moyzisch's MI5 PF KV2/169.
6. Erich Pfeiffer's MI5 PF KV2/267.
7. Osmar Hellmuth's MI5 PF at KV2/1722.

8. Paul Leverkuehn's MI5 PF at KV2/2664.
9. Otto Mayer's MI5 PF KV2/955.
10. Ibid.
11. Ibid.
12. Ibid.
13. Ibid.
14. Willy Goetz's MI5 PF at KV2/387.
15. Erich Vermehren's MI5 PF at KV2/956.
16. Ibid.
17. Ibid.
18. Erich Pfeiffer's MI5 PF KV2/267.
19. Ibid.
20. Ibid.
21. Ibid.
22. Thomas Ludwig's MI5 PF at KV2/2653.
23. Erich Pfeiffer's MI5 PF KV2/267.
24. Ibid.
25. Erich Vermehren's MI5 PF at KV2/956.
26. Gottfried Muller's MI5 PF at KV2/1734.
27. Willi Hamburger's MI5 PF at KV2/959.
28. Gottfried Muller's MI5 PF at KV2/1734.
29. Ibid.
30. Willi Hamburger's MI5 PF at KV2/959.
31. Ibid.
32. Ibid.
33. Ibid.
34. Walter Schellenberg's MI5 PF at KV2/95.
35. Ibid.
36. Erich Pfeiffer's MI5 PF KV2/267.
37. KOS ISOS at KV3/269.
38. Ibid.
39. Ibid.
40. Ibid.
41. Ibid.
42. Ibid.
43. Walter Schellenberg's MI5 PF at KV2/95.
44. Ibid.
45. Ibid.
46. Ibid.
47. Ibid.
48. Thomas Ludwig's MI5 PF at KV2/2653.
49. *The Guy Liddell Diaries*, 30 August 1942.

50. Ibid., 2 September 1943.
51. Fritz Lorenz's MI5 PF at KV2/310.
52. Ibid.

Chapter VI: The Klatt Mystery

1. Richard Kauder's MI5 PF at KV2/1497.
2. Ibid.
3. Ibid.
4. Ibid.
5. Ibid.
6. See *Crown Jewels* by Oleg Tsarev (London: HarperCollins, 1998).
7. SIS reports at KV3/98.
8. Ibid.
9. Ibid.
10. Ibid.
11. Serpell Report at KV2/1497.
12. Ibid.
13. Otto Wagner MI5 PF at KV2/284.
14. Ibid.
15. Ibid.
16. Ibid.
17. Veracity Report at KV3/98.
18. Ibid.
19. Otto Wagner's MI5 PF at KV2/284.
20. Richard Kauder's MI5 PF at KV2/1497.
21. Ibid.
22. Walter Schellenberg's MI5 PF at KV2/98.
23. Ibid.
24. Dick White Report at KV4/240.
25. Ibid.
26. Gilbert Ryle's Report at KV3/98.
27. Paul Blum's Report at KV2/1497.
28. Richard Kauder's MI5 PF at KV2/1497.
29. Ibid.
30. Ibid.
31. See *Crown Jewels* by Oleg Tsarev (London: HarperCollins, 1998).
32. Walter Schellenberg's MI5 PF at KV2/98.
33. Richard Kauder's MI5 PF at KV2/1497.
34. Ibid.
35. Ibid.
36. Ibid.

Chapter VII: Endgame

1. *The Running of Special Agents in the Field in North-West Europe* at KV4/215.
2. CELERY MI5 PF at KV2/674.
3. Guy Liddell's Diary, 19 March 1942.
4. Jack Curry report on German Secret Service, March 1942, at KV3/7.
5. Guy Liddell's Diary, 19 May 1942.
6. Ibid., 11 August 1942.
7. Ibid., 20 December 1943.
8. Ibid., 28 December 1943.
9. Ibid.
10. BRUTUS's MI5 PF at KV2/72.
11. Albert Gabas's MI5 PF at KV2/210.
12. Carl Eitel's MI5 PF at KV2/384.
13. John Marriott memorandum, 23 October 1944, at KV4/215.
14. Oscar Reile's MI5 PF at KV2/3016.

Appendix I

1. Baumeister Questionnaire at MI5 PF KV2/266.

Appendix II

1. MI5's NORDPOL Investigation at KV2/962.

Appendix III

1. *The History of the ROTE KAPELLE* at KV2/1972.

INDEX

345